The International Companion to Scottish Children's Literature

INTERNATIONAL COMPANIONS TO SCOTTISH LITERATURE

Series Editors: Ian Brown and Thomas Owen Clancy

Titles in the series include:

International Companion to Lewis Grassic Gibbon
Edited by Scott Lyall
ISBN 978-1-908980-13-7

International Companion to Edwin Morgan
Edited by Alan Riach
ISBN 978-1-908980-14-4

International Companion to Scottish Poetry
Edited by Carla Sassi
ISBN 978-1-908980-15-1

International Companion to James Macpherson and The Poems of Ossian
Edited by Dafydd Moore
ISBN 978-1-908980-19-9

International Companion to John Galt
Edited by Gerard Carruthers and Colin Kidd
ISBN 978-1-908980-27-4

International Companion to Scottish Literature 1400–1650
Edited by Nicola Royan
ISBN 978-1-908980-23-6

International Companion to Scottish Literature of the Long Eighteenth Century
Edited by Leith Davis and Janet Sorensen
ISBN 978-1-908980-31-1

International Companion to Nineteenth-Century Scottish Literature
Edited by Sheila M. Kidd, Caroline McCracken-Flesher, and Kenneth McNeil
ISBN 978-1-908980-35-9

International Companion to Scottish Children's Literature
Edited by Maureen A. Farrell and Robert A. Davis
ISBN 978-1-908980-41-0

The International Companion to Scottish Children's Literature

Edited by Maureen A. Farrell
and Robert A. Davis

Scottish Literature International

Published by
Scottish Literature International
Scottish Literature
7 University Gardens
University of Glasgow
Glasgow G12 8QH

Scottish Literature International is an imprint of
the Association for Scottish Literature

www.asls.org.uk

ASL is a registered charity no. SC006535

First published 2024

Text © ASL and the individual contributors

All rights reserved. No part of this book may be
reproduced, stored in a retrieval system, or
transmitted in any form or means, electronic,
mechanical, photocopying, recording or otherwise,
without the prior permission of the
Association for Scottish Literature.

A CIP catalogue for this title
is available from the British Library

ISBN 978-1-908980-41-0

Contents

Series Editors' Preface vii
Acknowledgements ix

Introduction 1
Maureen A. Farrell and Robert A. Davis
1. The Origins of Scottish Children's Literature 12
Maureen A. Farrell
2. 'Through the Midnight Sea': Some Dimensions of Scottish Children's Poetry 31
Robert A. Davis
3. Children's Scottish Historical Fiction 62
Beth Dickson
4. A 'Spell of Stories': Scottish Children's Fantasy 78
Sarah Dunnigan
5. Gaelic Plays for Children 1900–1950 99
Sìm Innes
6. Stevenson's Junior Fiction 115
David Robb
7. Mollie Hunter's Teen Fiction: Transitioning through Enchanted Humanness to Adulthood 130
Ralph Jessop
8. Adolescent Citizenship in Cathy MacPhail's *Mosi's War* and Claire McFall's *Bombmaker* 149
Fiona McCulloch
9. From Fairy Cauldrons to *An Gruffalo*: The Development and Challenges of Scottish Gaelic Children's Literature 166
Mairi Kidd
10. Scottish Children's Picturebooks Within a European and Global Context 176
Penni Cotton
11. Ambition and Identity: Scottish Children's Literary Prizewinners 191
Morna Fleming

Contents (continued)

12. Scottish Poetry in the Scottish Secondary Classroom: Seeing Beyond the Set Texts 206
    Jennifer Farrar
13. Scottish Children's Literature: Where Are We Now? 224
    Maureen A. Farrell

    Endnotes 233
    Further Reading 265
    Notes on Contributors 271
    Index 275

Series Editors' Preface

This series, developing steadily since its first volume was published by Edinburgh University Press in 2009, now comprises some twenty-three volumes, roughly classifiable under three broad headings: period volumes, author volumes and genre/topic volumes. Each has been edited and contained chapters by leading experts in the field. This, the twenty-fourth in the series, on the topic of Scottish children's literature, continues that record of high-quality contributions on aspects of key importance to the appreciation and enjoyment of Scottish literature.

In addressing the topic of Scottish children's literature, the editors have considered with care and discrimination the question of the nature of what 'children's literature' is. They have adopted a multi-perspectives approach: some chapters are historical, some generic and some focused on individual authors or groups of authors. In achieving this, the editors have encouraged commentaries which, while recognising ancient traditions, provide detailed discussions of writing for children over the last three centuries in chapters which refer, as appropriate, to writing in all three of Scotland's long-established literary languages, while not forgetting the importance of picturebooks within a global context. They conclude with overviews which consider developments since the mid-twentieth century in the nature of prize-winning novels, key issues regarding the contemporary teaching of poetry in schools and the possible future growth of the genre.

The International Companion to Scottish Children's Literature provides an apt addition to the sequence of subjects foregrounded in the *Companion* series we have had the honour of series-editing.

Ian Brown
Thomas Owen Clancy

This book is dedicated to Professor Douglas Gifford (1940–2020), a distinguished professor of Scottish Literature, an inspirational teacher, and stalwart champion of Scottish children's literature.

Acknowledgements

A volume of this kind accrues many debts. Our greatest are to our contributors for their unflagging commitment and dedicated scholarship. Alongside these stand our expert and supportive Series Editors, Ian Brown and Thomas Owen Clancy. Invaluable support has also been provided by Duncan Jones and Philippa Osmond-Williams.

The collection draws much strength and inspiration from the expanding academic interest in Scottish children's literature. Our own university has played an integral role in this and we record our deep gratitude to the colleagues who have contributed to and supported this work, particularly in the University of Glasgow's two successful Masters programmes – the Masters in Children's Literature and Literacies and the Masters in Children's Literature, Media and Cultural Entrepreneurship (Erasmus Mundus International Master) and the international research that accompanies these. Thanks are owed especially to Jim McGonigal, Evelyn Arizpe, Julie McAdam and Jennifer Farrar.

Beyond the University of Glasgow, thanks are also due also to a network of supporters – academics, authors, teachers and fellow enthusiasts. These include: Morag Styles, Theresa Breslin, and Ronnie Renton and fellow members of the Education Committee of the Association for Scottish Literature.

In bringing this work to completion, it is our sincere hope that the contents of this International Companion repay fully the trust placed in us over these last several years by our many friends and allies in this project.

Maureen Farrell
Bob Davis
Glasgow April 2024

Introduction

Maureen A. Farrell and Robert A. Davis

Context

When *The Edinburgh History of Scottish Literature* was published by Edinburgh University Press in 2007 it contained two chapters that considered Scottish children's literature: '"Half a trade and half an art": Adult and Juvenile Fiction in the Victorian Period' by Colin Milton in volume 2, and 'The Lost Boys and Girls of Scottish Children's Fiction' by Maureen Farrell in volume 3. These were probably the very first chapters to appear in a history or anthology of Scottish literature specifically focusing on Scottish *children's* literature. Most promisingly, the 2024 publication of *A Companion to Scottish Literature*, edited by Gerard Carruthers, includes a chapter on children's literature by Sarah Dunnigan.[1] In it, she comments that despite some attempts to redress this balance it remains 'a critical map whose cartographies remain to be charted in detail'.[2] This book is a contribution to that task.

The absence of a volume of this kind on Scottish children's literature is not as strange as it may first appear. The study of children's literature as an academic discipline in general is a relatively recent phenomenon, emerging most strongly from the 1970s onwards. Since then, it has proliferated. In the last five decades scholars have been mapping and exploring the huge academic field of children's literature to the point where there is now a sufficiently large and respected community of children's literature scholars and critics worldwide to elevate the standing of the discipline to the highest academic level.[3]

Within the accepted canon of children's literature, considerable status has been accrued by 'English' and American children's literature in particular. The term 'English' has been placed in inverted commas here because up until very recent times Scottish children's literature was subsumed into that category: the work of Scottish authors has been included in what should be more accurately identified as 'British Children's

Literature'.[4] Indeed, writers such as Sir Walter Scott, George MacDonald and J. M. Barrie produced works that have since become children's literature classics and they themselves had significant influence on diverse children's authors including writers such as Lewis Carroll and C. S. Lewis. While the work of Scottish authors has been included in British children's literature, it has not been widely recognised specifically for its distinctively Scottish character.

Recent events in Scottish society, the debates about devolution, the reinstatement of the Scottish parliament in 1999, the momentous 2014 referendum debate on Scottish independence, the 2016 Brexit referendum and its consequences for Britain's exit from the EU in 2019 all signal a watershed in the theme of 'local governance'. Each has drawn renewed media attention to the various expressions of Scottish culture and their status on the international stage.[5] Since devolution in 1999, Scotland's literature sector, in particular, has undergone an unprecedented period of rapid, sustained and dramatic expansion, a process paralleled by the growing profile of Scottish writers internationally. During the same period, Scottish children's literature and Scottish children's writers have perhaps not received the same level of critical attention, though their progress has been just as significant. In 2000, the Modern Language Association of America recognised Scottish literature as a national literature; presumably Scottish children's literature is included as part of that, but it was not specifically highlighted. The time seems right to address this kind of omission and this volume is a first step towards locating Scottish children's literature solidly in the heart of both Scottish literature and children's literature. The idea of an *International Companion to Scottish Children's Literature*, hence, arose as part of a cultural conversation about a body of work that has been critically and educationally neglected. Scottish children's literature has a distinguished, but largely unrecognised, history, a vibrant present and an inviting future which will begin to be showcased in the chapters in this volume.

The International Companions series offers students, scholars and general readers fresh insight into key authors, periods and topics within the corpus of Scottish literature. In addition, the series offers linked collections of authoritative and readable studies of aspects of Scottish Literature that are both succinct and yet which draw confidently on the most recent research. Within the series it has long been recognised that there is an urgent need for a single-volume companion to *Scottish Children's Literature* which offers both a general introduction to its riches and also provides some analysis and contextualisation that allows the student and general reader to develop a coherent overview of its scope and nature. This volume, which has been in development over the last six years, draws on the fresh insights offered by recent scholarship and takes account of contemporary developments in recognising the contribution of Scottish children's literature to the field of children's literature generically – as well as to the heritage of Scottish literature itself.

The present Companion will begin to stake out the terrain of contemporary Scottish children's literature but not in a forensic way. It covers some of the major authors, genres and works in Scottish children's literature, serving as an introduction to the field, both describing and exploring the canon for a new audience with a clear purpose: the identification and analysis of Scottish children's literature within an informed academic and critical framework. The field is examined historically, comparatively, generically: introducing it and raising questions and concepts by excavating underlying patterns of literary and cultural development. The foremost intention is that this book will initiate a conversation which will range beyond the confines of the volume itself, extending to Scottish children's literature the literary critical status and interest it surely now merits.

Of course, a volume of this kind cannot claim to be exhaustive, it is not an encyclopaedia with an aim for comprehensive coverage and inevitably there will be areas that receive minimal or no attention. These absences in themselves will act as catalysts for further research and publications to contribute to the growing study of the field.

Scotland's Languages

The introduction to a volume on Scottish children's literature cannot avoid discussion of one of the most important and challenging topics: the question of language. This question has been and continues to be a central one in the reception of Scottish literature both domestically and in international English-speaking markets. Much of the debate surrounding the state of contemporary Scottish fiction generally inevitably raises questions of a linguistic nature.[6] The issue of language in Scottish *children's* books is also a complex one. In any nation where one language is in effect the official one, yet where more people speak another language, there is bound to be confusion and periodically discord. In Scotland, the problem is compounded by the fact that the Scots language, unlike Gaelic, exists on a linguistic continuum along with Standard English. In 2024 a further consultation on Scotland's Languages was initiated. The attached

Bill included the Scottish Government's proposals to give Scots legal status alongside Gaelic and English, something that should be perceived as a significant opportunity for recognising linguistic diversity. An added factor in contemporary society for writers depicting Scottish children, then, is the acknowledgement that there are in fact at least three indigenous languages in regular use in Scotland: Gaelic, Scots and English.

Scots language is a set of forms into which the Germanic language, known to modern philologists as Old English, has developed within urban and rural lowland Scotland, and regions such as Caithness, Orkney and Shetland.[7] It is the language of a people with a distinctive and fascinating social history reflected in a folk culture of exceptional richness. Scots is not a dialect – for the simple reason that it includes numerous different dialects – but it has also been asserted that neither is it a language in the full sense that English and French are languages: it does not, for example, have a standard system of spelling and grammar.[8]

Scots is often defined negatively, as consisting only of pronunciations, grammatical features and vocabulary items that are not found in standard literary English.[9] Scots speakers typically retain pronunciations that have disappeared or were never used in England and use distinctive grammatical constructions and vocabulary. There are currently three related varieties of 'language' derived from earlier varieties of English used commonly in Scotland: Scots, Scottish Standard English (SSE) and English of the kinds spoken in England – Anglo-English. These are not discrete sets of categories but more often a continuum of usages. Scottish Standard English is historically a different entity from Scots. The majority of the contemporary population speak some kind of Scottish English but will write English Standard English or a close approximation thereto.

Traditional criticism, expressed most stringently in the twentieth century by F. R. Leavis, assumes that literature as a whole, as well as each successful work within it, can be tested by the criterion of whether or not it forms an organic unity. Since this unity is revealed in this critical tradition at the level of language, the fact that Burns and Scott wrote not only in Scots and English, but also by mixing Scots and English, necessarily means that their work, and the work of many Scottish children's authors, will fail such a narrow test of organic unity. There is also, as Derrick McClure pointed out in 1996,[10] the added paradox that 'traditional Scots forms may be valued in the work of Burns and Scott but denigrated in the speech of children'.[11] McClure's insight surely reflects attitudes hostile to Scots revealed in a 1946 Scottish Education Department report – whose influence lasted for many years – when it asserted that 'the first duty of the infant teachers [in Scotland], and the continuing duty of all primary teachers, is to implant and cultivate fluent speech in standard English',[12] going on to assert that Scots speech 'is not the language of "educated" people anywhere, and could not be described as a suitable medium of education or culture'.[13] It is perhaps for this reason, more than any other, that publishers have wrestled with 'Scottish' literature and its likely appeal furth of Scotland: it highlights that the linguistic dilemma for Scottish children's writers is more acute than in almost any other literary category. Language style can be an important marker of identity. Children learn to use language or languages in culturally shaped ways and through language are introduced to a particular tradition of oral and written literature and to particular sets of knowledge and values.

Attitudes towards the Scots language have changed in recent years, particularly in the educational context, and as might be expected, this change of attitude has been reflected and refracted by Scottish authors writing both for children and adults. Because of the powerfully didactic elements in children's literature, of course, this change has a significant impact on literature for children. Where previously an author might have struggled with the decision about the language to be used because of its potential effect on readers as either a barrier or gateway to understanding the story, they now have, effectively, permission to use the full range of language appropriate to the context of the stories. These language choices are not without consequences. Publishers may still decide that the language choice impedes understanding, and thus either request linguistic changes or refuse to publish for an international audience. Authors also may choose to ignore these difficulties and, as some always have done, maintain the linguistic integrity of the text in terms of its setting in both place and time. It is the special history of the Scots language that has made Scottish writers so culturally alert to the co-existing differences, and disparities in power, between it and English, between what is said and how it is written; what is written and how we speak; and when and in what genre we do one and not the other.

If the Scottish voice is quite clearly part of a sense of Scottishness, unique to Scotland and forming a bond between children, their home and their world, then Scottish languages and literature can surely contribute to a child's sense of national, and so personal, identity. Studies of children's literature have to begin with children learning their language and learning to play with it in the fashion of their cultures. Thus, Scottish children's literature must be fully present, so that children are made aware of the richness and potential of the Scottish voice in literature and, in turn they can become interested in seeing it maintained. It is in the education system and the media that the complete recognition of Scottish linguistic diversity must begin, and it is through an inclusive attitude to language that literature seeks to define the relationships between children and culture. Children learn to read their culture right from the start of their education and discover quickly how reading overlaps with their lives.

Scotland's Children

The rationale for a collection of this kind inevitably also highlights the question of a 'Scottish Childhood' and of 'Scottish Children', interacting in complex ways with the literature designed for, and consumed by, those children over extended periods of time.

Broadly understood, the historic narrative of childhood in Scotland conformed between medieval and modern times in large measure to the patterns seen elsewhere in Europe – marked conspicuously by the operations of the key institutions of family and community on the lives of young people. These were expressed, for example, in laws concerning cross-family fosterage and the obligations laid on responsible adults for the physical security and flourishing of children in the community.[14] It remains difficult to determine, however, the extent to which these rubrics made appreciable difference in practice to the lives of the young in subsistence agrarian societies where life was routinely hard and often short. A previous generation of Scottish historians complained over a prolonged period that the history of the Scottish family had yet to be written.[15] While much has been done in recent decades to remedy this shortcoming, significant gaps remain in our understanding of the experience of childhood for large sections of the Scottish population over lengthy periods of time. Very little yet exists, for example, to match Nicholas Orme's trilogy for English childhood, despite the work of Janay Nugent and Elizabeth Ewan.[16]

It seems clear, nonetheless, that the relative absence until comparatively recently of children's voices and testimony from the Scottish record testifies in its silence to the multiple layers of their cultural abjection and exclusion. We have moved in our knowledge in the last generation significantly beyond the cultural pessimism of the histories of childhood misleadingly promulgated by some of the followers of Philippe Aries, recognising more fully than before the experience of affection, love and belonging of which many children were certainly beneficiaries in their families and their common life in medieval and early modern times. Nevertheless, none of this disguises the sharply subordinate position of children and young people in highly stratified societies, subject to the strict authority of parents, elders and religious figureheads of all types who commonly paid scant attention to their interests and perspectives, declared or otherwise. Against a backdrop of high infant mortality and premature death, existence for most Scottish children until well into the nineteenth century would have been arduous and uncertain – dominated by early initiation into work and shaped by scarcity, disease and fierce intermittent conflict.[17]

In one key domain, of course, it has been claimed by historians and affirmed in the popular imagination that the experience of Scottish children has been since (at least) the middle of the sixteenth century distinctive: education. Education is hence an important and recurring motif in this collection. A fragmentary vernacular national narrative punctuated by insecure memories of the Wars of Independence, Mary Queen of Scots, the Highland Clearances, Enlightenment and industrialisation has also celebrated prominently the coming of 'a school in every parish' milestone as a signature event in the nation's story – extrapolated to the later 'branding' of a much-prized 'Scottish Education' across the territories and dominions of the British Empire and Commonwealth.[18] Heated debates among historians have of course led inevitably to various waves of revisionism questioning the origins, scale and effectiveness of the 1560 Knoxian revolution in education.[19] Nevertheless, enough has survived of the original claims to retain recognition of the strong place of formal schooling in the lives (and equally importantly the imaginations and aspirations) of Scotland's children from the early modern period onwards and attributable in large measure to the innovations of the Protestant reformers. Conceding its inconsistency, its piecemeal resourcing and immense regional, class and gender imbalances over several centuries, we can still point to comparatively high levels of national literacy, participation in elementary schools and respect for the institutions of education, most especially the ancient universities.[20] There seems therefore to be little doubt that the creation of an identifiable readership for children's literature was deeply interwoven in the national psyche with the strategic spread of basic literacy and the steady creation of generations of competent child-readers in schools and homes.

Again, as in other comparable societies, considered attention to, and respect for, children's voices and children's testimonies in Scotland necessarily had to wait for the rise of a 'rights discourse' in European

Enlightenment and Revolutionary thought from the late eighteenth century onwards. As the rights of man extended first to contemplation of the rights of women and, sporadically – often dismissively – to the possibility of the rights of children, Scottish philanthropic and paternalist endeavour driving the expansion of schooling began to take more seriously the 'witness' of children to the difficult conditions they were facing in field and factory.[21] This witness could take many forms: from the shrill, ventriloquised child-voices of certain strains of Scottish Romanticism, to the reforming zeal of activists such as Robert Owen, Thomas Chalmers and David Stow, seeking sincerely (if often naïvely) to get close to the felt realities of childhood often in conditions of pervasive deprivation. Increasing state annexation of these progressive impulses gave rise in the twentieth century to the widespread social and psychological science concern with children's accounts of their own experiences, their statements of their often-conflicted desires and goals, and their broader profile of needs.[22] Education and Health became the national vehicles, in Scotland and elsewhere after the two world wars, for giving shape and substance to this new understanding of, and commitment to, children and the 'good childhood'. 'Child-centredness' emerged as the core value of a welfare enterprise which in many respects sought to measure its effectiveness on the scale of children's wellbeing. Such a shift in the cultural climate meant that as an increasingly integrated post-war global movement began to press for formal United Nations recognition of the Rights of the Child, Scotland was among the first nations to embrace wholeheartedly this institutional expression of a new covenant between the generations and the affirmation of children's agency entailed by it.[23]

The actual experience of childhood sedimented out of these historical and contemporary forces is, of course, an immensely varied one and twenty-first century Scotland continues to meet this variety with both celebration and concern. Scottish children's literature has often been an important locus for, for example, the examination of social and economic inequality. It has often been the means of giving voice, current or retrospective, to the voiceless and the forgotten. It has figured repeatedly in campaigning for better treatment of disadvantaged or abandoned children. It has warned of danger (social, communal, environmental, global) and called out injustice. At the same time, avoiding a fatalistic outlook amidst such stark realism, the literature has also been a vital channel for capturing and communicating the pleasures of childhood – in play, companionship, adventure, imagination, discovery and place. Once again, we see in this collection discussion of many of these dimensions of Scottish childhood, past and present.

Scotland and its Literatures

Acknowledging the centrality of literature to the manifold developments described above, it is necessary to provide a stipulative, working definition of Scottish literature, one which will be used to inform the text selection within this volume. It is derived from the prior primary research of one of the editors:

> A Scottish text can best be described as a coherent and substantial body of writing, in many possible modes and genres, which deals centrally with issues of life and experience in Scotland, is set in Scotland, or which exhibits recognisably Scottish attitudes towards Scotland or the world at large. Such writing will engage the reader in the identification of and reflection on the wide range of cultural communities and individual experiences which constitute a distinctive national culture. While mainly produced by Scottish writers, texts need not be limited to Scottish authorship; the experience of non-Scots living and working in Scotland or commenting on Scottish life and culture from outside, when coherent and substantial, can justifiably be regarded as a valuable contribution to Scottish Literature. Additionally, Scottish born writers can write material that is not overtly Scottish in nature but if told in their own true and unique Scots voice then it should be considered a Scottish text.[24]

Using this definition, examples of Scottish children's literature include: *Daughter of the Sea* (1996) by Berlie Doherty, a non-Scottish author setting work in Scotland; *The Wilderness Wars* (2018) by Barbara Henderson, a non-Scottish author who describes herself as 'Scots by inclination' living and setting work in Scotland; *Caged* (2016) by Theresa Breslin, a Scottish author writing material that is not overtly Scottish; the *Harry Potter* books (1997–2007) by J. K. Rowling, a non-Scottish author living in Scotland, though Douglas Gifford argues that the 'values she embraces and the conflict in her world between good and bad clearly follow fundamental Scottish novelistic themes';[25] *Welcome to Nowhere* (2017) by Elizabeth Laird, exhibiting Scottish attitudes to the world at large; *Cold Tom* (2002) by Sally Prue, a non-Scottish author using an original Scottish text ('Tam Lin') as source material. Nicola Morgan, another non-Scot who has lived and set her work in Scotland, has supported just such an expansive conceptualisation, arguing that trying to identify what constitutes a Scottish book is only difficult if you confuse 'Scottish' with 'local'. The definition offered here avoids that position and defines Scottish literature as confident, outward-looking and inclusive.

What should become obvious from this brief overview of some of the issues raised here is that the chapters within this volume, commissioned under specific thematic titles, resulted in the writers tackling the material in ways that they found meaningful and sometimes that resulted in indirect and unexpected perspectives that nevertheless were relevant to the thematic topic. The fact that the contexts are varied and the chapters emerge with distinctive and original viewpoints suggests a freshness in approach to an important, if largely unrecognised, history of Scottish children's literature.

Content

The thirteen chapters in this volume run the gamut from the origins of Scottish children's literature through chapters considering aspects of Scottish children's poetry; historical fiction for children; Scottish children's fantasy; Stevenson's junior fiction; Gaelic children's literature; Scottish children's picturebooks; consideration of the work of Mollie Hunter; an examination of Cathy MacPhail's work representing young adult Scottish literature; recognition of the strength of Scottish children's literature as revealed in Scottish children's literary prizewinners; and finishing up with a brief overview of where we are now, reflecting on the health and potential of Scottish children's literature today and into the future. Clearly, the chapters can be 'dipped into' following interest and inclination. Alternatively, some chapters lend themselves to a linked or thematic sequence such as, for example, linking Sarah Dunnigan's chapter on Scottish children's fantasy literature with Sìm Innes's and Mairi Kidd's chapters on Gaelic children's literature. There are many possible combinations. Given the range of the contributions, some of the chapters inevitably reflect particular moments in time or specific educational and cultural arrangements which of course are subject to change. This is a deliberate editorial choice intended to show that some features of the Scottish children's literary tradition have a long and enduring pedigree, while others capture particular historical intersections and experiences which will not long outlive the structures that support them. Thus, we note that the regulations for Scottish education are provisional and subject to reform, as is the Scottish Qualifications Authority (SQA) itself. Jennifer Farrar's chapter on Scottish poetry in the secondary classroom is a case in point. It reflects the situation before the SQA's planned refreshment of the list of set texts in the 2025–26 school year – but nevertheless addresses important issues relating to notions of canonicity and inclusion in a modern, multicultural society. We also note that publishers come and go and that publishing practices in specialist areas evolve over time.

Readers may feel there are some obvious omissions, and as editors we would not argue with that, but considering the purpose of this volume as an initial showcase for the wealth of material which constitutes Scottish children's and young adult literature, we hope that it sets the scene and whets the appetite for further critical and creative engagement with this exciting domain.

CHAPTER ONE

The Origins of Scottish Children's Literature

Maureen A. Farrell

British children's literature is recognised as having a long and distinguished history or, rather, English children's literature has this accolade. Certainly, in reading the many histories of children's literature that abound one would be hard pushed to find Scottish children's literature acknowledged or the work of Scottish authors recognised. Only in recent years has this issue begun to be fully addressed. This volume is an example of one of the ways this is being done.

The Development of Children's Literature

The development of children's literature follows a similar pattern around the world. In the early stages of printed literature hardly any books produced specifically for children are generated. Gradually, books for educational purposes or courtesy books begin to appear, then, what are sometimes termed 'text' books. Children, as they learn to read, also take on adult books that appeal to them – a process helped by the fact, as outlined by Sheila Ray, that early printed material in any society is likely to draw on traditional stories that appeal to every age group.[1] Religion is also an important factor in the development of printed literature and, often, the earliest books specifically for children tend to be simplified versions of religious books or publications designed to support religious or moral instruction. Poetry, ballads and nursery rhymes also appear in the early stages of development of children's literature. Gradually, stories specifically written for children begin to appear and eventually they become more varied and soon special interest material begins to emerge. Maria Nikolajeva points out that in European countries this process has taken about five hundred years.[2]

The development of children's literature is also centrally linked to social, educational and, above all, economic factors. In Britain, children's literature really began to flourish in the nineteenth century when the population was growing, educational opportunities were increasing, technological advances made both paper and printing more readily available, and the influence of Locke and Rousseau and the Romantics fed through to children's books. The move towards universal education and the increase in size of the middle class helped create a reading public and a viable market for children's books. The advent of literary magazines proved a cheap and effective way of getting reading materials into the hands of children. By the end of the nineteenth century, full-colour picturebooks were becoming available at competitive prices. But the real flowering of children's literature in Britain occurred in the twentieth century.

The advances made in children's literature in the early part of the twentieth century were curtailed almost completely by the world wars. But the process of change has been going on since the end of the Second World War. Since the 1960s, there has been a huge increase in children's literature in Britain, with writers from the constituent countries, whose common language is English, moving easily across national boundaries. However, the literature they produced was always identified as 'English' children's literature, albeit with an international dimension – in common with children's literature throughout the world.

In the early part of the twentieth century, children's literature was still marginalised, undervalued and generally excluded from mainstream literature. As Sandra Beckett argues, the rise of children's literature, like texts by women and other minority groups, 'owes a great debt to post-modernism and its tendency to eliminate barriers, level hierarchies and give equal voice to all'.[3] Since 1970, children's literature has grown steadily as a significant field of scholarship: the first British research conference on children's literature was held in 1979. Now freed from many of the traditional restrictions, rigid moral codes and taboos of the past, children's literature offers a wide range of topics including philosophical, political, socio-cultural and economic issues aimed at a more clearly defined audience that includes both children's and young adult literature.

With these developments, the issue of the definition of children's literature seems to have grown in prominence. Defining children's literature is one of the most contested topics within its study and since this issue has been extensively debated in other forums, rather than rehearse this debate again, a more fruitful strategy here is to offer a stipulative definition of children's and young adult literature that will be used in this chapter and throughout the book.

> Children's literature is a body of literature, in a range of modes, intended for child or young adult audiences which, either deliberately or inadvertently, addresses or depicts the concerns, interests or experiences of its intended audience. The subject matter should engage, entertain, enthuse, change, challenge, inform or provoke responses from its readers. The primary purpose of the texts should be for enjoyment but may also provide relevant pedagogic opportunities for readers.

Scottish Children's Literature

As noted earlier, the process of developing what is now recognised as children's literature in Europe has taken about five hundred years. However, as with all such entities, 'Europe' is made up a large number of constituent elements, not all of whose children's literatures developed at the same time and not all of whose children's literatures have achieved equal recognition. Even within Great Britain the children's literatures of the constituent nations of Scotland, Wales and Ireland have tended to be overshadowed by those of England. Harvey Darton's seminal work *Children's Books in England* (1998 [1932])[4] includes coverage of the work of *some* Scottish authors – Stevenson, MacDonald, Barrie and Crockett for example – but their work and national identities are subsumed under the canopy of 'English'. The work of Scottish authors for children has historically been in the vanguard of the development of children's literature in Britain, yet is rarely mentioned and hardly ever acknowledged in mainstream studies of the subject. Julia Briggs in her chapter in *Children's Literature: An Illustrated History*[5] does acknowledge the large Scottish contribution to writing for children from the 1860s. There is however little evidence of, or discussion about, the nature of that 'large Scottish contribution'. There seems to have been virtually no acknowledgement in standard reference texts of the existence of a tradition of Scottish writing for young people, a tradition that stretches over some 180 years. Exceptions are Stuart Hannabuss's short survey in 1996 (second edition 2004)[6] and two ground-breaking reviews of Scottish publishing policies for children's books and comics by Jane Potter and Helen Williams[7] and Joseph McAleer.[8]

Even in two major encyclopaedias of children's literature, *The International Companion Encyclopaedia of Children's Literature* (2004)[9] and *The Oxford Encyclopaedia of Children's Literature* (2006)[10] the entries for Scottish children's literature are minimal. There are three pages of information in the former and entries on eighteen Scottish writers and illustrators in the latter, a list which does not include J. M. Barrie. Matthew Grenby has noted that:

> Although a substantial amount of critical analysis has now been carried out into particular Scottish children's books, for instance, no full-scale bibliography for children published in Scotland, or about Scottish subjects exists.[11]

He comments that the Scottish tradition of children's literature has been, until recently, 'silently subsumed' in what is commonly labelled English children's literature. In this expression the terms 'British' and 'English' are conflated tellingly. The distinctive cultures grafted on to English culture, often with unhealed scars, are almost completely eliminated as cultural sources or influences. Perhaps the essential differences between Scottish and British children's literatures have not been articulated because of the lack of specific archival work on Scottish texts. Until recently, Scottish, Welsh and Irish children's literatures have earned references as, in Heather Scutter's words, 'timeless and de-historicised fonts of Celtic myth, legend and oral tradition'.[12] The Irish have tackled the issue head on over the last thirty years and identified a thriving and distinctive canon as well as an internationally renowned academy of scholars in the area. Equally, Scottish children's literature is much more than 'myth, legend or oral tradition' both traditionally and historically and, more interestingly, continues to be so.

Scottish Children's Literature and the Question of Language

To reprise and amplify points made in the introduction: any discussion of Scottish children's literature must include some discussion on the topic of language. The question of language has been, and continues to be, central in the reception of Scottish Literature for both adults and children, both domestically and in international English-speaking markets. This raises linguistic questions. Language – vocabulary particular to a nation, expressions and so forth – becomes an important factor in the construction of literary nationality as it is a vehicle of nationality in itself. A sense of national identity is often largely expressed by language and so knowledge about the languages of Scotland is particularly important in developing and building an understanding and appreciation of cultural heritage. There are three historic and current spoken and literary languages in Scotland: Gaelic, Scots and English. Children's literature can be written in any of these languages. The issue of the Scots language in Scottish children's books is a complex one. In Scotland, the problem is compounded by the fact that Scots, unlike Gaelic, exists on a linguistic continuum alongside both English Standard English and Scottish Standard English.

The linguistic dilemma, then, for Scottish children's writers is acute. Language style can be an important marker of identity. Children learn to use language or languages in culturally shaped ways. Through language, they are introduced to a particular tradition of oral and written literature and to particular sets of knowledge and values. As the issue of the Scots language has come to the fore in recent years and its place within literature has been reset, the place of Scots has also been reassessed within Scottish education and, consequently, within Scottish children's literature.

As might be expected, this changing attitude has been reflected and refracted by Scottish authors writing both for children and adults. Because of the powerfully didactic elements in children's literature, this change has, of course, the greatest impact on literature for children. Where previously an author may have struggled with the decision about the language to be used because of its potential effect on readers as either a barrier or gateway to understanding the story, they now have, effectively, permission to use the full range of language appropriate to the context of the stories. These language choices are not without consequences. Publishers may still decide that the language choice impedes understanding and, therefore, either request linguistic changes or refuse to publish for an international audience. Authors also may choose to ignore these difficulties and, as some always have done, maintain the linguistic integrity of the text in terms of its setting in both place and time. It is the special history of the Scots language that has made Scottish writers so culturally alert to the co-existing differences, and disparities in power, between it and English, between what is said and how it is written; what is written and how we speak; and when and in what registers and genres we employ one and not the other. To a great extent these issues of language have played out in Scottish children's literature since its beginnings.

The Origins and Development of Scottish Children's Literature

Scotland has its own distinctive literary history and traditions as well as a particularly strong oral tradition of ballads, songs and storytelling based on myths, legends, key events – such as battles – religious stories and versions of biblical stories. The Scottish emphasis, from the time of John Knox in the sixteenth century, on education, and particularly literacy education for the purpose of reading the Bible, means that it is only to be expected that there would be a strong literary tradition of writing for children. Initially of course, the material produced certainly mirrored the development of children's literature outlined earlier. Books containing stories from the Bible, publications designed to support religious and moral instruction, primers, educational or courtesy books, all give way to textbooks and eventually to material specifically written for children. Earlier, Robert Henryson, poet and pre-Reformation schoolmaster in Dunfermline, had written his *Morall Fabillis*, a group of tales based on the traditions of Aesop and Renard, in Scots in the fifteenth century. Despite the fact that the Aesop fables were among the most obvious printed matter that could be adapted for children, Henryson's version cannot easily be dubbed children's literature. Notwithstanding their humour, their pre-occupation with religious and philosophical questions does not make them immediately accessible to children.

The emergence of Scottish literature written specifically for a child audience can be traced to the early nineteenth century, to Sir Walter Scott's *Tales of a Grandfather* (1828–30)[13] which offered an engaging introduction to Scottish history, and thence to the publication of *Holiday House* by Catherine Sinclair in 1839.[14] At the same time as these books were being written and published, nation states were assuming their modern form and cultivating particular kinds of literature as commensurate expressions of national cultures. The juvenile reading audience in Scotland grew in size and commercial importance from the mid-nineteenth century as religious suspicion of the effects of fiction on the young diminished. It grew further from the passing of the 1872 Education (Scotland) Act which, as well as establishing English as the language for education, also made school attendance compulsory for all children. In addition, the slow development of public libraries in Scotland after the Act of 1853, which permitted the raising of a rate to support them, was boosted by donations from the Scottish-American multi-millionaire Andrew Carnegie. His positive experience of access to private libraries as a poor immigrant to the USA led him in the last decades of the century and into the early twentieth century to offer local authorities throughout Britain the capital to build libraries on the sole condition they would take responsibility for their future maintenance. The importance of the role public libraries played in creating an appetite for books and in shaping the tastes of young readers from decidedly non-literary backgrounds must, as Colin Milton has demonstrated, not be underestimated.[15]

The earliest Scottish texts, other than chapbooks, specifically written for child audiences were the four series of Scott's *Tales of a Grandfather* mentioned above and published in 1828, 1829, 1830 and 1996 (the last was left unfinished and unpublished at the time of the author's death and was published only in the twentieth century by the University of Iowa). These texts were published eighty-five years after John Newbery published *A Little Pretty Pocket Book* (1744),[16] commonly regarded as one of the first English children's books as modern audiences would recognise them. Unlike this miscellany of tales and puzzles, Scott's stories were intended to be a narrative history of Scotland. Scott was partly inspired by John Wilson Crocker's *Stories Selected from the History of England for Children* which had been published in England in 1822,[17] and partly by having a specific audience for the book in mind, his six-year-old grandson John Hugh Lockhart, known as Hugh Littlejohn.

Scott had very particular views about the expectations of a child audience. He firmly believed that young readers did not like being 'written down' to their level and that they preferred a challenge to their understanding and curiosity. He hoped to cater for both juvenile and popular audiences and thus, he wrote on 8 July 1827 to 'find a way between what a child can comprehend and what shall not yet be absolutely uninteresting to a grown reader'.[18] As a consequence, these tales make a significant contribution to the debate about, and practice of, writing for children. More particularly, Sir Walter Scott's strong views about appropriate content and register for writing for children and his concern about the potential impact of the available books on young readers led him to make an important remark to another Edinburgh-born author, Catherine Sinclair. In the preface to *Holiday House* Sinclair records Sir Walter Scott's vision of children at the time and his concern that:

> in the rising generation there would be no poets, wits or orators, because all play of the imagination is now carefully discouraged, and books written for young persons are generally a mere dry record of facts, unenlivened by any appeal to the heart, or any excitement to the fancy.[19]

It may be useful to consider this remark in the light of Scott's own deliberations about whether or not to let 'romantic fiction rest' and to turn to composing 'histories for boys and girls which may be useful as fictions for Children of a larger growth which can at best be only idle folks' entertainment' in his journal entry for 7 January 1828.[20] One can only assume he did not intend his own histories would be 'dry records of facts'.

From a historical point of view, the book Catherine Sinclair wrote, having been influenced by those remarks, *Holiday House*, is one of the most important books in the history of children's literature: it was written with the specific intention of changing the quality and kind of reading supplied for young people. It is frequently identified as a turning point in children's literature and as a bridge between earlier, more obvious, didactic literature and the more liberated work of authors like Lewis Carroll and others. Recognised as a foundational text in general accounts of children's literature, the novel's Scottish setting and context and its place within the Scottish literary tradition are rarely mentioned or acknowledged in literary criticism.

The first acknowledged 'golden age' of children's literature in the English-speaking world took place between 1860 until around 1926. Scots writing for children during this time include R. L. Stevenson, George MacDonald, Andrew Lang, J. M. Barrie, S. R. Crockett, John Buchan, Kenneth Grahame, R. M. Ballantyne and Ian MacLaren. Particularly influential at this time was George MacDonald. From 1869 to 1873, he edited the magazine *Good Words for the Young*, founded in 1868. *At the back of the North Wind* (1871)[21] was first published here and the pressure to fill its pages produced MacDonald's best work for children. *The Princess and the Goblin*, *The Light Princess* and *The Princess and Curdie* were all serialised here, along with other, more realistic, fictions including Stevenson's *Treasure Island* (1883). Totally liberated from any didactic purpose, *Treasure Island* rode roughshod over what had previously been the rules for children's writing. In this adventure tale, Long John Silver is a much less obvious villain than previous exemplars, displaying some heroic qualities. The boundaries between good and bad, black and white became blurred, yet the text is written with great sensitivity to the narrative needs of his young audience. Stevenson's friend Andrew Lang edited a highly influential series of fairy and folk tales, beginning with *The Blue Fairy Book* (1889). He followed this with an original fairy tale of some humour and distinction, *Prince Prigio* (1889). These books furnished readers with a wealth of classic fairy tales and reintroduced many traditional stories. The richness of Scottish authors' contribution to the development of children's literature continued in the work of J. M. Barrie whose *Peter Pan*, both as literary work and central character, changed considerably over time. The story developed across four forms and for four different audiences:

- 1902: Chapters 13–18 of *The Little White Bird* (episodic narrative for adults)
- 1904: *Peter Pan, or the Boy Who Wouldn't Grow Up* (play performed at the Duke of York's Theatre, London)
- 1906: *Peter Pan in Kensington Gardens* (six chapters from *The Little White Bird*)
- 1911: *Peter and Wendy* (full narrative version in novel form)
- 1928: *Peter Pan, or the Boy Who Would Not Grow Up* (published play script)

Peter is represented in multiple ways, with his identity morphing and changing across these works to a considerable degree. Even the author himself could not remember which version came first. In a preface to the 1928 play script, Barrie wrote:

I have no recollection of writing the play of Peter Pan, now being published for the first time so long after he made his bow upon the stage. […] I cannot remember doing it. I remember writing the story of Peter and Wendy many years after the production of the play, but I might have cribbed that from some typed copy. ('To The Five', Dedication, *Peter Pan, or the Boy Who Would Not Grow Up*)

In whatever format however, it has become one of children's literature's 'classic' texts. Another 'classic' text is *The Wind in the Willows* (1908) by Edinburgh-born Kenneth Grahame. Writers like Grahame, MacDonald and Barrie who left Scotland reflect an, at times, borderline sense of Scottish identity in terms that open up much larger questions about the unstable and liminal nature of identity itself, a question too complex to address in this context.

The well-established Scottish contribution to writing for children might suggest that the concept of childhood in Scotland was significantly different from elsewhere, or perhaps it was that the Scots placed books and reading high on the educational agenda. Education extended literacy down the social scale and cheaper publishing costs expanded the market and improved the quality of popular reading material.[22] Publishing for children reflected economic and demographic growth as well as a society arguably more responsive and sensitive to children's needs. Children began to be allowed to choose books and their choices included, among others, adventure stories, school stories, fantasy and fairy tales, family and historical stories. Explicit moral lessons in children's fiction were rapidly becoming outmoded and the insistent moralising of Victorian fiction for children had, by the end of the nineteenth century, become a standing joke and, especially in Scotland, an obvious target for parody.

Before then, by the middle of the nineteenth century, at the time of the most rapid spread of literacy in Britain, Scottish printers were taking the lead in identifying and developing new literary markets. Blackie, Nelson, Collins and Chambers were all family firms established in early decades of the century when there was a growing body of working and lower-middle-class readers as well as expanding juvenile and educational markets.[23] Early experiences of these publishers encouraged sympathy with the educational aspirations of ordinary people. They were shaped by a religious and social ethos based on Presbyterian egalitarianism, overlaid by the power of the laird, rather than the explicit hierarchies of England's Episcopalian national church. All, except the Chambers brothers, were linked with radical Presbyterianism and after 1843 supported the break-away Free Church; all regarded their activities as publishers as, broadly speaking, educational and part of a wider commitment to social improvement. Most of these firms were involved in anti-slavery and temperance causes or initiatives like the improvement of working-class housing in Edinburgh. This gives the lie to the persistent notion that nineteenth-century Scots evangelicals were social and political reactionaries, intent on resisting progressive ideas and developments. All of these publishing houses recognised what is now called the 'knowledge economy' that was beginning to develop. They did not, though, restrict themselves to publishing only the work of Scottish authors, nor were their publications restricted only to the juvenile market.

By the beginning of the twentieth century, therefore, children's literature was well established. The impact of two world wars, however, had an obvious effect: children's authors were otherwise engaged and practical issues such as paper and labour shortages were challenging. In fact, during the Second World War the premier children's literature award, the Carnegie Medal, withheld the award in 1943 and 1945 for lack of suitable candidates, though Scottish author Eric Linklater's *The Wind on the Moon* won the medal in 1944. However, by the 1950s a second Golden Age had begun and Scottish writers during this period include Naomi Mitchison,

Linklater, Mollie Hunter and Joan Lingard. While there are very few Scottish women represented in the first Golden Age of Children's Literature, their contribution increases steadily through the 1950s and 1960s until today female authors are in the majority. In terms of productivity, since the beginning of the twentieth century there is a range from occasional, one- or two-book authors such as J. J. Bell, J. B. S. Haldane and Marion Campbell to skilled professionals who have sustained work of impressive quality over a period of years – Honor Arundel, Mollie Hunter, Allan Campbell McLean, Eleanor Lyon, Kathleen Fidler, Joan Lingard, Iona McGregor, Eileen Dunlop, Hugh Scott, Teresa Breslin, Elizabeth Laird and Alison Prince. Some, like Jane Duncan, Nigel Tranter, Mitchison, Linklater and Jackie Kay moved successfully between adult and younger readerships. The work of some of these authors – Mollie Hunter in particular – is considered in greater detail in other chapters in this volume.

Although the discussion to this point has focused on works of fiction, Scottish poetry for children is also worth examination. From Stevenson's *A Child's Garden of Verses* (1885), considered one of the most influential children's works of the nineteenth century and never out of print, to the work of contemporary poets such as Jackie Kay or Matthew Fitt, Scottish children's poetry has flourished. This includes the wealth of timeless folk rhymes collected by Norah and William Montgomerie in *The Hogarth Book of Nursery Rhymes*.[24] Minor poets William Miller, Alexander Rodger and James Ballantyne of *Whistle Binkie* notoriety offer a few good Victorian items. Another key figure is of course William Soutar, but J. K. Annand and 'Sandy Thomas Ross' have also made memorable contributions.

In recent years a new vitality has been injected through the work of Kay, Carol Anne Duffy and Fitt. But many of our established poets have occasionally written for children. Does it indeed make any sense to think of poets as having any particular segment of readership in mind? Consider for example some of the playful little contributions of writers such as Edwin Morgan, Ian Hamilton Finlay and Tom Leonard. The Scottish Poetry Library holds a wide range of children's materials and is active in promoting interest in poetry generally. It has also commissioned from contemporary poets a delightful thematic anthology of new poems for young people, *The Thing That Mattered Most*, published in 2006. Other useful short collections are Anne Forsyth's *Scots Poems for Children* (2001)[25] and the 1982 ASLS anthology *Ram Tam Toosh*, edited by Alan Macdonald and Ian Brison.[26] Another ASLS anthology, *Voices of Scotland* (2019), edited by Morna Fleming and Lorna Smith, provides a selection of poems aimed at readers aged between ten and fifteen, including works by John Barbour from the fourteenth century to Alec Finlay from 2012. Chapters by Robert Davis and Jennifer Farrar, also in this volume, explore this topic in greater depth.

It would be impossible to leave the consideration of Scottish children's literature in the twentieth century without mention of the long tradition of illustrated children's books. This includes everything from the comics published by D. C. Thompson, including one of the world's longest running comics, *The Dandy*, first published in December 1937 – which ran in print form until December 2012 – to prize-winning picturebooks from writer/illustrators such as Debi Gliori, Julia Donaldson and Mairi Hedderwick, whose work is considered later in this volume. Two of Scotland's comic strips originating in 1936 are still running in the *Sunday Post*. *The Broons* and *Oor Wullie* were originally scripted by R. D. Low who set the balance of surreal detail and narrative, humour and insight, while Dudley D. Watkins drew the cartoons until his death in 1969. Since then, new artists and writers have created fresh strips in the Watkins mould. *Oor Wullie* follows the adventures and misadventures of a small boy of eight or nine years with spiky blonde hair and black dungarees who is constantly in trouble with his teachers and the local police, gets into fights against the local bullies and is generally a character embodying values of irreverence, friendship and fairness. *The Broons* is a domestic comedy-cum-soap-opera about a large argumentative but close-knit family: Maw, Paw and their eight offspring ranging from adults in their twenties down to the Bairn, a toddler, live together in a small flat. Most of the humour derives from the timeless themes of 'the generation gap', stretching the money as far as possible, and the constant struggle for each family member to live in a very small flat with the other nine *Broons*. In the end, the family always support one another, getting through life with a gentle good humour as they argue among themselves. The characters from these comic strips have achieved iconic status, certainly within Scotland, and live on in the twenty-first century.

Scottish Children's Literature in the Twenty-first Century

There have arguably been more, and better, books published for children in the last forty years than in the previous four hundred. The children's books of today are more inclusive, more aware of the rights and interests of the readers, more risk-taking, more linguistically adventurous, more digitally relevant, while at the same time maintaining respect for classic texts set within carefully acknowledged contexts. There is a very strong Scottish presence among them. Particularly since the 1980s, there has been an explosion in the number of Scottish authors writing for children, including some authors willing to risk writing in their 'home' voice for mass audiences as they seek publication for their work. Scotland has also benefited from the fact that J. K. Rowling came to live and work in Scotland and dreamed up a certain boy wizard in an Edinburgh cafe. Julia Donaldson was for many years a resident of Bearsden and her book *The Gruffalo* (1999)[27] is fondly embraced as being Scottish. Originally from Edinburgh, Kate Wilson now works in London at the publishers Nosy Crow where she champions Scottish authors and illustrators publishing the works of Pamela Butchart, Ross Collins and David Solomons. Other publishers intent on helping to reflect the glorious history of Scottish children's literature include the Canongate Kelpies imprint which in the 1980s and 1990s set about bringing together a huge range of titles set in Scotland and from Scottish authors. Floris Books has revived the imprint in recent years with a mix of new commissions, debuts sourced via an annual competition and back lists. Teen and young adult material has strong voices with established work by Catherine MacPhail and Catherine (Cathy) Forde joined in recent years by Claire McFall whose novel *Ferryman* (2013) was an enormous surprise hit.[28] Even more recently the ranks have been swelled by the addition of Elle McNicoll, a Scottish neurodivergent writer whose debut novel *A Kind of Spark* (2020)[29] won the Blue Peter Book Award and the Overall Waterstones Children's Book of the Year in 2021. This book was also named Overall Book of the Year by Blackwell's, beating titles in the adult market. In 2022 McNicoll established the Adrien Prize, a prize for traditionally published books with a disabled lead character. Increasingly, Scottish children's writers are strong advocates for their own and society's causes, some of which are particularly pertinent to the languages of Scotland.

In recent years, children's publishing in Scots has been transformed by the Itchy Coo imprint of Black and White Publishing. Engaging translations of A. A. Milne's work, three *Asterix* titles and the work of Roald Dahl – including *Geordie's Mingin Medicine* (2007), *The Eejits* (2008), *The Sleekit Mister Tod* (2008) and *Matilda* (2019) – have joined original titles for young children including *Katie's Ferm* (2007) and *Rabbie's Rhymes* (2008). In 2010 Alexander McCall Smith's children's book *Precious and the Puggies* was available exclusively in Scots for its first year of publication, following a unique collaboration between its author and the translator James Robertson, the English version of the book being published only a year later. Robertson's translation of *The Gruffalo* (2012) has been a particular hit, spawning a raft of versions in different dialects of Scots from Glaswegian to Orcadian, Dundonian and Shetlandic. *The Diary of a Wimpy Wean* appeared in 2018 and translations of books by David Walliams, and Lemony Snicket have now been produced. *The Boggin Beginnin* (2021) is the first of Snicket's '*Series of Scunnersome Events*', a highly effective translated description. There are now translations of Hans Christian Andersen's Fairy Tales in Scots, Grimm's Fairy Tales in Scots, and even a Scots version of Paddington Bear has appeared. In the twenty or so years of Itchy Coo's existence, they have produced more than seventy titles including the first ever Braille book in Scots, the first ever graphic novel entirely in Scots, *Kidnappit* (2007), a version of Robert Louis Stevenson's classic adventure story, as well as a much-loved series of board books. Itchy Coo demonstrated that there *was* a market for books in Scots, and that when Scots was introduced into the classroom children responded with recognition and enthusiasm.

Currently, there has been something of a transformation of official attitudes towards Scots within the education sector, especially in primary schools. Recognising and engaging with the language that many children bring to school, rather than repressing it, encourages their linguistic curiosity and versatility, helps with inclusion and challenges the idea that their words or pronunciation have little value. The appetite of younger readers for reading in Scots seems to be growing from strength to strength. Contemporary Scottish children's fiction insists on the writer's right to reclaim and reshape language to speak for those previously neglected. No longer does the Scottish child have to be diglossic, having one language for school and school literature and another for home, with only sparse literature available in the language of home. New visions of Scotland can be expressed in vibrant modern language that is, nonetheless, distinctively Scottish.

Despite the Gaelic Language (Scotland) Act's being enacted by the Scottish Parliament in April 2005, confirming Gaelic as a national language of Scotland, this enactment has not made the tracking of the history of Gaelic children's literature any easier. This may be largely because the myth that Scots Gaelic is largely an oral language has misdirected attention, but also because of issues of language skill levels among historians and critics of children's literature. Later in this volume Mairi Kidd and Sìm Innes challenge that myth in their chapters on Gaelic children's literature and Gaelic children's drama and identify a written heritage largely unknown to a non-Gaelic-speaking readership and often, until relatively recent times, suppressed or ignored. They also highlight the potential for a Gaelic children's literature primed for new life in the twenty-first century.

At the same time, though, the interest in contemporary Scottish children's literature is not based exclusively on linguistic issues but rather on broader, more pressing thematic concerns. It is a sign of the vitality of modern Scottish children's literature that it is more difficult than ever to restrict it to neat definitions, categories or traditions. Instead, we have individual voices expressing themselves with originality and growing self-confidence. Writers are able to transform local experience into global experience but with the added advantage of the inimitable uniqueness of the Scottish voice. After all, when reading the literature of an 'other' culture, what the reader is seeking is the voices of the people who live there. Another – and some might argue, fundamental – change is that with the growing confidence of Scottish writers and of Scottish identity, there is no longer the need to write exclusively using specifically Scottish settings, Scottish concerns or using Scots language. Many, particularly young, writers seem to feel no need for direct involvement in (re)definitions of Scottishness. They are implicitly pushing the idea of Scottishness of identity, place and time outward in terms of themes and settings – sometimes even entirely beyond Scotland. Contemporary Scottish children's writers are writing about Africa and Bosnia; their historical fiction is set in Italy and Palestine and covers everything from the Medici to the Great War. Fantasy continues to be a strongly represented genre, but the fantasy is now assured enough to use inter-textuality both as a self-referencing tool and as a means of self-parody. Self-parody should be considered perfectly healthy in the context of a nation, confident and assured of its non-stereotypical national identity and within Scottish children's fantasy there is a rich world of irony, self-mockery, allusion and sophistication.

The Scottish children's writers working today are open to change and development; their ideas come from a diverse range of sources; they cross borders – literal and figurative – and re-shape previous assumptions. To that extent their material is typical of *all* contemporary Scottish fiction. It should be recorded, though, that the tradition of caustic analysis of Scottish identity and community remains a feature especially in the work of writers like Catherine MacPhail and James Jauncey. Nor are all recent children's publications only historical or fantasy texts. Urban realism also features in Scottish children's literature. Modern fictions of Highland and Island and even national decline appear in, for example, Julie Bertagna's

Soundtrack (1999) and Breslin's *Saskia's Journey* (2004). Regeneration all too often seems impossible in several of these texts, set against the context of ominous global and post-war changes in power relations, both societal and familial, and in social and national identity.

Unlike its adult counterpart, Scottish children's fiction has never really focused regularly on the negative representations of Scottish character. While it may mirror the fascination with doubles, common-sense, hard work and education, recent fiction in particular tends to be encouraging in mood and encompasses a remarkable range and variety. New writing manages the relationship between the urban and the rural in ways that do not require separation but rather can be mutually affirmative. Action is allowed to move without discrimination between the city and the country, privileging neither. Authors, where they use a Scottish setting, are exploiting a wider variety of locations including those that are rarely used, such as the outer islands or the extreme north and south of the country. Contemporary Scottish children's literature is dynamic and adventurous and distinguished by its willingness to see an inclusive rather than an exclusive variety of Scotlands.

Because Scottish children's fiction has never really let go of fantasy or supernatural literature, it has not had to 'recover' it, as has been the case within adult Scottish fiction. However, the forms that such literature takes have grown and developed and can now manifest themselves as anything from the traditional – exploiting ideas of second sight and symbolic magic – to bringing old legends and myths to life or, indeed, on into weaving traditional supernatural tales into novels. Magic realism – where elements of the marvellous, mythic or dream-like are injected into an otherwise realistic story without breaking the narrative flow – continues to be in vogue internationally and the Scots have always been aficionados of the genre. Modern magic realist fantasy has been exploited by Scottish children's writers, such that the bizarre and the impossible allow new perspectives on relevant issues – for example, race, gender and identity, as in Kay's *Strawgirl* (2002). There are also examples of modern variants of Scottish Gothic in Debbi Gliori's comic, six-book series about the Strega-Borgias: *Pure Dead Magic* (2001), *Pure Dead Wicked* (2002), *Pure Dead Brilliant* (2003), *Deep Water* (2005), *Deep Trouble* (2005) and *Deep Fear* (2006). This series demonstrates a solid awareness of older Scottish Gothic novels as well as an ability to bring these completely up to date by including both cinematic and literary intertextual references in a style Gliori makes her own. The humour of these books is probably the single most attractive factor for young readers, along with the local setting that is always intriguing – with the idea that their ancestral pile, StregaSchloss, really might be located in Scotland and under attack from everything from the Mafia to changelings.

Apocalyptic extrapolations set in a future Scotland where all public order has broken down appear from authors such as Bertagna in *Exodus* (2002), *Zenith* (2007) and *Aurora* (2011), Jauncey in *The Witness* (2007) and Forde in *Tug O' War* (2007). In some cases, Bertagna's in particular, concern about international environmental issues such as global warming provides the impetus for futuristic eco-novels set in the dystopian world of a submerged Glasgow, and contributes to the sub-set of Scottish children's fiction deeply critical of contemporary ideologies and world politics:

> In the scorching hot summers of the '30s and '40s the oceans rose faster than anyone ever expected. All the predictions had been wrong. And all the political agreements that were supposed to prevent global warming had fallen through [...] Suddenly it was all too late. Great floods struck, all over the world [...] Governments began to collapse everywhere. Economies crashed and everything that held society together started to fall apart.[30]

Bertagna's is a de-territorialised Scotland, deprived of one of its most powerful, traditional and iconic imaginative resources – the landscape – blending into the pluralised, globalised cyberspace of the post-modern age. The 'virtual' domain of the 'cyberwhizz' allows the erosion of traditional divisions between the local and the global, creating a new zone of what Carla Sassi calls *glocal* space,[31] where the language of narration represents the only evidence of a nation conceived in territorial, cultural and ethnic terms. The characters' names – Partick, Ibrox, Caledon – provide the 'lost' locations in Bertagna's work, and Mara's resemblance to the 'face in the stone' provides a context for the development and re-working of myth and legend inspired by the city's coat of arms and the story of Glasgow's foundations.

Also concerned with the environment is Barbara Henderson's *Wilderness Wars* (2018), a fast-paced eco-thriller with a hint of the supernatural. At its heart are questions like: Should we respect our remaining wild places more? Should we think twice before thoughtlessly imposing our will on them? In the novel, the main protagonist Em is a twelve-year-old girl who relocates with her younger brother and parents to the fictional island of Skelsay, a remote island off the coast of St Kilda. Em's father is site manager for the construction of the Skelsay Skies Resort, a 'ten storey luxury hotel' topped by an 'entirely' glass rooftop with 360-degree views. The build is iconic in its design, materially intensive and environmentally destructive, posing significant threat to the local ecosystem with wider impacts extending beyond its bounded spatial and temporal site.[32] Significant protests, including 'legal action' from 'high profile environmental charities', have taken place but planning has been granted. The strong implication is that the promise of 'hundreds of permanent jobs' has swung the decision. Em comes to believe that the build is destroying the unspoilt nature of the island. She is concerned because she believes that nature is waging war against humans in revenge and is afraid her family and the rest of the workforce and their families may not survive. She tries to warn her parents and teacher that they are all in danger, but they ignore her. Em's fears are realised when a tidal wave sweeps the island and it is left to the children to lead the adults to safety. There are two fatalities, but the rest of the workforce is airlifted back to the mainland unharmed, and the main plot ends happily with disaster seemingly averted, though the build is completely submerged. Henderson does add a Postscript: Five years later, Em and her friends Zac and Harvey return to Skelsay. All are now, according to Henderson, eighteen. The boys row around the island while Em looks at the view and reflects on the past. Her statement that the island is now returned to its peaceful wilderness concludes the novel.

The re-discovery, revaluation and re-shaping of older narrative strategies, themes and magical possibilities suggests that Scottish children's writers are also redefining their relationship to Scottish history: new and postmodern responses to the past are beginning to appear. Revisionist recreations of traditional material from the tobacco trade in Frances Mary Hendry's *Chains* (2000) and Burke and Hare in Nicola Morgan's *Fleshmarket* (2003) to the Covenanters in the form of the Wigtown Martyrs in Morgan's *The Highwayman's Curse* (2007) reveal through deeply humane fiction some of Scotland's most painful past. In the case of *Chains*, Scotland's shameful, and largely neglected until the twenty-first century, part in the slave trade in the eighteenth century is made prominent as part of the narrative. Contemporary Scottish historical children's fiction can also turn outwards as, for example, in the work of Elizabeth Laird in *The Secrets of the Fearless* (2005). This starts out in Edinburgh but is principally concerned with the exploits of a young lad, press-ganged into the navy at the time of the Napoleonic Wars, and set mainly outside Scotland. Historical writing for children is sufficiently self-confident, with Breslin commenting that 'Scottish authors make links between Scottish character and foreign setting through these central figures – even when the narrative is not directly Scottish'.[33] Like other genres, Scottish children's historical fiction continues to thrive.

Conclusion

A great paradox of our time is the fact that, notwithstanding the technical progress and the enormous growth in communication, children's literature in various countries, including Scotland, is becoming more reflectively national. The Russian scholar Maria Nikolajeva has stated that there is a tendency in every country to overestimate its native literature and give it more room in historical surveys, reference books and university courses.[34] In this regard Scotland seems, at least up to the present, to be an exception. A nation is always working – even unconsciously – to reproduce itself in its literature. How then could Scottish children's literature be missing from the prestigious roll call of national children's literatures? Of course, what this chapter contends is that it is *not* missing. Perhaps the more accurate explanation is that it has been mislabelled – or even more ironically – misidentified.

A question must then be asked about what the best strategy is to ensure that Scottish children's literature survives, flourishes and is recognised in this vital role. Should it let itself be integrated into the transnational metropolitan English literature which has such a strong international reputation today? Or should its Scottishness be cherished, curated and used instrumentally in the promotion of particular values and attitudes associated with its country of origin? Alternatively, should Scottish children's literature keep striving at the unfinished task of securing its rights as a minority literature within Britain? Whichever option is preferred by critics, the omens are certainly encouraging for the confident confirmation and enhancement of a distinctive Scottish children's literature clearly located at the heart of the nation's cultural and educational institutions. Children's literature, far from comprising a mere afterthought within Scotland's creative psyche, plays a fundamental role in the shaping of that collectively imagined space known as Scottish Literature and the culture and people that literature seeks to represent. Scottish children's literature has a distinguished history, a vibrant present and an inviting future – justly celebrated, at last, for its pivotal role in the ongoing development of the nation's educational and cultural identity.

CHAPTER TWO

'Through the Midnight Sea': Some Dimensions of Scottish Children's Poetry

Robert A. Davis

> Swim, star, swim, through the midnight sea
> (James McGonigal, 'Little Star')[1]

Scotland, Poetry, Children

Scottish children's poetry, like the children's poetries of many other nations, is, across its myriad beauties, freighted with paradox. Aside from the fact that extensive coverage of children's poetry still lags behind the discussion of prose fiction and other genres in children's literary studies, there are definitional slippages and ambiguities that sometimes blur understanding of the literature and which are ineradicably inscribed on its long Scottish history. While this chapter is not intended to yield an exhaustive account of that history, it does reference several of its milestone moments and explores some of their legacies among a number of contemporary children's writers. In assuming this task, the chapter invites readers into the living tradition of poetry for children in Scotland, to experience some of its many renderings of the relationship between the three constituent terms – Scotland, poetry, children – and the assorted effects of their integration in a body of verse that is of frequently considerable quality and interest.

In her influential 2019 discussion of one of those key historic moments, Kirstie Blair has highlighted the significance of the traditions of nineteenth-century anthology production in both their selective channelling of an older Scottish oral (and musical) tradition for which children were an important audience, and their foreshadowing of a new type of engaged and literate child readership associated with the extension of literacy and the increased national regulation of popular education.[2] Yet the two major and contrasting collections on which her discussion mainly focuses – Andrew Lang's (1844–1912) *The Blue Poetry Book* of 1891 and Robert

Ford's (1846–1905) *Ballads of Bairnhood* of 1894 – reproduce many of these same paradoxes to be found in Scottish children's poetry and indeed in other national children's poetries across the industrial period.

As Blair points out, Lang's anthology set a very strict concept of 'poetry for children', declaredly excluding from its content the presumed distractions of children's actual experiences, activities, perceptions of the world in favour of a canon of verse – albeit rich in Scottish material – that every reading and reciting child ought to know and appreciate, such as Scott's 'Young Lochinvar' and Campbell's 'Lord Ullin's Daughter'. Lang of course was a major Scottish thinker, folklorist and public intellectual, immersed in the learning of Continental anthropology under the influence of E. B. Tylor and J. F. McClennan and heavily vested in a view of national literatures, language and identity as old as the Romantic project of von Arnim and Brentano's *Des Knaben Wunderhorn* of 1805.[3] In this cluster of motivations, 'childhood' carried many meanings associated with, for example, the distant yet prized infancy of the nation (especially nations struggling to recover lost or suppressed sovereignties), the race, and the routinely 'infantilised' indigenous subjects of the imperial gaze, legible almost exclusively through the syntax of imperial power. Such manifold and often contradictory cultural and political work being done by the concept of childhood at this time leant itself to the recreational-educational mission of the anthology model as a resource for the formation of new generations of subjects and citizens in homes and schools.

Ford's in key respects quite different undertaking in his *Ballads of Bairnhood* also reflects the goals of the anthology principle, albeit pursuing in general a more demotic, diverse and contemporary content. His chosen title reflects another impulse in this nineteenth-century literature in gesturing towards and seeking to assimilate some of the older ballad and oral-sung traditions of the Scottish past, including the elevation of the Scots tongue, into the reading of children. This became in some settings a controversial feature because Ford also highlighted his respect for the pseudo-Burnsian *Whistle Binkie* heritage of popular literary collections (1832–1890), later condemned by many leading Scottish writers for its allegedly derivative and demeaning sentimentalism and conservative kailyard stereotyping, damaging to the enculturation of young children.[4]

Here was signalled another Scottish vector in the literary 'uses of childhood' so prominent in the nineteenth century and its literatures for the young: an ostensive homage to the archaic past and its oral legacies as the precious repository of national identity, nevertheless implying simultaneously the further hierarchical infantilisation of that past, its cultural products and its custodian populations. A national literature for children rooted in a distant era becomes a signifier of the arrested cultural development of a pre-scientific, pre-rational society, in a style that was to reappear writ large in the voluminous writings of James Frazer. At the same time, Ford has come to be praised for the versatility and vernacular energy of his collecting and preserving, reverberating through other anthologies of the time and capturing a genuine and thriving working-class oral folk culture, at work absorbing, renewing, improvising, publishing and extending an abiding tradition of popular verse and song immediately accessible to children and, like lullabies, frequently reflective of the child-centred demands, the disciplines and the rewards of everyday life. That these aspects of the anthologising customs of the period have come to be epitomised in the popular performance, in both English and Scots, of William Miller's (1810–1872) 'Wee Willie Winkie' of 1841 – still widely recited by and to Scottish children – serves only to underline that these paradoxes of purpose and reception go all the way down into the texture and experience of the verse itself:

> Wee Willie Winkie rins through the toon,
> Up stairs an'doon stairs in his nicht-gown,
> Tirlin' at the window, crying at the lock,
> 'Are the weans in their bed, for it's now ten o'clock?'[5]

Thus, the late nineteenth-century anthology fashion can be seen as not only reflective of contemporary attitudes to the place of Scottish (and other) poetry in children's lives, but also reproductive of it. At the centre of the educative aesthetic here lies that other zone where childhood can supposedly be corralled and interpreted – the nursery. If a large proportion of the anthology materials is indeed best understood, as several critics have argued, as 'nursery verse',[6] in a construction that a later generation of researchers would investigate and categorise,[7] it nonetheless anticipates and then participates in a wider renewal of the pastoral genre in late nineteenth- and early twentieth-century British literature. Within this literature, the subset 'indoor pastoral' of the nursery as a locus of childcare, nurture, amusement and initiation would become particularly cherished.[8] Even while actual nurseries as domestic spaces or emergent pre-school institutions remained largely an affordance of the affluent, the figurative site of the nursery came to supply the metaphors for a way of curating and fashioning early childhood, especially in the exposure of young children to age-appropriate language, literature and song.

The standard repertoire of nursery verse of this period of course recycled an old pastoral lexicon, associating children with, variously, safe and stimulating natural spaces rich in ruralist sentiment; with flowers and gardens and fresh air and animals and birdsong; with parents and domesticity and lullabies and sleep; with elemental landscapes and soundscapes rich in the representation of their cultures and places of habitation; with mostly healing (sometimes escapist) imaginary surroundings only intermittently shadowed by forces indifferent or hostile to the juvenile human presence. Some commentators at the time and later bridled at the mismatch between this literature and the environment in which most Scottish people lived and toiled[9] and it is at least arguable that when many of the young Scottish men, in particular, raised on such verse found themselves in the throes of industrial warfare, the passionate reworking by some of them of the pastoral genre, in Scottish war poetry of 1914–1918, owed something to an implicit protest against these consoling childhood pieties.[10]

One volume of poetry has, famously, come over time to embody the best of the Scottish nursery poetic – read either as the culmination of a popular, flexible and unjustly neglected genre, or as the wholesale redemption of a decadent and clichéd tradition. That volume is Robert Louis Stevenson's (1850–1894) 1885 *A Child's Garden of Verses*.

Stevenson's Secret Garden

A Child's Garden of Verses sits at the nexus of the literary and cultural forces summarised above. Its enduring reputation (it has remained in print since first publication) with the reading public (if not quite always with literary critics) is at least in some significant measure attributable to shifts in the perception of children's literature and of poetry for children that it clearly helped to initiate and then accelerate. For although *Garden* reprises from its very title onwards many of the standard motifs and thematics of the romantic nursery pastoral that reach back to William Blake (an obvious influence) and Robert Burns, and also echoes the established tropes and preoccupations of much Victorian Scottish 'childhood' and cradle-song poetry, it reanimates all of these legacies and repurposes them in a complex and original response to childhood that simultaneously celebrates and modernises the heritage on which it draws. The result may well be one of the most interesting and important works of Scottish literature of the era and one of the best and most influential books of poetry for children ever composed.[11]

There are several factors at work here that can be briefly explored in this chapter. First the context of the volume needs to be set in terms of Stevenson's wider intellectual interests in what was in his time emerging as the twin disciplines of the psychology and the anthropology of childhood. As Julia Reid has demonstrated,[12] and in keeping with the imperial cultural politics referenced above, Stevenson was initially drawn to the (subsequently discredited) late Enlightenment theory of recapitulation, in which the life cycle of the individual reprised the biological and social development of the human species. In a series of important and revealing essays of the 1870s – 'Notes on the Movements of Young Children' (1874), 'Child's Play' (1878) and 'Memoirs of Himself' (1880) – refracted through his enthusiastic acquaintance with the experimental ideas of Rousseau, Pestalozzi, Spencer and Darwin – Stevenson clearly moves on from strict recapitulation to ally himself with a broader 'evolutionist' account of childhood which is nonetheless still rooted in the romantic primitivist perception of the praiseworthy and privileged affinities between the child's mind and the worldviews of 'savage' or pre-scientific peoples.[13] Such an essentially animistic defence of the imagination of the developing child has understandably posed worrying problems for modern tempers, but it is harnessed in *Garden* to a correspondingly attentive 'anthropological' observation of how the detail of the child's mind works in its navigation and its transformation of everyday experience. This is one of the pivotal drivers of the volume as a collection of verse concerned with just such experience and certainly comprises a major source of its overall appeal. While the encompassing theory clearly mattered to the intellectually voracious Stevenson, it is the practice of the constituent poems and their patient disclosure and illumination, line by line, of the child's interactions with his environment and his own first-person reflective consciousness that absorbs the reader in the universe of the collection. What matters in poems such as 'The Wind', 'My Treasures or 'My Ship and I' is less an atavistic pan-animistic projection of elemental force and more something intrinsically intimate, personal, playful and even domestic: the investiture of natural or manufactured objects such as everyday weather events or occasional toys with personality and capacity which, while beyond the ordinary, remains steadfastly rooted within it:

> I saw you toss the kites on high
> And blow the birds about the sky;
> And all around I heard you pass,

> Like ladies' skirts across the grass—
> O wind, a-blowing all day long,
> O wind, that sings so loud a song!
> ('The Wind', *Garden*, p. 27)

> For I mean to grow as little as the dolly at the helm,
> And the dolly I intend to come alive;
> And with him beside to help me, it's a-sailing I shall go,
> It's a-sailing on the water, when the jolly breezes blow
> And the vessel goes a divie-divie-dive.
> ('My Ship and I', *Garden*, p. 59)

Stevenson's catalogue of verse in *Garden* has rightly been celebrated for its thoroughgoing fidelity to the world of the child, communicated in a variety of authentic voices and tonalities.[14] The poet's registering intelligence can seem preternaturally attuned to the fashioning of childhood from a series of early and foundational subjective-reflective experiences. These embrace the multiple domains of play, of the circadian rhythms of the day and the night, of the immediate sensory encounter with household surroundings. They extend also to the corresponding observation and discovery of other living creatures in the landscape outdoors; to the impact of the elemental presences of sky and sun and stars, to the adventure of books and story, of fairy tale and mystery, reaching finally beyond the security of the territories of nursery and garden to the sometimes refractory, even genuinely menacing, forces of which the child can ofttimes struggle to make sense and meaning. The result in the collection is a materialisation of childhood at the heart of a series of concentric circles, the shared centre of which is unmistakeably *home* and the outer circumference of which is a distinctly '*unhomely*'/uncanny zone – half in this world and half out of it – with which the child's mind, Stevenson implies, is specifically developmentally harmonised and to which it is uniquely emotionally receptive.

A celebrated representative poem such as 'The Swing' (*Garden*, p. 39) captures several of these related features in its structure and content:

> How do you like to go up in a swing,
>   Up in the air so blue?
> Oh, I do think it the pleasantest thing
>   Ever a child can do!

> Up in the air and over the wall,
>   Till I can see so wide,
> Rivers and trees and cattle and all
>   Over the countryside—
>
> Till I look down on the garden green,
>   Down on the roof so brown—
> Up in the air I go flying again,
>   Up in the air and down!

The invitatory interrogative of the opening couplet of the poem is simultaneously an opportunity to relive a common childhood experience and a beckoning into the occasion of the poem itself, where its rhyme-scheme, intricate and deceptively monosyllabic diction, and enjambement unite the flowing child-voice of the text with the attention, recollections and presumed appetites of the reader. The shared 'like' of the first line is part of an appeal made by 'The Swing' to a recurrent property of the collection as a whole: that is, to the *embodiedness* of childhood: its accentuated, exuberant sense of movement and its freshness of sensation typified in the weightless arc of swung motion, which, as Javier Moscoso argued in 2023,[15] endows the 'flying' child, especially, with a privilege that the sedate and regulated mobilities of adulthood tend normally to relinquish. The shifting optics of the poem incline also to recap the broader patterns of the anthology: anchored in the security of house and garden, returning automatically to the (seemingly) safe starting place, yet affording glimpses, poem by poem, of the teeming and less governable, 'air so blue' vistas that lie tantalisingly beyond, and which the child's imagination will elsewhere in the book seek cautiously to enter, describe, populate, and even in places subdue. The child is here hence characterised by gifts and attributes with deep roots in the Scottish and European Romantic traditions and imprinted on the nursery aesthetic: the elevation of primal infant pleasure and spontaneity, the proximity to nature, the incantatory effects of rhythmic repetition. We are asked in effect by the poem not simply to recapture the physical joy of the motion of swinging, but to identify with the self-contained singularity that is the swinging child himself in the perfect, joyful absorption of that moment. Thus, the poem speaks primarily to a state that truly, it suggests, only other children can appreciate. Yet, it simultaneously offers those eavesdropping readers who have left childhood and swings behind the compensation of its own lyric reproduction of that self-same timeless elation.

'Home' may be Stevenson's first and innermost circle of containment and the place of both departure and return. It plots in many respects the coordinates of a comfort zone signposted by familiarity, satiety and the mostly benign oversight of dimly realised background adult carers and parents. The absent, dislocated or cruel parents of Blake's *Songs* have been replaced in *Garden* by the distant, yet generally benevolent, mothers and fathers (and their hired peasant servants) of classic Scottish Victorian bourgeois family rectitude and solicitude. At the same time – and in this regard undoubtedly reflective of Stevenson's own upbringing – 'home' casts its own distinctive and unsettling shadows across both the day and the night in *Garden*. A significant instance of this is chronic illness, from which Stevenson was a lifelong (and finally life-limiting) sufferer and which is certainly again one of the registers through which the poetry communicates with children, past and present. Here the book tempers and validates further its powerful Romantic idealisations by facing candidly the realities of paediatric sickness and isolation whilst steadily marshalling a therapeutic and obstinately vigorous resistance to them from the resources of language and individual will. 'The Land of Counterpane' (*Garden*, p. 17) epitomises such childhood entanglements of anxiety and fancy, where the child's bed is simultaneously a place of distress, refuge, invalidity, convalescence, while also a setting for the exercise of the healing and consolatory powers of solitary invention:

> When I was sick and lay a-bed,
> I had two pillows at my head,
> And all my toys beside me lay
> To keep me happy all the day.
>
> And sometimes for an hour or so
> I watched my leaden soldiers go,
> With different uniforms and drills,
> Among the bed-clothes, through the hills […]

The defiant energies of the imagination, contesting the limitations of ill-health and confinement, can occasionally release into some of these 'bedroom' poems a sporadic violence which has unsettled some readers,[16] perhaps precisely because that sense of turbulence and frustration overcome is channelled chiefly through the seemingly innocent objects of a child's toys. Yet these manufactured toys, becoming of course a growing cross-class and gendered consumer fixture in the

Scotland of Stevenson's youth and after, are in 'Counterpane' less the distracting escapist playthings intended to numb the symptoms of disease and more the talismans of an empowering and pervasive childhood artistry through which sickness is sublimated and individual autonomy reasserted. The initial violence is, as it were, illness itself and its disabling afflictions on the child's body; the second is the juvenile mind's retaliation and its countervailing anti-ableist avowal of life and all its, as yet unrealised, possibilities. We recall that one of the major and anti-escapist themes of *Garden* is the appeal of what lies 'beyond'. For the most part, it can only be reconnoitred from the safe spaces of house and garden, yet its increasing magnetism in the collection champions a childhood that is not the expression of an arcadian refusal of maturity, or a resignation to permanent bodily impairment and dependency, but a proposal to carry forward uninhibited into adulthood the potent imaginative capabilities of the child, sedimented in the psyche over time by both good fortune and adversity:

> Just as it was shut away,
>   Toy-like, in the even,
> Here I see it glow with day
>   Under glowing heaven.
>
> Every path and every plot,
>   Every blush of roses,
> Every blue forget-me-not
>   Where the dew reposes,
>
> 'Up!' they cry, 'the day is come
>   On the smiling valleys:
> We have beat the morning drum;
>   Playmate, join your allies!'
>   ('Night and Day', *Garden*, p. 77)

The soldiers, armies, 'allies', 'wars', drums, 'grinning guns' ('To Minnie', p. 98), castles, marching songs, 'Heroes, fights and festivals' ('Travel', p. 13) of the collection have alerted several readers to its cultural locus in a domestic and community setting that, for all its pervasive solace and succour, is inescapably the beneficiary – and in key respects a civic cornerstone – of empire.[17] Scotland itself as a location in the text seems at the same time sensorily and topographically remote, blurred and indeterminate, yet curiously and strangely enveloping, in the imagery of the verse; remembered in the 'Envoys' poem, 'To Minnie', as the 'honest, homely Scottish shore', as though the country were a sustaining birthplace, a *locus amoenus*, a nebulous but nonetheless dependable site of departure and return, that the poet can forever carry with him through the poetics of memory. Neighbouring England, that testing senior partner in empire, is a passing simile for the scale of distant and exotic tropical forests in 'Travel' ('Wide as England'), confined to a fleeting figure of speech intended to gesture to the alluring otherness and diversity of, for the child, a much bigger and marvellously enticing world.

Of course, in Stevenson's time that wider world was in many places parcelled and portioned as colonial property or exploited client nations and a nineteenth-century imperial register is certainly periodically audible in the collection, especially in the recurrent lexicon through which it names and labels distant places and peoples as actual destinations and rendezvous that the eager child longs to see or of which he passionately dreams. *Garden*'s condescendingly diminutive 'Little Indian, Sioux or Crow / Little frosty Eskimo / Little Turk or Japanee' ('Foreign Children', p. 33), its 'Each little Indian sleepy-head' ('The Sun's Travels', p. 34), and its 'negro hunters' huts' ('Travel', p. 14) refer to recognisably real locations and communities, not all of them flourishing with the autonomy, amenity or leisure-time enjoyed by a Scottish middle-class boy swaddled at the heart of an empire that he might quite reasonably one day expect to traverse or indeed administer.[18]

That said, the poetry itself in *Garden* subtly underscores for us the sense of moral proportion with which these elements of the collection should be assessed.[19] The child's lead and tin soldiers do undeniably retain a faded imprint of the national victories to which their painted uniforms imply they are a tribute (again a vaguely undifferentiated echo of the Napoleonic struggles of which there were still living veterans in Stevenson's childhood), drawing the child into games of reconstructed battle. However, throughout the collection those mimicries of conflict, with their intermittent militaristic cadences, are restrained by the playful powers of the child's synthetic imagination, muting violence and repurposing the patriotic toy figures for designs quite different from those intended by their adult makers. 'The Dumb Soldier' (*Garden*, p. 85) 'hid [...] underground' in the garden hence serves in his inanimate insensibility almost as a textbook example of what psychoanalysts call a 'transitional object', the original martial signification of which is made magically subordinate to the 'subjective omnipotence' of the child.[20] The toy soldier is not commanding the mind of the child, the mind of the child is boldly recycling the toy for its independently chosen ends:

> I shall find him, never fear,
> I shall find my grenadier;
> But for all that's gone and come,
> I shall find my soldier dumb.
>
> [...]
>
> Not a word will he disclose,
> Not a word of all he knows.
> I must lay him on the shelf,
> And make up the tale myself.

A similar ambivalence adheres to *Garden*'s broader prospectus on overseas places and peoples. The cleverly self-satisfied juvenile egotism with which 'The Dumb Soldier' ends can in other poems project voices which, for all their calculated, knowing naivete, summon locations and children from beyond the speaking child's horizon of first-hand acquaintance that are discursively and disconcertingly implicated in a naturalised imperial imaginary. Here such voices sentimentally call forth 'little children saying grace / In every Christian kind of place' ('A Thought', p. 2), or patronise the 'Little heathen Japanee' with the supercilious query 'O! don't you wish that you were me?' ('Foreign Children', p. 33). Yet, the key point remains that these are only minority voices in a larger, antiphonal chorus. True to its motivating principles, *Garden* both accurately reflects the implicit 'picture book' pedagogies by which affluent Scottish children were educated Anglocentrically in the imperial geography of the nineteenth-century world, yet also repeatedly and impatiently smudges the boundaries of that world, casting into doubt, with a child's restless eye, its assigned rational categorisations and signposting its unexpected proximity to the mysteries and personalities of the non-rational:

> We may see how all things are,
> Seas and cities, near and far,
> And the flying fairies' looks
> In the picture story books.
>   ('Picture-books in Winter', *Garden*, p. 62)

The omnivorous appetites of the child reader or listener subvert the established genres and taxonomies by which 'we may see how all things are' to be conventionally classified and managed, often mischievously spurning such schoolroom distinctions as arbitrary discursive constructs and thereby liberating the mind of the child from the restrictive authority of unsatisfying accounts of reality in favour of daringly alternative poetic narratives. The poem 'Foreign Lands' (p. 8) illustrates just this kind of transgressive possibility. Climbing a 'cherry-tree' in the garden, the child's elevated perspective initially affords him a view of the kinds of dilating landscapes predicted by the title, 'That I had never seen before', where 'The dusty roads go up and down / With people tramping in to town'. However, in a surfeit of imaginative energy typical of the wider collection, the perceptions of the child suddenly ascend in the verse to a new vantage beyond even these panoramas of the rational-imperial gaze,

> To where the grown-up river slips
> Into the sea among the ships,
>
> To where the roads on either hand
> Lean onward into fairy land […].

The figural child in the book, we can recognise, is clearly a securely rooted and cherished resident of its eponymous and shimmering Garden and the sequestered house it graces, granted perhaps occasional excited forays to its uncertain edges and rare glimpses of the diverse 'grown-up' vistas beyond its fences. However, in the multiple forms of juvenile identity either laid upon him by an expectant adult generation or with which he freely and playfully experiments, the child is never really a servant or emissary of empire, but much more naturally and self-fulfillingly a loyal subject of the heterotopia called 'Fairyland': Foucault's 'places outside of all places'.[21] It is through Fairyland's shifting and magical frames of reference and emotional meaning that the child forcefully enlarges his conceptions of the Real and his appreciation of the role of his own unique imaginative powers in comprehending, questioning and shaping it.

This same sense of a liminal threshold between the rational and the magical is tangible in *Garden* not only at the physical and symbolic perimeters of the child's roaming perception but throughout all of the locations he inhabits, including within those seemingly most hallowed and sheltered central spaces which confer repose and security. The juxtaposition of the everyday and the marvellous pulls the reader, as assuredly as it seems to draw the child, recursively and repeatedly back to the intimate core locations of the house, the bedroom, the bed, the dark, the orbital of sleep, and even the dreaming mind itself. It is hence not only at the extended far-flung limits of awareness that the child encounters and embodies the heterotopic zone of the uncanny, but equally in the very heart of the 'home' from which his poetic excursions originate. This explains why *Garden*'s glittering, protean cluster of night-time poems evades introspection or silence and expresses at times the most elemental, even cosmic, continuities of the collection:

> When the golden day is done,
> Through the closing portal,
> Child and garden, flower and sun,
> Vanish all things mortal.
>   ('Night and Day', *Garden*, p. 77)

The 'vanishing' of those bright day-time hours that so many of the poems have joyously chronicled and celebrated does not close down poetic consciousness, but extends its parameters inwards and downwards into the registering, processing, generative psyche of the child in all its wonder and uncertainty. In this innermost plane, mortal vanishings do not signify darkness and emptiness, but plenitude. They afford an access, a 'portal' indeed, to heighted forms of perception that are activated by the suspension of light and reason and the corresponding awakening of the child's nocturnal imagination in its fluent intercourse with the associative powers of dream and oracle. Here fearful ghostly riders gallop ominously 'Late in the night when the fires are out' ('Windy Nights', p. 10) for no discernible purpose and towards no recognisable destination. The wheeling constellations, with their 'crowds' of 'thousands and millions of stars' 'that looked down upon me / And that glittered and winked in the dark', threaten almost to breach the rational-celestial bounds within which they are named and contained, filling 'the pail by the wall … half full of water and stars' and almost overwhelming the sensory capacities of the rapt, observing child, who is marooned dizzyingly with 'the stars going round in my head'. In this hypnogogic night-time condition, the inner subjectivity of the child and the outer workings of nature and culture, of home and abroad, meet in a synthesis that strongly argues for the voyage inwards manifesting as the archetypal or originary journey for which the collection's other speculative expeditions have each been but a preparation or foreshadowing:

> My bed is like a little boat;
> Nurse helps me in when I embark;
> She girds me in my sailor's coat
> And starts me in the dark.
>
> At night, I go on board and say
> Good-night to all my friends on shore;
> I shut my eyes and sail away
> And see and hear no more.
> ('My Bed is a Boat', *Garden*, p. 37)

These lines define not the enclosed juvenile or privileged subject, then, of a maritime British Empire rehearsing from his sequestered bedroom his confidently anticipated future mercantile or world-straddling adventures. Instead, they posit on the threshold of the night a child-citizen of a much older and liminal Scottish polity more closely affined, perhaps, to the astral gazetteer of Robert Kirk's allusive and suggestive *The Secret Commonwealth* of 1692: that great early modern scholarly compendium of the tales and portents of the distinctively Scottish 'weird' and their popularly attested influence over the lives and destinies of mortals. In the terrain of Kirk's haunted hinterland – a kind of archaic and alternative Old Scotland hovering everywhere at the edges of rational and national perception – the enchanted and invisible denizens of faerie sport effortlessly with generations of children initiated by parents and nurses into the popular traditions of national myth-making, rural folklore and peasant second-sight. Distinguished residents of this republic of letters and imagination, Scotland's children, so Stevenson's *Garden of Verses* finally proposes, are licensed by these legacies to make their childhood itself a vehicle for cultural preservation and generational resilience before the strident and consuming demands of modernity.

Scots Voices

We have seen that the nursery verse traditions of the nineteenth century – with their roots in an older Scotland of oral recitation, customary storytelling, and rich folk wisdom – proved a resourceful and versatile genre for the consolidation and renewal of poetry directly intended to entertain and stimulate the minds of children. These ambitions, and these literary practices, sit at a tangent to certain other bodies of poetry discussed elsewhere in this collection which, although not written *for* children, have been repeatedly and fruitfully shared (especially through the schooling system) with audiences of children and young adults, thereby playing an important role in inscribing an impression of 'Scottish poetry' on successive younger generations of readers. The older 'whistle binkies' styles, despite the frequently fierce caveats of their critics, maintained over decades the lineage of nursery and vernacular verse on which later writers could build, while also sustaining and promoting the continuing creation of poetry in the Scots language aimed primarily at younger people. This has turned out to be a vital heritage over more than 150 years of writing and reading. Scots language poetry for children has been one of the major channels for supporting and developing writing in Scots more generally and for ensuring the wider vitality of the language as a vehicle of literary craft and artistic achievement.[22] Moreover, it is also clear from recent studies that Scots language verse played an important role historically, as the structures of Scottish society changed, in inflecting aspects of the older nursery verse tradition away from its typically pastoral and ruralist ambience towards a more inclusive appreciation of 'the folk' in the communication of their wider proletarian and urban experiences. Such poetic hospitality to an increasingly modern and differentiated understanding of culture and society leant vigour and purpose to the renewal of Scots language writing and extended its registers beyond the curated forms to the voluble and colloquial life of the street, the playground, the community, the workplace and the home in an increasingly industrialised Scotland. These transitions did not entail an abandonment of the older material or ways of writing, but rather a diversification and extension of their literary content and focus.

Two writers stand out in this rich lineage whose work reflects its longstanding vitality, its literary continuities, and its capacity both to create and to entertain new, young audiences drawn from a changing Scotland. William Soutar (1898–1943) and James King Annand (known as 'J. K.': 1908–1993) were both attached to the broader, shifting movements of the Scottish Literary Renaissance of the first decades of the twentieth century, with Soutar in particular emerging as a leading light within it in both his Scots and English compositions. The two men also forged important reputations as accomplished poets for children and young people, maintaining and revitalising the Scots poetic registers in which they wrote with such facility and flexibility and demonstrating to younger readers and future writers the capacity of the language to engage meaningfully with facets of childhood, some of which were enduring and some of which were distinctive, place-based and modern.

Soutar's renowned 'Bairnrhymes'[23] modulate specifically for his child readers the Scots lyric voice for which he earned considerable literary renown in his wider poetic corpus. A representative text such as 'A Bairn's Sang' (p. 65) openly invokes the older inheritance of Scots nursery verse preserved and celebrated by Ford and his successors. It hence succeeds highly effectively in conjuring in its Scots diction the sung rhythm, movement, ritual repetition and tangible personae of enthusiastic singing and game-playing young girls: their 'merry-metanzie' (likely French 'Me tange' or 'touch me') taking their actions back to ring-dance ceremonials of a probably French washing game imported immemorially into Scottish grammar school playgrounds in the fifteenth or sixteenth century:[24]

> Round and around and a three times three;
> Polly and Peg and Pansy:
> Round and around the muckle auld tree;
> And it's round a' the world whan ye gang wi' me
> Round the merry-metanzie:
> And it's round a' the world whan ye gang wi' me
> Round the merry-metanzie.

At the same time, Soutar's dexterity in the language also enables him to project this vernacular energy through vivid portrayals of the realms of work and domesticity that sit so permanently and adjacently to the sphere of child's play in the typical lifeworlds of his audience, and where the freedom of fun and games meets and interacts with the disciplines of family and community governance. At one end of this reality, a poem like 'Black Day' (p. 92) captures wryly a stark and lasting fixture of much Scottish child-rearing over the generations:

> A skelp frae his teacher
> For a' he cudna spell:
> A skelp frae his mither
> For cowpin owre the kail.
>
> A skelp frae his brither
> For clourin his braw bat:

> And a skelp frae his faither
> For the Lord kens what.

The Scots lexis and the list-rhyme repetition ('A skelp frae…') do not lose their volatile, even humorous sense of the ridiculous and the inexplicable here as the child reflects on his seemingly unjust fate. However, they also convey a pervasive reality often subdued in the more sentimentalised reaches of the nursery aesthetic on which 'Bairnrhymes' draws and all but excluded from Stevenson's *Garden*: the presence of corporal punishment in the daily lives of Scotland's children. The familiar violence speaks to the experience of the child reader as much to its anonymous universal Scottish 'everychild' subject. For both categories, a 'skelp', while perhaps relatively low on the scale of physical chastisement, nevertheless is (or was, until Scottish Government outlawed these practices in 2020) all too routine a feature of life, underlining in the poem the realities of social and domestic hierarchy, adult authority and juvenile exclusion in a comparatively light-hearted, yet nonetheless immediately, stingingly, recognisable form.

Further along and towards the more benign end of the spectrum of socialisation, a poem like 'Aince Upon a Day' (p. 69) records the more homespun parental styles of admonitory moral education, which nonetheless still carry with them a strongly retributive caution: in this case warning the small child that the infractions of gossiping, stealing and telling lies will incur the disapproving, 'naming and shaming' surveillance and censure of animate nature itself:

> Aince upon a day my mither said to me:
> Dinna cleip and dinna rype
> And dinna tell a lee.
> For gin ye cleip a craw will name ye,
> And gin ye rype a daw will shame ye;
> And a snail will heeze its hornies out
> And hike them round and round about
> Gin ye tell a lee.

Behind even an occasional verse like this lies again the playful proximity of that folk realm at the threshold of which the lines between rationality and mystery, the natural and the supernatural, grow hazy and to which the liminal imagination of the child is supposedly uniquely susceptible. Yet, one key to Soutar's success as a writer for children in the Scots idiom is to keep these folk and fantasy elements grounded firmly in the common life, the learning and the appetites of the young as these are lived and negotiated in their homes and communities. A poem like 'A Penny to Spend' (p. 88) is a glimpse of those very material and sometimes consuming longings of young children in a largely subsistence society when a rare surplus penny can take the child, Dod, 'owre the brae to Forgandenny / And Grannie Panton's shop', where he can feast on that great popular (and now increasingly reproved!) indulgence of many generations of Scotland's children – sweets: 'Sae lickery for the lips; / Zulu-rock and curly-wurlie / And everlastin stripes'. The sources of these all-too-infrequent surpluses are attested in poems like 'The Cutty' (p. 91) or 'Sea Shell' (p. 96), where the often costly labour on land and at sea – albeit recorded in the context of their softening daily irony and plangency – by which marginal communities maintain their economic existence is indirectly, yet movingly, acknowledged. This is a reality that impinges overtly and hauntingly on the lives of children in 'Bairnrhymes', for whom another assuredly and permanently blurred boundary is of course that between play and work. Little wonder, then, that there are occasional moments when Dod, ironically echoing Stevenson's much more privileged child daydreamer, can admit,

> I lang for yon day whan I'll be a loon
> And naebody to daur me;
> Wi' a fare-ye-weel to this auld, grey toun;
> And the weys o' the world afore me.
>   ('Yon Day', p. 86)

Undoubtedly, however, Soutar's finest contributions to the literary nourishment of his child readers and listeners stem from a capacity prized in the wider corpus of his Scots writing to convey the full lyrical and expressive beauty of the language. He does this in a series of the 'Bairnrhymes' poems scattered throughout the collection as whole which celebrates nature, landscape, the sky, the weather, the day and the night in terms perfectly recognisable both to the older Scots arcadian tradition on the lexis and imagery of which he draws and, indeed, to the Stevenson who also takes his reader into the nocturnal fastness of the 'childhood uncanny' where the familiar and the strange seem eerily contiguous.[25] 'The Gowdan Ba'' (p. 68) domesticates the 'muckle müne' shining in the night sky by placing it comfortably and contemplatively within the named landscape of 'the Carse o' Gower' and the 'fluther o' the Tay'. Yet, the later poem 'Sang' (p. 103) resorts to an older incantatory language of magical instruction from the deep deposits of the Scots folk imaginary in order to invite its child-reader to 'Hairst ['harvest'] the licht of o' the müne':

> To mak a siller goun;
> And the gowdan licht o' the sün
> To mak a pair o' shoon:
> Gether the draps o' dew
> To hing about your throat;
> And the wab o' the watergaw
> To wark yoursel' a coat [...]

The imperatives in the poem impart the favoured rhythm of a spell; a spell which is really the transformative power of the language to clothe the child-reader in the enchanted elements of nature. The final promise of the poem vouchsafes this belief in the boundless magic of metaphor by promising to the consenting reader nothing less than mysterious entry 'through the open door / In the wa' at the world's end'.

This concern with an expressive impulse within the Scots poetic of childhood that presses at boundaries, limits and borders does in Soutar have a family resemblance to Stevenson's experiments in the uncanny (a word we remember of Scots origin, coined in this spelling by the poet Robert Fergusson in 1773) discussed above. 'In the Nicht' (p. 94) dwells repeatedly with the child reader on 'the queer hour', 'a be yoursel', where the child's sense of hearing is keenly attuned to a series of unnerving sounds that Soutar captures uniquely in his own tender devotion to the distinctive and euphonous Scots vocabulary: the 'dinnle' of a church bell; the 'knappin' of the wall clock; the 'knockity-knock' of the child's own heart; the 'chark' of the fieldmouse; and finally the 'wheemerin' of the anthropomorphised wind, calling *'lat me in!'*

The 'queer hour', somewhere between sleep and waking, is another of these threshold locations where the reader is brought to the perimeters of perception, and indeed the outer reaches of language itself, delving deeply and profitably into an old and unmatched Scots lexicon (in much the same way as did the translators of Freud's *Unheimliche*) in order to render faithfully the psychoacoustics of the night as experienced by the child in all its intimate marvels and fears. One of the most poignant and enigmatic of all the later poems in 'Bairnrhymes' takes this impulse still further, to the very edges of the poet's powers of expression before the mysteries of the world as the child encounters it:

> Though a' the hills were paper
> And a' the burns were ink;
> Though a man wi' the years o' Ben Voirlich
> Wrocht at the crambo-clink;
>
> Getherin the world's glory,
> Aye there afore his e'en,
> In the day-licht, and the grey-licht,
> And the cannel-licht o' the müne;
>
> Lang, lang, or the makin were ended
> His rowth o' years were by;
> And a' the hills wud be midden-heaps,
> And a' the burns dry.
> ('Gloria Mundi', p. 82)

Soutar's striking opening metaphor of his cherished Scottish landscapes becoming the tools of the poet's craft speaks to the bonds with place and people that forever underpin the core values and sentiments that his poetry seeks to share with his child readers. Hence a poem that celebrates the natural 'glories of the world' and ponders at its heart if they can ever be truly captured by paper and ink in fact in its central stanza's bold, yet subtle, repetition of the circadian cycle of 'day-licht ... grey-licht ... cannel-licht', from morning till night, exhibits precisely the watchful capacity of the Scots language ('Getherin') to perform something approaching just this impossible feat. Again, with his characteristic poetic virtues intact, Soutar, having adroitly demonstrated these powers to his readers and gifted them in his words a language of seeing, allows the poet's ambitions again to recede, in a gesture of characteristic literary humility and self-effacement.

Soutar's younger contemporary, J. K. Annand, does not possess the older poet's lyrical range or sustained attention to observation and interiorised literary reflection. His poems in the celebrated 1989 collection *A Wale o Rhymes* are for the most part amusing, light-hearted fare with familiar themes from the genre: finger, action, number and skipping rhymes; nonsense verse; often humorous poems about animals, birds, games, eccentric people and special occasions and festivals. While there is plenty of fun and comedy, the poems for the most part celebrate a pleasant, largely soft-focus and often escapist view of childhood. They can seem frequently niche and incidental. Annand does perform some important tasks, however, and thus remains a significant figure in the further alignment of the Scots poetic voice with the vernacular commonplaces of twentieth-century Scottish children in their seemingly unremarkable daily lives. Moreover, he can sometimes rise to a richer literary attainment, drawing more deeply on the Scots traditions and presenting them vigorously and invitingly to modern audiences.

Even Annand's more occasional verse does dwell regularly and appealingly in the everyday rhythms of childhood. The poem 'Bus Queue' (p. 20) catches not only a fixture of everyday life but also conveys both the resourcefulness of queuing children playing 'I Spy' games to pass the time, while the impatient adults grumble, and their underlying amused indifference to whether 'the schule bus never came' at all. The complaining adults at the stop don't speak, it transpires, 'for aa the ither folk'. Boredom and the distractions from it are of course much-observed features of childhood on which many writers have dwelt, but Annand takes its measure in a poem like 'Dressin Up' (p. 26) by once again noting the resilience of children 'On dreary wat days' rummaging in 'a kist up in the garret' to find clothes which enable the poem's three protagonists to play at a wedding ceremony!

An attractive feature of several of the poems in *Wale* is, indeed, this wry juxtaposition of the social world seen seriously by over-pressed adults with its more carnivalesque perception by playing and musing children alert to features to which adults have become inured. Poems from *Wale* which focus on jobs and occupations in society, such as 'Conductress' (p. 67) and 'Polis' (p. 70), express the young child's amusingly oversimplified understanding of work, the eternal adult question of 'what you want to be when you grow up', and also the young child's elliptical observation of what indeed it would be like to occupy such roles. The girl who dreams of being a Conductress (ironically, a job long extinct in Scottish transport), 'When I grow up and leave the schule', tellingly contrasts it with 'work in onie mill', and is attracted chiefly by what she has observed as a passenger of its sounds and rhythms, which the poem then skilfully reproduces:

> Move up the bus.
> That's the very thing.
> Thripence to the circus,

> Fowerpence to the zoo,
> Hae your fares ready
> And I'll thank you.

The (presumably male) child contemplating the Police combines his very mixed experience of daily exchanges with them as they track down on his streets 'gamblers and goalies' with a naïve envy of their imagined 'muckle strappin' authority and excitement on the beat, or behind the wheel of a police car:

> When we're the traffic polis,
> Motorists hae to thole us
> And draw up unco quick.

Annand's clever command of this mostly quite incidental material of children's quotidian lives and impressions is ably demonstrated when he extends his career lists to the half-imaginary figure of the 'Spaceman' (p. 79), becoming in the mid-twentieth century an 'occupation' located liminally for most ordinary Scottish children somewhere between science fiction and televised reality. We glimpse also in this poem Annand's genuine facility with the Scots tradition, as his poem is, despite its title, replete with an older 'lunar' imagery ('Gowd and siller ore') and informed by a noticeably and recognisably archaic folk narrative of buried treasure and mysteriously acquired wealth:

> I think I'll be a spaceman
> And trevel to the mune
> To poke aboot the craters
> And see what I can fin'.
>
> They say it's fou o diamonds,
> Gowd and siller ore;
> I'll lade them in my spaceship
> Till I hae quite a store.
>
> Then I'll come hame a rich man
> And dander up the street
> Noddin my fancy helmet
> To ilka sowl I meet.

This same ironic alignment of tradition and modernity is present in another of the volume's best poems, 'Nessie' (p. 38). Here the ambiguous Scottish monster and emblematic national tourist attraction, 'discovered' and popularised of course by the twentieth-century analogue technologies of handheld and mass media, is presented to the reader in language which partially echoes older fairy narratives, partially juxtaposes these with modern investigative science – and succeeds thereby in ironising both:

> Nessie the Loch Ness Monster
> Wad seem to be gey blate,
> And doesna like the scientist chiels
> That come, and sit, and wait.

The resultant concluding advice to the child reader artfully preserves in its equivocal intonations the uncertainty and scepticism in which the monster's existence remains shrouded, empowering the child reader (and maybe therefore also the poet?) to be the strictly unscientific agent of its shifting, liminal presence before the eye of the creative imagination:

> But gif ye want to see her
> Pretend ye dinna care,
> Keek oot the corner o your ee—
> Ye'll see her soomin there.

From sometimes overlapping and sometimes quite divergent approaches to their art, both William Soutar and J. K. Annand helped braid the living legacies of Scots language writing into the mainstream of modern Scottish children's poetry. In consequence, we can see in their literary heirs both continuity and innovation in Scots poetry writing, strongly reflective of a living and evolving practice. This is a practice rooted in the principles of access to the 'kist' of a plentiful past alongside attentive interest in the present, the modern day in all its detail. It blends into its distinctive Scots aesthetic much that we have seen refracted through Soutar and Annand: a bustling sense of loquacious energy; a watchful concern for the ways in which children see and interpret adult behaviour towards them; a deprecating humour and receptivity to the comic soundtrack of Scottish childhood; a joy in the youthful engagement with nature, which at its best can combine full immersion in the ordinary with those glimpses of the visionary that the fresh and supple Scots vocabulary seems especially well equipped to communicate. The exceptionally talented and wide-ranging former Makar, Jackie Kay, herself a product of mixed race and adopted cultures in Scotland, and fluent in Scots versifying throughout her work, demonstrates one aspect of this embrace of the Scots heritage in her entertaining poem 'Hauf A Dozen'.[26] In the spirit of Soutar's repeatedly skelped little boy, the poem describes a child 'sent tae buy: / hauf a dozen eggs' and 'tae hurry back hame / tae my mammy or I wuid / get six o' her best'. In a poem that cleverly and wittily encodes the typical arithmetical confusions of a young child learning anxiously to count, in the face of 'caved in' eggs and the promised parental retribution for them, she signposts purposely her unplanned and sobering moment of ironic instruction:

> I'm aye at sixes and sevens
> I'm scatty like a chicken.
> And till that day I didnae ken
> That six was hauf a dozen.

Sheena Blackhall's poem 'Skyscraper Family'[27] ventures further into the domestic and municipal realms of mid-twentieth-century Scottish urban childhood, its title acknowledging the many working-class families whose lives came to be lived in the shadow of the high-rise council flats that proliferated in the major cities in the wake of post-war slum clearances. Her poem echoes some of the observational and quizzical methods of Annand, when bringing to bear a distinctively mordant and enquiring Scots intelligence on to a singular and looming contemporary object:

> Skyscraper family, it maun be a bore
> Bidin twenty storeys frae yer ain front door.
> By day ye've gulls for neebors, syne ye've stars at nicht
> Save on the electric wi the meen for licht.

Blackhall's words exhibit that almost metaphysical capacity of the Scots idiom to integrate wonder and humour, curiosity and scepticism; the oft-invoked moonlight of the rustic Scots tradition here jokingly referenced as a means of saving money on electricity bills – a regular preoccupation of the residents of these draughty brutalist buildings. The poem succeeds in depicting the breathtaking modernist spectacle of the skyscrapers whilst never failing sympathetically to humanise them and their elevated occupants, pinpointing obliquely some of the questions to which the town planners did not perhaps devote sufficient attention: 'Fin the bairn greets, dae ye hung her on a cloud? / My, it must be lanely, up abeen the crowd!'

Anne Armstrong's 'Cat Food Rap'[28] is another excursion into the zone where the eldritch past of the Scots poetic patrimony meets the commonplace realities (and the musico-poetic rhythms, indeed, as the punning title suggests) of modern life, to considerable humorous effect. Rescuing a mouse from the mouth of his cat, the poet's speaking persona greets, in fact, a grateful fairy who promises a fitting reward in return for the solution to a series of trick questions:

> 'Can ye show me the ram, that disnae hiv a fleece?
> Can you show me chips, that were never fried in grease?
> Tell me where are the windaes nae sun shines through?
> And where is the moose, that never ever grew?'

The poem's clever allusions to the ancient genre of the folk riddle, in which Old Scots verse abounded, is here both honoured and parodied. In return, and respecting the long-hallowed rules of the test, the speaker tries faithfully to answer in the same ritual spirit – only to discover that the answer from the fairy to all four questions is in fact to be found in 'a computer, whit d'ye say ti that?' Annoyed at being hoodwinked out of his just reward, the boy notes in his deadpan conclusion that he 'lifted up the fairy an A fed her tae the cat.' The comic revenge at the end of the poem stresses its game-playing, mock-ceremonial literary ancestry. It also underscores the skill with which a contemporary and quick-witted sensibility can repurpose aspects of that same heritage to engage amusedly with a technological language that has become today an otherwise unremarked part of everyday parlance.

We can see aspects of this interchange of past and present come full circle in Liz Niven's fine poem, 'Feart'.[29] This is a work that takes us back into the darker thematics of the tradition as we have documented it here, embracing its traffic with the night, the fairy folk, the fearful imagery of thunderstorm and haunted locations and the unknown to which children have a supposedly special sensitivity:

> In the pit mirk nicht at the fit o the stairs,
> A heard a wee noise that jist made the hairs,
> oan the back o ma neck, staun straight up oan end
> ma teeth start tae chatter, ma hert fair bend.

Yes, as with other verse we have looked at in this chapter, this is also a poem which cunningly manages the emotions and the tension it has released, not by disrespecting or merely deflating the Scots gothic conventions it so calculatingly calls up, but by recognising that for modern children they often sit within a world that is as much disenchanted as magically infused; an 'Enlightened' and scientific world where reason routinely resists superstition in pursuit of explanation. The resultant compromise with which the poem ends hence serves not to scoff at the child's nocturnal fears, but to assuage them in the recognition of familiar and comforting truths: that the seemingly ghostly presence in the room is in fact 'A wee black baw o fur and fluff / [...] Ma new wee kitten [...] fair famisht fir her food'. While this resolution has a distinctly 'contemporary', even 'secular' feel to it, we can appreciate on reflection that fear and laughter, suspense and sentimentality, the unknown and the mundane, have existed in a kind of poetic equilibrium all through this distinguished body of indigenous literature.

Contemporary Resonances

The notion of what we might term a 'renewable tradition' that somehow 'writes back' to itself – respectfully, ironically, questioningly, testingly and sometimes *protestingly* – may simply be another means of describing one of the central defining 'dimensions' of Scottish children's poetry with which this chapter experimented at its outset. When Bashabi Fraser writes about 'My mum's sari',[30] she writes as a woman of mixed Indian parentage and elective Scottish allegiance – a so-called 'New Scot' – addressing Scottish children in terms with which Stevenson, Soutar and Annand would each in their own way have fully identified. Declaring that 'I love my mother's sari on the washing line / Flapping like a giant flag, which I pretend is mine', she names and embraces proudly her own ethnic particularism. Yet, she also recognises in the associations of the named garment the near-universal domestic mischief and its consequences that are a part of many local childhoods:

> I love to wash my dirty hands at the kitchen sink
> And wipe them on mum's sari before she can even blink.
>
> But when she takes her *anchal* and ties it round her waist
> I know it's time for battle and a quick escape is best!

Matthew Fitt's celebrated and much-anthologised comic piece, 'Captain Puggle'[31] is in lively dialogue with the nonsense verse tradition that runs through the history of Scottish children's poetry and in each of its languages. Yet, this is a captain not of an exotic pirate galleon, fairy band or military company, but an aeroplane:

> Captain Puggle flees his plane
> Frae Tumshie Airport tae Bahrain
> Gets the Smiths and their wee wean
> Brings them aw back hame again.

The poem's seemingly random inventory of locations national and international – from Barra to Crete and Spain – playfully references a Scotland grown more global and cosmopolitan in its outlook on the world, even as it has grown internally more diverse in the makeup of its communities and the multiple childhoods they foster. Once again, difference sits alongside and in productive relation with universality as the tradition addresses from out of its reservoir of imagery and story, wit and wisdom, a changing culture and society.

Perhaps no living children's poet has sustained a more searching, vigilant and reflective conversation between past and present, heritage and (post-)modernity, than Carol Ann Duffy. Duffy's approach to writing poetry for children originates in her career-long interest in the subject of childhood, which is entwined with much of the wider corpus of her verse. In these important continuities in her work, we can rightly see a kind of doubling-back on to the impulses and interests that informed Robert Louis Stevenson's desire to write poetry directly for children on the threshold of a new era of psychological and anthropological knowledge. The result, gathered up in Duffy's richly rewarding *New and Collected Poems for Children* (2009), is surely one of the most significant and distinguished bodies of verse for children and young people seen in Scotland in recent decades.

Like Stevenson, Duffy makes it clear that she believes in childhood innocence, but this is not the often mawkish, overemotional (and occasionally predatory) voyeurism and nostalgia of the Victorians and their heirs (which Stevenson also spurned). Rather it is a frequently resilient, empowering and even at times adversarial innocence; what she terms 'innocence as birthrights',[32] from out of which children, strengthened by story and language and art, can find new styles of engagement with, and resistance to, the often refractory world around them – including, sometimes, the superficially sincerely solicitous designs of protective, caring adults towards them. An authorial positionality of this kind makes a poem like 'Don't be scared'[33] both a homage to, and an intervention in, the literary inheritance it so clearly conjures:

> The dark is only a blanket
> for the moon to put on her bed.
>
> The dark is a private cinema
> for the movie dreams in your head.
>
> The dark is a little black dress
> to show off the sequin stars.

The dark and its fears, which have figured so prominently in the literature we have appraised throughout this chapter, is here deftly and soothingly neutralised from the first line adverb 'only' onwards. It is not that the fears of this particular child are dismissed or trivialised, but that the healing spell of language applied by the poet can refashion the manifold anxieties of the night and the dark into persuasively alternative benign and reassuring metaphors, finally lulling the child into the protected security of sleep: 'so smile in your sleep in the dark. / Don't be scared.'

Whitley[34] and other close readers of Duffy's children's poetry rightly point out that her intertextual reworkings of the forms and the thematics of the past are more than merely corrective or therapeutic. As Angela Carter did for adults in prose, so Duffy in verse for children seeks to open a portal on to the imperishable realm of fairy tale and folklore: one which validates fully the authenticity of its darkness and the visceral impact of its terrors as part of a fluent intercourse between human, chthonic and celestial influences and the psychic lives and inner dramas of children themselves. Intermittently, the poetic task here does indeed become one of containment and reassurance, but only because the full otherness and danger of the world as children often experience it is comprehensively and starkly rendered. The poem 'Whirlpool' (p. 86) – one of Duffy's most discussed children's texts[35] – offers little by way of such succour or compensation, chiefly because of its unflinching regard for the depth of the child dreamer's mounting realisation of horror:

> I saw two hands in the whirlpool
> clutching at air,
> but when I knelt by the swirling edge
> nothing was there.
> Behind me twelve green-black tall trees shook and scattered their
>   rooks.
> I turned to the spinning waters again
> and looked.

The poem smudges dream and reality, assisted by its ballad rhythm and classic pastoral imagery. This is a familiar rendezvous point for both loving trysts and vengeful murders. The rising sense of tension and horror in the verse goes increasingly unappeased as each stage of the nightmare draws us more deeply into a seemingly stricken forfeiture of selfhood and an unregulated watery metamorphosis: an eventual drowning in the endless possibilities of being, which in other contexts might be miraculous, but in this one portends for the child only dissolution and death.

It would be misleading to characterise Duffy's conversation with the tradition as exclusively or disproportionately 'dark'. Her poetic range is much wider than this and precisely by virtue of her receptivity to the full emotional and symbolic spectrum of what she has interiorised (and often interrogated too in her adult poetry) Duffy is able mobilise it on behalf of a much more assertive and agentive construction of childhood. Addressing the tradition obliquely, and in a language here laced with Scots, serves to encourage children, for instance, in 'Vows' (pp. 47–49) quirkily to resist assigned generational or gender destinies:

> I will not marry a Duke
> who walks like a duck.
> I will not marry an Earl
> who feels like an eel.
> I will not marry a Knight
> who jumps like a gnat.
>
> [...]
>
> I will not marry a Maiden
> who mings like a midden.
> I will not marry a Lass

> who bites like a louse.
> I will not marry a Girl
> who glares like a ghoul.

In the same way, the girl in 'A Bad Princess' (p. 45) who,

> stomped through the woods
> in a pair of boots
> looking for trouble –

'... and ready to bubble', channels both the wicked and stupid aristocratic females of fairy-tale romance and the recognisable teenage bullies of a modern high school. This synthesis holds until she of course meets the much tougher and mysterious 'Tree Girl', whose older, autochthonous greenwood energy, and casual disregard of arbitrary social hierarchy, soon sends the vain Princess fleeing predictably 'into the arms of the dull young Prince', to be his wife.

In her 'adult' verse a great and original poet of the season of Christmas and its many festive paradoxes, Duffy in the poem 'The Babysitter' (pp. 90–92) exploits the preternatural liminality of the season to immerse the child reader yet again in the 'Once upon a time' marvels and promises of the fairy story. However, the apparently essential 'timelessness' that this established narrative formula commonly excites and initiates is immediately qualified in the first line of the poem by the down-to-earth conversational historicity of the phrase 'nearly fifty years ago'. The promiscuous mixing of genres, registers, realism, nonsense, puns, memoir and fantasy conventions that ensues in the poem is consciously set at liberty to extend literary permission to its entreating girl protagonist, 'Bobbie B. May', to embrace fully the unforeseen miracle for which we are informed she prays 'day after day' – *'please send Elvis to babysit'*. Disappointed by a series of inadequate 1950s surrogates visiting her home, Bobbie remains through the year steadfast in her faith until, assisted by the added seasonal magic of 'One Saturday near Christmas', Elvis Presley does indeed appear at her door ready to babysit and to serenade her with a selection of his famous hits. Bobbie B. May hence comes to epitomise those many child personalities throughout Duffy's verse for young people who with due and appropriate reverence adopt sincerely the grammars of custom and tradition but who then daringly reinvent or transgress them to encode distinctively modern desires and yearnings. Regaled by Elvis's songbook, Bobbie slips in and out of the dreamscape on which such poems depend in even their most magic realist modes of apprehension, finally to be rewarded in terms that yet again merge past and present, myth and modernity, popular cliché and satisfying originality:

> Against the midnight sky a shooting star
> slashed like a hand on the strings of a guitar.
> When Bobbie woke up
> Elvis was gone.
> She walked in his foot prints in the firm white snow,
> she wandered round the house where he'd sung his songs.
> But on Christmas morning by the tinselly tree
> were a little pair of blue suede shoes
> addressed
> to Bobbie B.

The adventurous, miraculous experience of one imagined young person, Bobbie B. May, seems a fitting point to bring this exploration to an at least temporary conclusion. For the many dimensions of Scottish children's poetry continue to multiply and in often unpredictable forms. Similarly, the many versions of Scottish childhoods also continue to proliferate and diversify in ways that Carol Ann Duffy's poetry seems spectrally to anticipate and celebrate while – as the same poetry also reminds us – improvising on patterns we have known and felt immemorially. Perhaps these are inevitable properties of the strange nexus between community, art and power where childhood and poetry meet and where our next iterations of a specifically Scottish childhood, and an accompanying Scottish children's poetry, will be together confidently forged.

Primary texts cited

J. K. Annand, *A Wale o Rhymes* (Edinburgh: Macdonald Publishers, 1989).
Robert Ford (ed.), *Ballads of Bairnhood* (Paisley: Alexander Gardner, 1894).
Robert Kirk, *The Secret Commonwealth of Elves, Fauns, and Fairies*, ed. and introduced Marina Warner, (New York: NYRB Press, 2019).
Andrew Lang (ed.), *The Blue Poetry Book* (London: Longmans, 1891).
Robert Louis Stevenson, *A Child's Garden of Verses* (Harmondsworth: Penguin, 2009).

CHAPTER THREE

Children's Scottish Historical Fiction

Beth Dickson

Introduction

Scottish historical fiction for children from 1800 to the early years of the second millennium reveals a wealth of literary riches. Fictional characters drawn from all walks of life and periods of history – Wallace and Bruce, piemen and dressmakers, judges and criminals, engineers and local councillors, teachers and taxi-drivers – inhabit the novel as its durable form gives countless hours of enjoyment to readers before and into the media age. Conflicts found in Scottish adult historical fiction – Episcopalians and Covenanters, Jacobites and Hanoverians – also provide settings for children's fiction. Just as much as adult historical fiction, children's novels are comments on, and products of, the time in which they were written.[1] The literary form of children's fiction is part of the romance genre where, though very realistic problems may be treated in the novels, their endings are resolved imaginatively in numerous variants of the sentence, 'And they all lived happily ever after'.[2] Thus the genre is characterised by hope rather than the despair which could easily be induced by reflecting on history.

This overview will span the period between the early nineteenth century and the early twenty-first century by considering a range of novels, at least two of which come from each half century of the two centuries under discussion. In order to explore the wealth of the genre, and to present a coherent account, the overview will chart two socio-political issues which span the period: changes in the role of women and changes from religious to materialistic ideologies. Firstly, however, it will discuss the cultural changes in modes of production which characterise the shift from a word-based culture to a multi-modal one.

Production

What a children's historical novel consists of – how and why it has been written and published – changed during the period. As a form, the novel, originating in the eighteenth century, came into its own during the nineteenth century providing learning and pleasure for growing numbers of readers. Its educative function was significant in making the form respectable. In *Tales of a Grandfather* (1827) Walter Scott (1771–1832) writes history for younger readers, rather than fiction *per se*. This text shows a transition between history writing and fiction as, arguably, Scott's fictional skills in rendering romantic atmosphere, drawing noble heroes and execrable villains, which exerted such a powerful attraction on adult readers of his fiction, are not absent from this text.

If Scott is the grandfather of children's historical fiction, then Grace Kennedy (1782–1825) is its grandmother, as *Anna Ross: a story for children* (1824) was published before the first part of *Tales of a Grandfather*. The action of *Anna Ross* is set in 1815 as news of a British victory at Waterloo filters north to Edinburgh. While Scott's use of literariness blurs the distinction between history and fiction in an attempt at legitimisation, Kennedy, in her introduction, justifies the novel on the grounds that it provides religious parents with a means of impressing important truths on the minds of their children. At the time many readers believed that, as fiction was deliberately imagined, it was a species of untruth and therefore 'lies', pernicious and abhorrent to right-minded people. This view underlies the response of one of Kennedy's early reviewers:

> We cannot persuade ourselves that we have overvalued the production, even on the supposition that it was merely an effort of the imagination; but if it turns out as we suspect, to be founded on fact, then its value is enhanced in a degree which it will be no easy matter to specify or appreciate.[3]

It is clear that Kennedy has judged exactly the fictional product which readers will accept, even as her reviewers struggle with distinctions between fact, truth, lies and the real on one hand, and their obvious enjoyment of the text on the other. Like Scott she uses the importance of the content being conveyed as a justification. In the hierarchy of the times, religion was accorded greater weight even than history. A brief note on her life compiled by one of her publishers provides Kennedy's justification of fiction:

> The framework of fiction was adopted by our Authoress in the earnest hope that a species of writing which possesses irresistible charms to multitudes of readers, and has been rendered subservient to the dissemination of error, might be rendered as extensively useful in the communication of truth.[4]

She carefully distinguished between the attraction of the form and its purpose. If the purpose of form is upright, then attraction is a strength rather than a weakness.

Scott's style of writing for children is complex. In his Preface to *Tales of a Grandfather* he explains that, although using a simpler diction for the 'Tale of Macbeth', he decided to use a more 'elevated' style when he found his young relative preferred it. 'There is no harm [...] in presenting a child with ideas somewhat beyond easy and immediate comprehension. The difficulties thus offered, if not too great or too frequent, stimulate curiosity and encourage exertion.'[5] In his very affectionate dedication to his grandson, John Hugh Lockhart, Scott seems to believe that the child of about five or six would understand most of the volume but may have needed some things explained to him.

Scott's text does require advanced reading skills. In terms of accessibility, using a SMOG test (Simple Measure of Gobbledygook), a test designed to measure the readability of texts,[6] *Anna Ross* and Janis Mackay's twenty-first century *The Accidental Time Traveller* (2013) are similar in levels of accessibility but *Tales of a Grandfather* is about half as difficult again as either of them. What makes *Anna Ross* more accessible than *Tales of a Grandfather* is the nature of vocabulary and the formation of the sentences. Scott uses more words with more than two syllables and his sentences are written with long main clauses, subordinate clauses, and are often built up by phrases in apposition. Kennedy's sentences are similar in length but they often comprise a series of simply expressed phrases separated by dashes. Although her sentences can have as many as seven dashes, these could easily be re-punctuated as shorter sentences which would bring them much closer to modern sentence lengths.

Not only are some of the earlier texts written in a style which may seem dense to modern child readers, they also contain a range of references thought to be common to their contemporary readerships. As late as 1930, in *The King's Curate* Dorita Fairlie Bruce expects her readers to understand such an obscure Biblical reference as 'bowing down in the House of Rimmon' (accommodating oneself to a religion one does not follow). Underneath these earlier texts which require advanced reading skills, of course, lies the biblical text which acted as an aural and reading primer for many children.

Twenty-first-century fiction demonstrates the transition from a word-based to a multi-modal society. The text of *The Accidental Time Traveller* is written in short sections with shorter sentence lengths than the earlier texts. The text is broken up playfully by a variety of fonts which reproduce road signs, the names of shops, text messages – which themselves use a mixture of alphabetical and numerical digits such as '2moro' – and a representation of a topic written into a search engine box. The font size is larger than earlier texts so there is more white space on the page.

The balance of text to illustration also changes during the period. *Anna Ross* contains a few line drawings contributed by the author but twenty-first-century texts display much more visual content. The text of *The Accidental Time Traveller* is accompanied by little illustrations of objects which are important for the plot, reinforcing its main elements and adding visual but non-text-based interest for the reader as visuals become the norm for all readers, rather than a concession to the young.

The later texts mimic alternative contemporary modes of production in communication in order to create a bridge between the literary past and the multi-modal present. The reading challenges of earlier texts lie not so much in the nature of the vocabulary as in the absence of white space, the smallness of the font, archaisms, the range of references, and the sheer abundance of text which suited the mono-modal context in which textual forms dominated and did not have to compete with the range of communicative possibilities in a multi-modal world.

Women

Although the main characters in *Anna Ross* are girls, a number of nineteenth-century novels demonstrate an untroubled assumption about a link between education, history, and boy readers. This assumption characterises G. A. Henty in *In Freedom's Cause* (1843), who addresses his audience as 'My Dear Lads'. Scott, too, writes for boys, explicitly for his grandson; Stevenson wrote for his step-son. R. M. Ballantyne in *The Lighthouse: being the story of a great fight between man and the sea* (1865) expects a male readership, whom he educates in the engineering processes necessary to build the Bell Rock Lighthouse:

> A balance-crane which was fixed in the centre of the tower, and so arranged that it could be raised along with the rising works. This crane resembled a cross in form. At one arm was hung a movable weight, which could be run out to its extremity, or fixed at any part of it. The other arm was the one by means of which the stones were hoisted. When a stone had to be raised, its weight was ascertained, and the movable weight was so fixed as exactly to counterbalance it. By this simple contrivance all the cumbrous and troublesome machinery of long guys and bracing chains extending from the crane to the rock below were avoided.[7]

The length and detail of this description is enough to enable readers to construct their own mini versions and demonstrates a strong link between fiction and education. Boys were being educated in masculinity. Areas such as engineering, warfare and adventuring were constructed as male and male values were strength, loyalty, bravery, and perseverance against the odds. However, as Kate Flint has shown, novels for boys were also read by girls.[8]

Moreover, girls are much more visible in these novels than the conventional account allows. Grace Kennedy, writing as early as the 1820s, enables us to modify that account considerably. She wrote religious works – mainly for adults but some for children. She shares some similarities with English writers of the same period such as Mary Martha Sherwood (1775–1851). Both writers demonstrate a belief in the absolute necessity of adults and children in making an explicit decision to accept the tenets and responsibilities of the Christian faith. They share beliefs in redemption and damnation; are shrewd observers of behaviour and write engagingly. Kennedy, like her English counterparts, was translated into a variety of European languages: French, German, Dutch and Danish.[9]

Within this deeply religious context, in *Anna Ross*, Kennedy creates a female protagonist who is the agent of her own story: she has to decide which side of her family she wants to live with. This decision is of cosmic significance. Anna has to make it; and only Anna can make it as the decision is an expression of her individual faith which will affect her post-mortem fate. Because of the Protestant emphasis on the individual's responsibility before God, this was a decision which women had to make for themselves. Much of the emotional and rational weight of this decision is not obvious to later readers. The narrative is contextualised by Christianity to the extent that it is actually programmatic, almost allegorical at times. Each family is an expression of a form of response to the religious ideology of the time. The Rosses stand for a rather superficial attitude to religion and the Murrays for a deeper, thoughtful devotion. Although the influence of *Pilgrim's Progress* can be detected in the novel, Kennedy's talent for observation of habits and language tends to make the allegory not so obvious. Despite this historical context, which is normally viewed as generating very narrow and stereotypical views of women, Anna is the focus of attention, and in this imaginative space her thoughts, needs and desires can be expressed and explored.[10] Anna is drawn to the more religiously committed family rather than the society whirl of her wealthy Edinburgh cousins. She enjoys not having to depend on maids and being able to dress herself. She likes washing up 'quite as well as lying on a board to keep her figure straight'.[11] She enjoys being able to learn grammar, geography, arithmetic and French much more than being socially accomplished. Thus, within a religious context, commonly thought of as constricting human liberty, lie education and a willingness to reject to some extent, social conventions which stereotypically define and confine women: the rational pathways to equality for women.

Even in the work of G. A. Henty, a writer of adventure stories for boys, there is a much more flexible attitude to gender than might have been supposed. *In Freedom's Cause*, an entertaining tale of derring-do during the Wars of Independence, Archie Forbes is a stereotypically resilient, courageous and loyal hero. Often considered as a paradigm of masculine values, this narrative significantly modifies the stereotypical account of girls because girls, too, can defeat enemies with ingenuity and courage. Archie falls in love with Marjory, a feisty character in her own right, who, as Archie says, has no 'time for milliners and mantua-makers'. When Archie is away fighting with Bruce, Marjory organises the remaining servants to defend the castle and says that 'orders from me' are quite sufficient for the defenders. She equals Archie in risk-running and is able to rescue him when he has been incarcerated in an iron cage outside Berwick. Although a binary within Henty's view of femininity seems to exist between action/agency and signs of femininity such as fashionable dress, so that Marjory does at times seems an honorary boy, in this novel Henty does not present courage as an exclusively masculine value. Deirdre H. McMahon suggests this flexibility about gender characterises his colonial writing.[12] His prolific storytelling capacity was able to imagine an equality of agency, the implications of which took longer to characterise British society more generally.

R. M. Ballantyne's attitudes to gender are more obviously conventional than Henty's. Ruby Brand, the hero, 5' 10" and 'muscly' (p. 13), is the strong protector. His girl-friend, Minnie, is first pictured with Ruby when 'the relative position of their noses, mouths and chins' were in 'a position which would have been highly improper and altogether unjustifiable but for the fact that Ruby was Minnie's accepted lover' (p. 13). The physicality of this clinch demonstrates degrees of freedom in relations between men and women which attached to different stages of a relationship which would ultimately lead to marriage.

By the early twentieth century, girls were addressed as audiences in their own right. In 1930, *The King's Curate* by Dorita Fairlie Bruce (1885–1970) comes alive through the lively characterisation of Anne Carstairs. Anne often rides out over the moors; she is an able sailor; likes attending the Covenanters' hill-preachings, sometimes, she thinks, more for the danger than the religion. It may be that *Tales of a Grandfather* is a source for this characterisation. Scott writes, 'The romantic and dangerous character of this species of worship recommended it to such as were bold and high-spirited' (p. 596). If there is a connection, then Bruce's subversion is that it is a woman who embodies this character, not men, as Scott assumes. That her behaviour is seen as problematic is shown through Anne's mother – who is dismayed by her 'mad pranks' (p. 164) – and through Alison Mellish, a victim of Presbyterian persecution, who is stereotypically feminine. Her illness throughout the novel emphasises her passivity, while in her a more conventional femininity is more clearly seen.

In Patrick Mellish, the Episcopalian parson, Anne recognises 'a gentleman', someone of a similar social class (if exiled from it) as herself. Patrick and Anne marry. Patrick receives his lands again and Anne, though easily as capable, far-sighted, and determined as her husband, re-affirms the belief that a woman needs a man to complete her. Thus, the character confirms early twentieth-century social order by having a husband, the sign through which she may express her strong personality legitimately. Although viewed from the succeeding century this may appear a limited freedom, it is the case that only a century previously, Grace Kennedy was making the first imaginative moves which made Bruce's fiction possible.

In the mid-twentieth century, a more feminist perspective becomes apparent. In Iona McGregor's *An Edinburgh Reel* (1968), Christine is the heroine. She dislikes being teased for being uneducated by her Edinburgh cousins since she did learn some history, Latin, and literature at her rural estate before travelling to Edinburgh where she lives in somewhat reduced circumstances. Her father is a Jacobite returning from France to settle again in Scotland now governed by Whigs. Her father finds it difficult to accept the civilian employment he is offered; he is still inclined towards Jacobitism although he is aware of the dangers of this; and when he and Christine do not see eye-to-eye, she is afraid he might use corporal punishment. Interestingly, on the one occasion he is about to hit his daughter, he restrains himself. He realises that she is growing up and that she is entitled to her views on matters. It is more important that Christine should express her views and he should learn how to disagree rather than impose his own view backed up by patriarchy. Christine falls in love with Jamie from a family who live upstairs in the Edinburgh tenement, Davidson's Land. Because of the plot Christine attends a cockfight, for which Jamie calls her 'a disnatured, unwomanly creature' (p. 161). Although in this incident Christine is acting out of duty rather than choice, the novel does demonstrate a willingness to investigate the darker side of female identity, pushing at the boundaries of women's liberation, which marked 1960s Britain. Women's freedom is expressed through control of what happens to their bodies and freedom to make their own decisions.

Donald Lightwood's *The Baillie's Daughter* (1990) demonstrates some of the hidden tensions around female identity. In terms of sexuality and before reliable forms of contraception existed, women were vulnerable to unwanted pregnancies and pregnancies which resulted from rape. Janet, the heroine, was born outside of wedlock. Her mother was made pregnant by the man for whom she worked as a maid at the time when her employer's wife was pregnant. When Janet's mother realised she was pregnant, she left the house immediately. There was no sympathy or support for her. Janet as a young adult coincidentally finds herself in the same household as her mother had been, working for the man who is in fact her biological father. Janet is employed as a maid/companion for the Baillie's legitimate daughter, Lizzie, who has Down's Syndrome. The Baillie is the father of both girls, who are therefore half-sisters. The vulnerability of a person in a subservient situation is visited on Janet, this time through the mother who begins to think of replacing Lizzie with Janet so that she can have a 'normal' daughter. In order to escape from this trap, Janet is supported by Cope, a freethinker who argues that she does not have to stay in this social trap and provides the means for Janet to pursue a life of her own choice. For Lizzie, rejected and murdered by her mother, there is no freedom unless death is considered such. It was not until 2004 that Scotland passed the Education (Additional Support for Learning) (Scotland) Act which provided children who experienced barriers to learning with a legal framework which would identify and address such issues.

Novels from the early years of the new millennium contain more progressive ideas about women. In Janis Mackay's *The Accidental Time Traveller*, Agatha Black is based on the historical figure of Marjorie Fleming (or 'Pet Marjorie') from Kirkcaldy (1803–1811), who kept note-books filled with her observations and opinions. Agatha, who accidentally finds herself in twenty-first-century Peebles, has strange, rather comic turns of speech, which mix archaisms and Scots. Saul, the boy she meets, decides that the simplest way to account for Agatha is to turn her into a boy so he can take her to school. However, Agatha hesitates: 'I am but a girl, it's true, but one used to taking care of herself. I will be grand' (p. 43). Saul is quick to explain 'not that girls were bad, but I had never brought a girl home before and girls were not allowed to join the gang' (p. 42). He cuts Agatha's hair (a cultural sign of femininity in both time worlds) and gives her some of his old clothes. That the writer still feels the need to explain the boy's action at the end of the novel is shown when his mother says, 'You didn't need to pretend she was a boy' (p. 199). Saul does learn his lesson. Agatha introduces him to Agnes, a girl on the margins of society. Through Agatha, Saul has learnt that girls can be intelligent, good at telling stories, and physically adventurous. After Agatha has returned to her own time, Saul continues to be friends with Agnes.

Philip Caveney's hero Tom Affleck, in *One for Sorrow* (2015), travels back in time to Edinburgh in the late 1800s where he is trying to ensure that Robert Louis Stevenson completes the writing of *Treasure Island*. There he meets Catriona McCallum as an old woman, a character he had already met as a girl in Caveney's earlier novel *Seventeen Coffins* (2014), set in 1836. In the interim Catriona has become a science-fiction novelist, praised by Jules Verne. Tom tells Catriona that he has found this out at the National Museum of Scotland:

'Cat, you're going to be a big name in feminism.'

'In what?' she murmured.

'Er ... You remember when we first met how you used to say that women should have the same rights as men and how they should be treated as equals? Well, in the future, they will be and it's because of people like you that it happened ... or will happen.' (116)

From being decorous or subservient in the early nineteenth century, by the twenty-first century women are seen as equals with an equality established in law through the work of writers and political campaigners. Finally, Tom becomes so fond of Catriona that he elects to go back in time to when she was a girl so that they can have a life together in a parallel space and time. Is it perhaps significant that these boy protagonists seem only to be able to connect with girls in other time zones? And that the otherness of the female gender is still being signed as 'other' through the exoticism of belonging to another period in history? Or is it the power of the happy ending which simply forecloses discussion on intractable issues and determines to be hopeful rather than despairing? This selection of twenty-first-century texts contains much modified versions of stereotypes. They give girls and boys some room to breathe and if they raise more questions than answers, they provide the imaginative yeast for critical thinking.

Ideology

In terms of ideology, children's Scottish historical fiction fits into general English language and European patterns. De Maeyer (2005) defines modernity as the process by which, from the mid-seventeenth century until around 2000, various aspects of life – political, relational, social and cultural – ceased to be understood solely from a religious point of view.[13] This chapter argues a similar case for Scotland. For the earliest novels, an apparently monolithic Presbyterian establishment controlled the beliefs and values of the majority of Scots. But, as with any hegemony, there are always gaps in the extent of its coverage and contradictions in its beliefs and values which demonstrate the existence of other people with different views. The conflict between the Catholic Church in Scotland and the forces of reform plays itself out endlessly in historical fiction. The forces of reform did become politically and religiously dominant in the decades after 1560, but a rebellious, banished, proscribed and hidden Catholic minority continued to exist, and to be an expression of issues of plurality which became central to Scottish society from the late twentieth century onwards.

In his 'tale' of the Massacre of Glencoe, Scott examines the theme of political, and therefore religious, hypocrisy through the judicial murder of members of the Clan MacDonald in 1692. The written orders that all must die 'have rarely been penned in a Christian country' (p. 402). The Scottish establishment was made up mainly of Protestant, Lowland supporters of the English crown while those who had rebelled were Catholic and (mainly) Highland with ties to majority Catholic countries on the European continent. Scott uses the characterisation of Master of Stair as a microcosm of the hypocrisy of the Protestant state. Scott describes Stair hypocritically conducting family worship at the same time as the MacDonalds were being massacred, thinking that he had nothing to feel guilty over in 'the death of a few Highland Papists, whose morals were no better than English highwaymen' (p. 408). However, Scott notes that subsequently the MacDonalds, when they had the opportunity to revenge themselves on their enemy, chose rather to guard Stair's property, thus fulfilling the Christian principle of loving one's enemy. The Establishment is preserved, though stained; and the rebels, though politically doomed, are more upright in their faith. Given that within this religious ideology virtue is more important than political prestige, the historical victims are the spiritual victors. The balance of this chiasmus is Scott's attempt at resolution. Scott, more generally, was not without his contemporary critics who believed him to be so sympathetic to a Catholic point of view, that his depiction of Protestants and Covenanters made them seem uncouth when at the time many people felt that they had the best of the argument.

Henty seems to stumble across the implications of Catholicism in Scottish history without as much forethought as Scott. The hero of *In Freedom's Cause*, Archie, finds out that Marjorie, with whom he is in love, has been sent to a convent for refusing to marry the man her family have selected for her. In the manner of anti-Catholic propaganda, the nuns are depicted as being unkind and hostile to the girl's wish to think for herself. However, as the novel progresses the tone softens as Henty has to deal with the implications of the fact that Bruce, the undoubted hero of the hour, was himself a Catholic. Rather than describing Bruce's killing of John Comyn as the unchristian act of a barbarous Catholic king, Bruce is described as being 'repentant'. This Christian response affirms the reality of Bruce's faith as the writer accommodates his respect for the archetypal Scottish hero. At the end of the novel, Henty points out that Queen Victoria, the reigning monarch, is descended from Bruce. That badge of honour assimilates Bruce into the historical ranks of the Great and the Good, leaving aside any awkward questions about his religious faith. It also shows Henty's willingness to be flexible about issues of ideological equality. Yet their persistence is a sign of an unresolved historical tension.

In Ballantyne's *The Lighthouse* there is the faintest indication of a contradiction between Christianity and other forms of religious belief, rather than the tension being found internally within Christianity itself as in Scott and Henty. The general context is still a dominant Presbyterian culture where the value of work is clear. The novel depicts the care taken over the departure from the norm of Sabbatarianism. Robert Stevenson 'requested' his men to work on Sundays with prayers being provided on site. Eventually all the men worked Sundays in order to cut the duration of working in hazardous conditions to construct a lighthouse on the Bell Rock. Although there is a culture of Bible-reading and churchgoing in the novel's background, at sea one of the men puts forward an evangelical view of faith which attempts to persuade the others to a more personally engaged religious commitment. He is listened to respectfully, then one of the workmen says, 'it is not natural to us, and not easy, to rise from nature to God's nature' (p. 104). This somewhat enigmatic observation seems to suggest that a god expressed by the power of the wind and sea might not be entirely like the Christian one. However, this thought, which like the seven-day working week is a feature of a future secular society, is not elaborated by the narrative. Ballantyne, like Henty, affirms the status quo and the novel ends on an emphatically Christian note comparing the completed lighthouse to the star in the Nativity story 'which brought the shepherds to the Light of the World and the Rock of Ages' (p. 287).

Dorita Fairlie Bruce, mainly known as a writer of school stories for girls, also wrote a series of historical novels set in the fictional parish of Kirkarlie, based on West Kilbride in Ayrshire. *The King's Curate* depicts the conflict between Covenanters and Episcopalians. This conflict derives from the earlier conflict between Catholicism and Reform. Although Protestantism became the dominant religious expression, the later debate was about how the reformed church should be governed. Episcopalians, who believed the church should be governed by bishops appointed by the monarch, opposed Presbyterians, who believed the church should be governed by a group of men chosen from its congregation. Thus, Patrick Mellish is sent to Ayrshire as the Episcopalian priest for the parish which prefers a Presbyterian form of church government. Since this has been outlawed, many local people (Covenanters) have taken to meeting in the hills above Redkirk (based on Largs) to be free of imposed religious authority. The influence of this impulse to self-government has been traced in the historical growth of the idea of democracy both in Scotland and America. Anne Carstairs, the daughter of a local landowner, attends the hill-preachings. Mellish's father was the local landowner whose lands were sequestrated under Cromwell, so when he eventually marries Anne the religious and historical conflicts are resolved through a marriage which ensures that the landed class preserves its social position and authority. Thus, what was a religious conflict is resolved in terms of gender and class.

Thus, the religious conflict, though foregrounded and not ahistorical in detail, is ahistorical in its glossing over the violent physical and spiritual agonies of the time. This rather anachronistic version of Scott's balanced chiasmus signals that the writer's main focus is not on the historical arguments. Rather the literary focus is on the characterisation of Anne Carstairs and the view Bruce wants to express about the position of women.

By the mid-twentieth century, the Christian context provides an evaporating backdrop rather than a dramatic foreground. *The Wide Blue Road* (1957) by Marion Campbell (1919–2000), set in the thirteenth century, leads up to the battle of Largs (1263), a key episode in Scotland's Scandinavian past. The story concerns Richard, son of a Norman lord, who is chosen by the Scottish knight, Sir Hugh, to be Hugh's page and be educated in the chivalric ethic of honour and courage. Before the battle, the Scots lords confer at Stirling and the bishop of St Andrews prays that 'God will direct their councils' (p. 102). Sir Hugh, who has sworn an oath of friendship with the Norse lord Biorn, believes that the Norsemen are 'as good Christians as anyone' (p. 24) and, again in an incident at sea, a transitional place between cultures, Richard has to think about Zaid Mahommed, a Saracen healer. Sir Hugh says of this foreigner, 'we may call them infidels, but is there another man in the ship who prays five times a day come rain or snow?' (p. 114). As well as there being contradictions between Scots and Norse Christians, there are those also between Christianity and other religions.

With Donald Lightwood's *The Baillie's Daughter* an entirely new note is struck. The novel is set in St Andrews in 1852 and concerns the religious hypocrisy of socially privileged parents who have a daughter, Lizzie, who has Down's syndrome. The suffering endured by Lizzie, who is hidden away because her parents would be embarrassed if their Down's Syndrome daughter were to appear in public, is sensitively rendered. Nothing is expected from Lizzie and so her personality, language and capacities languish until she meets Janet who befriends her and helps her to develop. Janet's unlikely friend Cope, as well as being a prize boxer, is a 'free thinker' who explicitly challenges Janet's belief in a God who acts in a world riven with suffering. Christians are depicted as narrow-minded, vengeful, and hypocritical, especially Lizzie's mother who, in an unexpectedly cruel psychological twist, murders her daughter and tries to replace her with Janet.

This novel faces head-on the idea of otherness in Lizzie's condition and argues that in the face of such difficulty, Christians do not act charitably and the religion itself only generates unsatisfactory, and sometimes harsh, answers to questions of human vulnerability and suffering. With the passing of the years, the way in which Scott portrayed aberrant Protestantism in Stair has come to represent all Christians, a conclusion which echoes Peter Hunt's view that by this time religion has 'taken on strong negative connotations'.[14] Christianity has become 'the other' from a secular worldview. Janet and Cope's happy ending satisfies the formal requirements of the genre. Yet, it is a deferred ending. Arguably, it is Lizzie's unspeakable murder which actually ends the story in a conclusion that is anything but happy. The shift from religious to free-thinking ideology critiques the hypocrisy of dominant religious ideology and severely pressurises the possibility of a happy ending. That there is a happy ending finally is the triumph of form over content and hope over experience.

Children's novels of the twenty-first century view Christianity as a muddled memory – eccentric, unsatisfactory and remote. Mackay in *The Accidental Time Traveller* accords significance to Beltane and the Winter Solstice, while music and storytelling are also important carriers of value. Saul returns Agatha to her own time by telling a story which along with flute music generates a trance-like state through which Agnes is enabled to return to her own time because 'Time is the true mystery of existence' (p. 39). In *One for Sorrow* (2015), Philip Caveney's time-travelling hero, Tom Affleck, arrives in Robert Louis Stevenson's Edinburgh in 1881. Visiting one house, Christmas trees are strange German habits being adopted by the Victorian middle class (p. 70). 'Onward Christian Soldiers' is a stirring tune played by a brass band in Princes Street and 'Jesus' is an exclamation of surprise (p. 99). *Darker Ends* (2015) by Alex Nye is the story of a sister and brother, home-alone in a farmhouse in Glen Coe. Their story intersects with those people fleeing the massacre of 1692 as the children tumble into a different fold of time trying to reach safety. Nye gives Maggie a sixth sense, able to hear noises in the mountains, thus her spiritual credentials are established. However, in a cemetery she wonders about God and then realises 'God is not at home' (p. 226).

The novels show the shift to more materialist or scientific viewpoints, which can be seen in the same struggle for happy endings as was seen in *The Baillie's Daughter*. The fantasy happy ending of *One for Sorrow* in which hero and heroine join each other in a fold of time where they are both the same chronological age values love. Saul and Agatha return to their own times at the end of *The Accidental Time Traveller*. Saul is left in the present with Agnes, a historical descendant of Agatha's, with whom he can be friends and demonstrate what he learned about historical difference in his positive attitude to the social and economic differences seen in Agnes, who comes from a family even poorer than his own. *Darker Ends* has an ambiguously unhappy ending. Very unusually, at the end of the story, the reader learns that both children, though they are active, are dead as far as this world is concerned. Their deaths are moderated by the fact that they are described as continuing to exist in another dimension of time. Hope is to be found in the half-lives of a series of ghostly characters which pervade the novel as Nye is reluctant to let Death be the last enemy. The romance ending of children's literature when confronted by a mainly materialist ideology does not entirely negate the happy ending but dents it, reduces its frequency and sites its existence in dimensions as yet unknown to physics.

Hence, we can see that over two centuries, Scottish historical children's fiction has shown the dominant religious ideology – Christianity – being replaced by other ideas which then push it to the margins of common values. Society transforms itself from being based on, and evaluating itself by, how nearly or distantly it kept to Christian values, to ideologies which are generally materialist in nature. There is an overlap in terms of ethics, perhaps, but there is a stronger vein of realism in the later books seen in the genuine struggle for happy endings.

Conclusion

From the early nineteenth century until the present, Scottish historical children's fiction demonstrates changes in the form of the novel and the process of reading; as well as ideological change in important aspects of what society thinks and values. Novels move from word-based cultures to visual, digital ones. They are often the seedbed for the forms which continue to parallel the purposes of books: radio, television or film. Reading itself undergoes change as it becomes meaning-making from texts which are not purely word-based. Digital technology becomes product, process and value as printing once was.

Over the same period children's historical fiction also demonstrates – critically – the changing role of women from being submissive and domesticated to achieving legal equality with men. Surprisingly, perhaps, rather than being inimical to this development, its seeds can be traced *within* religion from which, in some cases, steps towards gender equality are hewn out of older religious patriarchy. We have seen, in effect, the development of ideology from a monoculture of beliefs and values to a much more diverse Scotland. Religious ideology, closely associated with politics, affecting all aspects of life, moves from dominance to an existence in an increasingly secular Scotland as the 'other': a weak, confused and possibly dangerous voice at the edge of the fiction.

Even so, it is perhaps surprising to notice how early some brief accommodations to the 'other' were present in this tradition of writing. Scott's desire for equilibrium among Scottish historical forces began in the early nineteenth century and its influence can be traced well into the twentieth century. Kennedy's orphaned girl, Scott's Catholics and many more characters demonstrate the capacity of children's historical fiction to give a wide range of characters, whether mainstream or marginal, room to breathe and the right to speak. Children reading these novels inherit values of technology, equality and democracy. Armed with such values, children's fiction, though its romance values have been affected by secular doubt, shows an abiding desire, expressed through the romance itself, for a world which is better than the one we live in, one where hope triumphs over history.

Chronological list by publication of novels discussed
Grace Kennedy, *Anna Ross: a story for children* (1824)
Walter Scott, *Tales of a Grandfather* (1827)
G. (George) A. Henty, *In Freedom's Cause* (1843)
R. (Robert) M. Ballantyne, *The Lighthouse* (1865)
Dorita Fairlie Bruce, *The King's Curate* (1930)
Marion Campbell, *The Wide Blue Road* (1957)
Iona McGregor, *An Edinburgh Reel* (1968)
David Lightwood, *The Baillie's Daughter* (1990)
Janis Mackay, *The Accidental Time Traveller* (2013)
Alex Nye, *Darker Ends* (2015)
Philip Caveney, *One for Sorrow* (2015)

CHAPTER FOUR

A 'Spell of Stories': Scottish Children's Fantasy

Sarah Dunnigan

'It pays to remember, in this world, that magic is imagination. Imagination is magic.'[1]

In Naomi Mitchison's historical fairy-tale fantasy, *The Big House* (1950), a young boy tells how he 'fell through times of the world'.[2] And so he does: abducted by fairies, enfolded back into the historical realms of Jacobitism and early medieval Gaelic Scotland, until his wonder-tale ends, and he is returned to his own world – the Highlands in twentieth-century wartime. Mitchison's lyrical phrase captures the imaginative fluidity and transformative energies at the heart of the fantasy mode which partly account for its vital contemporary popularity; the story of a boy wizard, that began life in an Edinburgh café, might remain the most globally famous example but it belongs to a rich and diverse seam of other work.[3] As a genre, fantasy is notoriously thorny to define: transhistorical and transcultural in its reach and depth (the otherworld voyages of classical Greek literature or medieval supernatural romances are also 'fantastical'), rooted accordingly in both traditional oral and literary print cultures and, especially from the nineteenth century to the present day, bleeding into other genres (including, for example, science fiction, fairy tale, utopia / dystopia, Gothic, cyber-fantasy, magic realism).[4] Whilst Lucie Armitt, discussing the tendency to denigrate fantasy literature as 'childish', asserts that fantasy is not 'innately childlike',[5] throughout its historical and cultural development, in Scotland as elsewhere, it has often been intended specifically for a child readership. This body of fantasy writing is the subject of the present chapter but it is necessary to point out that the child-adult readership distinction is itself fluid; as the narrator of Ross MacKenzie's *The Otherworld Emporium* notes, the eleven-year-old Susie stands 'near the border threshold of one of the most important borders in life: the border between childhood and adulthood, between magic and the everyday'.[6] Since the concept of 'the child reader' cannot be thought of as a singular or monolithic identity,[7] the readership for the fictions discussed in this chapter is understood as varied and intersectional. The primary material also encompasses what has come to be called 'young adult' (YA) literature, a deeply popular and autonomously recognised genre in the contemporary publishing industry. For reasons of limited space, the chapter does not include early-reader picturebooks, a topic addressed later in this Companion by Penni Cotton. It is important to note that their visual and graphic worlds frequently embody, and take inspiration from, the fantastical languages of fairy tale, myth, and folklore.

For the purpose of this chapter, fantasy is understood by an overarching definition: a fiction which involves a magical and/or 'otherworldly' dimension (where the latter alludes to a variety of imagined, alternate realities). In a well-known essay, one of twentieth-century Britain's most famous fantasy writers, J. R. R. Tolkien, referred to the 'primary' and 'secondary' worlds of fantasy.[8] This chapter explores fictions which articulate a self-enclosed, autonomous fantastical world, and those which depict journeying between 'real' and 'fantastical' realms, as well as what Farah Mendlesohn describes as immersive, portal quest, intrusive, and liminal fantasies.[9] However realised, all these fictions have in common the creation of a wonderland, underworld, dream-space, or alternate reality – whether George MacDonald's Victorian fairylands, George Mackay Brown's ancient Orcadian realms, Ross Mackenzie's 'Nowhere'-rooted, time-travelling, magical Emporium and its Victorian steampunk aesthetic, or Julia Bertagna's Weave, an 'ice-blue static' cyberspace 'far beyond realworld'.[10] These secondary worlds – frequently replete with their own magical objects such as 'a vial of unicorn blood', or a box with a golden hazelnut for a soul – usually possess their own internal logic and rules which may still prove uncanny, strange, and even authoritarian to the text's protagonists and readers.[11]

With the exception of Maureen Farrell's work, the history of Scottish fantasy writing specifically for children has rarely been explored.[12] This is in striking contrast to the prolific number of studies devoted to English and North American children's fantasy literature, especially in relation to the 'Golden Age' period and the contemporary young adult fiction.[13] Colin Manlove, however, suggests that Scottish fantasy can be considered an imaginatively coherent and autonomous mode through the recurrence of particular themes and preoccupations, echoed by Margaret Elphinstone in her millennial reflection on the pervasiveness of a Scottish fantasy tradition.[14] Inevitably, this chapter has limitations and boundaries. Whilst it cannot be comprehensive in its coverage – space does not permit discussion of children's fantasy which takes Scotland as is its imaginative setting by writers of non-Scottish origin[15] – it seeks to convey a sense of the historical dimensions of fantasy as a genre for a young readership so that the roots of its current, and well-known, flowering (beyond Rowling, in the work of other gifted writers such as Julie Bertagna, Martin Stewart, Ross McKenzie, and Lari Don, for example) are placed in perhaps a less familiar seedbed. Whilst it could have begun with Robert Henryson's late medieval *Fables* as a primer for children, the chapter locates its historical arc in the early nineteenth century. Discussing some of the major impulses and movements in Scottish writers' deployment of fantastical modes, the chapter briefly highlights the mode's persistent structural and thematic fascination with motifs of journeying and landscapes, and the importance of intertextuality and allusiveness more generally. It then identifies three key features which recur in this body of work: the role and importance of child protagonists; the ways in which fantasy powerfully enables a child readership to confront and experience 'difficulties' and how its portrayal of 'alternative worlds' can serve a variety of utopian or 'redemptive' purposes; and, finally, the strikingly persistent use of traditional folklore and belief by Scottish fantasy writers. Throughout it seeks to suggest that the particular imaginative structures and motifs of children's fantasy – the possibilities of young reader identification with (for example) the heroine of MacKenzie's *The Colour of Hope* (2022), who longs to be a spellcaster, or Ropa, the brilliantly imagined heroine of T. L. Huchu's *The Library of the Dead* (2021) who delivers messages to, and from, Edinburgh's dead – help nurture empathy, agency, and empowerment.

A Brief History of Scottish Children's Fantasy

Fantastical taletelling intended for, or inclusive of, children inheres in the stories, lullabies, ballads, and folk-rhymes transmitted through living tradition and oral culture.[16] In that sense, its specific origin cannot be pinpointed and it has a heritage, as we shall see later, which is capable of being infinitely reimagined. The tale of 'the reyde eyttyn vithit the thre heydis', as described in a little-known mid-sixteenth-century Scottish political text, surfaces as 'The Red Etin' in nineteenth-century fairy and folktale anthologies (including Andrew Lang's *Blue Fairy Book* (1889), the first in the famous series), and was among the stories apparently loved by James V when he was little.[17] But if we see print culture as the formal record of traditional culture, then the emergence of chapbook literature (largely from the seventeenth century onwards) – popular, portable, accessible, and relatively cheap – is therefore important. Surviving chapbook collections point to the popularity of fairy tale chapbooks in eighteenth-century Scotland, predominantly drawn from the French *conte des fées* tradition (rarely the elaborate, metafictional adult tales created by women writers but frequently the versions by Charles Perrault which helped to shape the canonical fairy tale tradition).[18] The earliest known Scottish chapbook, printed in Edinburgh in 1682, is *Tom Thumb, his life and death*.[19] The subject of Thomas the Rhymer, his abduction into fairyland and attainment of prophetic gifts as told in medieval romance and ballad tradition, also became a popular subject for chapbook literature. These would have enjoyed a dual child-adult readership though, as Valentina Bold notes, there is also a small but specific number intended for a juvenile readership.[20]

That it should largely be fairy tale and fantastical literature which drives the creation of children's literature in Scotland is interesting. In wider European and English contexts, the genre's suitability is a vital source of contention in eighteenth- and nineteenth-century debates over the instructional and pedagogical value of children's reading. This well-known, and well-charted, debate sees fantasy as the inhibitor of children's rational, intellectual, and moral faculties, encouraging delusion and daydreaming of various kinds. It is ultimately an 'old' debate, rooted in earlier anxieties about the truth-distorting powers of imaginative writing more broadly – in Glasgow in 1644 Zachary Boyd expressed dismay that children are 'fed on fables[…] baudry ballads […] youth's poison'[21] – and then harnessed to wider moral and philosophical discussions in the eighteenth and nineteenth centuries about the nature of childhood. Interestingly, some Scottish educationalists and writers played a part in this debate. For example, Elizabeth Hamilton (1756?–1816), better known for her adult novel, *The Cottagers of Glenburnie* (1808), in *Letters on Elementary Principles of Education* (first published in 1801) discusses the role of imagination in children's literature, noting how '[a]n early taste for the wonderful naturally disposes the mind towards credulity'.[22] Moral and religious impulses dominate early to mid-nineteenth-century children's literature (the Grimms' *Household Tales* were duly edited or bowdlerised); but in her Edinburgh-set novel *Holiday House. A Book for the Young* (1839), Catherine Sinclair (1800–1864) innovatively presents two happily curious and disobedient children.[23] Mid-way through its realist narrative, Laura and Harry listen to 'Uncle David's Nonsensical Story about Giants and Fairies', a comically grotesque, pseudo-moral fairy tale in which Master No-book learns an irrevocable lesson when 'Teach-all' triumphs over 'Do-nothing' – two rival fairies who lure children through the temptations of virtue and moral decadence respectively. The boy (whose worst nightmare at the story's outset involves 'sitting down to devour an enormous plum-cake' which 'all on a sudden' turns into 'a Latin Dictionary!'), becomes compliant, 'diligent' and 'happy' by the end; but only after he has been hung up, gothic-style, on a 'prodigious hook', with a view of the 'dead bodies of six other boys', in the larder of an avaricious giant.[24]

A different vein of radicalness is found later in the work of George MacDonald (1824–1905), the Aberdeenshire novelist, poet, and children's writer who made one of the period's most telling and important interventions into the debate about fantasy's suitability for children. In his essay 'The Fantastic Imagination' (1893), MacDonald expounds a radical theory of fairy tale which sees its value, beauty, and power as non-instrumentalist and non-utilitarian, lying not in any narrow prescriptive or didactic message but in the way its meaning is understood naturally or organically within each reader: '[...] what can it matter that neither you nor your child should know what it means? It is there not so much to convey a meaning as to wake a meaning'.[25] In a non-hierarchical, non-prescriptive way, child and adult readers are bound in an emotional and intellectual continuum. This theory was mirrored in his own practice as a fairy-tale writer for children. His was a deeply Romantically-inflected and spiritual view of childhood which, as we shall shortly see, allowed for the sensitive emotional as well as moral growth of his child-protagonists. Dreaming and imagination are presented as healing and cathartic, transacted within fantastical landscapes and fairylands which are the stuff of Victorian fairy ethereality but also harbour dark and terrifying visions. MacDonald is unafraid to take children into complex otherworlds – to encounter the grotesque 'cat-a-mountain' in 'Cross-Purposes' (1867) or the 'creatures of the air' which terrorise the princess Rosamond alone in the cottage in 'The Wise Woman, or The Lost Princess: A Double Story' (1874) – usually with the aid of benign but testing feminine guides and magical helpers. His fictions are also often laced with humour, as in 'The Light Princess' (1864) and its ironic, self-referential witch; a queen much cleverer than the king; and its mockery of science and materialism. MacDonald is therefore a vital figure in the development of children's fantasy.

The folk collecting movement and the legacy of Romantic antiquarianism may seem an unlikely source of inspiration for children's fantasy writing, but collections such as Robert Chambers's *Popular Rhymes of Scotland* (first published in 1826, then subsequently enlarged and reprinted), which contains stories, nursery rhymes, lullabies, and folktales ostensibly first heard in 'the nursery', told to him by his nursemaid. In one way, this might be seen as the 'infantilisation' of folk culture traditions; but another view would see it as an imaginative rehabilitation or reconfiguring of the place of childhood and children's stories. It also becomes a way of preserving some of the most striking traditional Scottish fairy and folktales; for example, 'The Well at the World's End', 'Kate Crackernuts', 'Rashin-Coatie'. There are different printed variants: 'Rashin-Coatie', a Scots variant of the 'Cinderella' tale, appears in Lang's collection and in the English folklorist and collector Joseph Jacobs's *More English Fairy Tales* (accordingly these brought such stories to a new 'British' child readership). In the version published in Sir George Douglas's *Scottish Folk and Fairy Tales* (1898), under 'Nursery Stories', there is a Grimm-like episode of startling violence where the magical red calf instructs the heroine to kill her sister rather than himself, contrary to her cruel parents' wishes: 'everything was ready – the ugly lassie holding his head, and the bonnie lassie armed with the axe. So she raised the axe, and came down on the ugly sister's head; and in the confusion that took place she got on the calf's back and they ran away'.[26]

By the turn of the century, Scottish traditional literature, and folk and fairy tales in particular, had received new creative energy from the Celtic Revival as well as the enduring legacy of the nineteenth-century fascination for traditional and Gaelic materials. This had an influence on children's literature. Ballad collections specifically for children began to appear: for example, the anthology by Mary Macgregor, beautifully illustrated by Katharine Cameron. Its preface impresses on children the stories' long lineage, which can be kindled again through their own experience and understanding:

> It is long, oh! so long ago, that they were sung up hill and down dale by wandering singers who soon became known all over the country as minstrels [...] In court, in cottage, by princes and by humble folk, everywhere, by every one they were greeted with delight [...] It was in the old books that thus came to be written that I first found these tales, and when you have read them perhaps you will wish to go yourself to the same old books.[27]

These prose retellings stay close to the language of the original ballad variants, but they are inflected with the storytelling rhythms sympathetic to children (the 'Queen of the Fairies [...] was very cross, very cross indeed';[28] 'Young Tamlane' enchants not only maidens but 'many a fair-haired child' from whom he steals toys).[29] Many of these editions of ballads and folktales for children, such as Elizabeth Grierson's *The Scottish Fairy Book* (1910), with illustrations by the Welsh artist Morris Meredith Williams, name Chambers's collection and J. F. Campbell's *West Highland Tales* as their sources, but are mindful that they are 'new to the children of this generation', and often include Scots dialect.[30]

The early twentieth century witnessed the proliferation of illustrated children's books by artists associated with the turn-of-the-century aesthetic movements, such as Jessie M. King, reminding us of the importance of the visual, material, and sensory dimensions of otherworld storytelling. It also saw the creation of one of Scotland's most enduring fantastical creations – Peter Pan – whose place in the history of fantasy, and children's literature more generally, is obviously profound. For Jacqueline Rose, Barrie's work exemplified all the possibilities and contradictions of children's literature itself whereby adults create an impossible and distorting illusion of childhood.[31] In its incarnations from children's story to 'fairy play', the Peter Pan narrative means many things: a fable of enchantment, freedom, anarchy and celebration but also of loss. For Peter, the 'strange boy' who brings Neverland 'too near' to Mrs Darling at one point,[32] is not only the embodiment of imagination but of death too. The decades of Peter Pan's popularity also saw the publication of the much-loved *The Wind in the Willows* (1908) by the Edinburgh-born Kenneth Grahame (1859–1932), who had also written children's fantasy stories in the earlier *The Golden Age* (1895) and *Dream Days* (1898), Violet Jacob's (1863–1946) collection of fairy tales for children, *The Golden Heart, and other stories* (1904), in which Hans Christian Andersen's influence can be sensed, and the northern and Scandinavian-inspired stories of the prolific Shetlandic writer Jessie Saxby (1842–1940).[33] Mitchison's *The Big House*, discussed in more detail below, can be considered a landmark text in postwar children's fantasy for its sensitive interweaving of Scottish history (particularly Gaelic culture) and folklore with a compelling narrative dynamic which follows the tasks and trials of two wartime Highland children to rescue fairyland's captives.[34] In her recent edition of Mitchison's *The Fourth Pig*, a Carter-esque collection of inventive fairy tales and retellings of the tradition, Marina Warner notes how she 'relished transgression and a certain degree of delinquent extremism'.[35]

Mitchison's play adaptation of the Scottish folktale, 'Kate Crackernuts' (for 'family theatricals') does indeed relish the fearless powers of its prince-rescuing heroine and, more importantly, her fierce loyalty to her 'sick' sister (p. 158), her defiant self-belief ('see what Kate has for thee!', p. 158), and her rebuke of the proverbially cruel stepmother ('Mother, I see the dark immerse you', p. 127). Eric Linklater's *The Pirates in the Deep Blue Sea: A Story for Children* (1965) is a Stevensonian-inspired, Hebridean-inflected boys' adventure story transposed to an energetically fantastical 'sea-bottom' world, a counterpart to the magical quest narrative of two young English girls in *The Wind on the Moon* (1944), which won the Carnegie Medal. This mid-to-late century fantasy is expanded in the prolific work of Mollie Hunter (1922–2012) (the subject of a separate chapter in this volume but see especially *The Haunted Mountain* (1972), *A Stranger Came Ashore* (1975), *A Furl of Fairy Wind* (1977), *The Enchanted Whistle* (1985), *The Brownie* (1986)), and in the children's stories of George Mackay Brown (1921–1996) whose frequently Orcadian, folkloric-inspired tales might be thought to recall MacDonald's strain of spiritualised, symbolic fantasy.

Children's fantasy is a diverse, hybrid mode but, like the shapes and forms of folktale, traditional literature, and romance and mythic narratives in general, there are broader patterns of narrative and structural resemblance which underpin almost all of these texts. The story itself – its delineation and closure, the means of its telling and often its narrator – is often a point of heightened awareness for the reader. The narrative shape frequently forms around a journey or quest (there may be more than one) undertaken by the central protagonist (or protagonists, as in the shared final quest of the three children in MacKenzie's *Nowhere*): for example, in MacDonald's *The Princess and the Goblin* (1872), Irene's magical thread leads her to Curdie, entrapped within the goblin mine; in Andrew Lang's fairy tale, 'The Gold of Fairnliee' (1888), Jeanie's desire to rescue Randal from Fairyland initiates a dream-like journey through the forest ('Deeper into the wood she went, and now it grew so dark that she scarce saw anything; only she felt the fragrance of briar roses, and it seemed to her that she was guided towards these roses').[36] In Martin Stewart's *Riverkeep* (2016), the fifteen-year-old Wull embarks on a dangerous journey along the waters which he and his father once guarded together after the latter is terribly injured.[37] This becomes both a literal and figurative voyage of discovery and transformation for Wull, Pappa, and their companions, and while its particular consequences are worked out within the intricate, violent, and dark world of Stewart's 'coming-of-age' fantasy, it exemplifies the characteristically transformative nature of the archetypal fantasy narrative journey. And in *Aurora* (2011), the last book in Julie Bertagna's futuristic dystopian fantasy of environmental crisis, multiple journeys are untaken by different generations: daughter seeks father, mother seeks daughter through cyberworlds and drowned cities.[38]

In addition we, as readers, know and expect that the distances crossed by travellers within and between fantastical realms will have emotional and psychological meaning, just as the fantasy spaces themselves are often portrayed in sensorily heightened way, as in *Riverkeep*'s Gothically murky, fleshly, and eerily alive world. (The motif of the sensory fantasy world is interestingly reversed in Lang's 'The Gold of Fairnilee' where Randal's eyes are touched with a water which 'destroy[s] the "glamour" in Fairyland',[39] while MacKenzie's recent *The Colour of Hope* is set in a world from which all colour has been stolen). Fantasy spaces often possess a distinct topography, frequently marked by borders, thresholds, and portals which come to signify liminal experience. In Lang's 'The Gold of Fairnilee', the landscape is layered out of literal geographical, historical, and otherworld realms (the worlds of the Borders' Roman heritage, Flodden battlefield, and fairyland are unearthed by the children). In MacDonald's highly symbolic narratives, for example, water, staircases, and mirrors frequently appear. In the first of the *Emporium* trilogy, MacKenzie has Lucien Sharpe describe his Emporium as 'tree'-shaped: 'The hall of staircases you just walked through – that is the trunk. Branching off it are the passageways, hundreds of them, where the Wonders lie', powered by the 'piece[s] of Imagination', absorbed from the Emporium's customers.[40] Particularly in contemporary fantasy, these realms are often proximate to, or resemble, familiar cities and landscapes, close to home: the Emporium first lands amidst the 'fat drops' of '[g]rey Glasgow rain', speculating at the end if '[P]erhaps one day' it 'will visit the place where you live' (pp. 16; 278). Glasgow's cathedral and university re-emerge in Bertagna's phantasmagoric drowned underworld; a litany of local landmarks and areas reappear as characters' names (e.g. 'Old Candleriggs'); and its heroine, Mara, proves a descendant of, or reincarnates, Thenew, mother of St Mungo, and Glasgow's founder. In T. L. Huchu's *The Library of the Dead* (2021), Edinburgh's familiarly Gothic underground architecture, the spaces of the Grassmarket and Calton Hill are vividly reincarnate as spaces where both the dead and the inhabitants of the realm of the everyThere predate on the city's children.[41] Jackie Kay's *Strawgirl* (2002) encases the magical within the everyday (the northeast farming community of its heroine, Maybe) from the moment that 'a girl made entirely of straw' emerges, in a beautifully uncanny Grimm-like moment, 'out of the plain gold hay' to meet Maybe in her loneliness. Strawgirl's fragile, liminal status between earthly and unworldly realms (no one can see her except Maybe) is captured in her bodily responsiveness to the changing physical landscapes ('Strawgirl's eyes [...] had changed to the colour of autumn fruits [...] as if [she] had her own harvest, a harvest of body and soul').[42]

Another shared quality of all these fictions is their intertextuality and allusiveness. In MacDonald's case, for example, this is partly a result of working within the inherited fairy-tale mode which presents a core narrative spine along which motifs, tropes, narrative variations are added and embellished according to the culture or storyteller which nurtures it. So we find the shards of previous stories in, for example, 'The Wise Woman' ('Hansel and Gretel', 'Snow White', *Alice in Wonderland*); 'Hansel and Gretel' and 'Jack and the Beanstalk' in 'The Giant's Heart'; James Hogg's poetic fairy tale 'Kilmeny' in *At the Back of the North Wind*.[43] For the child-reader, this has the almost reassuring effect of encasing the story in a kind of 'echo-chamber' whilst the newly minted imaginative dimensions of the story can appear more sharply (later we shall see how vital this is to the reiteration and reweaving of traditional folklore and myth). In the *Emporium*, Daniel refers to himself as another Peter Pan, 'the boy who never grew up' (p. 234) on realising that the Emporium protects him from ageing. Further, the act of storytelling itself is invested with a power of its own – in George Mackay Brown's collection we are told that 'stories told in the sea' have a particular magic. The figure of the storyteller herself or himself is often key (either the text's frame-narrator or other protagonists who tell inset stories): to draw on MacDonald again, in 'The Carasoyn', an old woman, carding wool, 'kept telling Colin one story after another, till he thought he could sit there all his life and listen' (p. 198); or the narrator of *At the Back of the North Wind* who enters the story frame at the end to vouch for his own knowledge and experience of the wondrous boy, Diamond. In that text, too, the communal telling and sharing of fairy tales is itself a means of catharsis and of healing, as illustrated by the episode in the children's hospital. And Diamond, too, becomes a storyteller of a kind in conveying the wonder of North Wind, though his listeners (his child companions) are more disbelieving. This doubting of the 'credibility' of the fantastical experience is interesting: in MacDonald's *The Princess and the Goblin*, Irene's magical grandmother tells her not to be impatient that Curdie cannot yet see her enchantments: '[...] in the meantime you must be content, I say, to be misunderstood for a while. We are all very anxious to be understood, and it is very hard not to be.'[44] In 'The History of Photogen and Nycteris: a Day and Night Märchen' (1879), MacDonald ends with a character's unanswered question ('"[...] who knows [...] that, when we go out, we shall not go into a day as much greater than your day as your day is greater than my night?"', p. 341). This evokes MacDonald's own 'theory' of the fantastic mode where the meaning of a fairy story is unfixed, dependent on the receptivity and responsiveness of the (child) reader herself.

Contemporary fantasy, too, is metafictionally layered. Stewart's *Riverkeep*, for example, begins each chapter with a quotation or extract from the river ledger-book or an encyclopaedic or geographical book (almost always invented, but helping to strengthen the vividness and autonomy of the novel's alternative world). It has its own invented language as well in which the river creatures and boats have their own distinct names (seula, bohdan, bradai, not least the mormorach, the water-monster itself; evocative, beautiful words, with Scandinavian and Gaelic inflections, which deepen this otherworld's imaginative identity). And the vital, life-affirming gift of stories in worlds shorn of meaning is also affirmed in many of these texts. This is the case in Bertagna's trilogy where Mara first discovers the dead 'paper mountains', with nesting birds, of the drowned city's library (the so-called 'Wizard Hat'). She gifts these books to the 'ratbashers', the wordless, abandoned, and supposedly feral children shut out of the New World's walls. The terrifyingly futuristic New World in which Mara must begin her heroic quest has been cleansed of stories (the 'search-ball' fails to recognise the very word, 'story'). Before Mara and her beloved Fox are separated, she bequeaths him Gorbals's 'netherworld' poems, and to her young daughter, Lily, is the source of tales which impel her on a quest to find her missing father (Fox). And in *Aurora* (the trilogy's final book), storytelling is a narrative catalyst and redemptive agent as Fox, in his capacity as the radiowaves' Midnight Storyteller, narrates books and stories which belong to the New World's extirpated and censored past, heard 'deep in the cyberjungles of the rebel Noosweavers' (p. 143),[45] and by his formerly estranged mother, now the empire's 'rogue Guardian', who comes to his aid. In the first book of the *Emporium* trilogy, Lucien Sharpe reveals the Book of Wonders to Daniel, a kind of magical creative sketchbook for his ideas so talismanic that his arch-enemy will steal it, and Daniel and Ellie (Sharpe's daughter) need to recover both it and the vanished Sharpe. So 'enchanted and entwined with the shop' are its pages that a Wonder literally appears in the Emporium after being inscribed;

and Daniel himself is entrusted by Sharpe to write and actualise a Wonder into existence. There is also 'The Library of Souls' which 'holds on its many shelves the life story of everyone who has ever lived, everyone who *will* ever live'. This Gothic '*city of books*', amidst 'countless canals of ink' patrolled by a spectral 'hooded librarian', is visited by Daniel and Ellie before its spectacular collapse as they try impossibly to discover the end of Sharpe's narrative. The cavernous rocky underground space of the titular 'library of the dead', in the first of Huchu's Gothic series, 'was built as the repository of all of Scotland's magical know-how'.[46] Accessed via David Hume's mausoleum in Old Calton's burial ground, it gives an ironic nod to the philosopher's supernatural scepticism while deftly reflecting the literary, intellectual passions of the fantasy's heroine, Ropa, as much at home in the bookish world of Scottish Enlightenment science as the Zimbabwean heritage of her Gran's oral spirit magic.

Fantasy's Child Protagonists

Robert Louis Stevenson's observation that '[i]t is the grown people who make the nursery stories'[47] articulates a dilemma common to children's literature in general: how does the adult writer create a fictional world of events and character (who may themselves be children) which is sympathetic and open to young readers? Fantasy literature is full of curious, adventurous, and brave children (in Lang's 'The Gold of Fairnilee', Randall actively seeks out the fairy queen). But fantasy also frequently carves out a bond with the reader by making a 'sensitive' child, who might be considered 'other' in some way, at the heart of its story. In Mollie Hunter's *The Kelpie's Pearls*, for example, the young boy, Torquil, is the only one who understands the loneliness of the *cailleach*, Morag, and her need to protect the kelpie.[48] The orphans of fairy and folktale are mirrored in the frequently bereaved, lonely children of these texts: for example, Randal is also fatherless, alone with his grieving mother at the story's start, and described as a 'fey' and 'strange child'. In MacDonald's *The Princess and the Goblin*, Irene is motherless so the bond between father and daughter is particularly strong ('he [...] held her to his heart', p. 77), whilst a ring inherited from her mother (via her grandmother) acts as a magical talisman and protector. The child Diamond, in Macdonald's *At the Back of the North Wind*, is a sensitive, creative child misunderstood by other children, who sings poetry heard at the back of the north wind to his baby siblings. Diamond is an intensely realised incarnation of the pietistic and angelic child whom we find elsewhere in his fantasy writing, stemming from his belief in the divinity of children and the spiritual nature of childhood. In that sense, Diamond is a symbol rather than a multi-dimensional child protagonist. But elsewhere MacDonald importantly has children as narrative 'focalisers', the 'experiencing' centres of the fantastic. In 'The Wise Woman', for example, the 'princess' and the 'shepherdess' are taken on transformative and frequently alarming journeys by their 'wise' but demanding guide (who sees 'through it all what you were going to be', p. 294). Though they begin very differently, their stories come to mirror each other, blending and intertwining. Disturbingly, too, they are also about the emergence of other alternate identities – those which are 'better', more mature and, crucially, more empathic. Because of 'her own ugly Somebody' (p. 243), the princess Rosamond keeps failing the Wise Woman's tests, which become increasingly terrifying. This can be seen as a moralistic fairy tale, but its child protagonists are also portrayed as emotionally layered and complex, made vulnerable by inadequate parenting (Rosamond has experienced 'more bad than good' (p. 238); Agnes starts off fearless because she has never learnt to use her imagination, pp. 258–59). Rosamond and Agnes exemplify the maturation process undergone by many fairy and folktale protagonists. But the concept of the 'shadow self' as opposed to 'the true self' (p. 288), a dominating theme of MacDonald's writing shaped by the influences of German Romanticism and Hans Christian Andersen, is importantly articulated through the exaggerated but still recognisable vulnerabilities of children.

In opening up a space for such interiority, then, fantasy – like the darker capacities of fairy tale – has the potential to allow its child and young adult protagonists (and their readership) to confront difficult subjects, including mortality. In Victorian children's literature, encounters with death are frequent. MacDonald's *At the Back of the North Wind* presents us with Diamond's death but it is different from the 'deathbed' sentimentality or disturbing piety of dying children in other contemporary texts. It works as a consolation for bereaved parents but also for children, too, for the experience of dying itself is not fearful when embodied in the loving, protective figure of the maternal north wind. The northland tree which Diamond can climb (and share with others) in order to see the people he loves back home (pp. 126–27) is a tender image of the notion that the living and the dead are inseparable. MacDonald's fairy tales conceive of death as an inevitability which is not to be feared but welcomed as part of wider and harmonious cyclical patterns; in that sense, MacDonald presents a vision of death to children which is both religiously informed and symbolically redolent of the organic processes of death and rebirth in fairy tale.

The figure of the child or young adult confronting the spectre of death is prominent in contemporary fantasy too. For Daniel, in the first of the *Emporium* trilogy, life with Mr Silver presents the 'opportunity to be someone else, even if it was just for a while. And if he was someone else, maybe he wouldn't feel so alone' (p. 46). Bullied by others in the children's home, Daniel is grieving for his parents. When he disobeys Lucien Silver and seeks independently to create a Wonder, a 'room where they're still alive' (p. 104), he is rebuked and told that '"Magic cannot bring back the dead [...] The dead are beyond the reach of magic. Do you understand?"' (p. 105). That the *Emporium*'s magic should be circumscribed in this way is interesting: the process of coming to terms with such loss must unfold naturally over time, helped by his friendship with Ellie, as lonely as he is. And when the cruel Sharpe tries to inflict the 'same death [by drowning] that his father had suffered, alone in the dark with nobody's hand to hold' (p. 256), his own courage, and the Emporium's residual magic in creating 'an echo' from his memories, save him. At the end, when Daniel and Ellie (whose own father, Silver, 'dies' into 'hundreds of blank book pages', p. 276) are ready to venture out into the 'big world', Daniel is secure in the new knowledge that his father has 'been with me all along. He always will be' (p. 277). In Stewart's *Riverkeep*, the young Wull is confronted with a different kind of loss: not exactly the death of his 'Pappa' but his transformation into 'something', or someone else. This is harrowingly wrought: Wull sees his formerly strong, brave father reduced to a 'hunched shape [...] sagging like wet-cloth against the seat-back [...] His eyes were hidden behind the hang of his hair. They were not Pappa's eyes' (p. 26), and he was barely able to speak or feed himself. As the young boy is compelled to assume the inverse parental role of carer, with enormous sympathy and delicacy the novel portrays Wull's estrangement from, yet enduring tenderness for, his unrecognisable father.

In other characters, too, *Riverkeep* is unafraid to portray different kinds of traumatic loss; the young woman, Remedie, for example, has lost a weeks-old child. The magic she has worked on her buried child returns him in the form of a baby made out of 'yew-wood' whom she now constantly cradles. When the others mock this 'thing', this 'wooden doll' (p. 222), Wull is quick to defend both Remedie, the child, and the validity of that love. In Kay's novel, Maybe must find ways to navigate 'a world without a dad in it' (p. 49); the quest narrative is as much internal as embodied in surreptitiously magical events, unfolding a process of growing around grief, enabled by Strawgirl's love and companionship. In *Night Shift* (2017), Debi Gliori reframes the classic quest trajectory within the picture-book medium to depict a young girl's journey, without 'compass' or 'map', hounded by the dragons of depression. It ends with her discovery of a single 'feather. Black and white. Stripy and beautiful. Neither black, nor all white', a simple, powerful talisman to reflect that slowly 'something shifted'.[49]

Fantasy therefore has the capacity to represent in singularly heightened and symbolically projected ways common experiences of loss and grief, alienation and loneliness; its representational mode may be 'unreal' but the emotional experiences it portrays are vividly real, gifting readers the possibilities of affective identification and agency. In the next section, we shall see how fantasy can be utopian, imagining solutions and alternatives to questions which are not only psychological but social and political in import too. It is worth noting, though, that the growth and transformation experienced by child protagonists in the fantasy world is not always welcomed or enjoyed. In *The Big House*, Su and Winkie for a time become the swan-maiden and the Chief in the otherworlds: Mitchison deftly portrays how their quotidian, and class-bound, selves struggle to inhabit their new realms (e.g. the swan-maiden, Susan, yawns as she is made to climb a hill) which bring the experience of freedom and transgression too. But there is a broader point as well: the experience of being 'other' makes Su feel 'lonely'; and whilst Winkie gladly embraces his new clan warrior identity, in the novel's darkest moment, he shocks Su in his newfound capacity for violence. Empathy and understanding therefore grow in different ways in fantasy's children, and the alternate universe is not always preferred to the familiarity of 'home'.

Fantasy's Alternative and Redemptive Worlds

On the surface, children's fantasy may seem an unlikely 'political' genre. But its apparent 'unworldliness' makes it a powerful means for exploring, in characteristically symbolic and projected ways, 'worldly' concerns such as class and gender, and a diversity of other social and political concerns. Children's and young adult fantasy is no exception to this, as Fiona McCulloch has demonstrated.[50] The Victorian fantasies of MacDonald and Lang depict poverty and hardship (in the former, the ruthless materialism and selfishness of contemporary society is targeted; in the latter's 'The Gold of Fairnilee', the struggles of families in post-Flodden Scotland is portrayed). And, as we shall see, contemporary

Scottish writing has embraced the mode's timely political potential. Firstly, however, two examples from George Mackay Brown and Naomi Mitchison respectively illustrate a universal and timeless politicised reflection, and one very specific to Scotland's history. In Mackay Brown's story, 'The Everlasting Battle', a young princess from the north, Hildr, willingly absconds with the prince of another kingdom, Hedinn. Her furious father raises an army in pursuit of her. Father and husband engage in violent conflict over who is her rightful possessor. Horrified by this, she seeks recourse to her own magical powers when all other interventions have proved useless; in despair and anger, she inflicts the enchantment of eternal war on both armies ('[I]mmortal tormented heroes, they were flung from stone to pain, and back again', p. 133). The spell is only broken centuries later by a Christian king so the tale's conclusion exemplifies the deep-rooted spirituality of Mackay Brown's other fictions; but it has also pitted masculine violence and narcissism against a selfless and peace-loving femininity. Mackay Brown is very much George MacDonald's heir in his children's fairy tales; but this is also a timeless fable about the futility of war and conflict, and the need for love and reconciliation ('when the face of love appears the world is quickened with blossom', p. 134). On the other hand, in *The Big House*, Mitchison weaves through the children's adventures in fairyland traumatic events specific to Highland history. In particular the plight of the Gaelic language in the nineteenth century is highlighted: relocated in time to the previous century, the children are being taught in English rather than Gaelic in school. Susan also marvels at how her nineteenth-century self discovers Scots words which 'ran off her tongue' (p. 36). And throughout the text evinces sympathy for the poor and the rebellious: in the Napoleonic era, a poor tailor, perceived as a 'spreader of anarchy', is conscripted to the army, and Susan is horrified by her cousins' indifference to his plight.

In the twenty-first century YA fiction in particular has been keenly responsive to the climate emergency which is mobilising young activists across the globe. Environmental degradation and global warming are the subject of Julie Bertagna's powerful fantasy trilogy, begun in 2002.[51] The preface to the first novel, *Exodus*, at once draws its reader into its topicality by telling of a once beautiful planet called Ur, which 'ripened into Earth', and which 'grew hot and fevered'. The story begins at that 'fragile moment before the devastation begins' [n.p.] in 'midwinter 2099'; it moves swiftly to 'April 2100' where we enter the beleaguered world of the trilogy's principal heroine, Mara Bell, where fuel and natural resources have all run out, the school has been swallowed up by the sea, and the waters are catastrophically rising again. Mara's quest is to find refuge for her family and her people, to search for the fabled 'New World' which towers in the sky above the drowned cities and ultimately to sail north to the sanctuary of the 'forgotten highland forest at the top of the world' (p. 171). The devastated remnants and signs of 'the world's drowning' (p. 173) are everywhere portrayed (in the 'sea-urchins" strange, recycled clothes, in the Treenesters' outlawing of 'tree-killing' (p. 173), carried out by the 'ancestors' who are to blame for the degradation. Bertagna's work also presciently portrays the human cost of environmental catastrophe in the displaced peoples and refugees who fill the underworlds and are deliberately excluded and locked out from the 'sky-city' created by Caledon, Fox's grandfather. In a moment which eerily anticipates the American election of 2016, Mara's realisation that '"I'm a refugee"' (p. 269) comes when she sees 'the great wall built [...] to keep out' people like her (p. 265). The New World's horror lies not just in its representation of a futuristic technological dystopia, which atomises its people's lives and shreds meaningful communication, but in exposure of its fear and hatred of the dispossessed and powerless, and of anyone or anything which is 'other' than its own conformist and uniform identity. Its compassionless world is responsible for creating a community of child slave refugees whilst its 'sea-police' ruthlessly murder the urchins sheltering in the cathedral. What, if anything, then, can be offered to counter the horror of what might be described (to use the novel's own term) as a 'necrotten' authoritarian and capitalist state? Bertagna's work is not proselytising but suggests that acts of rebellion and resistance will incrementally bring about change. Some of these are dramatic such as Fox's 'cyberflood' revolution; others are achieved by individual acts of self-realisation (towards the end of *Exodus*, Mara doubts herself only to draw strength from hearing her mother's voice, urging her that 'my daughter is made of the same stuff as my mother', p. 304; this is a matriarchal narrative for Mara's own daughter, Lily, will continue the resistance in the final book). For Fox, collective action and a recognition of shared solidarity is the answer to shattering 'fear and apathy': 'this is who we were [...] this is who we are [...] all on the same Earth, under the same sun, moon and stars' (p. 143).

Although manifest in quite different ways, a similar utopian vision can be seen threading back to the earlier fantasies. MacDonald's fairy tales frequently suggest the interconnectedness between the human and natural worlds in a proto-environmentalist sense. And they end, not just with a final cathartic journey and transformative experience, but with a coming together of characters in mutual recognition and solidarity: 'And now she saw Richard's path as he saw hers, and between the two sights they got on well' (p. 115). Relationships between female and male child protagonists in MacDonald offer a model of mutual tenderness, strength, and equality. 'The world *can* be changed', says Mara in Bertagna's *Aurora;* and children's and YA fantasy configures many different ways in which narratives of power and normativity might be challenged and reimagined. Kay's *Strawgirl* can be read as a tender tale of queer love. The girl with 'eyes [...] as bright and as pagan as conkers' (p. 103) helps Maybe to defend herself against the racist bullies; magicks 'the pair of them together like two beautiful birds with open wings' (p. 135) on lunar journeys which ultimately save the farm and the way of life which belonged to Maybe's father; and then leaves, only when Maybe's own healing journey has so progressed that she is ready to embrace the companionship of another girl, Hayley – who has an uncanny familiarity about her. In Rachel Plummer and Helene Boppert's collection, *Wain* (2019), the shifting, pluralistic, and beautiful worlds and bodies of traditional folktale and ballad are re-told, laying out a canvas, both poetic and visual, of identities, experiences, and emotions for a young LGBTQIA+ readership.

Fantasy's Folkloric Heritage

Scottish children's fantasy, as we have seen, keenly imagines alternative, redemptive worlds and modes of being. Its hero/ines and adversaries, human, creaturely, and otherwise, might include fairies, witches, wizards, Death-Eaters, werewolves, or cyber avatars. Yet with striking frequency they are also drawn directly from Scotland's folkloric and mythic heritage, demonstrating, as Maureen Farrell has observed, how 'retold stories also have the potential to disclose how old stories suppress the hidden, the untold and the unspoken'.[52] Theresa Breslin and Lari Don, for example, have prolifically re-imagined a variety of mythic and folktale traditions for young readers. Ballad traditions, as already discussed, offer rich materials for chapbook culture and find a place within the popularity of nineteenth and early twentieth-century retellings for children of traditional and medieval myth and narrative. There are manifold reasons for their popularity: beguiling and beautiful stories, they often put female strength, power, and desire at their core (in the figures of the Queen of Fairies and Janet), and manifest a highly distinctive fairy world forged out of Scottish folk belief.[53] MacDonald's stories draw attention to the latter (which Scott's *Minstrelsy* had already emphasised): playfully so in

The Princess and the Goblin (when we learn that the goblins have become 'softer', 'like the Scotch Brownies' (p. 241)); and more darkly, in the later story of 'The Carasoyn' (1871), where the fabled cruelty and capriciousness of 'Scotch fairies' is realised in a changeling narrative that has moments of horror as well as humour. The tales of 'Tam Lin' and 'Thomas the Rhymer' in particular are the nourishing roots of many tales about fairies:[54] Lang's 'The Gold of Fairnilee', mentioned earlier, where the conclusion to Jeanie/Janet's winning of Randal/Tam Lin back from fairyland suggestively seems to evoke the reunion of Gerda and Kai at the end of Andersen's 'The Snow Queen', therefore fusing different kinds of 'northern' folkloric fairy tale; in Dianne Wynne Jones's much-loved *Fire and Hemlock* (1984), and in other retellings by North American writers such as Janet McNaughton and Elizabeth Marie Pope;[55] and in Lari Don's *The Tale of Tam Linn* (2014). Significantly, recent decades have also seen the publication of collections of children's stories by major tradition-bearers, such as Duncan Williamson.[56] Beautifully illustrated editions for children of traditional wonder tales have been produced whilst Matthew Fitt and James Robertson have brought to renewed linguistic life the fairy tale corpus in *A Wee Book o Fairy Tales*, while Donald Smith's collection, *Wee Folk Tales in Scots* (2018), gathers some of the most well-loved traditional märchen and story in vivid retellings.[57]

Twentieth- and twenty-first-century Scottish children's fantasy has another deeply mined vein of traditional oral heritage, a phenomenon also in Gaelic children's literature addressed by Sìm Innes in his chapter in this volume – the stories and folklore of the sea's inhabitants and, in particular, retellings of the selkie legend, a creature half-human, half-seal, as attested in Janis Mackay's *The Selkie Girl* (2014), Lari Don's *The Secret of the Kelpie* (2016), and in recent YA writing by Joan Lennon (*Silver Skin* [2015] and Gill Arbuthnott (*Beneath* [2014]). In his preface to his collection, *The Two Fiddlers. Tales from Orkney* (1974),[58] Mackay Brown writes that he has explicitly been inspired by collections and studies of Orcadian folklore. The tales are therefore an imaginative bricolage of recorded folklore and Mackay Brown's own invention so that his own imaginative sympathies for children's storytelling are melded with the historical and cultural significance of the northern islands themselves. In that sense, Mackay Brown's work reaches back to a tradition rooted in the Grimms whereby children's wonder stories are also records of fragile cultural memory (many of his stories allude to an Orkney transformed beyond recognition in the face of modernity, prosperity, and industrialisation). But these selkie stories are much more than nostalgia; they refract some of the themes and ideas which we have seen are fundamental to children's fantasy – loneliness, alienation, and the importance of empathy. In the frame story from *The Two Fiddlers* (1974), a reputed sea-cave witch turns out to be Jenny, a lonely and motherless girl from 300 years previously; 'a wild creature' who had shunned Edinburgh schooling and the prospect of a conventional marriage because she was 'in love with someone else [...] with one of God's creatures' – a selkie-man.[59] One day she vanishes into the sea. Time and again in Mackay Brown's selkie stories, those who manage to breach the separation between human and creaturely worlds, 'open[ing] the door of the sea' are the vulnerable, the misunderstood, and the rebellious ('The Sea-Bride', 'Cheems'). In the harrowing Norwegian-set tale of 'The Seal King' (a neomedieval, chivalric retelling of the selkie legend), a free-spirited woman, who loved 'to go with my hawk to the hill', is possessed by king Odivere's dark magic and compelled to enter a loveless marriage. In his absence, she gives birth to a little seal-child through her joyful alliance with the seal-king, Imravoe. On his return, Odivere has the boy killed; and just as she is about to be executed, she is rescued by the creatures of the sea who protect her through sympathy and communion with her: 'a single pulse of pity beats through the cold world-girdling element, and seal, pearl, whale, and sea-blossom devise with their God-given instincts that which will restore beauty and wholeness to the breached web' (p. 94). This is a fable about innocence and enduring love but can also be seen to anticipate the eco-critical and environmentalist concerns of contemporary children's fantasy.

Conclusion

At the end of Hunter's *The Kelpie's Pearls*, the boy Torquil sees what no one else can: Morag riding by on a black horse, 'young again [...] looking towards a great light that shone out of the west' (p. 114). To everyone else in the community, she is simply the strange, reclusive old woman who has disappeared; Torquil, and we as readers, know that she and the kelpie have gone to the fairy otherworld of Tir-nan-Og. The narrator tells us that Torquil's precise memory of these experiences will diminish with age and the passing of time; but that 'the secret door of the dreamworld' (p. 115) remains open via imaginative remembrance – through feeling 'the spell of stories' (p. 116). In different ways, all these children's fantasy texts enact and demonstrate that enchantment while nurturing a free and pluralistic space for the re-imagining of identities, worlds, and futures. From the genre's early nineteenth-century inception to its contemporary resurgence, fantasy's spacious and inclusive otherworlds forge powerful connections with their readers, whether through sheer narrative drive, affective force and depth, or the variety of other means by which story-world and reader are relationally bound.

CHAPTER FIVE

Gaelic Plays for Children 1900–1950

Sìm Innes

This chapter will consider Scottish Gaelic children's plays written in the first half of the twentieth century, focusing in particular on the ways in which the playwrights reworked and adapted folklore as source material.[1] The use of folklore in literature is often complex and we will see here that Gaelic playwrights writing for children could use the rich traditions of Highland folklore to promote various agendas, including, at times, somewhat subversive ones.[2] The majority of the plays under study here were written shortly after the *fin-de-siècle* Celtic Revival during which the Gaelic language and its culture were simultaneously actively discouraged by the establishment and yet a source of fascination and exoticism for Scotland's intellectual communities.[3] A full survey or history of Gaelic children's literature in Scotland remains a desideratum. The source-based analysis presented in this chapter is based on my own new and ongoing primary research.

In areas of Scotland where the majority spoke Gaelic as their home and community language in the late nineteenth century and into the mid-twentieth, the majority of children arrived for their first day at school as monolingual Gaelic speakers. The 1891 census had recorded over a quarter of a million Gaelic speakers in Scotland and, as a result of the recent Highland Clearances and economic outmigration, there were many thousands more elsewhere. For instance, there were at least fifty thousand Gaelic speakers in one province of Canada alone, Nova Scotia, by 1901.[4] However, in Scotland, Gaelic as the language of school instruction, or indeed as a subject worthy of study in its own right, was either ignored entirely, or provision was extremely limited and marginalised, when mandatory primary schooling was introduced as a result of the Education (Scotland) Act of 1872.[5] This, of course, had a huge detrimental impact on the earlier nineteenth-century progress made towards literacy in Gaelic for the native-speaker population. This earlier progress had been carried out under the auspices of Lowland evangelical organisations, such as the [Edinburgh] Society for the Support of Gaelic Schools and General Assembly Schools, in order to encourage the reading of scripture.[6] After 1872, in addition to affecting Gaelic literacy and perceptions of the worth of Gaelic negatively in the eyes of the Gaelic communities, an English-language education also involved enculturation of children into the culture and values of Anglo-British society more generally. Ealasaid Chaimbeul (Elizabeth Campbell, 1913–1981), from the island of Barra in the Western Isles, details in her autobiography how difficult the absence of Gaelic at school was for children like her, who spoke no English, and that school taught her to view her mother tongue and the language of her region of Scotland as 'cainnt nan truaghan bochda' ('the language of poor wretches').[7] She also gives us glimpses into the kinds of intercultural communication that accompanied an education in English, detailing how it was the schoolteacher

> a dh'inns dhuinn an toiseach mu Bhodach na Nollaig a bhiodh a' tadhal air cloinn air 'tìr-mòr', a' fàgail aca san stocainn a h-uile seudam sìorraidh a thogadh cridhe cloinne. Có nach iarradh a bhith air 'tìr-mòr' an uair sin, ge bith càit an robh e. A rèir na naidheachd, cha robh Bodach na Nollaig math gu marachd agus, co-dhiù, is coltach gun robh an t-astar ro fhada, agus leis a sin dh'fheumadh sinne a bhith riaraichte gu leòr a bhith cluinntinn mu dheidhinn.[8]

> *who first told us about Father Christmas who visited children on the 'mainland', leaving them all sorts of treasures in their stockings to bring joy to the children's hearts. Who wouldn't want to be on the 'mainland' then, wherever that was! Apparently though, Father Christmas wasn't a great mariner and maybe the distance was too far because we had to be happy just hearing about him.*

Another Gaelic-language autobiography, by Aonghas Caimbeul (Angus Campbell, known as Am Puilean, from the Isle of Lewis, 1903–1982), provides further comment on the enculturation process in the early decades of the twentieth century:

> 'S e Gall, aig nach robh facal Gàidhlig, am maighstir-sgoile. Cha d'fhuair mise leasan Gàidhlig san sgoil riamh agus 's e faireachadh a bha agad gun dh'àlaich do chànan, d'fhine is do dhualchas ann an treubhan ainreiteach, borb, aineolach agus ma bha dùil agad slighe shoirbheachail a dhèanamh

san t-saoghal, gum b' e do bhuannachd an dìochuimhneachadh gu tur. Chan eil lorg agam fhèin air eachdraidh, goirid air an rud a sgrìobhadh mun Ghearmailteach Baron Munchhausen, cho eas-onorach, breugach agus seachranach ri eachdraidh Alba mar a bha i air a teagasg san latha ud. Thug a' Bhanrigh Mairead suairceas is sìobhaltachd gu cùirt Chalum a' Chinn Mhòir nuair a thug i a' cheud inbhe don Bheurla.[9]

The schoolteacher was a Lowlander who didn't speak a word of Gaelic. I never got a single Gaelic lesson in school and you got the feeling that your language, your people, and your culture were spawned among unruly, barbarous and ignorant tribes, and if you intended making a success of life, it would be to your advantage to forget them completely. I don't know of any other history, apart from that written about the German Baron Munchhausen, which is as dishonest, deceitful and misleading as the history of Scotland taught in those days. [History which told that] it was Queen Margaret who brought politeness and civility to the court of Malcolm Canmore when she gave primary status to English.

Of course, in direct contrast to the pressure applied to Gaelic communities to assimilate to Anglo-British language and culture was the contemporary rise in interest, among sections of Scotland's artistic and literary communities, in things Gaelic and Celtic during the same Celtic-Revival period.[10] We might think of somewhat separate but contemporaneous Celtic-Revival and Gaelic-Language revival movements in Scotland at the time. However, the interplay between the two movements in Scotland is under-studied. William Gillies notes that by the time of the *fin de siècle* 'Celticising music and art movements took inspiration from the Celtic world eclectically'.[11] Thus, we see the impact of a new national 'Celticism' in Scottish literature and drama in English. For Scottish writers who were Celtic-Revival enthusiasts the main wellsprings in terms of subject matter included: medieval Gaelic/Irish written literature; episodes from Scottish history, particularly Highland history; and modern Gaelic oral folklore, which was increasingly being collected and translated into English. For instance, two of Fiona MacLeod's (William Sharp's) published plays for adults were based on medieval (Irish) Gaelic literature: *The House of Usna* (1903) and *The Immortal Hour* (1907) used *Longes mac nUislenn* ('The exile of the Sons of Uisliu', i.e. the story of Derdriu) and *Tochmarc Étaíne* ('The Wooing of Étaín') respectively.[12] Bessie J. B. MacArthur's play *The Clan of Lochlan* (1928) has a Highland setting and uses the common Gaelic folktale of the seal wife.[13] Such use of folktales in twentieth- and twenty-first-century Scottish children's fantasy is a parallel phenomenon, addressed by Sarah Dunnigan in her chapter in this volume. We also see the impact of the Revival in the dramatic output of the Scottish National Players, founded in 1921, particularly their interest in historical plays in the earlier decades of the twentieth century, and this English-language output in turn had an impact on plays for adults in Gaelic.[14] The cognitive dissonance of a minoritised or colonised culture and its language(s) being at once both suppressed and yet appropriated/fetishised (or mimicked in reverse) by the more dominant culture is, of course, not unusual globally. In the US, for instance, indigenous peoples were decimated and their languages and cultures forcibly removed at residential schools, and yet facets of their culture were central to emergent Anglo-American identities. Native Americans were, and are still, 'simultaneously symbolic of and excluded from American collective identity'.[15]

I have argued elsewhere that Gaelic plays written for children at the turn of the century deserve our attention because of the particular educational and linguistic context in which the children found themselves. Since Gaelic-speaking children were really only meaningfully taught literacy in English, a Gaelic play could allow a sympathetic Gaelic-speaking teacher to do something in Gaelic with classes, as the children could learn lines without having to be able to read them comfortably.[16] As noted above, a full study of Gaelic children's literature is still awaited but it is worth noting that very little written Gaelic material aimed at children, beyond instructional readers – consisting of not much more than word lists – existed at all until later in the twentieth century. A good example of the early readers would be *An Ceud Leabhar a chum Leughaidh na Gaelic a Theagasg do Chloinn nan Gael/ The First Book for Children in the Gaelic Language* (1811).[17] Notable exceptions, with more than just word lists, include works for children written by and/or overseen by Calum MacPhàrlain (Malcolm MacFarlane), to be discussed below, such as *Companach na Cloinne* (1912), and see also Mairi Kidd in her chapter in this volume.[18] Despite J. G. MacKay's *Sgeulachd a' Choire* ('The Tale of the Cauldron', 1927), discussed by Kidd, it was not really until the 1970s that the situation began to change significantly. Ian MacDonald wrote in 1988 that the catalogue of Comhairle nan Leabhraichean/the Gaelic Books Council at the time

> showed some 300 titles wholly or partly in Gaelic in print at the end of 1987. Of these, over 100 were books for children, three-quarters of them produced in the 1980s and nearly another quarter dating from the 1970s.[19]

Thus, what did the Gaelic plays for children, under scrutiny in this chapter, written between 1900 and 1950, set out to do? We will see that they were often an attempt to fight against the enculturation and that they hoped to engender respect for Gaelic culture. However, some were more explicit about the fight against the linguistic and cultural change agenda than others. A further factor for us to consider is the extent to which the Gaelic writers in this chapter, writing as they were at the very end of the nineteenth century and the early decades of the twentieth century, may themselves have been influenced by Celtic Revival ideas. We can explore if the writers of Gaelic plays for children, introduced here, presented something reflective of Gaelic tradition; and to what extent it was something anachronistic or archaic representing an attempt to revive or engineer aspects of Gaelic culture that were no longer meaningful anyway. It is worth pointing out that no matter the content or relationship to Gaelic folklore, every work discussed in this chapter, in this educational and language attrition context, was activism on behalf of Gaelic.[20] All of the writers hoped that their creative labours would help to ensure a future for the Gaelic language in Scotland.

The imaginative horizons of the writers of the emergent wave of Gaelic children's plays in the first half of the twentieth century focused on characters from Gaelic folklore, arguably also influenced by the Celtic Revival. Gaelic folklore with medieval literary antecedents was also explored. A flurry of Gaelic children's plays utilised traditions of the sìthichean ('fairies'), the sìthean ('fairy hill') and tàcharanan ('changelings'). These traditions were often quite dark, as we shall see, since Gaelic culture's fairies were dangerous and threatening, though they could at times be useful creatures. Folklore narratives and characters could serve a variety of didactic purposes in the hands of the playwrights.

An Sìthean Ruadh ('The Russet Fairyhill') was written by Maighstir Ailein (Father Allen MacDonald, 1859–1905) and published in 1906, shortly after his death.[21] MacDonald was originally from Fort William but served as parish priest in South Uist and then Eriskay.[22] He was a keen folklorist. The characters in his play re-enact a common Gaelic folktale in which two men with kyphosis (humps on their backs) receive quite different treatment from the fairies, partly based on their ability to add to a piece of music sung in the sìthean, 'Diluain, Dimàirt' ('Monday, Tuesday'). This Gaelic folktale is a variant of an international variant: ATU 503 'The Gifts of the Little People'.[23] The play is not particularly didactic, although there is a reasonably elaborate description, and amount of time, paid to good manners as regards hospitality and visiting. The first man is particularly careful on entering the sìthean:

> DOMHNULL (*a' gabhail a stigh*) Gu 'm bu slàn do 'n tigh 's do 'n chuideachd.
> BEAN-SHITH Gu 'm bu slàn dhuibhse, a dhuine chòir, agus làn dì-ur-beatha do 'n t-Sithean Ruadh. Teannaibh a nuas, is dianaibh suidhe a bhos goirid dhomh fhein.
> DOMHNULL Tapadh leibhse, a bhean-uasal, ach tha mi cho math 's a dh'iarruinn far a bheil mi.
> BEAN-SHITH Cha b' e cùl na còmhladh aite aon duine a thigeadh a chur seachad greis de 'n oidhche comhla ruinn. Teannaibh a nuas; teannaibh a nuas.
> DOMHNULL B' olc a fhreagradh e dhomhsa ar diultadh, a bhean uasal; agus is mise ni sin suidhe ri 'r taobh, 's a chì mi fhein sona dheth an cead fhaighinn.
> BEAN-SHITH Tha cathair mhòr shocrach an so.
> DOMHNULL Nach i tha math?[24]

> DONALD (entering) *Salutations to the house and household.*
> FAIRY WOMAN *Salutations to you, dear man, and welcome to the Sìthean Ruadh. Come down and sit down here near to me.*
> DONALD *Thank you, dear lady, but I am as good as could possibly be here where I am.*
> FAIRY WOMAN *Behind the door isn't the place for a visitor who has come to spend part of the evening with us. Come down, come down.*
> DONALD *It would become me badly to refuse you, dear lady, and I'll do just that and I'm delighted to have permission.*
> FAIRY WOMAN *There is a large comfortable chair here.*
> DONALD *Isn't it great!*

Domhnull advises the other man, Cormag, as to how to behave on entering the sìthean:

> DOMHNULL Cha 'n 'eil agaibh ach sibh fhèin a ghiulan gu modhail iomchuidh mar gu'm biodh sibh ann an tigh duin' uasail.[25]

> DONALD *You just have to conduct yourself appropriately and politely as you would in a gentleman's house.*

Cormag ill-advisedly ignores this advice and barges in, sitting in the comfortable chair, leading to one of the fairies, Murchadh, to ask, 'Cò 'm' bodach grànnda gun mhodh a thainig a stigh. Cha robh guth air beannachadh no eile, ach gabhail lom direach suas dh' an aon aite as urramaiche stigh.'[26] ('Who's this ugly old man without manners who came in? Not a word of a greeting or the like but just bursting in and going straight for the best seat in the house.') Although it does not all hinge on manners, the polite man, Domhnull, is rewarded in the play since his hump is removed while the impolite man, Cormag, is punished with Domhnull's hump added to his own.

Catrìona NicIlleBhàin Ghrannd (Katherine Whyte Grant, 1845–1928) embedded a Gaelic folktale concerning the legendary hero Fionn mac Cumhaill within her children's *kinderspiel* of 1908, *Dùsgadh na Féinne* ('The Awakening of the Fianna').[27] Whyte Grant was from Appin and travelled extensively. Her introduction explicitly rejects English-language paradigms as 'neo-fhreagarrach don Ghàidhealtachd' ('unsuitable for the Highlands') outlining that she had based her *kinderspiel* on existing children's Gaelic games and rhymes.[28] Fionn and his *fianna* warriors have a long and productive history known to us from medieval manuscripts and in later folklore.[29] Whyte Grant's embedded folktale, in which Fionn and his warriors are found dormant in a cave awaiting the call to return to fight, was seemingly common in the nineteenth- and twentieth-century Highlands. It is a version of the international motif of the 'sleeping hero' or 'king in the mountain' (ATU 766 'The Seven Sleepers'). As early as 1848 the tale of Fionn asleep in the cave had already appeared in print translated into English.[30] Whyte Grant serves as an early example of Gaelic playwrights who used drama to ensure continued attention to threatened facets of Gaelic culture, folklore and custom.[31] In her case she used it to comment on landlordism and the impact of the Highland Clearances. Thus, tradition could be used in the Gaelic children's plays both conservatively and radically: to preserve but also to incite. Here we see one child explaining to the others the destructive craze of clearing villages and pastoral agriculture to create deer forests, with clear criticism of landowners seen to be too removed from the Gaelic-speaking residents:

> FIONNAGHAL Na'n robh na Fianntan beò, cha tachradh e!
> SÌLE Ciamar a tha fhios agad?
> FIONNAGHAL Cha reiceadh aon diubh dùthaich an gaoil; oir b' aon iad
>   fèin 's am pobull.[32]

FIONA *If the Fianna were alive, it wouldn't happen!*
SHEILA *How do you know?*
FIONA *None of them would sell off their beloved homeland; since they were as one with the population.*

Another radical, or in places anti-establishment, play for children is *Am Mosgladh Mòr* ('The Great Rising', 1914–15) by Calum MacPhàrlain (Malcolm MacFarlane, 1853–1931). It is an ambitious multi-character allegorical vehicle used, as the introduction tells us, to show 'the denouement of the Gaelic movement as hoped for by the enthusiast'.[33] Further instalments were published after the first, and indeed a later second edition in 1925.[34] We know that it was performed by schoolchildren in some areas.[35] The core frame is a version of ATU 410 Sleeping Beauty with a rightful queen under a spell, prophecies, a giant, a bean-shìth ('banshee'), seven dwarfs and more. As I have argued elsewhere, this play uses a trope common at the time of the *fin-de-siècle* Celtic and Gaelic revival summarised in 1896/97 by the writer Lachlan Macbean (1853–1931) as follows, 'Until quite lately, we seem to have been a race under some evil enchantment. We were ashamed of our Gaelic, ashamed of being Highlanders [...] but all this is changed; the spell is broken.'[36] *Am Mosgladh Mòr* is somewhat heavy-handed with the child actors tasked with singing words, such as those sung by the returning hero Geurchuis:

> Mo chean air an t-sluagh sin
> d'an dual a bhith còir;
> Na treun fhir gun taise
> 's na mnathan gun ghò;
> An daorsa cha'n fhuiling
> fo dhuine tha beò;
> 'S cha cheannaich an t-òr iad:
> Cò 'n cinneadh a th' ann?
>
> An cinneadh coibhneil carthannach;
> Ge daibhir, doirbh an crannachur,
> Is dìleas, dàimheil, daingeann iad;
> 'S cha 'n eil samhuil ann.
>
> Mo chean air a' chànain
> a ghràdhaich mi òg;
> 'S i 's binne ri seanchas,

'S is ealainte ri ceòl;
'S i b' anns leis na bàird
A chum dàin chur air dòigh;
'S is blàth bhriathrach beò i:
Co i chànain a th' ann?

Cànain aosd ar n-athraichean;
Ged chaidh i seal am fannachadh,
Cha leigear leinn a maslachadh
Le glomhar 's glas-ghuib Ghall.[37]

Hail to that population / Who are naturally decent / The brave men never soft / And the women without fault / Their captivity won't be suffered / By any man alive / They cannot be bought with gold / Which race is it? // The kind charitable race /Although their lot is wretched and difficult / They are loyal friendly firm / There is no match for them // Hail to the language / I have loved since youth / It is the most eloquent for storytelling / It is the most artistic for music / It was the preferred language of the poets / When composing poetry / It is warm loquacious vibrant / Which language is it? // The ancient language of our fathers / Although it weakened for a while / We won't let it be shamed / By Lowland muzzles or gags.

Later, the play has one of Geurchuis's warriors, Bollsgaire Builg, sing 'Oran do 'n Ghaoith' ('Song to the Wind') a humorous, but nonetheless poignant, song containing an evergreen warning that those of high rank or in officialdom often seem to be saying something important because of their standing or positions of authority, and yet their words are often nothing but wind:

Tha mòran dhaoine anns an t-saoghal tha mu'n cuairt
Nuair bhios urra mòr an òir ag òraid ris an t-sluagh
A bheir creideas do gach facal their am bladair baoth,
'S gun annta fios no foghlum ceart ach gaoth, gaoth, gaoth.[38]

Many people in the world pay heed to the rich elite / When they address the population / Believing every word the vapid prattler says / When in fact they have no actual knowledge or education but only wind, wind, wind.

This is undoubtedly an important life lesson but a subversive one here, given the intended audience of children; and given, also, that MacFarlane was heavily involved with An Comunn Gàidhealach (The Highland Association), and editor of their periodical *An Deo-Ghréine*.[39] An Comunn relied on the patronage of the rich aristocratic elite from the outset: the first president was Lord Archibald Campbell, son of the eighth Duke of Argyll.[40] Yet, here we see MacFarlane exhorting Gaelic-speaking children not to trust that rich elite.

Ruaireachan (Ruaireachan is the diminutive form of the male name Ruairidh) written in 1924 by Dòmhnall Mac-na-Ceàrdaich (Donald Sinclair, 1885–1932) from Barra is also an adaptation or reimagining of a Highland folktale.[41] At its core is the tale classified as F22 'Man Goes into Fairy Dwelling and Spends Year or more Dancing'.[42] In the play a young human child, Ruaireachan, wanders away from the other children to chase a rainbow. He is accompanied by some talking birds who provide comic relief, as they are constantly bickering with each other. The child strays too close to Cnoc an t-Sìthein ('the fairy dwelling hill') hearing the unearthly music of the sìthichean and is taken inside. A leanabh sìth ('fairy child') is left out on the moor in his place. Ruaireachan is made to forget his real family, along with the birds, through the use of fairy music that makes them dance. The fairy woman refers to taking the child to Eilean Uaine, Tìr nan Òg and Uamh an Òir, all well-known as otherworldly locations. It is only after the passing of a year and a day that the child is rescued from the sìthean by the sudden appearance of a dove carrying mungan ('pearlwort'), identifying itself as 'calman glas à Ì' ('a grey dove from Iona'), named Sonas Sìth ('Happiness Peace'). The calman from Iona is evocative of St Columba, since the names Calum/Colm/Columba are all related to calman ('dove'). Sonas Sìth attaches some iron into the door of the sìthean, a common trope allowing future escape, and frees the enchanted child and other birds by reciting the following which evokes Columba:

> Le feart cumhachd Rìgh nan Dùl
> An ainm Chaluim naoimh ion-rùin
> le geal-bhuaidh a' Mhungain mhìn
> Fuasglaim sibh o gheasa sìth.

With a powerful charm of the Lord of the Universe / In the name of holy fittingly mysterious Columba / With the pure power of dainty pearlwort / I release you from fairy enchantments.

Sinclair here has drawn on folklore otherwise attested from his home island, since the use of the pearlwort flower to fight the power of the fairies is attested in the repertoire of a well-known tradition bearer from Barra called Nan Eachainn Fhionnlaigh (Nan MacKinnon, 1903–1982).[43] Furthermore, the counter-charm recited by the dove in the play appears to show that the author may have drawn on the kinds of incantations and other popular religious folklore published by Alexander Carmichael from 1900 onwards in *Carmina Gadelica*. For instance, Carmichael's 'Beannachadh Buana' shows a particular level of shared vocabulary and similar metrical structure with Sinclair's countercharm as can be seen from the verse below:

> Air sgàth Mhìcheil mhil nam feachd,
> Mhoire chneas-ghil leac nam buadh,
> Bhrìde mhìn-ghil ciobh nan cleachd,
> Chaluim Chille nam feart is nan tuam

For the sake of Michael head of hosts, / Of Mary fair-skinned branch of grace, / Of Bride smooth-white of ringleted locks, / Of Columba of the graves and tombs.[44]

Carmichael's presentation of popular religious folklore, such as the above, collected in the Western Highlands, particularly in the southern Hebrides, has come under some scrutiny for its tendency towards the obtuse and the archaic, in ways that highlight its Celtic Revival context.[45] This reflects Sinclair's own tendency to embellish his writing with rich vocabulary and idioms which, while a fantastic resource in the context of language loss, make the plays difficult, and perhaps made them difficult even at the time. Indeed Michelle Macleod has written on Sinclair's tendency, in his writing, to act as 'language archivist'.[46] This is not to negate or diminish Sinclair's accomplishments in any way in his use of Gaelic folk tradition, but it gives us a glimpse of the kinds of source materials he may have used. It also highlights the particular strands of Gaelic culture that were being promoted to children. For Sinclair, a children's play in Gaelic was not only a chance to give young people exposure to imaginative drama in the language but also an opportunity to teach some rich but, in all likelihood, antiquated vocabulary and idiom.

An Ceòl-Sìthe ('The Fairy Music') (1925) by Iain MacCormaig (John MacCormick, 1869–1947) also features a somewhat demonic fairy playing enchanted music that makes humans lose control and dance continually. MacCormaig was originally from the Isle of Mull although he later lived and worked in Glasgow. He is the author of the first Scottish Gaelic novel, *Dùn-Aluinn*, published in 1912, and he produced much original Gaelic content and translations into Gaelic, including translation of two Shakespeare plays.[47] In this play a sìochaire (another word for 'fairy') gets into the house of a tailor because the metal corran ('reaping hook') is missing from above the door. The tailor threatens to have the rest of the village go and burn down the sìthean which is the traditional trick used to get rid of unwelcome sìthichean. This fails though and the sìochaire makes the tailor, his wife and others dance to his music before sending them all into an enchanted sleep. We see a high level of intertextuality in this play with all sorts of other Gaelic folklore mentioned, including fairy deer and references to Fionn and his warriors asleep. The two sons of the tailor return from hunting where their hunt had been thwarted by fairy mist with nothing to show for it but a feather from the wing of a wild duck.

> DUBH-FHALT (*thig esan a steach, agus togaidh e a làmhan le iongnadh*) A Rìgh nan Dùl! Ciod e tha 'n so? A h-uile duine fo chromadh an tighe agus srann aca air an cathraichean, mar gu 'm biodh ann an Fhéinn. Nach iad a dh'òl an deoch cadail gu dearbh. Haigh! Ho! Ho ró! Dùisgibh dùisgibh. Haigh, haigh!

> BLACK-HAIR (enters and lifts his hands with surprise) *O Lord of the Universe! What is this? Everyone under the roof of the house snoring in their chairs, like the Fenian heroes. They all certainly drank the sleeping potion. Hey! Oy! Wake up, wake up. Yoo-hoo!*

Dubh-Fhalt manages to wake them, and the parents recognise the feather as belonging to their other lost daughter, stolen as a young child by the fairies and transformed into a duck. They return to the hill to try and find the sister. On the way, they come across a bean-nighidh ('washer woman'), a common spectre whose appearances often herald future deaths, as she is seen washing the shrouds. In Gaelic tradition, if you grab hold of her, you can force her to share her supernatural knowledge. The brothers do this, and she tells them that their sister takes the form of the wild duck during the day but at night she returns to human form and passes the night in the fairy hill. She tells them that the way to get their sister back is to go into the fairy hill with a cockerel which will ensure their safe passage out, because if the cock crows inside the hill at dawn, the fairy hill will remain open against the will of the fairies for a whole year. They manage to find their, now adult, sister and bring her home but she does not recognise anything until her mother sings a rhyme she liked as a toddler, and it triggers her memory of her former life. *An Ceòl-Sìthe* is, therefore, an often-thrilling romp through, and reworking, of a number of conventional supernatural and fantastical Gaelic characters and Gaelic folklore motifs.

Over the decades following the Great War, we start to see something of a movement away from the more fantastical native Gaelic folklore and/or medieval Gaelic heroic literary heritage as source material. Perhaps this reflects the waning influence of Celtomania in Scotland more widely from the 1920s onwards. For instance, the children's plays, vignettes and songs composed by Catrìona Dhùghlas (Katherine Douglas, known as Ceitidh a' Mhaighstir, 1893–1965) used a variety of English-language sources. Her father Ian MacNab had been the headmaster of Kilmuir school in Skye.[48] Douglas was a collector of Gaelic songs, apparently a pensions officer, and so in much contact with older people in the vicinity, she also helped prepare local children for competitions at the Royal National Mòd.[49] The Mòd is the annual showcase festival of An Comunn Gaidhealach, akin to the Eisteddfod in Wales. Her children's literature appears to date from the 1930s to 1950s. She herself won a variety of literary prizes at various Mòds in this period.[50] She was also known for her comedy sketches written for adults and performed at local cèilidh houses in the north of Skye.[51] Douglas's works for children show little interest in the various supernatural creatures native to Gaelic folklore and instead we see notes such as the following appended to her verses 'An Sionnach agus An Ròcais' ('The Fox and the Crow'), that it is 'bho Uirsgeulan Aesop anns a Bheurla' ('from Aesop's Fables in English').[52]

In Douglas's short play for children, *Greusaiche nam Brògan* ('The Cobbler of the Shoes') (exact date unknown), a woman has been left destitute and is living on the shellfish she can gather from the shore, having suffered a string of broken engagements: starting with the shoemaker who left her for the dairymaid, but then the dairymaid dumps the shoemaker for the farmer. She was betrothed next to the tailor who breaks it off to go with a woman called Maile Ruadh na h-Aibhne, who has since jilted the tailor for the soldier. The shepherd left our main character for the daughter of the maor ('factor') and the hunter left her for someone called Flòraidh. Thus, our main character has not had much luck and the plot is almost telenovella-esque. The use of archetype characters such as the dairymaid and so on is very reminiscent of Gaelic folk songs of love and loss, popular in the cèilidh tradition. In fact, Douglas herself was recorded singing a number of songs from this genre such as 'Agus ho Mhàiri' in the 1950s.[53] Thus, Douglas's play still uses Gaelic folklore as source material, even if the slightly more folk-realism end of the tradition. There are also some features in *Greusaiche nam Brògan* from non-Gaelic sources. For instance, the stage directions tell us as follows:

> Tha a' mhaighdeann ris am bheil an t-oran so ga sheinn 'na 'Cinderella' bhochd. Tha an t-aodach a th' oirre na luideagan.
>
> *The maiden to whom this song is sung is a sort of poor 'Cinderella'. Her clothes are in rags.*

In fact, she is referred to as 'Cinderella' for the rest of the piece and we see in what follows a Charles Perrault/Andrew Lang/Disney-style of fairy godmother, complete with magic wand, who improves on the rags:

> 'Cinderella' a-nis a' seinn:
>
> > Tha iad uile 'n deidh m' fhagail,
> > 'On tha mi bochd 's gun chàirdean,
> > 'S gam sharach anns an traighe,
> > Ri faochagan is bairnich.
>
> Tha ban-sìth a' tighinn a-staigh agus a' seinn an dara cuid dhen rann:
>
> > O chaomhag bhochd gun chàirdean
> > Is cràiteach leam mar tha thu,
> > Cha bhi thu fada' sa chàs seo,
> > Is bidh gaol aig fear gu bràth ort.
>
> Tha a' bhan-sìth a' cur paidhir de bhrògan àluinn mu choinneamh 'Cinderella' a tha a-nis gan cur air a casan ruisgte. Air don bhan-shìth a slat a chrathadh [...] 'Cinderella' a tha nis a' seasamh a-mach air a còmhdach mar bhean-bainnse.
>
> 'Cinderella' now sings:
>
> > *They all left me,*
> > *Since I am poor and without relatives,*

Wearing myself out at the shore
Collecting whelks and limpets.

A fairy enters and sings the second half of the verse:

O poor girl without relatives,
Your situation pains me,
You won't be in this condition long
And a man will love you forever.

The fairy puts a pair of beautiful shoes in front of 'Cinderella' who puts them onto her bare feet. The fairy waves her wand [...] 'Cinderella' now stands dressed as a bride.

We see, in *Greusaiche nam Bròhan*, almost the opposite of the trend observed above, in which culturally specific Gaelic ecotypes of international folktale types were used as source material for children's literature. Rather, in this case, features of what became the most-common version internationally of a folktale (used by Disney in 1950), in English and in other languages, were used when in fact Gaelic folklore ecotypes of Cinderella (ATU 510A) existed.[54] Perhaps *Greusaiche nam Bròhan* postdates the release of the Disney film and reflects that particular cinematic zeitgeist. Furthermore, in the earlier plays for children discussed in this chapter, such as *Dùsgadh na Féinne* and *Am Mosgladh Mór*, the quest for material success was warned against, the children being asked not to turn their backs on Gaelic in return for wealth. However, in *Greusaiche nam Bròhan* the future happiness of our unlucky-in-love Highland pauper Cinderella is ensured through her marriage to a wealthy outsider, 'sgiobair Galld' 's na h-Innsean' ('a Lowland skipper [arrived from?] the Indies'), who provides her with silk gowns and gold rings.

In conclusion, this survey of select Gaelic plays written for children in the first half of the twentieth century reveals an imaginative horizon populated in the earliest period by Fionn mac Cumhaill and his *fianna* characters who, although popular in folklore, also had a particular level of esteem provided by a medieval literary manuscript heritage. In the plays which followed, the supernatural creatures, such as the fairies, of Gaelic folklore took pride of place and were appropriately menacing, as their cultural context dictated. Our final example shows that by the 1950s Gaelic folklore was still utilised, but when the marvellous or fantastical was needed, gentle non-Gaelic versions of the fairies, for instance, might appear. It is tempting to draw a chronological line between *Dùsgadh na Féinne* and *Greusaiche nam Bròban* and conclude that this change in the source material tells a tale of cultural change from Gaelic to Anglo-British or even Anglo-American, at least in terms of the models used. However, this belies the fact that, as shown in this chapter, even the seemingly culturally specific folktales in Gaelic used for the children's plays were themselves Gaelic versions of international migratory folktales and motifs. This necessitates scrutiny of the hybrid nature of any demotic culture. The impact of the Celtic Revival's romanticisation and exoticisation of Gaelic and Celtic culture on those writing in Gaelic may be in evidence here also. Certainly, these early Gaelic children's plays allowed the writers to foreground features of Gaelic folklore and even linguistic richness already obsolete or perceived to be in danger of obsolescence. This pattern might be seen to be in accordance with Gaelic plays for adults from the same period accused of mummifying cultural traditions on the brink of extinction.[55] However, as part of their activism to support Scottish children's maintenance of their Gaelic language skills some of the authors also included anti-authoritarian and explicitly political material. These Gaelic plays for children could simultaneously be thrilling and often frightening.

CHAPTER SIX

Stevenson's Junior Fiction

David Robb

Robert Louis Stevenson (1850–1894), of course, was not the first to write adventure fiction for the young. *Treasure Island* in particular was instantly recognisable as a late example of a 'desert island' genre. This had begun with *Robinson Crusoe*, especially after Daniel Defoe's (c. 1660–1731) novel came to be regarded more and more as a book particularly suitable for children. Johan David Wyss's (1743–1818) *Der Schweizerische Robinson* (1812) had an early translation by William Godwin (1816), Frederick Marryat's (1792–1848) *Masterman Ready* appeared in 1841 and R. M. Ballantyne's (1825–1894) *The Coral Island* in 1858. Stevenson, however, is often thought of as a writer who abandoned the instructive and religious dimensions of earlier books and wrote purely with a view to providing the sort of entertainment which children (boys in particular) might relish. And that, looked at in one way, is indeed what he did. Looked at another way, however, it was the earlier writers who were writing specifically 'for children': they were adults with didactic intent, admittedly, but it was 'the young' who were very much in their sights. Stevenson, free of didacticism and religiosity as he was, presents a more complicated picture.

Stevenson's reputation as a writer of books for the young might be expected to be the result of a special and unpredictable twist to his genius, but when one considers the four novels which he wrote for young people, *Treasure Island* (written 1881), *The Black Arrow* (1883), *Kidnapped* (1886) and *Catriona* (or *David Balfour*) (1892), it becomes apparent that they fall into place in the larger scheme of his astonishingly diverse output. Writing for children, or younger readers, was simply an aspect of his impulse to write to entertain, to write so as to follow what he conceived to be the essential nature of fiction, and to write to make money. There is such imaginative continuity between these four works and so much of the rest of his writing that it was for long a common view that as a writer he was only finally beginning to write a proper 'adult' novel when he suddenly died in the course of creating *Weir of Hermiston*, which was finally published in 1896.[1] Of the four books under consideration, the latter two are unlikely to be narrowly confined to any 'children's literature' category by any reader, wherever they were first serialised and whatever the ages of their central characters: they must also be seen as substantial additions to the adult genre of historical fiction initiated by Walter Scott (1771–1832), and as works moulded in part by the examples of other nineteenth-century writers including William Thackeray (1811–1863) and Stevenson's particular favourite, Alexandre Dumas (1802–1870). The imaginative closeness of *Kidnapped* and *Catriona*, in particular, to *The Master of Ballantrae* (1889) is clear enough, and if that novel also now has about it something of the air of 'children's classic', it is only one of many nineteenth-century historical novels which (one is tempted to say) share that fate. Indeed, it was a feature of the Victorian literary world that historical fiction was the type of 'adult' writing deemed particularly appropriate for younger readers, thanks to its leanings towards outward events and away from the complexities, dangers and embarrassments of the inner lives of men and women, realistically depicted.

If there is the possibility of confusion and complexity in the categorising of Stevenson's writing for children, it is a confusion which reflects his times in general, as regards fiction for readers of different ages. It was a Victorian development to see those very 'adult' products of the eighteenth century, *Robinson Crusoe* and *Gulliver's Travels*, as 'children's literature', and by the end of the century even the manly and scholarly Scott was established as reading fodder for the young. By 1888, R. H. Hutton could describe *Ivanhoe* as 'the most brilliant tale for boys which genius ever penned'.[2] So it is perhaps no surprise that Stevenson, with his instinct for fictional 'romance' and his vision of the enthralled young reader as the writer's quintessential audience, should produce a body of work which seemed to engage with youthfulness from the beginning. His 'A Gossip on Romance' founds its account of the power of fiction on its opening description of the way child readers like himself and his friends had devoured 'incident' and escapist locations:

> I liked a story to begin with an old wayside inn where, 'towards the close of the year 17—,' several gentlemen in three-cocked hats were playing bowls. A friend of mine preferred the Malabar coast in a storm, with a ship beating to windward […].[3]

From here, his thinking and preferences evolve in the essay to consider the relative importance of the other dimensions of fiction (character, setting, etc) but he makes it clear that for him striking incident is the key element in the greatest, the most imaginatively powerful, storytelling.

> This, then, is the plastic part of literature: to embody character, thought, or emotion in some act or attitude that shall be remarkably striking to the mind's eye. This is the highest and hardest thing to do in words; the thing which, once accomplished, *equally delights the schoolboy and the sage* [my emphasis], and makes, in its own right, the quality of epics.[4]

Indeed, it was an age which developed and valued the notion of 'children of all ages'. The periodical in which Stevenson published, in serial form, *Treasure Island*, *Kidnapped* and *The Black Arrow*, began in 1879 as *Young Folks: a boys' and girls' paper of instructive and entertaining literature* but modified its full title in 1884 to *Young Folks paper: For old and young boys and girls*. In his essay on fairy tales, 'The Fantastic Imagination', George MacDonald (1824–1905) declared 'for my part, I do not write for children, but for the childlike, whether of five, or fifty, or seventy-five'.[5] As we know, *Treasure Island* was begun as wet weather entertainment in Braemar for both young and old, young Lloyd Osbourne and Stevenson's father Thomas. And if my own experience is anything to go by, this most famous of boy's books is capable of providing greater pleasure to the adult reader than it did to the child – and I would say the same, perhaps even more so, regarding *Kidnapped*. It was the example of *Treasure Island* which prompted H. Rider Haggard (1856–1925) to seek to emulate Stevenson by writing *King Solomon's Mines* (1885), thereby initiating a writing career of adventure romance in novels which cannot be seen as narrowly targeting the young. Rather, what was emerging was a type of novel written primarily for adults but accessible to young readers: John Rowe Townsend points to the fictions of Arthur Conan Doyle (1859–1930), Anthony Hope (1863–1933), John Buchan (1875–1940) and H. G. Wells (1866–1946).[6] It seems to have been the essential ambiguity (as regards readership) of Stevenson's writing which opened up this new development. Oliver S. Buckton has argued persuasively that *Treasure Island*, imaginatively springing from its famous map, created a new type of readership: it was taken up by 'boys', he suggests – that is, by grown men who found in its fiction, its invitation to fantasy, an opportunity and excuse to revert to the outlook of boyhood.[7] Whether or not we accept Buckton's further belief that this widespread regression of mind and feeling was linked to the expansion of empire, it seems clear that Stevenson's complex and potent creation instigated a powerful new phase of reading entertainment for adult male readers in particular.

If Stevenson's prioritising of 'incident' was one of his key ideas regarding his art, another – a related one – was his perception that art does not 'imitate' life but creates a simplified, clarified vision with its own shaped meaning. As he argued publicly with Henry James in 'A Humble Remonstrance', the artist must 'half-shut his eyes against the dazzle and confusion of reality':

> Life is monstrous, infinite, illogical, abrupt and poignant; a work of art, in comparison, is neat, finite, self-contained, rational, flowing and emasculate.[8]

And when he looked back on the writing of *Treasure Island* in 'My First Book', it was the process of simplification which he remembered.

> It was to be a story for boys; no need of psychology or fine writing [...]. Women were excluded [...]. And then I had an idea for John Silver from which I promised myself funds of entertainment: to take an admired friend of mine [...] to deprive him of all his finer qualities and higher graces of temperament, to leave him with nothing but his strength, his courage, his quickness, and his magnificent geniality, and to try to express these in terms of the culture of a raw tarpaulin.[9]

The reductive transformation of W. E. Henley into the world's most famous fictional pirate encapsulates the way in which Stevenson's instinct for the relationship between life and art enabled him to find writing for the young thoroughly congenial.

Of these four books, however, some simplify life more than others, and their heroes differ correspondingly. Jim Hawkins is the youngest: he is a boy thrust into an adult world of danger and skulduggery, small enough to hide in an apple barrel. It is his wilful, impulsive acts of disobedience and ill-discipline which decisively influence events, but, as he says (recounting his behaviour from his adult perspective) 'I was only a boy'.[10] Dr Livesey eventually realises that it has been Jim's irresponsibility which has saved the good characters from the pirates: 'There is a kind of fate in this [...]. Every step, it's you that saves our lives.' (p. 161) – an imaginative vindication, for Jim and for his boy readers, of their proneness to disobey their elders. And the fictional 'world' of this youngest hero is that of a young Victorian boy's imagination: pirates, buried treasure, etc.

On the other hand, Dick Shelton in *The Black Arrow* is almost eighteen, a fully grown adult with a freedom of action and mobility which are beyond Jim, to the extent that, when called upon, he can take heroic command of a company of soldiers in the thick of a medieval battle. His 'world' is less the product of a child's daydreams, more a reflection of encounters with the novels of Scott (especially *Ivanhoe*) and the history plays of Shakespeare (with, suggests John Sutherland, *Hamlet* and the tales of Robin Hood thrown in).[11] The story is notably more violent than *Treasure Island* (which, of course, has its bloody moments) and Shelton, unlike Jim, does his full share of blood-letting. Also, unlike Jim, of course, he has love and beauty to contend with. Altogether, *The Black Arrow* is a very different novel.

But so are the two David Balfour novels which offer the young reader, and the rest of us, yet another experience. Like Dick, David is notably older than Jim, old enough to be sent out alone into the world on the death of his father but perhaps not yet fully grown to adulthood – Alan reminds himself (with some emotional exaggeration) that he is 'just a bairn' as David's strength finally gives way in the aftermath of the quarrel.[12] Yet *Kidnapped* and *The Black Arrow* are (once more) very different novels: instead of being conjured out of a handful of predictable literary predecessors, *Kidnapped* is a product of Stevenson's deep engagement with Scotland's past, and the past of the Highlands in particular. The result is a historical novel which provides a much denser rendering of the past than he had attempted in *The Black Arrow* – dense and knowledgeable to the extent that it can be thought of as a serious successor to Scott's writings. At its heart is a correspondingly 'rounded' (to use an old-fashioned critical term) pair of central figures, convincingly emerging from a well-understood past. Alan's Highland pride perhaps leans a little towards cliché. Yet, to most readers he convinces as the embodiment of (and guide to) a distinctive and alien culture; David's Lowland Whiggishness is observed, on the other hand, with total and confident accuracy.[13] Various features illustrate the deep differences between, on the one hand, *Kidnapped* and *Catriona* and, on the other, the two earlier novels. For example, David has a thorough moral dimension (obvious in his desire to rectify injustice in *Catriona* but clear, too, in *Kidnapped* when he understands how shabby had been his treatment in Cluny's Cage at the hands of Alan and Cluny); Dick Shelton has far less. And (to take another example) when David is variously endangered and bewildered in the Highlands and then in the more mysteriously threatening world of post-Culloden Edinburgh, that political and legal minefield, the contrast with the simple day-dream dangers and hazards confronting Jim and Dick in their more artificial fictional worlds could scarcely be clearer.

What we must conclude, I suggest, is that Stevenson had no single approach to writing for the young. He had no unvarying concept of a youthful readership, nor had he only one way of rendering the world for young audiences, or one type of young hero with which they might identify. Indeed, *Catriona* was written for a periodical aimed not at boys but at girls. This may well explain the book's new prominence of young female characters, but they exist in the novel as aspects of David's expanding encounter with the world's complexity rather than as foci for the imaginations of female readers. We might say that *Catriona* attempts to deal with more of the kinds of problems and issues which could confront an adult than any of its predecessors do, but in saying that we are further acknowledging the sheer variety of these books.

At first glance, the two David Balfour novels might not seem so different from the others after all: all four turn to the past and are therefore, in simple terms, historical novels. It is only David's adventures, however, which approach the serious commitment to a precisely envisioned past with which late nineteenth-century readers were familiar in the writings of, say, Scott or Thackeray. Stevenson's instinct for the fictional uses of history is indicated in that account of his juvenile tastes quoted earlier. Precision about dates was not required, and a tale could be located satisfactorily almost anywhere in a given century. That boyish preference for eighteenth-century inns, in fact, might well have been the germ of the opening of *Treasure Island*. *The Black Arrow*, on the other hand, initially tempts the reader into thinking that the tale has far more historical and geographical solidity than it actually has. As it turns out, we cannot say much more than merely that it is set, as its subtitle informs us, in the fifteenth century, during the Wars of the Roses. We are told enough to be able to deduce (or to be informed by an assiduous editor such as John Sutherland) that it opens in May 1460, although the clues about that date scarcely clarify the chronology. There is no explanation for the civil war, nor does one party or the other appear to have any particular justice, or extra appeal, on its side. It is as if the confusion which generations of playgoers have felt while immersed in Shakespeare's Henry VI plays had been made into a founding condition of the fiction: Dick shifts his allegiance from one side to the other for purely personal reasons and happily retires from the national fray at the end of the book. *The Black Arrow* assumes no interest in the conflict itself: there is none of that informative, indeed educational, purpose which is usually hinted at, however faintly, in a properly solid historical novel. Scott's longer, over-arching view of history is absent here, nor is there anything approaching the seamless combining of a national historical narrative with a purely fictional personal story such as we find in *Henry Esmond*. In particular, the early portion of that great book offers a comparison which highlights how differently Stevenson used historical material: Thackeray portrays the boy Esmond's first involvements in the plotting to restore James II in such a way that both aspects of the story, the personal and the 'historical', progress with the utmost ease. In fact, none of Stevenson's four novels for the young places its characters or its action at any of history's notable turning points. The nearest Stevenson gets to such a standard move in historical fiction is to involve David and Alan in the slaying of the Red Fox. Striking as this true incident may be, however, it was scarcely one of the crucial events of Scottish history – indeed, it was a crime and a mystery probably of greater interest to the lawyer in Stevenson than to the historian.

The absence in these novels of the historical content which would satisfy a real historian is a feature of Stevenson's fiction as a whole. Yet he was constantly drawn, in his imagination, to the Scottish past. Edward Cowan makes it clear that while Stevenson was never going to make a historian (despite his application for the Edinburgh Chair of History and Constitutional Law in 1881), his preoccupation with Scotland's history was central to his imagination and creativity.[14] His historical imagination had one particularly individual feature, however: it was intimately bound up with his response to place, as Cowan also makes clear:

> he was utterly entranced by place [...]. Louis was intrigued by the idea that 'there is a fitness in events and places', that the right kind of thing should fall out in the right kind of place. He was particularly attracted by 'the genius of place and moment'.[15]

Location, therefore, and its variety in these novels, proves as central to their individuality as their diversity of heroes. The title of the first and most famous of the four, after all, refers to the principal scene of the action.

Behind each of the various settings is a corresponding variety of source-types. As already noted, *Treasure Island*'s opening chapters are a confident elaboration of Stevenson's boyhood predilection for tales which begin mysteriously in eighteenth-century inns. And the daydreaming culminates in his creation, from pure imagination, of the highly specific topology of the island itself. The famous map, Stevenson's unexpected first step in the development of his novel, provides the essential conditions for all the adventures, all the twists and turns, of Jim's story. As he later admitted in 'My First Book',

> The map was the chief part of my plot. For instance, I had called an islet *Skeleton Island*, not knowing what I meant, seeking only for the immediate picturesque; and it was to justify this name that I broke into the gallery of Mr Poe and stole Flint's pointer. And in the same way, it was because I had made two harbours that the *Hispaniola* was sent on her wanderings with Israel Hands.[16]

Its origin a playfully drawn map – a pure landscape of the imagination – and its course of events discovered within it, rather than planned and calculated by the adult mind, *Treasure Island* seems to have been written in the spirit of a game, played out like the games of cowboys-and-Indians some of us used to play in a corner of the local park, or in the streets, lanes and gardens surrounding our homes (in the 1950s, admittedly, before we became sensitive about terminology, or about the toy guns in our hands). It is no wonder that Robert Crawford can say that

> *Treasure Island* is a book not just to read but to play at. It is full of an energy that comes from play; from hide and seek, from boys' toys such as swords and boats, from fancy dress, from chases.[17]

Readers can respond in that spirit, because it was written in that spirit – the spirit which (sword or gun in hand) can transform a prosaic urban street, or rain-soaked Braemar, into a landscape of adventure.

Stevenson's essay on his first book ends, still, with its map and with his sense of the centrality of 'maps' – that is, his grasp of the settings of his fictions – in his creative processes.

> The tale has a root there: it grows in that soil; it has a spine of its own behind the words. Better if the country be real, and he has walked every foot of it and knows every milestone. But, even with imaginary places, he will do well in the beginning to provide a map. As he studies it, relations will appear that he had not thought upon. He will discover obvious though unsuspected short cuts and footpaths for his messengers; and even when

a map is not all the plot, as it was in *Treasure Island*, it will be found to be a mine of suggestion.[18]

'Better if the country be real, and he has walked every foot of it': here, perhaps, is a clue as to why *The Black Arrow* seems to be less successful than the other three works being considered here. *Kidnapped* is set in a very real Scotland, and in locations known to Stevenson, thanks in part to his Edinburgh upbringing and also to those journeys he made with his civil engineer father. Edinburgh, East Lothian and the southern Highlands, too, are the settings for arguably the most successful parts of *Catriona*. *The Black Arrow* is set in Suffolk, where Stevenson had spent around five weeks during the summer of 1873 staying with relatives in Cockfield Rectory. This was not a long time to explore an unfamiliar county: Cockfield is inland, eight miles from Bury St Edmunds, and while we know from his letters that he explored the immediate vicinity on foot, both alone and in company with his new friend Sidney Colvin, and also that he visited Melford and Lavenham, small towns a few miles south of Cockfield, he can have had very little opportunity to get to know properly the area around Tunstall (thirty miles away from Cockfield as the crow flies), or the coast yet further beyond it to the east, where much of the novel is set. He had, no doubt, a strong recollection of the general character of the area, because the weeks he spent there were memorable and intense: not only was he living through the aftermath of the emotional cataclysm which had overtaken the Stevenson household when he admitted his religious unbelief, but he was introduced to Mrs Fanny Sitwell with whom he fell thoroughly in love and also to Colvin, whom he had already idolised and who rapidly became one of his closest and most influential friends. Stevenson began to write *The Black Arrow* in May 1883 while in Hyères, ten years after his Suffolk sojourn: the result is a mingling of generalised recollection of the Suffolk scene filtered through impressions derived from Shakespeare's history plays, and (as John Sutherland sensibly speculates) the close perusal of a map.[19] The text, a curious mix of certainty and uncertainty, conveys strongly a sense that the author has a firm grasp of his landscape, but the reader is unsettled by being unable to relate the action to any securely possessed geographical knowledge of his or her own. Treasure Island is a fantasy terrain in which the reader is happy to be abandoned; David Balfour's Scotland is a solid presence for author and reader alike. (His Holland is a slightly different matter.) Late medieval Suffolk is neither one nor the other.

Potentially troubling to the adult reader, the sheer sketchiness of its time and setting, however, may have been just what Stevenson's young readers required: a fictional world written about as if it had the solid certainty of the everyday world yet possessing a fluid uncertainty and excitement which the everyday world normally lacks. Consider again Stevenson's enthusiasm for maps as part of his inspiration: maps have a demonstrable relationship with the solid earth yet, in their abstractness, can be peopled infinitely and unpredictably with humans and their doings. Their worlds of solid actuality can contain, in imagination, all sorts of adventures if the right imagination sets to work. Stevenson knew this from the start – hence *New Arabian Nights* (1882) with its weird adventures in familiar places. And in the Suffolk landscape both recollected and imagined from his reading (and his map-gazing), he had at his disposal a simplified and malleable environment, a 'world', which seems to have appealed particularly to his young readers, as the initial responses to *The Black Arrow* and *Treasure Island* (in *Young Folks*) demonstrated. The Dedication of the former to his wife Fanny, on the occasion of its printing in an American edition, is signed 'R. L. S. / Saranac Lake, / 8 April 1888': in it Stevenson observes that

> in the eyes of readers who thought less than nothing of *Treasure Island*, *The Black Arrow* was supposed to mark a clear advance. Those who read volumes and those who read story papers belong to different worlds. The verdict on *Treasure Island* was reversed in the other court; I wonder, will it be the same with its successor?[20]

Furthermore, Stevenson now knew his young readership better, for this time he clearly had the example of the journal's prize author Alfred R. Phillips (fl. 1880s–1890s) in mind both as a guide but also as a rival to be outdone. Phillips was the author of many serialised novels for the young: in the hardback reissue of his popular tale *Don Zalva the Brave* (serialised 25 June 1881–15 April 1882, published in book form 1885), five other similar reprints of his novels are also advertised. *Don Zalva* is set in fifteenth-century Spain, with Christians and Moors in uneasy co-existence. What is striking, however, is the lack of detail both as regards history and geography. The setting is made as simple as possible: the Waverley Novels are obvious forebears, but Scott's specificity and engagement with historical context is lacking. This sketchy Spain is merely an environment in which the hero can fight with monotonous frequency and equally monotonous success – in every chapter, essentially. Phillips's formula of shaping each chapter/instalment around an episode of simple and striking excitement, and of varying the scene with great frequency, was not lost on Stevenson: *The Black Arrow* moves, in narrative and geographical terms, more swiftly than *Treasure Island*, while possessing a degree of verbal liveliness and zest far superior to the plodding style of Phillips.

The fact that *Treasure Island* had not gone down so well with young readers seems to have piqued Stevenson; as he wrote to Colvin on 8 October 1883: 'great Success of the *Black Arrow*, another tale demanded, readers this time (the Lord lighten them) pleased.'[21] And to the editor of *Young Folks*, James Henderson, who wanted another tale when *The Black Arrow*'s serialisation finished, a request with which Stevenson could not instantly comply: 'At least I am really glad to have so far succeeded with your readers, and I hope "the next time I come round again", to please them yet better' (20 October 1883). That same month, he wrote to W. E. Henley:

> I am now a successful writer in *Young Folks*; I have additional terms offered me: 30/– a chapter, and Alfred R. Phillips has plunged at once into an unsparing imitation of the scene and language of the *Black Arrow*. N.B. I have done him good. Fact. That popular author has pulled himself together with both hands and is, at least, in this first chapter, writing with redoubled care.

The Suffolk scene and the 'tushery' in which the dialogue is steeped, so easily mocked and yet so entertaining, are indeed prominent amongst the elements which stay in the mind when the book is put down: along with the re-imagining of Shakespeare's Richard of Gloucester, they are important aspects of the creativity which the artist in Stevenson brought to the task. His sense of superiority to Phillips, tied in with his consciousness of the tussle over creative worth and mass popularity in which the two writers were silently and distantly engaged (a tussle made all the more precarious in that its locus was the specialised one of children's writing), came out in a letter to his parents a couple of months later, as he commented on an inaccurate published statement by Henderson to the effect that Stevenson was already writing a new story for the journal.

> My rival poor Alfred R. Phillips must think this is much ado about nothing and gird at fate's injustice. I feel real sorry for Phillips; he has been trying so hard and doing so fairly well in his new story, spurred up by the *Black*

Arrow, I am sure, and horrid feelings of jealousy. Rest, rest, perturbed spirit! The readers of *Young Folks* will always prefer him to me. But I must write to Henderson and praise his last. (?15 December 1883)

It must be rare for *Kidnapped* to be published without an accompanying map of David Balfour's wanderings: the sense of journeying, of the contest between hero and natural landscape – indeed, of the sheer experience of travelling ('to travel hopefully is a better thing than to arrive') with no certainty of the goal – lies so completely at the centre of its imagined experience. One might speculate that the success of *The Black Arrow* made this subsequent, much finer, novel possible, for Stevenson's reputation with his young readers had clearly been established and he could feel confident in satisfying them, even as he created a novel which he must also have been conscious of as a worthy contribution to the tradition of Scott. *The Black Arrow* was something from which he could profitably move on. *Kidnapped*'s hybrid nature, and the doubleness of its implied readerships (enthusiastic young persons *and* adult, more discriminating readers) was perfectly clear to its author. To Charles Baxter he described it, in a phrase which highlights its mysterious ambiguity, as 'a kind of a boy's story' (14 February 1886), while to Theodore Watts-Dunton, who had criticised it by claiming that it did not come imaginatively alive until the Highlands were reached, he wrote: 'I began it partly as a lark, partly as a pot-boiler; and suddenly it moved, David and Alan stepped out from the canvas, and I found I was in another world' (early September 1886). *The Black Arrow* may have helped in a more precise way, also. Its first book, 'The Two Lads', is another tale of flight, as a mis-matched pair struggle across a dangerous landscape: Dick Shelton and 'Jack Matcham' (the disguised Joanna) strive to reach the sanctuary of Holywood Abbey. This adventure constitutes the bulk of the novel's Book One and Stevenson must have felt secure thereafter that the tale of a challenging and laborious journey against the odds would prove popular.

Stevenson's intensive bout of reading about Highland history at the end of 1880 provided an inspiration very different from those behind the two earlier books. The confident intensity of the storytelling of *Kidnapped*, and its near-miraculous poise in balancing entertainment for the young and adult reader alike, stem from its double background in the youth-orientated writing he had now successfully achieved and the adult studying he had undertaken. *Kidnapped* balances so much that was in play in Stevenson's writing for the young. Its hero is neither near-childlike as Jim Hawkins is, nor is he freshly grown-up like the Phillips-derived Dick Shelton: David is utterly poised – physically, emotionally and experientially – between the youthful and adult states. Its settings were known to Stevenson to a considerable extent, but the very nature of its story, a long and varied journey experienced in a brief space of time, forced Stevenson to think in cartographic terms. Furthermore, the previous few years had produced much writing, and steady publication: his confidence in himself as an artist had been confirmed both by his new prominence in British letters and also by his well-considered theoretical discussions about fiction and romance ('A Gossip on Romance' in 1882 and 'A Humble Remonstrance' in 1884). His first attempt at a full-scale novel for adults, *Prince Otto* – with which he was initially well-pleased – had recently appeared. He was at the top of his game, as he knew when he described *Kidnapped* as 'infinitely my best, and indeed my only good, story' (to George Iles, 29 October 1887). Except, as he admitted to his father (May 1886), there was more to write about David and Alan.

Confirmation, if any be needed, of how basic to Stevenson's imagination was the sense of place comes in his sketch of how he intended to carry on their story:

> I had to give up *David Balfour*, but by Colvin's suggestion, left the end for a sequel, which, if the first part is successful, I should be able to do with both pleasure and effect. It will deal with Edinburgh, Gullane, Bass Rock, Leyden and Dunkirk, and should have a deal of go. (23 May 1886)

Catriona (i.e. *David Balfour*) follows closely on the events of *Kidnapped*, starting self-consciously a few minutes from the end of the previous novel, yet fails to find the same equilibrium between writing for boys and for (and about) adults. For one thing, Stevenson appears to have been grappling as seldom before with female characters: it was written not for *Young Folks* but for *Atalanta*, a journal for girls edited by 'L. T. Meade' (Elizabeth Thomasina Meade Smith – 1844–1914 – a successful female writer of girls' stories) and designed as a successor to *Every Girl's Magazine*. Furthermore, as commentators agree, its exploration of the political and legal calculations which result in the unjust hanging of James of the Glens draws a lot of energy from Stevenson's close encounter with the grubbiness of politics and statecraft in Samoa. These two pulls, both rather fresh in Stevenson's writing, help explain the hybrid nature of the book. His commitment to the story of the Inverary trial is not in doubt: it completes one of the main loose ends of *Kidnapped* and is fuelled by his new cynicism regarding public life and national governance. It seems a long way from the juvenile world of *Treasure Island*. But so is his exploration of David's affairs of the heart. Did the thought of a female readership prompt his creation of Prestongrange's daughter Barbara Grant, let alone Catriona herself? Stevenson's conception of a fictional love affair, especially one for young lady readers, maintains a safe emotional distance between boy and girl: for his hero, being in love is to be lovelorn and teased perpetually, by Barbara because that is her character, and by the complex historical circumstances in which he is entangled. It wasn't that a Phillips-style story could not admit of girls and love, but fictional amorousness was allowed only the simplest proprieties – and so it had been in *The Black Arrow*, in a considerable portion of which the heroine is disguised as a boy (so that love is no issue) before she is transformed into a distanced ideal, a pledge of Dick Shelton's heroism and a (mere) object of rescue. In *Catriona*, Stevenson clearly wanted to explore hearts in love but could not go anywhere near love's physical dimension. Perhaps, therefore, it could only be for a magazine for girls that he could conjure up the chasteness of the co-habitation of David and Catriona in Leyden. One can agree both with Catriona's father when, informed of the co-habitation, he says, with considerable understatement, 'This is a very unusual circumstance' and also with Stevenson himself in a letter to Colvin on 18 May 1892: 'David Balfour's love affair, that's all correct – might be read out to a mothers' meeting – or a daughters' meeting, and would be thought delicate by a strumpet.'[22]

Nevertheless, one suspects that publication in a girl's journal had surprisingly little influence on Stevenson's creative impulse: by this stage, he was an artist following his artistic trajectory rather than a writer striving to write to a brief. If, in the nature of *Treasure Island* and *The Black Arrow*, there is a blurring of their appeal to (on the one hand) boys and (on the other) to adults, a blurring which occurs to an even greater extent in *Kidnapped* and *Catriona*, there is in the latter two a concomitant blurring as regards boy readers and girls. If *Catriona* is tilted, however slightly, towards a female readership, that suspicion arises as much from one's knowledge of the journal of its first publication as from any marked tendency within the text. The love-matter is not so insistent that most boys would be put off by it, if they enjoy the rest of the novel. Nor, one suspects, were (or are) girls likely to feel excluded from *Kidnapped* because it lacks a prominent female character: it stands as a coherent and inspired work of art, accessible and appealing to every sympathetic reader. It may seem appropriate to categorise these works as 'books for children', but their over-riding classification should be 'works of art, Stevenson-style'.

CHAPTER SEVEN

Mollie Hunter's Teen Fiction: Transitioning through Enchanted Humanness to Adulthood

Ralph Jessop

Understanding is Argus-eyed, and shrewd in realising the child's need for story-characters through whom he can identify with the rest of humankind, and so discover who *he* is, how he 'belongs'.
(Mollie Hunter, *Talent is Not Enough*, p. 10)

Commoners are the very stuff of history. [...] Let them speak, for a change!
(Mollie Hunter, *Talent is Not Enough*, p. 14)

Mollie Hunter is one of Scotland's most outstanding authors of children's fiction.[1] She was born (Maureen Mollie Hunter) at Longniddry, East Lothian, on 30 June 1922, and later moved to Drumnadrochit, near Inverness, with her husband. Publishing some twenty-seven novels between 1963 and 1998, four plays, and several picturebooks, she also gave a series of lectures in the United States, published in *Talent is Not Enough* (1976). In 1974 she won the prestigious Carnegie medal for *The Stronghold* (1974), receiving the Dutch Zilveren Griffel award for a translation of the same novel in 1978. Symbolising something of the recognition she received during her lifetime, a portrait of her by Elizabeth Blackadder is currently held in Edinburgh's Scottish National Portrait Gallery. She died at Inverness in 2012, aged ninety.[2]

Attracting international interest during her lifetime, her novels have been warmly celebrated by several scholars, including Peter Hollingdale.[3] An excellent introduction to her work by Betty Greenway was published in 1998.[4] But subsequently Hunter has received very little critical attention.[5] Though her novels may continue to attract a small readership, they currently appear to be sharing the fate of so much children's literature, ephemeralised by changing fashions, socio-economic and geopolitical transformations, and the plethora of recent high-quality novels for teenagers. Now hailing from bygone eras of the situatedness of her work's production and its various historical settings, a likely assumption, that her stories are too far removed from the present-day reader, is bound to prevail unless considerable scholarly and promotional endeavours refute this prejudice. However, attentive *readers* of her fiction are likely to discover narratives that cross boundaries of culture and periodicity. Reaffirming, informing, and encouraging the reader's humanness, Hunter's work explores intercultural and seemingly timeless phenomena of the child's enchanted condition of make-believe participations in supernatural/magical narration, and of transitioning out of this into adulthood. In doing so, Hunter reaches towards our growing awareness of modernity's precarity.

Hunter's historical fiction is gripping, highly compelling for both child/teen and adult readers alike. Her stories absorb attention through complex plots, frank portrayals of her characters' humanness, and spectacular scenes involving witchcraft and the supernatural. The climacteric excitement of some of her denouements is intensely engaging. The authenticity of her characters – ordinary, fallible, kind, loving, resilient – is warmly humane, reassuringly life-affirming. Furthermore, her stories are deeply immersive due to their reliance upon a complex set of general, iterative relations between: realism; supernaturalism/make-believe; her characters' struggles to survive within protective yet threatening/threatened communities; character development that narrates significant perceptual changes commensurate with child-adult transitions, from a state of childhood enchantment to one of adulthood disenchantment; and, the reader's growing awareness of such changes in perception, involved in his/her own experience of the adult world, the changefulness of cultural contexts, and the child-adult transition.

A notable aspect of this perceptual change is the teenage character's loss of belief in supernatural/magical narration. Typified as a personal shift from enchantment to disenchantment, this loss is refracted in the meta-narrative of the historic transformation of (residually) pre-modern communities, into a disenchanted modernity (compare *Talent is Not Enough*, henceforth *TINE*, pp. 75–77).[6] Thereby, traces of a pre-modern past of enchantment, within the reader's present social condition and the child's still surviving involvements in make-believe's enchantment/mystification/playful disruptions of the mundane, continue to undermine or abrade the apparent hegemony of a modernity that threatens to destroy both the relevance of the past, and the child's need for various forms of imaginative play.

Bringing reader and text together through these relations concerning humanity's and the individual's struggles with, or experience of, various manifestations of recurring conditions of human existence, Hunter's fictional representations of peoples of the past encourage a high level of reader-immersion, through what may be broadly summarised as the humanness of her subject matter. If this humanness of her narratives speaks to her readers, her stories transcend the national/cultural boundaries suggested by their Scottish-centred subject matter.[7] They are therefore likely to overcome initial prejudices about her novels being outmoded due to the situatedness of both her work's production and her characters' historical settings. But Hunter's work undoubtedly has a problem: though fully deserving extensive literary-critical discussion and a new generation of young readers, the work of this exceptionally talented, progressive, and sophisticated Scottish children's author currently lacks widespread national and international recognition.

The humanness of her novels is discernible in how Hunter's characters transition from childhood to adulthood. This transitionary condition encourages the reader's immersion in stories that are effectually refracting his/her consciousness of a similar, personal narrative of change between childhood and adulthood (see *TINE*, p. 28). But emergence into adulthood in Hunter's novels involves a major perspectival shift, or modification of the child's perception of the world, through becoming aware of the importance of social contexts.

The problem of the contingency of context is foregrounded through suggestions of modernity's overmastering power of social transformation to overset communities' entire modes of existence. This predominant characteristic of modernity continues with unabated vigour into the reader's present experience. Thus, Hunter's historical novels resonate with the reader's experiential induction into the realities of the present's conspicuous precarity through its relentless displacements of the past. Striking familiar chords of concern, with young and adult readers alike, Hunter's texts variously play upon the deep bass notes of a long, meta-narrative of the human species' opposing struggles to maintain or displace social continuities, epitomised in the notion that the progress of the species involves a struggle for survival, exhibited in contesting or furthering modernisation. *The Stronghold*'s tribal struggle against Roman invasion, or *The Third Eye*'s signs of impending socio-economic changes that will all but eliminate traces of a pre-Christian agrarian existence, are just two examples of survival struggles that crucially refer to the contingency, ultimate demise, and yet endurance of Scotland's communities of the past.

In Hunter's teen fiction, whether set in Iron Age/first-century Orkney (*The Stronghold*) or 1960s Inverness (*The Kelpie's Pearls*), as undeniable facts of life, humanity struggles with and continues to survive a plethora of contingent conditions, potent forces of change, significantly modifying or threatening to eliminate otherwise seemingly stable communities. Examples of such struggles are evident in: the after-effects of warfare in *A Sound of Chariots* (pp. 38–40, 50);[8] impending modernisation in *The Third Eye* (p. 116);[9] the threat of enslavement in *The Stronghold* (pp. 9, 17);[10] risks to the individual and community of the Press Gang ships, and generally of outsiders, in *A Stranger Came Ashore* (pp. 38, 43, 63–64);[11] external distrust, threat of rape, and shocking violence against the travelling community in *I'll Go My Own Way* (pp. 16–18, 114, 171–72);[12] growing scepticism about the warlock and witches in *The Thirteenth Member* (pp. 62, 66, 128–32);[13] the coming demise of an independent Scottish monarchy in *You Never Knew Her as I Did*; the dispossession of thousands of Scots during the brutal Highland Clearances in *A Pistol in Greenyards*.[14] Such general forces of change pivotally function as major morphotic social conditions of distinctly metamorphic characters within 'the uncertainty of the between years' (*TINE*, p. 16). Her characters are undergoing transitions into adulthood within contexts indicative of the future's consignment to the past, of ways of living that Hunter's novels reanimate.

The beliefs and norms of the community are coherent, but not absolute. Norms are questioned, modified, or overset by characters who reach towards the future (for example, *The Stronghold*, p. 25). Hunter's re-imagined communities of the past are therefore mutable as once self-subsistent contexts within which her characters struggle to survive. But they are ultimately heading towards extinction. Her novels thereby induct her teen reader into an awareness of the contingent status of the human condition, as inescapably subject to forces of social and individual change signifying the community's future demise.

However, giving agency and a voice to otherwise occluded and silenced children, Hunter's teen novels provide richly textured relations between character and context, suggesting their analogous relationship. Through fictional recreations of lost childhoods, combined with the reader's potential awareness of present-day similarities with this reanimated past, along with the more closely analogous relation between the text's fictive historiographies of various child-adult transitions and the reader's present/remembered experience of this transformational condition, these analogous relations are replete with potential reader–text intimacies.

Hunter's teen fiction thereby amply enables immersion in her stories' meaningfulness for the present-day young reader.

Informed by a consciousness of modernity's victory over the various existences, beliefs, and ways of living her communities of Scotland's past reanimate, these communities provide conduits into enchanted (residually) pre-modern modes of existence, alternative to the increasingly rampant modernity of the 1960s–80s (when Hunter was writing). Hunter's communities of the past therefore provide portals into supernatural narratives, or what Hunter herself calls fairylore (*TINE*, p. 80). Such supernaturalistic understandings of the world – the stuff of children's make-believe games and 'their natural fascination for the fantastic, the hilarious, the exotic, the adventurous' (*TINE*, p. 23) – are reaffirmed as integral to a pre-modern condition of enchantment, but also of continuing importance to countless childhoods of the present. As children's authors before her, and since (such as Phillip Pullman in, for example, *Northern Lights*),[15] Hunter is striving to maintain the child reader's plastic world of make-believe as a hallowed capacity to interpret the world differently through becoming conscious of what apparently lies beyond consciousness.

Assuming deep continuities between the child of modernity and the lost, ignored, silenced children of the past, Hunter romantically fosters and protects modern childhood's residues of pre-modern enchantment. Her stories therefore encourage the present-day child's capacities to make-believe, participate in supernatural narration, transition into adulthood, and survive modernity's forces of change and corrosions of the child's need for that imaginative play involved in, or prompted by, a literature of their own: 'one of the mediums through which young minds eventually reach maturity' (*TINE*, p. 19). The child/teen reader is being encouraged to indulge in the naturalness of his/her state of enchantment as a protective alternative to the reductively empiricist, anti-human ethos of a modernity which destroys the child's deeply precious make-believe capacities. But, while her texts protect the legitimacy of this enchantment, they also smooth the way towards a disenchanted adulthood.

Acknowledging and fostering the young reader's transition into adulthood as involving a loss of enchantment and corresponding perceptual change concerning the contingency of social contexts, a further aspect of the child's impending adulthood in Hunter's work involves becoming a moral agent in a community involved in genuine struggles with forces of change. Child/teen characters become active participants in Hunter's plots, engaged with serious matters, burdened with significant responsibilities, as occurs in *The Third Eye*, and *I'll Go My Own Way*, in which Cat assists her mother in a graphic account of childbirth (p. 141). But Hunter subtly conduces the teenage reader towards becoming fully human: resilient, capable of surviving life's vicissitudes and enjoying its pleasures, socially integrated, thoughtful, perceptive, critical, kind, and a moral agent.

Her realist narration situates characters as members of communities, struggling with numerous, sometimes grim aspects of worldly experience, such as the appalling poverty of the Irish labourers in *The Third Eye* (pp. 43–44). Such struggles involve intangible dimensions of belief and emotion. Presenting reality, with at times distressing yet nonetheless reassuring frankness, her novels invariably respect – through challenging – the emotional capabilities of the teenage reader. Hunter's realism thus extends far beyond a mere transmission of historical fact; it is permeated by an admirably high expectation of the young person's intellectual and imaginative capabilities. This often also involves the child's reliance upon, belief in, and enjoyment of the natural environment, animals, and the supernatural, through which her characters are germinating their ultimate emergence into becoming moral beings in adulthood, capable of acting, apt to make mistakes, but vitally able to participate in what it is to be human. Candidly or subtly suggesting certain unbearable truths about the human condition, her robust realism is also evident in portrayals of the sensuousness, beauty, and dignity of the imperfect, suffering, and resilient humanity of ordinary people. Through how she crafts the child's incipient moral agency within an enchanted condition that relishes participation in supernatural narration, Hunter's art powerfully respects, loves, and nurtures the child's unfolding existence.

Existing within real worlds of challenging/threatening conditions that demand action (a prominent example being Coll's invention of the Broch in *The Stronghold*), the child character perceives such conditions through an imaginative consciousness that variously refers to folkloric traditions of fairies, magic, witchcraft, and visions. The child character thereby extends beyond an empirically and/or culturally constricted perception as a way of better interpreting and coping with a socially determined reality. Hunter's child/teen characters often perceive reality through the lens of make-believe, through a playful readiness to see beyond the mundane world into the otherworld of supernaturalism's alterity.

The child's imaginary is so important in Hunter's novels that it attests to a deep conviction that his/her lifeworld of make-believe and participation in folkloric narratives, is critical to the possibility of a more humane adulthood and humanity's urgently needed redemption.

In her later reflections on her art, she appears to regard the adult's retention of childhood enchantment romantically, as the rare preserve of the few adult dreamers, 'strangers to their fellows [...] the incomprehensible ones' (*TINE*, p. 77). But, regardless of this constriction, her novels accord such genuine respect for the child's propensities towards supernaturalism/make-believe that they strongly suggest the great importance to humanity generally, of preserving and enhancing the child's realm of imaginative play.

Hunter's characters and the events in which they are involved or witness, provide lost or evanescing childhoods of the past for the reader's own make-believe. Though historical fiction and other genres similarly memorialise and craft memories for the reader, her stories' interconnections of past and present effectually enweave the reader's imaginary within past childhoods, recalling the lives of predominantly ordinary people in mainly rural communities.[16]

This memory of a communally structured existence brings to the reader's consciousness, childhoods that are alternative to the reader's present, in being more substantially permeated by a (residually) pre-modern condition of enchantment. To become immersed in Hunter's narratives is to assimilate a memory of socially and epistemologically different times and places, recreating 'some part of the past as a living link in the chain of human experience' (*TINE*, p. 40). The reader's remembrance becomes one of a human existence, typified by an organic set of relations and a much less restricted epistemological universe in which, buttressed by the community's belief system, the child's imaginative play participates in supernatural narration, to make connections with the past.

Several of Hunter's narrative techniques or emphases are generally cognate with her texts' remembrance of the fibrous texture of the pre-modern trace of enchantment, embodied by the rural, communal, supernatural-orientated, intergenerational, and organically interconnected past ways of living and childhoods her narratives script. Such narrative techniques/emphases – for example, her uses of prolepses and analepses, dialogues that intimate changing perceptions, presentation of mutual dependencies between characters or of a special intimacy with animals or the natural environment, and treatment of heroism (crucially inflected by social dependencies and love)[17] – emulate and pay homage to the socio-environmental interrelatedness of her communities. Furthermore, as her texts memorialise these past/lost worlds as finely interwoven matrices of interrelating elements, such interconnectedness is yet further replicated through the incorporation of memories. Hunter utilises memory in interesting ways. For example, the extraordinarily powerful psychological realism of Bridie's harrowing grief in *A Sound of Chariots* is emotively and technically breathtaking in its handling of memories – this novel deserves a whole chapter on its outstanding utilisation of memory.

In *You Never Knew Her as I Did*, Will Douglas narrates his memories of serving Mary Queen of Scots and assisting her escape from imprisonment. This memorialising narrative is framed by Will's much later adult situation on receiving news of Mary's execution in 1587. But Will's adult remembrance of the Queen's imprisonment also suggests an alternative, adult reading of the narrative, about the personal and national tragedy of Mary's ultimate beheading. Highlighting his own flaws – a gambler, drinker, carefree jester, and actor approaching his eighteenth birthday – Will emerges as an increasingly competent strategist, dissembler, and survivor (pp. 38, 42, 172, 192–95).[18] His competence is actualised by love and devotion, quickened by the Queen's kindness in calling him her 'little orphan', instead of the accurate, but degrading, 'bastard' used by others (p. 47). As a key agent in the plot, Will's developing competence and resilience (p. 154–55) is integral to his emerging adulthood, as is his awakening to Mary's outstanding beauty (p. 153). As with so many of Hunter's narratives, the more conspicuous details of the plot serve as first-order (child-orientated) material for a second-order (adult-orientated) other narrative.

Foregrounding action and adventure, a later edition re-titled the novel *Escape from Loch Leven* (1981).[19] However, its original title (*You Never Knew Her as I Did*) suggests an alternative, adult-orientated reading that complements the teen adventure story. Attending to Will's devotion to Mary, the narrative becomes Will's testament of love, intensifying the reader's sense of the tragedy of Mary's execution. Will's love of the Queen suggests her sexual power, but also her vulnerability to the rise of a markedly misogynistic form of patriarchy (see p. 120), and how her captivity, mistreatment, and execution comprise a tragic dimension of Scotland's neglected history of a pivotal moment, both for women and as antecedent to the later demise of national sovereignty through the two forms of Union in 1603 and 1707.

Recounting adult memories of his younger/teen perceptions and actions, the dualistic relationship of involved categories (of child and adult) is embodied by Will's dual identity as a narrator. This enables overlapping child and adult readings of the novel. However, integral to the child-adult transition of Hunter's principal characters generally, her stories repeatedly signal child-adult transitions in perception, from the naïve perceptions of youth to the more sophisticated (disenchanted/realist) perceptions of adulthood. This change in perception is immensely important to Hunter's general treatment of the child-adult transition and relies upon or may be informed by the perceptually transformative experience in the enormously influential Allegory of the Cave, in Plato's *Republic*.[20]

Plato's Allegory of the Cave describes a condition of uncritical, misinformed perception as one of epistemic imprisonment within a cave of misleading representations. Socrates describes emancipation from this bondage as initially painful. The individual prisoner, following his forced release from the Cave of deception, gains a newfound sense of perceiving a hitherto disguised reality. Ultimately, through establishing a critical dissonance between the profoundly misleading perceptions within the cave and those made possible after the prisoner's release into daylight, the allegory suggests that liberation from one's past, imprisoned perceptions of a grossly misrepresented reality is utterly transformative.

Hunter was aware of the child's make-believe fascination with caves, and of 'innumerable folktales of dwarfs guarding treasure deep in the mine under a magic mountain' (*TINE*, pp. 12, 61). Caves have of course been used in a number of prominent works of children's literature, such as R. M. Ballantyne's *The Coral Island* (1858), Mark Twain's *The Adventures of Tom Sawyer* (1876), R. L. Stevenson's *Treasure Island* (1882), J. M. Barrie's *Peter Pan* (1904), and J. R. R. Tolkien's *The Hobbit* (1937) and *The Lord of the Rings* (1954–55). Caves symbolise elements of human experience so primal that readers of all ages are likely to identify the literary use of a cave as, for example, a portal into another world, suggesting adventure, danger, escape. Much as Plato's Cave is only part of Platonic epistemology, Hunter treats perception as not entirely confined to what can be physically observed, or positively known – some characters see beyond the realm of consciousness. Importantly, the whole notion of being conscious of what lies beyond consciousness is embodied in, for example, *The Third Eye*, in Jinty's 'fey' nature and capacity to see beyond the horizon of worldly perception (pp. 21, 142, 185, 218). But whether or not Hunter is directly alluding to Plato's Cave, the perceptual transformation in the Allegory nevertheless remains interpretatively important to understanding her treatment of the child-adult transition.

In *The Ghosts of Glencoe*, the narrator, Robert Stewart, is aged just sixteen years. He is a proud soldier, dressed as an officer, full of youthful confidence and a sense of his social superiority. Though answerable to senior officers he is also in charge of men. Billeted at Glencoe, shortly before his fellow soldiers infamously massacre many members of the Clan MacDonald, his social status makes him markedly different from present-day expectations of a teenager. Nevertheless, Robert is initially naïve. But, prior to being brutally awakened by the massacre, his initial misperceptions are crucial dimensions of his transition into adulthood. His perceptions of the MacDonalds, the massacre, and of himself, change radically. Capable of perceiving what is really happening, he becomes a moral authority.

Robert's condemnation of the massacre is doubly haunting, as he raises avenging ghosts to haunt Glenlyon's future while also haunting the reader:

> What ghosts haunt you, Glenlyon? Does MacIan stand, murdered, beside your bed at night? Does his lady wander with bleeding hands through your sleep? [...] Whose face do you see in the dark [...]? Is it Inverrigan's staring sightless at you from a-top a pile of corpses? Or is it the face of a little boy upturned in useless pleading to you as a dagger pierces his tender neck?[21]

Realising he had either ignored or misread the signs foreshadowing the impending massacre, Robert becomes responsible. He takes a necessary step towards exercising his moral agency and judgement in resisting the atrocity and indicting his fellow soldiers, who were acting under orders to eradicate their hosts. Such orders ought to have been disobeyed by Robert's seniors. He thus mediates and encourages the reader towards an important awareness of moral evil's dependence upon compliance.

The massacre is being re-imagined via a post-Holocaust consciousness of, to use Hannah Arendt's now famous phrase in her *Eichmann in Jerusalem*, 'the banality of evil', and the inadmissibility of the so-called Nuremberg Defence, namely, that perpetration of certain acts was permissible because demanded by superior orders.[22] *The Ghosts of Glencoe* thus raises a post-Second World War concern (that led to the Milgram experiments in 1963) about the deeply troubling problem of being overly deferential to authority. The many instances in Hunter's other novels of young characters telling white lies or being rightly disobedient accord with this concern. Evoking feelings of great moral repugnance, Robert is a complex exemplum of the moral rightness of risking everything in opposing the seemingly irresistible slide into sins of omission or commission. In *The Ghosts of Glencoe*, such sins result from a variety of human failings, but pre-eminently in this genocidal situation from that troubling weakness of insufficient criticality and undeveloped morality that conjointly underlie complicity with wrongful authority.

Robert's experience of re-perception also involves reinterpreting the vision of MacEachern (p. 74), which he had initially judged to be mere superstition. Part of Robert's development of a sophisticated moral understanding therefore includes a broadening of his domain of legitimate knowledge to accommodate radically alternative ways of understanding the world. The Clan's ancient belief system, their state of enchantment (epitomised in the vision of MacEachern), is not the delusive/superstitious condition Robert had naïvely assumed. In sharp contrast to the brutality and moral weakness of an uncritical complicity with superior orders within the ascendant forces of Scottish modernisation, the MacDonalds' communally constructed humanity is signified by their hospitality, clothing, manners, knowledge of other languages, but also by their enchanted state through the inclusion of visions – or seeing beyond the realm of a materially-constricted consciousness.

In *The Enchanted Whistle*, Hob's partially enchanted condition also involves an ability to be conscious of entities beyond this-worldly consciousness. Hob is seductively invited into a cave by the shape-shifting Ferlie (Scots for fairy). This cave is described by the Ferlie as 'the entrance to the ferlie world', a world beyond mundane experience, of 'a longing for something ye canna name' – a realm beyond language and consciousness (p. 105).[23] The place that Hob then enters contains an archway beyond which there is a 'bright light'.

In Plato's Allegory of the Cave, light from outside enters the cave and enables shadow-shapes to be cast upon the cave's wall, re-presenting certain physical objects. The prisoners in the cave are thus profoundly misled by solely encountering highly misleading re-presentations. When one of the prisoners is dragged out into the sun, he struggles to see properly. Initially blinded by the sun's rays, he cannot believe what he sees. In Hob's case, this process of enlightenment is being re-enacted in reverse; Hob is confronted with initially blinding and unbelievable phenomena *within* the Ferlie's cave: 'He had to close his eyes again and blink until he got used to it, but when he could look steadily at the ferlie world he could hardly believe his eyes' (p. 106). The Ferlie promises Hob that, in this Otherworld, he will enjoy the complete, self-pleasing freedom of non-spatial and non-temporal insubstantiality, a place (reminiscent of some of the fairy tales by the brothers Grimm) that 'can be any place ye want [...], for here it is always the time and place you like best to be in' (p. 107). Hob will be able to wear fine clothes, 'eat the rich food we eat, and have the same freedom to come and go unseen that we have' (p. 107). According to the Ferlie, part of Hob already belongs to the Ferlie's Otherworld. Hob's pre-existing partial participation in this enchanted world, formerly enabled him to 'hear music in the wind, in the voice of the river, in the bees' hum and in singing grasses' (p. 108).

Hob is therefore ambivalently both this-worldly and other-worldly, a combination of being imaginative (a dreamer) and yet bound by his mundane existence, ancient/eternal and modern/temporal, enchanted and disenchanted. The Ferlie world within the cave 'is a land of dreams [...] the world of perfect beauty and eternal youth that mortals dreamed of and lost so long ago that they have forgotten even the dream of it' (p. 108). But Hob has not yet become disenchanted. Now, within the Ferlie's cave, he is at the brink of becoming *entirely* enchanted, a prisoner emancipated from the world's realities. If he chooses the Ferlie's world, in preference to the harsh realities of his life with the cattle reiver, Archie Armstrong, Hob will enjoy a life of eternal happiness in which, as the Ferlie seductively tells him: 'there is no sickness or sorrow [...] so what more *could* you ask for?' (p. 109). However, the Ferlie's question is aptly ambiguous: both rhetorical (nothing more than eternal happiness *is* desirable), and yet answerable (something important is absent in the Ferlie's 'land of dreams'). Hob can be conscious of indeterminable possibilities beyond conscious experience. Thus, he intuits there is something wrong about this Otherworld within the cave. He doubts – 'I'm no sure', 'there was something about it that chilled him and warned him not to yield to the Ferlie's tempting' (p. 109).

This tiny splinter of scepticism – fundamental to an otherwise impossible criticality – enables him to gain a further insight that sears through the spectacle's tempting beauty and the Ferlie's seductive promises of freedom and eternal happiness. Figuring out what is wrong with this Otherworld, Hob finally rejects the Ferlie's temptations through realising he does not 'want to stay in a world without love' (p. 110). This would be a trite or (given the hardship of Hob's life) an absurd reply to the Ferlie, but Hob's choice is made through a re-perception of the former harshness of his existence. For, in sharp contrast to the Ferlie's loveless world, amidst the grimness of Hob's reality, love does exist. Love is the correlative of the real world's suffering, making a mortal existence preferable to the automorphic dream world of unfettered, self-pleasing happiness within the cave: 'If there is no sickness or sorrow or death in your world, Ferlie, then there is no love in it either, for it is when such things strike at people that they are warm and kindly to one another.' (p. 110). The dialogism of reality's co-relativism is thus preferable to the loveless monism of the otherworld, but also to a reality of mere materialism. Hob's choice of this dialogical standpoint on the correlative nature of love and hate/suffering, affirms a belief in human goodness, encouraging the young reader to have faith and participate in humanity's capacity to respond to suffering – with love.

This pivotal moment is crucial to Hob's development from a child's state of partial enchantment to a young adult's disenchantment. In the dream-world of solipsistic delusiveness, Hob will only encounter representations of what he unilaterally wants this Otherworld to be. The dialecticism of a real, human existence is thus subtly intimated in Hob's rejection of the Ferlie world. In addition, this real world cannot be always, if at all, what Hob wants it to be: the suggestion is that the real world is thus unpredictable, infinitely capable of surprising us, for good or ill. The dynamism that Hob prefers is, in broad outline, Hunter's underlying conception of reality as consisting in an inherently unpredictable and uncontrollable dialectical interplay within the unity of opposites.

The symbolism of the cave at the end of *I'll Go My Own Way* suggests an apparently more tenuous allusion to Plato's Cave. Towards the end of the novel, the principal female character, Cat, and her husband, Charlie, consummate their marriage in a cave (p. 193). Hence, the place in which they become fully adult is symbolic, the space within which the couple are transformed into their formal adult roles of husband and wife. But, reading the text in this way, the cave's transformative significance becomes multiple: their marriage signifies or promises a momentous individual and social transformation through the couple's potential modernisation of the Travelling people's marital norms. The couple reject the brutal patriarchal subjugation of wives by their husbands, presented in the story as a common practice. Cat and Charlie also reject their people's turn to modern motor-driven forms of transport, leaving the cave to start their married life in a manner reminiscent of their ancestors – travelling in a horse-drawn cart, separate from Charlie's wife-beating, drunken father and his family.

The gynocentric/sexual symbolism of the cave is also suggested as the couple are completely united in their marriage by the mutuality of their lovemaking: 'she was hungry for him as he was for her, so that she did not mind the pain; and the love-making that followed was as fierce and ecstatic for one as it was for the other' (p. 193). The symbolism of the cave in *I'll Go My Own Way* is thus gynocentric/sexual but also, reminiscent of Plato's Cave, it is a place of significant transformation, awakenings, realisations – the 'sunrise light striking into [the cave] wakened Cat' the morning after her first night with Charlie (p. 193; and see 193–95). This marriage promises a sensual, gender-equal, non-violent, progressive marriage that will return the couple to a pre-modern mode of transport and of living. Cat and Charlie are returning to the ways, and even places, of their people's past. Rejecting a modernity that is increasingly beleaguering their nomadic, agriculturally rooted, and residually enchanted existence, their emergence from the cave is so transformative that the couple become elevated to a progressive symbol of hope for re-enchanting and renewing the way of life of the increasingly persecuted Travellers.[24]

Adult characters in some of Hunter's novels importantly link the present's disenchanted modernity with the past's pre-modern enchantment, such as the two main storytellers in *A Stranger Came Ashore*, Old Da and Robbie Henderson. In *The Kelpie's Pearls*, the witch, Morag MacLeod, connects 1960s Inverness (through the nearby crofting community at Abriachan where Morag lives) with the ancient past of Highland crofting communities, witchcraft, magic, the kelpies, and '*Tir-nan-Og*' (the 'land of heart's desire', or otherworld 'land of eternal youth') (p. 93).[25] The enchanted world of Morag's witchcraft, her intimacy with Nature, and the self-sufficiency of her crofting existence, countervail modernity's artifice, superficiality, industrial dependency, and its grim, adult suppressions of the wonders and rich pleasures of supernatural narration and an intimate relation with Nature.

One embodiment of this disenchanted modernity in *The Kelpie's Pearls* (notably associated with a stern Presbyterian Christianity) is 'the Woman', the unloving distant relative guardian of orphaned Torquil MacVinish. Contrasting with the venomous prohibitions and threats of this guardian, Morag humanely befriends the recently orphaned Torquil, provides a shed for his animals, and regards his intimacy with them as a valuable 'gift of understanding', 'that comes to those with the patience and kindness to learn the ways of wild creatures' (p. 18). This is just one instance of Morag's wisdom – the 'Pearls' in the novel's title adroitly suggesting the narrative's hidden pearls of wisdom.

The continuance of Torquil's 'gift of understanding' into adult life is enabled by Morag's protection through the narrative's supernaturalism, and finally by his adoption by the Naturalist, after Torquil witnesses Morag's magical escape with the shape-shifting supernatural being, the Kelpie (pp. 100–02). As an adult, Torquil begins to think 'he must have imagined it all', but he can still feel the peculiarly sensuous enchantment of his magical time at Abriachan. Briefly hinting at an adult-orientated reading, and within this, the presence of an unbearable loss, the narrator comments: 'a moment of longing for a world that has vanished is as much as anyone can bear' (p. 107). The story subtly parallels and interweaves overt with covert narratives, including: Torquil's bereavement, his gift of a peculiar affinity with animals, the spectacular magic of Morag's witchcraft and the Kelpie's supernatural powers, Morag's death (supernaturalised as her magical escape with the Kelpie), the loss of an ancient crofting community, and loss of both a society's, and an individual's, enchanted state. The narrative exquisitely contains disguised pearls of wisdom concerning the mortality of human existence, the terrible agonies of grief, and the protective power of supernatural narration, as a necessary escape and alternative understanding for the child character and reader, that feeds and preserves the child's need for enchantment. However, blending the supernatural/wondrous with the natural, Hunter's stories also nurture the child's enchantment through evocative descriptions of Natural Magic.

Hunter provides some delightful descriptions of experiencing natural phenomena unmediated by scientific explication, such as *'the Merry Dancers'* (the Northern Lights) in *A Stranger Came Ashore*. The invigorating sense of wonder at the beauty, spectacle, and mysteriousness of the Northern Lights' phantasmagorical display, interspersed by 'the sky's spells of total darkness', is emblematic of the darting, dancing action – or dramatic shifting of the reader's attention – that contributes to the brilliant intensity of the novel's denouement (p. 102). *A Stranger Came Ashore* ultimately closes with Robbie – now an adult storyteller of supernatural tales – and his practice concerning his audience's shifts between disbelief and credulity, of moving from one tale to another. Robbie evidently now understands supernatural narration quite differently from his earlier child's perception of an exciting involvement with the stranger, Finn Learson (the Great Selkie). Robbie has inherited the wisdom of the storyteller's art of telling tall/supernatural tales. Thus, he does not attempt 'to convince anyone against that person's will', shifting instead, to telling another tale (p. 104). The motion of the Northern Lights patterns several aspects of the narrative's exciting ending: its sense of urgency in rapidly moving from one action to another, the audience's/reader's playful shifting between belief and doubt, and the storyteller's art of withholding explanation to leave the tale undecided, mysterious, in 'total darkness'.

A particularly pleasing and potent instance of Natural Magic occurs in *The Third Eye*. The schoolteacher, Miss Carson, is strait-laced, exam-orientated, and her classroom is tense, but both Miss Carson and the class are elegantly transformed through the children's sheer pleasure and wonder at a pair of visiting swallows – 'two living arrows of midnight-blue and snow-white' (p. 77). The swallows build their nest on a ceiling beam and eventually rear their young. Surprisingly, Miss Carson allows the swallows to continue nesting and the children watch, listen, and work harmoniously, transformed by the swallows' presence. The children love their flitting to and fro, feeding their young, and the nestlings' 'wild fluttering and chirping as they made their first flight' (pp. 79–80). The birds provide a pleasurable source of distraction, yet the class 'had the feeling of learning faster than they ever had before', and the improvements in their work are noticed by Mr Hargreaves, the headmaster (p. 80).

The swallows' calming influence also transforms Miss Carson: 'from the stern sergeant-major figure she had been before, to someone strangely gentle' (p. 80). The Natural Magic of the swallows' transformative presence defeats Miss Carson's 'sergeant-major' instructional method. Driven by understandably genuine anxieties concerning the children's employment or higher education prospects, 'sergeant-major' teaching methods are being exposed as far inferior to the more nurturing, non-disciplinarian pedagogy that Miss Carson finds herself practising. Gently, but devastatingly, the Natural Magic of the nesting swallows displaces disciplinarian and overly instrumentalised educational practices, a reading supported by the decisions taken by the sisters of the principal character, Jinty Morrison, not to pursue Higher Education. They overtly thwart their mother's instrumental conception of education as merely a means to securing her daughters' material success and independence from men (p. 157).

Hunter's use of animals is various, from the magical, transformative presence of the swallows to challenging portrayals of suffering and even (in *The Stronghold*, pp. 68–71) fighting a wild boar to the death. In *The Third Eye*, the harvest rituals include the ancient practice of killing hares fleeing from the reapers: 'Hares were food, of course, but there was also something about the excitement of killing the last hares of harvest that seemed to make them special in the same way as the last of harvest itself was special' (p. 105). Hunter confronts the reader with a graphic description of the hares' terror – 'eyes bulging with panic' – and their slaughter:

> The sticks flailed out at them. The field became a bedlam of shouts, yells, curses, shot through with the screams of hares that had been wounded by a first blow and needed a second one to dispatch them. Blood spurted – hares always seemed to bleed freely. (p. 107).

Jinty shrinks from this scene,

> repelled by the blood and the dying screams. And yet it didn't last. Just one great explosion of violence, and it was all over. [...]. And there was a sense of rightness in the air – a satisfying sort of feeling, as if something that was proper and necessary had been accomplished. (p. 107)

Hunter is not suggesting that this practice of killing hares is to be condoned – the ritual was of its time (*TINE*, pp. 53–54). Comparison might be made between this scene and a witch's intimacy with Nature in *The Thirteenth Member*; significantly, the young, good witch, Gilly Duncan, calms a terrified hare attempting to escape being bludgeoned to death (pp. 27–28). In *The Third Eye*, the harvest ritual produces a complex set of differing perspectives on killing the hares. Necessary for food, exciting in its momentary madness, brutally violent, terrifying for the hares, gory, mercifully brief, partly ritualistic – Jinty's response is one of both revulsion and acceptance. The belief-system, values, and traditions of the community are therefore presented as warranted, through the people's understanding of this bloodbath as an emotionally 'satisfying' accomplishment 'as if [...] proper and necessary' (p. 107), but open to critique, an example of a once unquestionable reality in the process of being questioned and ultimately abandoned. Shortly after the event an additional perspective is included: Mr Elphinstone, the Church Minister, voices his anti-Pagan opposition to the pre-Modern and pre-Christian Corn Dolly harvest ritual and the associated ceilidh-style kirn's licentiousness. But the old Earl eloquently declaims against Elphinstone, accusing him of being a 'dry, narrow creature', of repressing in himself 'the wonder in the sweet flowering of lovers' bodies', and of his ignorance 'of the pain and sweat' that goes into harvesting the corn and making the Corn Dolly (p. 115). This climacteric moment in the text positions the emotionless inhumanity of Elphinstone in direct confrontation with the all-too-human Earl. Hunter is thus presenting her reader with a major division between the Apollonian (dry, rational, disciplined, and detached from the energies, instincts, and holistic fusions that unite the community) and the Dionysian (mythic, ecstatic, sensual, drunken, communally intermingled). Elphinstone's position, representative of Church discipline and stern prohibitions, is clearly being ridiculed, whereas the narrative strongly suggests sympathy for the Earl's broader consciousness of the community's traditions as integral components of the people's humanity.

The combined forces of the Church, the Law (the narrative is framed by the Procurator Fiscal's investigation of the Earl's death), and advancing modernity (the tractor replacing the horse, blacksmith, and fieldworkers) sharply oppose the Earl's humanness (p. 116). These forces of change are implicated in stunting human vitality by constricting the variegated experience and emotional richness of the community's more ancient, nature-orientated way of life. The Earl ultimately succeeds, defeating some major constraints as he does so: the ancient curse on his household; the Christian moral dogmatism against self-slaughter; and the Law, by tricking (via Jinty) the Procurator, to return a verdict of accidental death. However, Hunter is depicting a whole way of life, poised to vanish. Jinty's revulsion at the hare-killing, the old Earl's self-sacrificing defeat of his family's ancient curse (through his suicide), and the beginnings of yet more industrialised farming methods are just some of the ways in which Hunter sows conditions of ideological change, both within and external to a community, as contributing forces of its ultimate demise. The child reader may sense the text's pathos, while the adult reader is more likely to discern the extent to which *The Third Eye* is a lament for a lost world with an ancient lineage that Hunter clearly understood and cherished, but which (writing in the late 1970s) had largely disappeared.

Hunter's unstinting endeavour to re-create the past through re-animating the agency and voices of Scotland's forgotten and silenced children and the neglected lives of the ordinary people's struggles to survive, is evident in the research that underpins her work. But her use of this is judicious, helping to mediate a compelling *sense* of times past (*TINE*, p. 41). Graphic description and historical accuracy contribute to Hunter's realism, but more importantly, her fictional worlds convey a consciousness of reality's complexity in its mutability. Dynamically related to their communities, many of her protagonists struggle with their changing social contexts of norms, traditions, beliefs, values, and supernaturalistic para-narratives. In reaching back to past struggles with changing social contexts, and in foregrounding child-to-adult transitioning characters within these metamorphosing conditions, Hunter's fiction is importantly dualistic as it situates character in relation to context and maintains a dialogue with the reader's personal experience of both becoming a young adult and his/her developing awareness of existing in present times of potentially catastrophic change. Our situation re-informs her art's fascination with the child's enchantment as a crucial element in nurturing an incipient moral agency and criticality, fundamental to resisting dull compliance in times when complicity is becoming increasingly dangerous.

Encompassing an important additional duality of subtly related realistic and supernaturalistic narration, the highly complex interrelations within Hunter's narratives enable both diverse and deeply immersive reading experiences. Though her narratives may appear well rounded and complete, her handling of dual forms of narration – realistic and supernatural – comprises a holding together of binaries in ultimately unresolved paradoxical relation. Her narratives are thereby discursively, a-linearly processive, resistant to finalised readings. This interpretability of her narratives is consonant with the inclusiveness of her characters' humanness. Deeply permeated by some of the most elemental problems/concerns of adult and teenage existence, her work combines a specifically national setting with the more generalisable and thus inclusive humanness her characters exhibit. Understood as such, this is an open invitation to developing international interest in her wonderfully crafted stories. The humanness of her characters and of her writing generally, imply that Hunter's stories are maximally, if yet latently, international.

Hunter's narratives are also peculiarly amenable to extensive further research, critical reinterpretation, and adaptation. Apart from the numerous obvious candidates for future scholarly examinations of her work – for example, to do with their grounding in Scottish folklore, the nation's social and political history, and Hunter's life – the complexity of her dual form of realist-supernatural narration and the various other dialogical relations of her writing significantly contribute to her work's enduring potential to be interpreted anew. And, given the many spectacular scenes in her stories involving magic, witchcraft, supernatural agency, and authentic portrayals of human and animal suffering, courage, kindness, and love, several of her novels await high-quality film adaptations. This is the surest way now to ensure the international prominence and recognition Hunter's work so justly deserves.

CHAPTER EIGHT

Adolescent Citizenship in Cathy MacPhail's *Mosi's War* and Claire McFall's *Bombmaker*

Fiona McCulloch

Since devolution and particularly with the grass roots momentum of the 2014 independence referendum, I have argued that Scotland's young people have become increasingly interested and invested in matters of cosmopolitan citizenship, transforming often disaffected and disengaged youth into active adolescent agency.[1] Part of that drive has been instigated with the plethora of available children's and young adult (YA) literature where Scotland's future generation increasingly sees itself reflected in textual narratives that advocate a voice for those hitherto marginalised within literature and culture. Similarly, Maria José Botelho and Masha Kabakow Rudman argue that 'Children need to see themselves reflected so as to affirm who they and their communities are. They also require windows through which they may view a variety of differences. Books are one way they learn about the world.'[2] With a view to exploring ways in which adolescents can learn through such mirrors and windows, in this chapter I will consider Cathy MacPhail's *Mosi's War* (2013) and Claire McFall's *Bombmaker* (2014) in the light of Scotland's socio-political climate and consider how these texts pedagogically impact upon their intended readers as ideological modes of comprehending citizenship.

For Michael Gardiner, Deleuze and Guattari's concept of a 'minor literature' as a political force is a vital way of positioning post-devolution Scotland's postcolonial literary voice, since it becomes 'more literary than the major'.[3] As it exists within the interstices of more major literature, he argues, its spatial energy has the potential of 'always *becoming* something else'.[4] Even more minor, then, is Scottish children's and YA fiction, a genre often written by women and frequently disregarded, yet vital as a means of charting the trajectory of Scotland's future. Themselves minors, adolescents too have the malleable capacity to *become* ethical and empathetic citizens who actively develop Scotland's future, inspired by the fictional heroes and heroines with whom they engage. If post-devolution Scottish politics (described as 'a journey without a reliable map'[5]) is preoccupying itself with a future that is undetermined and full of potential as endless becoming, then children's and YA fiction is certainly pondering that future too for its readers. Such fiction, often encompassing the trope of mapping a journey, engages in a field of geopolitical struggle as it helps to persuade the reader of a particular ideological position. Like Gardiner's concept of *becoming*, O'Neill says 'Devolution has been described as a process not an event, and there is widespread expectation that it will develop over time'.[6] Similarly, children's and YA writer Julie Bertagna recognises 'Scotland is in transition, I suppose that must inform your imagination – I am writing about characters who are all in transition'.[7] A fundamental aspect of being in transition usually involves going on a journey, as Bertagna's title, *Exodus* (2002), suggests because one's ontological sense of oneself in the world can be shaped and altered by charting these shifting horizons. Utilising the trope of mapping a journey, adolescent Scottish fiction of this ilk is responding accordingly to its political landscape by portraying characters who are dynamically shifting boundaries, by undertaking journeys of endless becoming not unlike the imagined nation through which they often traverse.

Integral to a new vision for Scotland is, of course, its future generation and how they can be encouraged to participate in shaping its trajectory in a global world of transnationalism, climate change, conflict, and post-secularism. MacPhail's *Mosi's War*, like Theresa Breslin's *Divided City* (2005), directly responds to the demands of globalisation by featuring asylum seekers, particularly the boy mentioned in the title. To briefly recount the plot: Mosi and his parents are asylum seekers in Glasgow, fleeing from war-torn Somalia, and he slowly develops a friendship with a Glaswegian, Patrick Cleary. When Mosi inadvertently stumbles across notorious war criminal Papa Blood, who is clandestinely evading capture by living as an asylum seeker in Glasgow under a stolen identity, it transpires that he was a child soldier enslaved by Blood's malevolent regiment. The novel's opening sees Patrick witness an asylum seeker's suicide, only to realise later it was a murder by Blood, and this awakening brings the warlord to Patrick's flat to kill him, ensuring his ultimate silence to avoid capture. Patrick is saved by Mosi, who realises Blood's intention, so cementing a friendship between these boys which, in turn, advocates the need for alliance rather than alienation between different cultures living within the same city.

McFall's *Bombmaker*, published just one year after *Mosi's War*, concerns itself with the plight of eighteen-year-old Lizzie, a Scot living in London during a futuristic dystopia where the UK has been dissolved and Celts (Scots, Irish or Welsh) are considered illegal aliens if found in England. After being rescued from the 'GE, the Government Enforcers',[8] she finds herself at the mercy of a criminal underworld governed by the Welsh Evans brothers, Alex and Samuel. Having discovered an innate talent for wiring up bombs, Lizzie is forced to carry out explosions against the English Government, while simultaneously serving as Alex's sex slave. Eventually, though, she escapes to Wales with Samuel as the two embark upon a romance.

Clearly both novels place young people in dangerous situations and, as such, demonstrate that the world is an uncertain place that habitually abuses and exploits the vulnerable, including children and adolescents. Patrick and Mosi are not yet voting age, while Lizzie is, but she is disenfranchised by being considered a non-citizen, so each of them is outside of, and disempowered from, active political citizenship. Yet both texts seek to empower their protagonists through participatory measures, such as adding their voice to community concerns in *Mosi's War* or fighting for Celtic rights and disobeying English laws in *Bombmaker*. By doing so, both texts directly interrogate the lack of political influence that teenagers may feel in the face of adult authority and regulative regimes and, instead, offers them a spatial interstice of dynamic political engagement, albeit outwith the ballot box. Similarly, Judith Torney-Purta and Jo-Ann Amadeo argue that by providing participatory spaces for young people, an emergent citizenship is fostered that will continue to flourish throughout adulthood, noting that 'The settings especially relevant to early adolescents include not only the home, but also the school, the peer group, and both formal and informal organizations to which they belong in their communities'.[9] While the school is particularly pertinent to the emergent citizenship fostered in MacPhail's text – 'I do not care what is going on outside the gates of this school, but in here, we will be a haven of peace, diplomacy and tolerance'[10] – I would argue that it is also the space afforded by the fictional texts themselves that allows for the depiction and involvement of adolescent citizenship as the main protagonists imagine social spaces like the school, family and peers where civic participation can occur.

Likewise, for John Stephens, children's and YA fiction encompasses 'a struggle for the minds of young readers',[11] offering a dynamic space to challenge ideologically and intellectually their existing thinking and values, since 'a function of children's literature is to socialize its readers'.[12] Though this can disempower adolescents by reinforcing conservative hegemonic dominance, nevertheless fiction is often a site of transgressive counter-discourse, which strives to resist rather than reflect reactionary social systems and, in turn, allow teenagers fissures of politicised stimulation into which they can insert themselves and feel dialogically empowered by the thematic concerns of the texts. For instance, Breslin's *Remembrance* (2002) resists the hegemonic equation of patriotism with military heroism and offers a cosmopolitical alternative for her readers, just as MacPhail's text counters the discursive dehumanisation of immigrants. In *Mosi's War*, when racial tensions and bloodshed threaten to bubble over on the Glasgow housing estate where both Patrick and Mosi reside, Patrick's granny tells him about the hysteria of local children who started the rumour of 'The Gorbals Vampire' (p. 46) when she was a girl, while informing him: 'Vampires don't exist. And let me tell you, son. Real life is a lot scarier than any vampire story' (p. 113).

Though a realist novel, *Mosi's War* engages with the Scottish Gothic tradition by alluding to vampires and Glasgow's Necropolis in order to unmask the 'Real life' horrors lurking within contemporary Glasgow, namely racism and the bloodthirsty Papa Blood. Mosi recounts to Patrick the multiple atrocities of this warlord, as the repressed memories of his forced participation in Blood's regime surface, triggered by an encounter with 'The face that haunted every one of his nightmares' (p. 97). Like his name, Blood (who drinks the blood of murdered boy soldiers) oozes with sanguinary Gothic associations, a spectral revenant of Mosi's unconscious who disruptively transgresses into the safety of his waking world in Glasgow: 'The monster is here' (p. 101). His monstrous capacity is reinforced through Patrick's eyes, who 'gasp[s]' at never having 'seen anyone so tall' (p. 99). Akin to the Gorbals vampire, it is fitting that Patrick encounters Blood in the putrefying Gothic cemetery where, 'out of the darkness, as if it had emerged from the grave itself, a hand touched his shoulder' (p. 175). Though traumatised, Mosi and Patrick's unmasking of Blood exposes him to justice, effectively demonstrating their adolescent agency and participatory citizenship.

For McFall's protagonist, the political demise of the UK directly impacts upon her and throws her into a dystopian climate of English nationalism, where she is stigmatised as a social other. Lizzie is doubly marginalised as a young woman, her body reduced to a material commodity, even before she becomes Alex's property: 'I got myself back down to England, buying my way with my looks, my smile and my body' (p. 27). Once she falls prey to Alex, 'From that minute on, he owned me' (p. 31). The vulnerability of the female body is emphasised throughout Lizzie's precarious existence in London: 'A man had actually stopped, got out of his car and tried to drag me inside' (p. 28). As well as abusing Lizzie and having sex with, then murdering, another woman, we learn that Alex is 'making money hand over fist, cashing in on every dirty deal that just didn't exist before. You know he's trafficking people now, bringing Celt girls into the country, smuggling them in then selling them off to rich English tossers?' (pp. 189–90). In turbulent times of social instability, *Bombmaker* accentuates the message that it is those already marginalised within Britain who will suffer most acutely, particularly 'Celt girls'.

According to Glenda Norquay, while contemporary Scottish cinematic depictions of adolescent masculinity are concerned with transitional borderlands, specifically twentieth-century North-East Scottish literary depictions of femininity problematise rather than reinforce the spatial mappings of the threshold towards emergent womanhood. For female sexuality and identity, it becomes, argues Norquay, not so much a border crossing from one state to another as with masculinity but, rather, a shift towards 'undesignated territories'[13] that are marginalised or outsider spaces. In her Kristevan reading, these become not restrictive margins, but anarchic liberatory sites of semiotic resistance to the patriarchal social order, which is geopolitically driven by and reflected in the distinctive marginalised culture of North-East Scotland.

Norquay's consideration of a more assured masculine space set against an indeterminate, unfixed and dynamic spatial femininity is interesting in light of my focus upon post-devolution Scottish adolescent citizenship. To identify with one's community, after all, demands that one feels part of, rather than apart from, that social space. Since devolution, it is encouraging to see active heroines featuring in the likes of Bertagna's and Breslin's fiction. Politically, and particularly with the referendum debates, women, including Nicola Sturgeon's former leadership, are now envisioning a more gender-equal citizenship for contemporary Scotland, signalling that the geopolitical tectonic plates are shifting. However, Norquay's point about young women being outside of social spaces also certainly fits with Lizzie's lack of belonging and her fearful mobility across the peripheries of landscape and cityscape. Whether that becomes a site of liberatory resistance, though, is questionable since her geogendered marginalisation constantly threatens to erase rather than enrich her identity.

With the continuing turmoil instigated by the referendum on Brexit from the European Union in June 2016, McFall's novel seems disconcertingly prophetic. As narrator, Lizzie recounts:

> When the global economy collapsed, the world as we knew it changed overnight. China and the USA were at each other's throats, with Europe caught in the crossfire. Germany and France were pushing hard for laws and policies that would reel Britain in, make her a slave. So we left the EU [...] It didn't work very well. (p. 23)

Bombmaker offers an interpretation of the detrimental effects of neoliberal globalisation's demise and its aftershocks that bring division rather than unity in the face of adversity. Though it is problematic to discuss the enslavement of Britain within the EU (McFall may well be responding to its dominance by corporate power and the harsh treatment meted out by Brussels to Greece after its financial collapse), the punitive reverberations of exit from the EU certainly sounds familiar, with reference to an analysis of recent extra-textual events. Although the novel was published only at the onset of the Brexit process, in McFall's fictional Britain, 'After just five years the country was bankrupt, the people starving. The government in London made the decision to dissolve the United Kingdom [...] They cut off Scotland, Northern Ireland and Wales' (p. 23). In McFall's speculative dystopia 'bankrupt' Britain fragments while, at the time of publication in 2024, one might ponder the extent to which Brexit exacerbates current economic instability, airport and ferry queues, and staff and food shortages. Interestingly, while Scotland and Northern Ireland continue to be absorbed in protracted internal debates over their relationship with both the UK and the EU, having voted remain rather than leave, McFall's dystopia contemplates a scenario where Westminster itself ousts the Celtic 'fringe', leaving it to wither on the vine.

Instead of Celtic nations determining their own futures, they are disempowered by a hegemonic Anglocentric state that 'built great cement and steel structures that put the Berlin Wall to shame. And they cast out the Celts – sent us back to our hills and our heather and our empty pockets' (p. 23). Lizzie's systematic abuse mirrors a wider social malaise where political polarisation encourages fragmentation, hostile borders, and self/other hierarchies of power. She has a 'Celtic knot' (p. 24) branded into her cheek, reminiscent of the darkest periods of history where others are demarcated and stigmatised as lesser humans and thus subject to corrupt enterprise. As noted, though, her gendered body magnifies Lizzie further as a commodity to be exploited, emphasised with her emblazoned 'tattoo [that] was like a barcode' (p. 58): her 'barcode' reminiscent of consumer produce, she is prey to market forces. Before returning to London, she is deported to Scotland where,

> Like animals released into the wild, we were expected just to survive. Never mind that there was little in the way of government in Scotland any more, and absolutely no welfare state. There were no jobs, no money, no food. No chances. (pp. 26–27)

Despite laudable views on a need for cosmopolitan hope over divisive hate, McFall nevertheless apparently sells Scotland short here. Not only are the Celtic nations trapped in a quagmire of inertia in *Bombmaker*, but Lizzie too is a passive victim of her gender in a patriarchal society. The novel's cataclysmic failure to go it alone echoes Alistair Darling's pro-Union 'Better Together' (rebranded 'Project Fear' by independence supporters) campaign to derail confidence in 2014's pro-independence momentum by cautioning that an independent Scotland could not thrive. Yet, McFall depicts England not as an ally, but as a brutal hostile state, erecting a barrier to 'put the Berlin Wall to shame': reframing of its outlier nations as lesser humans and non-citizens ultimately refutes any notion of 'better together', since Celts are aggressively abandoned in a time of crisis. Likewise, Lizzie's mistreatment portrays an all-too-accurate picture of the corporeal, economic and psychological disenfranchisement of women and girls globally beyond the textual frame.

Despite having the ability to plant bombs and evade capture, Lizzie is helpless in the face of Alex's control, and only manages to escape with the assistance of his brother, Samuel. Initially escaping to Mark, a young man she inadvertently meets on a bus, she feels the need to repay his hospitality by offering her body, which he refuses until they properly date. However, Alex kills Mark before this relationship can be consummated, leaving Samuel as her only viable alternative escape route in her realisation that 'I've swapped one Evans brother for another' (p. 321). Though Samuel protests – 'Don't say that. Lizzie, it's nothing like that' (p. 321) – in essence, her physical dependency and bodily control does indeed shift to him, thus problematically casting Lizzie in the role of passive heroine who needs to be rescued and saved. In McFall's vision, female agency is limited by the strictures of patriarchy, just as Celtic mobility is constrained by territorial confines. Despite their escape to Wales, 'It seemed to me that we'd swapped one terrifying gangster for another in Rhys Davis [...] as much a criminal as he was a freedom-fighter' (p. 372), signalling that she is once again at the mercy of criminal men and a precarious future. Further, even though she is an outcast Scot, as Samuel's freedom-fighter sidekick she is not politically engaged with the process and participation is not initiated by her: 'the cause was noble, but it was Samuel's fight. Not mine. But then, at least I had Samuel' (p. 372). Although a fellow Celt, she does not feel a political investment or affinity, once again reducing her relationship to one based on gender dependency via a heroic male caretaker.

This is hardly a positive model of the female protagonist and begs the question of how it can help to politicise young, particularly Scottish, women, who may already feel disempowered from active citizenship. Potentially, though, McFall's dystopian narrative denies the possibility of a utopian heroine in her fictional lens in order to emphasise the realpolitik of patriarchy and how it actively ensnares women. Angela McRobbie warns that feminist politics is being subsumed in a quagmire of post-feminist consumerism, fuelled by government policies that deceptively disempower young women by encouraging them to compete in masculinist workspaces while becoming increasingly sexualised, and concluding that 'this convergence of commerce and government has quite fatal consequences requiring renewed feminist attention'.[14] McRobbie's observation serves as an apt precursor to McFall's futuristic dystopia where young women's trafficked reduction to body parts indeed has 'fatal consequences': the woman acquired for Alex's sexual pleasure is diminished to 'a blonde; legs bare and ample bosom on display' who is 'crowing with pleasure at having the attention of the most dangerous man in a room full of dangerous men [...] his hands rove over her indecently' (p. 126). When sated, Alex extinguishes her life, underlining the ultimate power imbalance where women's space evaporates 'in a room full of dangerous men'.

Similarly, not only is Lizzie reduced to bodily commodification (her undisclosed surname further contracts her selfhood) and passively inert in the face of adversity, but her country too is stagnant, immobilised by England's authority. Lizzie wonders if Wales is 'Like Scotland. My home. A country ruined, where it was everyone for themselves and survival depended on what you were willing to do' (p. 191), but Samuel responds 'Cardiff's not too bad. It's being held together by the gangs', although the wider country is 'Really bad. People are starving; no one's safe, not even in their own homes' (p. 192). Though Wales and Scotland are hostile terrains, nevertheless Cardiff offers a glimmer of hope, albeit from masculine underworld entities. Scotland, however, is a lost cause, dependent on rescue from a wider Celtic movement, just as Lizzie too is dependent on other Celts. In other words, both nation and heroine are regarded as passively feminine, being acted upon rather than actively navigating a route through the contractions of post-Brexit Britain. As with Norquay's view that women inhabit marginalised spaces, Scotland and Lizzie remain excluded from the social order, but McFall fails to allot Lizzie a resistant space of her own, instead insisting that, in a war of masculinist territorialism, the female body is devoid of autonomy. In terms of nation, despite the depiction of Anglo-aggression, the driving desire is for reunification of the UK, rather than a route towards defiant Celtic independence.

MacPhail's text is more optimistic for cosmopolitical communities in Scotland being driven by adolescent unity rather than fragmentary divisions, though its main focus is on boys' relationships. Mosi reduces 'Girls' to an anomalous trivialised entity, 'the same all over the world' (p. 78), and apparently devoid of any intellectual capacity. Such appalling misogyny from the Somalian boy's perspective is reinforced and legitimised by Glaswegian Patrick's sense of them as mystical: 'Girls. Patrick would never understand them' (p. 94), while he decides that Mosi's behaviour regarding the uncovering of Papa Blood 'was much bigger than girls. Much bigger' (p. 94). Politics, from this perspective, offensively positions itself in terms of gender hierarchies, where male considerations encompass world problems that trivialise girls and reduce their intellect. One could argue that many teenage boys are uninterested in girls as part of their developmental process until they mature, but such dismissal of girls is surely complicit in wide-spread gender inequalities both nationally and globally. As with McFall's text, *Mosi's War* does not utilise the fictional space to envision an empowered female positioning but, rather, to observe the existing squandering of their contribution to global citizenship.

Yet, the business regarded as 'bigger' and thus more important than girls *does* lie in the territory of masculine aggression. Papa Blood is, after all, the notorious male leader within a hostile world of masculinist factions. On the other hand, there is some positive female characterisation. For example, Bliss had 'become something of a heroine after she had arranged with her whole family and all their friends to link arms in front of her best friend Ameira's house and stop a midnight arrest of the whole family' and, as a result of this direct participatory action, 'Ameira's family's asylum application had been upheld' (p. 15). Bliss clearly engages in an emergent citizenship that cements her future foundations in her community and wider world: 'Bliss would be prime minister one day, Mosi was convinced of that' (p. 15). While dismissive of girls, Mosi simultaneously acknowledges Bliss's grass roots political activism, which inspires a wider community to action so that a political decision against asylum seekers is reversed. For MacPhail, it is incumbent for girls to gain political agency in order to create a more gender-balanced world. This correlates with Torney-Purta and Amadeo's view that adolescents can be politically empowered, despite not yet having a vote. Bliss's activism reflects her school's policy of diversity and 'Zero tolerance for any kind of racism, or bullying. Signs everywhere. RESPECT' (p. 16). The school depicted by MacPhail, in turn, responds to Scottish pedagogical policy, since, according to Alison MacKenzie, Penny Enslin and Nicki Hedge,

> Fostering global citizenship is a significant aim of education in Scottish schools [...] Scotland's Curriculum for Excellence (CfE) encourages pupils to have greater awareness of their local, national and global environments, and to value the diversity that these contexts present.[15]

To reiterate Stephens's thesis, such fiction is influential in terms of social policy and the ideological direction of young people as they chart their trajectory towards future citizenship.

Scotland's political system, however, recognised the influence of young people's voices during the independence referendum campaign and notably lowered the franchise to those aged sixteen and above. Similarly, Peter Hopkins posits that 'From the perspective of young people, the Referendum offered them the opportunity to have a say in a major political decision, and this was often the first chance they had to participate in such a significant decision'.[16] Despite the view that civic participation alone cannot empower adolescents, Hopkins regards suffrage as vital to 'enable young people to become fully recognised as political agents and for political geographers to integrate consideration of age – the agency of young people – into their work'.[17] Crucially, however, as Ebbi Ferguson points out, the EU referendum did not extend the vote to encompass adolescents, yet

> Young people – the people who will have to live with this decision for a lifetime – wanted to stay in. And unlike in the Scottish referendum, 16- and 17-year-olds didn't get a say on the most important decision of their lives.[18]

Ferguson continues: 'That's why Brexit is another example of how important it is to secure votes for 16 and 17-year-olds, and how outrageous it was they were shut out of their own future on this occasion.'[19] With reference to adolescent agency in Scotland, this outcome is even more problematic, given that the nation's (to date) resounding yet ineffective will to remain in the EU mirrors the refusal to allow young citizens a vote. In that sense, both Scotland and its adolescents' agency has been infantilised by an uncompromising British electoral system.

Nevertheless, Scotland's and its adolescent citizens' political appetite remains fervently engaged and, in the case of the latter demographic, reading fiction certainly contributes to its sense of social justice, community and global participation. In response to the question 'I find things out most often from ...', John W. Robertson, Neil Blain and Paula Cowan suggest many adolescents regard fiction as paramount: 'The relatively strong showing for books seems at first encouraging for those who worry over the decline of reading. However, the choice of reading was very heavily dominated by fantasy'.[20] Fiction, then, is a source of knowledge and information for teenagers and, as such, the work of 'tweenage' and YA writers is crucial in helping to shape the path of future citizens.

Despite Robertson, Blain and Cowan's regarding fantasy in a rather negative light, I have argued elsewhere that it is not an escapist genre but, rather, offers a space of engagement with concepts of citizenship.[21] The likes of Bertagna's *Exodus* trilogy firmly respond to very real political, environmental and cultural concerns, so it is utterly unhelpful to denigrate such a significant literary format given its crucial role in encouraging adolescent activism and citizenship. Bertagna's heroine, Mara, is particularly important politically in providing a positive and active role model for girls, demonstrating that they too need a voice in mapping the trajectory of the nation. Adult and children's fantasy writer Ursula Le Guin would certainly take umbrage at the above study's dismissal of fantasy's socio-political impact, arguing 'We read books to find out who we are. What other people, real or imaginary, do and think and feel [...] is an essential guide to our understanding of what we ourselves are and may become.'[22] Fiction, including fantasy, according to Le Guin, becomes a bridge that links young people to others, helping them to empathise and, in turn, to develop a sense of self.

Similarly, Maria Nikolajeva's study of cognitive criticism in children's literature concludes that 'Novice readers have limited life experience of emotions; therefore, fiction can offer vicarious emotional experience for readers to partake of, long before they may be exposed to it in real life.'[23]

In order to be an active citizen, adolescent reading is imperative, since it enhances and extends their political engagement, just as the act of reading invokes physiological shifts known as cortical remapping. The fiction itself becomes an intellectual, creative and geopolitical map through which young readers navigate their journeys to adulthood. YA fiction is aimed at a readership that is also susceptible to cortical remapping from exposure to external stimulus, such as developing knowledge through reading. Thus, rather than being a fixed, static entity, the brain's malleable capability of redeveloping one's mind-set is comparable to Scotland's trajectory of dynamic heterogeneity. Such cortically and geopolitically cartographical fiction charts Stephens's 'struggle for young people's minds' by opening neural pathways that envision an empathetic and ethical future potential. As such, the act of reading for a young person is a physiological as well as political neural pathway towards cultural enhancement and remapping. Bogdan Draganski and his co-authors' article, 'Temporal and Spatial Dynamics of Brain Structure Changes during Extensive Learning', found that medical students' grey matter increased significantly within a matter of months due to a greater acquisition of knowledge. They conclude,

> It is reasonable to assume that plasticity is a characteristic of the nervous system that evolved for coping with changes in the environment. Understanding changes in brain structure as a result of *learning and adaptation* is pivotal in understanding the characteristic flexibility of our brain to adapt.[24]

Children's and YA fiction, then, are clearly fundamental contributors to cortical remapping within such a vibrant malleable period. It becomes a viable intellectual tool or neural pathway that offers the realpolitik of social change. If reading medical books can remap the brain exponentially, presumably fiction allows for an even more interesting cortical remapping, given that it offers dialogical space for the reader to intervene and engage with the text rather than simply digesting the rote learning of facts. With that in mind, the intellectual trajectory of such fiction within contemporary Scottish culture is pivotal to comprehending adolescent agency.

Post-devolution and, more recently, post-referendum Scotland is ideally positioned culturally, politically and geographically to generate a dynamic space of unlimited potential that allows children's and YA fiction to thrive. Gardiner, above, regards post-devolution Scottish fiction as 'a literature of effect and becoming rather than one of static assumptions' so that 'the minor is invariably more literary than the major'.[25] Scottish literature, then, is dynamic and 'becoming' rather than static, much like neuroplasticity. Scottish children's and YA literature is doubly dynamic given its target readers are prone to the malleability of cortical remapping influenced by reading fiction. Rosi Braidotti also utilises the Deleuzian concept of endless becoming to discuss cosmopolitanism, where she regards the subject as a mobile and philosophically nomadic citizen who rejects static masculinist territorialism in favour of 'multiple belongings' to the world,[26] just as adolescent heroes and heroines often embark upon journeys. Such fluid resistance to territorialism, in many ways, maps the journeys of maturation encouraged in McFall's and MacPhail's literary imaginings.

Adolescent Scottish literature is a viable political force that often resists static assumptions and instead strives for a cosmopolitical outlook of fluid endless becoming. Far from utopian impracticality, fiction aimed towards future citizens will inevitably contain aspirational facets that, ultimately, encourage them to perceive a cosmopolitan outlook while interrogating the restrictive hegemonies beyond the texts. Creativity and imagination are the very seeds needed to envisage a world that offers spatial possibilities beyond the current impasses of globalisation, including neoliberalism and what the cosmopolitan theorist, Ulrich Beck, refers to as 'world risk society' like climate change or terrorism.[27] Such fiction, then, is politically engaging with contemporary concerns and challenges in order to navigate towards a trajectory of ethical possibilities. It maps Scotland's future by charting journeys that develop new ways of thinking for the nation and, in turn, communities that can sustain its readers as tomorrow's cosmopolitan citizens. O'Neill's earlier consideration of devolution as 'a journey without a reliable map' is comparative to Caribbean-American lesbian writer Audre Lorde's observation that 'What you chart is already where you've been. But where we are going, there is no chart yet.'[28] The journey becomes necessary for the outsider as a dynamically mobile experience which rejects the phallocratic fixity of the reliable map in favour of the unwritten plasticity that Braidotti would associate with nomadic thought. Intellectual development, then, depends upon the journey which, pedagogically, is the act of reading YA fiction so that Scotland's future citizens can open their remapped minds towards cosmopolitanism and resist insular isolationism.

It is through narrative, according to Benedict Anderson's 1983 *Imagined Communities*,[29] that we understand our identity in regard to nationhood. Stories help us to imagine by presenting a particular version of that community. Therefore, women's writing can offer an alternative perspective on that national imagined identity and help to shape a new direction that is inclusive of those hitherto marginalised from its dominant hegemony. As Aileen Christianson and Alison Lumsden argue, it '*cuts across* patriarchal constructions of Scotland to suggest alternative "imaginings" or constructions of nationhood and their relationship to it than those offered by their male counterparts. Frequently, it is women writers within national cultures who seemingly disrupt homogeneity.'[30] If women are redrawing the literary map of Scotland, then the way the nation is imagined is becoming more heterogeneous and mobile, and that is surely vital when plotting adolescent citizenship. Since YA and tweenage fiction is often written by women, it is a particularly important voice in that remapping as it harnesses the intentions of the nation's future citizens and encourages them to participate fully in Scotland's geopolitical journey.

Adolescent fiction's cosmopolitan vision offers a bridge between different communities that endeavours to accept diversity while seeking common ground. Though Mosi and Patrick are from very different backgrounds, their coincidence spatially and temporally in Glasgow allows those differences to contract in favour of a burgeoning friendship. As with Breslin's consideration of sectarianism and asylum seekers in *Divided City*, MacPhail urges her readers to humanise rather than demonise others. Initially the gulf between both boys is apparently insurmountable: though Mosi 'lived in the same block of flats as Patrick [...] they hardly saw each other except in class' (p. 4). Again, the school becomes a space where differences are pedagogically challenged to offer students alternative positions from dominant narratives that are fuelled by the media. Despite the school's attempts to alter the neural pathway of entrenched mind-sets, some still ventriloquise a hegemonic mandate: 'They spoke, some of them, as if the life of an asylum seeker meant nothing. As if asylum seekers didn't feel as other people felt' (p. 4). Similarly, according to Judith Butler, Western media manipulation 'frames' foreign nationals into a position that dehumanises them so that their demise is regarded impassively. For instance, during conflict, populations are divided 'into those who are grievable and those who are not. An ungrievable life is one that cannot be mourned because it has never been lived, that is, it has never counted as a life at all.'[31] MacPhail's narrative indicates the importance of fictional texts to shape adolescent thinking and act as counter-narratives to the dominant discourses embedded by media. Likewise, McFall's fiction demonstrates how uneasy self/other narratives within Britain could easily be framed to dehumanise and disempower those on the peripheries.

While in *Mosi's War*, the death of a Somalian asylum seeker is considered in a similar light to that depicted by Butler, since he 'meant nothing', in *Bombmaker* the 'ungrievable life' is brought much closer to home geopolitically. McFall considers the divisions existing *within* a populace that are then magnified and legitimised by government and media measures, so that former British citizens are regarded as 'animals' (p. 26). The narrative directly considers this outrage: 'I stared at her. She was one of *them*: the people who thought the government had got it right' (p. 25) in its partition of borders. The officer is one of 'The people who were quite happy to cut off millions and see them living in poverty and squalor like some Third World country' (p. 25). Lizzie's observation here simultaneously focuses upon the dehumanisation of Celtic nationals and the accepted treatment of non-Western states, though Lizzie remains problematically ambiguous about whether she endorses the dehumanisation of the 'Third World' or if she sees an affinity with it. What is clear, though, is how rapidly one's humanity and citizenship can be removed, just as the officer 'frowned, annoyed that I wouldn't respond, wouldn't apologise for my existence' (p. 25), regarding her intrusion as an unseemly blot on England's landscape so legitimising her expulsion, since she is 'standing in a country that no longer wanted' (p. 26) her. As with Butler's concern over media manipulation of reality, Celts are represented as dangerous sub-humans who must be cleansed from the land and 'shot without trial' (p. 70) if found to be encroaching upon England's borders. Lizzie notes, 'If he was to believe the news reports running almost nightly on EBC, I should be dangerous, untrustworthy, devious. Certainly not someone you should welcome into your home' (p. 207). By ratcheting up hostility and fear, the media ensures that Celts are regarded as a monstrous threat rather than ordinary people, so that their deaths are seen as the necessary protection of civilians against wild others.

To ensure that its ideology succeeds, any insurrection is subject to surveillance by 'the big brother communications monitoring the government claimed it didn't do' (p. 111), clearly signalling that this does occur in such an Orwellian society. As well as facial branding, Lizzie is in danger of being exposed because of her 'Scottish accent' and her inability to be 'the master of a convincing English accent' (p. 218). Already dispossessed, her Scottish voice is silenced in a state that only legitimises Anglo-dialects. Yet centralising her accent in the novel ensures that Scotland's voice dialogically engages with British politics and culture, refusing to allow its heteroglossic diversity to be silenced in a monotonous dystopian void. Much like Gardiner's view of post-devolution Scottish 'minor literature' becoming more significant as a marginalised voice, Lizzie's dialect and intonation renders her more impactful within a society dominated by the 'major' voice. As the focaliser and narrator of events, her Scottish perspective overturns the dominant Anglo-hegemony through which she navigates, conscious of her otherness yet disparaging of panoptical state power. It is here that Lizzie has the potential to inhabit Norquay's powerful outsider gender position – robbed of a stable homeland and, an illegal alien in England's social order, both her body and nationality are in jeopardy – where her voice provides a dialogic counter-narrative to challenge and overturn dominant Anglo-hegemony in *Bombmaker*'s war of words between Anglo hegemony and its others. Like Norquay's use of Kristeva's semiotic disruptive site, it is in 'the house of fiction'[32] that Lizzie finally finds a Woolfian room of one's own that empowers her to critique and resist marginalisation as a Scottish woman by creating a narrative space.

McFall's depiction of Lizzie's struggle in a dystopian state responds to Roberta Seelinger Trites's comments regarding the YA fictional format which concerns itself 'with investigating how the individual exists within society'.[33] According to Trites, YA fiction simultaneously arises alongside postmodernism's interrogation of dominant hegemonies and identity politics. As a genre that probes social constructions, it is inevitable that it will concern itself with adolescent agency as a means of challenging discourses of power and seeking to find alternative routes for emerging citizens. In a world where young people feel that their voice is often silenced, it is imperative that fiction can open up dialogic spaces that can envisage empowerment in the face of adversity. Ultimately, though, *Bombmaker* never fully articulates Lizzie's capacity to resist a hostile environment, since she is too often out-manoeuvred by gender restrictions. In a discussion of Canadian fiction and adolescent agency, Benjamin Lefebvre concludes: 'By focusing primarily on a protagonist's oppression, and ending at the moment when newfound freedom appears to be achieved, these texts signal that the quest for agency, belonging, and citizenship is always an ongoing project'.[34] Likewise, Lizzie's precarious freedom is intertwined with the tensions of adolescent agency and her relations to citizenship, exacerbated further by concerns over ethnicity and gender. More widely, adolescent agency will always be 'an ongoing project' of endless becoming that journeys through concerns like nationhood, sexuality, gender, and ethnicity. The lack of gay or lesbian characters in both *Bombmaker* and *Mosi's War* is a reminder that fictional spaces of queer representation pose a continual struggle for adolescent agency.

The Scottish Government's 2014 independence white paper was entitled 'Scotland's Future', and it is timely to consider fiction that also directs itself towards the nation's future citizens. Both nation and literature are clearly remapping the possible routes of Scotland's journey and the societal impact of that fiction is integral to a fuller comprehension of adolescent agency.

CHAPTER NINE

From Fairy Cauldrons to *An Gruffalo*: The Development and Challenges of Scottish Gaelic Children's Literature

Mairi Kidd

If John Newbery's *A Little Pretty Pocket-Book* (1744) is accepted to be the first book specifically for children's leisure reading, then young speakers of Scottish Gaelic had almost two centuries longer to wait before they received their own first book published to entertain young minds. While Calum MacPhàrlain's (Malcolm MacFarlane's) *Companach na Cloinne: Leabhran Sgoil anns am Bheil Sgeòil Thaitneach* ('The Children's Companion: A School Booklet with Pleasant Stories', 1912) was explicitly a school book (reader),[1] J. G. MacKay's *Sgeulachd a' Choire* ('The Tale of the Cauldron') issued in 1927, with sixteen coloured plates reproducing paintings by Gordon Browne, R.I., was different.[2] Prior to this publication, even explicitly didactic materials were limited, as the 1872 Education (Scotland) Act and subsequent developments in the nineteenth century made limited or no provision for the language.[3]

Sgeulachd a' Choire is a traditional story marketed by its publisher as one of the 'Ancient Legends of the Scottish Gael'. Perhaps it is natural that the oral tradition should furnish children with their first published work for, while they were deprived of written materials, Gaelic-speaking youngsters did have access to one of the richest oratures in western Europe. Perhaps it would be more accurate to say that *some* of them did; the degree to which some communities' religious traditions may have suppressed transmission of secular story and song is unclear. The image, however, is a common one, powerfully portrayed for example in Ruaraidh MacThòmais's (Derick Thomson's) poem 'Am Bodach Ròcais' ('The Scarecrow'), in which an evangelist enters the cèilidh house:

    Bha fear a sud
    ag innse sgeulachd air Conall Gulban
    is reodh na faclan air a bhilean.
    Bha boireannach 'na suidh' air stòl
    ag òran, 's thug e 'n toradh ás a' cheòl.[4]

There was a man there / telling a story about Conall Gulban / and the words froze on his lips. / A woman was sitting on a stool / Singing, and he took the goodness out of the music.

The oral tradition is essentially a commons, and it is not possible to point to many genres as being specifically 'for children'. To borrow Joanne L. Lynn's framing, lullabies have long been reckoned 'runes to ward off sorrow';[5] in Gaelic as in other traditions, themes vary widely and indicate that the song was as much for the comfort and enjoyment of the singer as for the child it was intended to soothe. Counting rhymes and other 'nursery rhymes' must be reckoned to qualify as the property of children, but traditions of mouth music and song often overlap, and were not limited to children. Cumulative tales such as 'Biorachan Beag agus Biorachan Mòr' seem particularly child-friendly (the name is not immediately translatable but is translated by J. Derrick McClure as 'Big Tappietoorie and Wee Tappietoorie' in one adaptation).[6]

Wonder tales are plentiful, including many familiar friends we meet across the world, and the Gaelic variants are loved, as everywhere, by adults and children. 'Leth-cheannach Nighean a' Chait' ('The Half Cat-Head Lady'), for example, is instantly recognisable as a version of the 'Cinderella' type (ATU 510A), 'Lasair Gheug' ('Flame of Branches') as 'Snow White' (ATU 709) and 'Na Trì Lèintean Canaich' ('The Three Shirts of Bog-cotton') as the story known in Grimm as 'The Six Swans' (ATU 451). *Sgeulachd a' Choire* derives from the extensive Gaelic store of fairy-lore and tales of other supernatural creatures such as kelpies or water-bulls. Some of this lore may have had particular significance for children, serving to warn against a particular stretch of water or the dangers of making promises of silence to strangers, for example, but again it was most definitely a tradition shared with adults.

Some material from oral tradition has been made available in the modern era, initially in hardcover collections intended for adult mediation such as *Oideas na Cloinne* ('Children's Learning'),[7] and *Aithris is Oideas* ('Telling and Learning').[8] A number of illustrated collections and stand-alone stories have been published for children's own use. Examples include:

- *Air do Bhonnagan a Ghaoil* ('On your Bare Feet, Sweetheart'),[9] a rhyme anthology
- *Bha Siod ann Reimhid* ('Once Upon a Time'),[10] *Am Bloigh Beag le Beannachd* ('The Little Portion with a Blessing'),[11] and *Mar a Chuala Mise E* ('How I Heard It'),[12] all collections of retellings

- *Am Peata Bàn* ('The White Pet Sheep'),[13] *Lasair Dhearg* ('Red Flame'),[14] and *Conachar agus an Torc* ('Conachar and the Boar'),[15] all stand-alone adaptations of individual stories.

International distribution of many tales has allowed for some serendipitous versioning; for example Malachy Doyle and Jane Ray's beautiful adaptation of an Irish story for Walker Books, *The Bold Boy*, relates closely to the Gaelic tale 'Bodach an t-silein eòrna' ('The old man with the grain of barley') and was published in translation as *An Gille Bragail*.[16] In the other direction, Gaelic has perhaps enriched children's books in English most through the seal-wife tales it shares with the Northern Isles and Scandinavia, a topic discussed by Sarah Dunnigan in her chapter in this volume, and which have inspired creators as diverse as Anglo-Indian author Sita Brahmachari, illustrator and wildlife artist Jackie Morris and picture-book creator Mordecai Gerstein in the USA.

Original Works and Gairm

Publishing for Gaelic readers received a huge injection of energy with the establishment of the periodical *Gairm* (the name means 'a Call') in 1952, followed by the establishment of a publishing list under the same name, which included children's books. The poet, writer and academic Ruaraidh MacThòmais (Derick Thomson, 1921–2012) was at the helm of *Gairm* until cessation in 2002 and was a key figure in developing writing and publishing.

As a publishing house, Gairm collaborated with educators on an early series of illustrated books about professions – *Am Fear-smàlaidh* ('The Fireman'), *Fear nam Fiaclan* ('The Dentist'), etc.[17] – which had particularly striking mid-century design. These were a high point in visual terms, although presumably dated quickly; design and production were otherwise more basic. During the 1970s and 1980s, short novellas for readers aged around 8–12 or in their early teens were also issued. Writers included Iain Mac a' Ghobhainn (Iain Crichton Smith, 1928–1998) and Maoilios Caimbeul (Myles Campbell, b. 1944), both well-known writers/poets in Gaelic more generally and, in Mac a' Ghobhainn's case, in English also. Both contributed short novellas in the science fiction genre, *Iain am Measg nan Reultan* ('John Among the Stars')[18] and *Clann a' Phroifeasair* ('The Professor's Children') respectively.[19] Mac a' Ghobhainn also contributed stories for younger readers.[20]

Recognising that market failure exists in Gaelic, Thomson also established Comhairle nan Leabhraichean/the Gaelic Books Council in 1968. The Comhairle disbursed funds and other support to writers and publishers, underpinned all further activity from writers and publishers over the next two decades, and continues to support activity today.

Until the mid-1970s, most children's book activity was through Gairm and Inverness-based Club Leabhar (the name means 'Book Club'), which issued a number of original and versioned titles. The former included Eilidh Watt's *Latha a' Choin Duibh* ('The Black Dog's Day')[21] and *Tothan* by Fionnlagh MacLeòid.[22] The latter included Judith Kerr's classic *Mog* in translation.[23] Later Leabhraichean Beaga (the name means 'Little Books') and others would join the ranks of publishers issuing work for children.

'Ever increasing, urgent needs'

In 1975 came the establishment of Comhairle nan Eilean Siar/Western Isles Council, and almost immediately the Pròiseact Foghlam Dà-Chànanach/ Bilingual Education Project was begun, aiming to reintroduce Gaelic as a holistic language of education, versus a 'subject' to be studied by native Gaelic-speaking children who were otherwise taught in English. The Project ran into an immediate difficulty with regard to materials with which teachers might teach: there were almost no books available. The race was on to fill the gap, and the directors initially took a pragmatic attitude informed by the pedagogical approach of the Project. Teachers and children created their own materials including stories using paper, pencils and basic technology such as slide cameras, and these were shared by such means as were available. An art teacher was seconded to help lay out materials prior to circulation. The overall effect, however, concerned the directors, who considered there was risk in Gaelic being perceived as a 'hand-me-down' language.[24] With the guidance of Iain Moireach (John Murray, 1938–2018), a Project director who had previously been an employee of Comhairle nan Leabhraichean, the Highlands and Islands Development Board was approached for support and Gaelic cultural organisation An Comunn Gàidhealach issued eight books in 1976 and 1977. These included *Tiugainn Cuairt* ('Let's Go for a Walk'),[25] and the *Cliath* ('Web') series, which combined storytelling with nature education and included a particularly terrifying title in which an unfortunate boy is kidnapped by an eagle; *Uilleam Bàn agus an Iolaire* ('Fair-haired William and the Eagle').[26]

These titles were all original; next the Project turned to versioning. In partnership with Jordanhill College and Longman Education, the *Monster* series by Ellen Blance and Ann Cook was secured for translation and appeared as *Spàgan*.[27] These books were immensely well-loved, not least, perhaps, because of the illustrations of their main characters – an amiable purple monster couple – by Quentin Blake. A reissue in 2009 perhaps coincided with the offspring of the original readership reaching the appropriate age to read the books themselves.

By this point it was clear that a formal structure was required to manage publishing output and Acair ('anchor') was established in 1977. The company rapidly issued a clutch of three original illustrated stories,[28] translations of illustrated retellings of Bible stories,[29] and an early reading scheme, *Grian* ('Sun').[30] The pedagogical approach of the Project continued to inform the books produced. *Grian* offered children not only materials reflecting their own environment, but actually drew from their own artwork. Titles such as *Làraidh agus Digear* ('Lorry and Digger') and *Searrach Èirisgeidh* ('The Eriskay Pony') were produced quickly and cheaply but, despite the basic production values, are fondly remembered by Western Isles pupils of the era.

The Bilingual Project staff and advisors themselves authored a significant number of titles during and after the Project and including fiction, picturebooks and non-fiction titles. Perhaps most interesting among these are *Mac an t-Srònaich* ('Stronach') by Dr Fionnlagh MacLeòid (Finlday Macleod) and Aonghas MacDhòmhnaill (Angus MacDonald),[31] and *Stamh* ('Tangle') by Anna NicDhòmhnaill and Aonghas MacDhòmhnaill.[32] The latter is a dreamy picture book with laminaria hyperborea (a type of kelp) as a central character and explores life under the sea. It is interestingly, if not wholly successfully, designed to make use of both black and white and colour spreads, presumably to reduce costs. The former explores the ways in which bogeyman narratives function to offer adults and children a 'safe' experience of fear. It takes as its starting point the semi-mythical outlaw murderer of Lewis, Alexander Stronach. Both books are experimental, particularly *Mac an t-Sròanaich*, in which the 'real' Stronach transforms in the artwork into an abstract, see-through figment of the imagination. Like *Spàgan*, it was reissued a generation later. Gaelic has produced few such original picturebooks since, presumably since the costs of artwork, design and print are prohibitive.

From its inception, the Bilingual Project was aware that lack of reading materials was especially acute once children reached the upper end of the primary school. It was decided that the bilingual nature of the Project should inform approaches; children would read fiction in English, completing their exploration bilingually, and would moreover have access to Gaelic-language radio adaptations broadcast by the BBC over several weeks. Rosemary Sutcliff's *Mark of the Horse Lord* and Ivan Southall's *Hills End* were both broadcast in this way.[33] Gaelic television saw its first ever children's broadcast in 1977, and TV and radio would remain key means of dissemination of story, poetry, song, and broader educational content.

Acair to Stòrlann

During the 1980s and early 1990s, Acair became the pre-eminent publisher of Gaelic books for adults and children. The aforementioned original books remained available, and versioning also began in earnest. (There had always been a degree of versioning in the form of 'pasteovers', translations laid out to cover original English text in picturebooks and distributed to schools either ready stuck in books or for cutting and pasting; these were almost universally disliked as a format although the translations were generally of high quality.)

Early translations from English by Acair included Eric Hill's *Spot* series,[34] and Carole Watson's *The House / The Shop / The Town*.[35] There was a short experimentation with versioning from Welsh, which saw a series from publisher Y Lolfa about a small witch[36] issued in Gaelic as 'An Stobag Bheag' ('The Little Granddaughter').[37] This had the obvious advantage of making new titles available to children which were not also available in their other language of English. (This approach was also adopted in Ireland, where many of the translated titles published by government-funded publisher An Gúm were sourced from Russia. This is, of course, heavily dependent on having access to an individual able to read both languages and efforts eventually foundered on both sides of the Irish Sea.)

For older children a range of easy readers/reading scheme extension titles originally published in English as the 'Yellow Bananas' were versioned. These included titles by Michael Morpurgo, Joan Aitken, Penelope Lively and many more well-known names from the world of children's literature in English.[38] These were followed by a small range of original Gaelic texts around the same reading/interest level. Authors included Maoilios Caimbeul (Myles Campbell, b. 1944), Anna Latharna NicIllIosa (Anne Lorne Gillies, b. 1944), and the aforementioned team from the Bilingual Project.[39]

Core school texts, meanwhile, were issued by specific education groupings involving the growing number of local authorities by then in receipt of Specific Grants for Gaelic Education to deliver Gaelic-medium schooling. These arrangements led, in 1999, to the establishment of Stòrlann Nàiseanta na Gàidhlig/The National Gaelic Education Resource Agency to procure, publish or otherwise bring about the production of resources for circulation to Gaelic-medium schools under a pre-publication purchase agreement with local authorities. This affected the fortunes of Acair for a time and resulted in increased focus on island and Gaelic history in their list, including titles in English.

Stòrlann's relatively generous budgets resulted in significant output in a short space of time, with activity initially focused on core literacy resources including a version of the *Storyworlds* reading scheme from Heinemann Education (now publishing as a Pearson imprint). This may have occasioned a level of withdrawal from children's book activity by other players, perhaps on the basis that responsibility for 'children's books' had been assigned to Stòrlann and therefore that other areas should take priority in the allocation of already limited resources. While the landscape had changed dramatically from the days of the Bilingual Project, however, it was not true that 'children's books' were in a particularly healthy state, and nor would it be fair to represent children's leisure reading as the responsibility of Stòrlann. In fact, a sensible policy decision was taken not to supply Storyworlds to the general public, as these were not intended for leisure reading or home use.

How We Live Now

The imbalance identified by the Bilingual Project team as long ago as the 1970s persists today, which is to say that younger children are relatively better-served than their older peers.

Acair actively publishes a strong list of picturebooks versioned from English, supplemented by a small number from Irish. Translations from English include modern classics such as *The Gruffalo* and other titles by Julia Donaldson and her regular collaborators,[40] plus newer names such as Joseph Coelho and Fiona Lumbers,[41] and Scottish artists with trade presence such as Ross Collins[42] and Morag Hood.[43] The company has become something of a specialist in picture book co-editioning and the quality is high, although there is some evidence that versioning into Gaelic renders text more complex. The ten syllables of 'A mouse took a walk in the deep dark wood …'[44] become twenty in Gaelic to preserve the rhyme:

Chaidh luchag bheag nan casan aotrom a-steach dhan choille dhorcha na h-aonar ... (Literally *the little light-footed mouse went into the dark forest alone ...*).[45]

This complexity perhaps contributes to the reality that market categories in Gaelic do not perfectly align with the same categories in English, so that picturebooks that might be categorised as 3–5s in English are generally categorised as 5–8s in Gaelic. Also relevant in this context is the fact that children reading in Gaelic are likely to be (a) second-language speakers learning Gaelic by immersion in primary school and/or (b) affected by a lack of access to books and media by comparison to that available in English, influencing the speed at which they acquire confidence and automaticity in reading.

Acair are generally the Gaelic publishing partner for Scotland-wide book initiatives such as Bookbug bags. To an outside eye, this is an area that appears indicative of a lack of attention to Gaelic at the decision-making stage. The worst culprit is perhaps a picture book called 'Tha Mucan-Mara air Bus',[46] which makes no sense whatsoever once translated from English, where 'The Whales on the Bus' may provide a pun based on a well-known children's song, but one undeliverable in translation. On the other hand, well-handled translation can produce creative results. A particularly charming example is the translation of 'Hugless Douglas' by David Melling, published by Acair.[47] The Gaelic title *Cudail Chan Fhaigh Mi* (literally 'A Cuddle I Cannot Get') plays on a widely-known and much-loved Gaelic song of loss and longing, 'Cadal Chan Fhaigh Mi' (literally 'Sleep I Cannot Get').

A small number of original picturebooks from Acair include Mairi C. NicAmhlaigh (Marie C. MacAulay) and Robin Bans's collaborations about a little girl named Teàrlag and her various associates,[48] and artist Catrìona NicIlleDhuibh's (Catrìona Black's) story about one boy and his toy tractor, *An Tractar agus an Liobht* ('The Tractor and the Lift').[49]

It might be noted at this juncture that Gaelic books are inclined to remain available very much longer than their English-language counterparts, as even a small co-edition or straight print run is likely to be at a level that takes many years to sell through. Titles by companies such as Leabhraichean Beaga, which are not active at the present time, are still available to purchase, sometimes decades after publication.

'Commercial' (i.e. non-educational) materials for the upper end of the 5–8 category, are limited. A number of small and micro-publishers have illustrated books which are not precisely picturebooks, and in which content is perhaps better aligned to the slightly older ages of children reading. These include titles by Ceitidh Hutton,[50] Lisa Storey,[51] and Gracie Summers.[52] Production values of these books, perhaps inevitably, cannot match trade titles in English.

Readers aged 8–12 are, again, not especially well served in the general market; 'Middle Grade' fiction does not really exist. Conscious of this fact, in 2015 two Gaelic academics and the present author founded Cuilean Craicte ('Mad Puppy'). A Community Interest Company, Cuilean Craicte supplied new titles through a crowd-funded bookclub model whereby subscribing families paid up-front for six titles, and their monies covered rights, digital print and (token) design fees. Translation, distribution, management and communications were all handled on a voluntary basis by the directors. Rights were sourced from dyslexia-specialist publishing house Barrington Stoke (the present author was then Managing Director there), as the short-extent, illustrated, high-interest/low reading-age books in which the company specialises suited both print budgets and accessibility considerations for second-language Gaelic-speaking children.

Cuilean Craicte issued two seasons of six titles to a membership of over two hundred families, publishing each one monthly and posting copies direct to subscribers with extras such as badges and colouring sheets. Video readings of first chapters and of related crafts were also created, and multiple events delivered at festivals including Edinburgh International Book Festival and Aye Write. Many of the original authors supported these, including a memorable event featuring Chris Bradford, author of *Young Samurai* (Puffin), whose 'Ninja' series for Barrington Stoke was a significant hit among Cuilean Craicte's readers (that year World Book Day saw many Gaelic-medium ninjas).[53] After the second season, a hardcover translation of Michael Morpurgo's 'Clare and the Captain',[54] illustrated in full colour by Catherine Rayner, was issued as a one-off. A third season of six books was supported by Creative Scotland's Open Fund, allowing directors to pay other translators to produce two of the six works, and an assistant to carry out the mailings which by then amounted to some 1,500 parcels. Their own translation, editorial and management (including fund-seeking) remained unpaid and the decision was taken to wind up the project as levels of activity were not sustainable on a volunteer basis. The last title issued by Cuilean Craicte was a translation of an *Oor Wullie* annual, *Uilleam Againne*.[55] It should be noted that Cuilean Craicte was unusual only in the intensity of its publishing schedule; much Gaelic publishing activity, other than Acair's and Stòrlann's, is unpaid or largely unpaid, and dependent on what might be termed the 'garden shed' model of distribution.

Teens have seen a similar concerted effort to address the gaps in their available reading material with a small series of novellas from Acair, supported by Comhairle nan Leabhraichean, that additionally sought to support the development of new writers with debuts by Ishi NicIlleathain (Ishi MacLean),[56] and Elaine NicFhearghais (Elaine Ferguson).[57] The strongest voice among the cohort is perhaps that of Catrìona Lexy Chaimbeul (Catrìona Lexy Campbell), who has authored children's books for a range of market categories and seeks to experiment in genres such as dystopian sci-fi.[58] Historically, some translation from Irish has been attempted for teens, including Ré Ó Laighléis's book *Punk*, published in Gaelic by Leabhraichean Beaga.[59]

A Gaelic Proverb: 'Is e obair-latha tòiseachadh, ach is e obair beatha crìochnachadh' ('beginning is a day's work, but finishing is a lifetime's')

At the present time, then, young Gaelic readers receive an exciting and colourful introduction to the language – if one that may challenge their language capacity – but almost fifty years on from the Bilingual Project, we have not solved the unfortunate dilemma that, as children's reading skills increase, books for them to read dry up. The situation is better in school, certainly, but no matter how well school supports reading for pleasure, all literacy development initiatives understand that reading is not just for school. If we are to secure the future of Gaelic, there is no question but that we must do more to ensure young readers have access to many, many more books deserving of their leisure time and attention.

CHAPTER TEN

Scottish Children's Picturebooks Within a European and Global Context

Penni Cotton

Introduction

There has been a significant rise in interest and research in the domain of visual and multimodal literacies which converges with discovery of the distinguished and neglected tradition of Scottish children's picturebooks. This chapter will address the previously ignored genre and place its advancement within both a European and global context. Distinctively Scottish elements of certain Scottish picturebooks will be discussed, alongside linguistic, literary and cultural aspects of individual visual narratives. Attention will be given to how a number of publishers have begun to focus on the development of specifically cultural features in their books, including setting, language, appearance, and the themes of heritage, change, continuity and modernisation. This will be linked to the ways in which young readers engage with enmeshed and entwined texts. Finally, reference will be made to current trends in visual texts, drawing attention to increasingly popular comics, graphic novels and new digital interactive picturebooks. For the purposes of this chapter, Barbara Bader's definition of a picturebook is followed:

> a text, illustrations, total design; an item of manufacture and a commercial product; a social, cultural, historical document; and foremost an experience for a child. As an art form it hinges on the interdependence of pictures and words, on the simultaneous display of two facing pages, and on the drama of the turning page.[1]

Over twenty years ago, at a European children's literature conference in France, Alan Hill was asked to share his thoughts on Scottish picturebooks that would enable children throughout Europe to understand more about ways of life in Scotland. In his contribution, he mentions distinguished picturebook authors like Frank Rogers and Debi Gliori but suggests that there are very few Scottish picturebook creators whose work is 'distinctively Scottish'.² He says that only the works of Mairi Hedderwick and Aileen Paterson regularly fall 'within a Scottish setting or cultural tradition'. In 1996, he placed emphasis on the fact that Scotland provided at that time 'barely ten percent of the total British market' and authors and publishers understandably tended 'to set their sights upon the greater sales potential of the wider market of Great Britain'.³

Picturebooks are a total design, incorporating the interaction between text and illustration, hence the joining of the two words, and their production worldwide has greatly advanced since the 1990s – the Scottish market is no exception. It is good to see that, in the twenty-first century, Mairi Hedderwick and Aileen Paterson are still producing wonderfully Scottish visual narratives, but many new picturebook creators have emerged. One only has to look at the Scottish Book Trust website to see the abundance of quality Scottish picturebooks that are now available. Three new publishing houses have appeared which promote Scottish culture. For example, Floris's 'Kelpies' catalogue indicates just how many new Scottish picturebooks are available from one publisher and also provides an excellent annotated map of Scotland showing exactly where almost a hundred of their books originate. These include traditional tales as well as more contemporary Scottish rhymes. The focus of Itchy Coo publishing, on the other hand, is mainly on the Scots language because they want to bring it to life for children, young people, and their teachers by revolutionising attitudes towards Scots-language teaching in schools. In contrast, Birlinn publishes a wide range of Scottish books, both for children and adults, and in recent years has begun to produce e-books.

In order to place Scottish picturebooks within a European and then more global context, it is necessary to take a brief look at some of the projects that have helped to promote the genre more widely.

Picturebook Collections in Europe and Beyond

In 1996, the first European picturebook collection (EPBC) was created with funding from the European Commission (EC) 'to help children throughout the European Union (EU) to understand more about each other and what it means to be European'.⁴ The idea was that they should do this by: reading the visual narratives of carefully selected European picturebooks; focusing on the universal themes that permeate the books; looking at the similarities between languages and cultures; and accepting/celebrating the differences. The Collection comprises twenty picturebooks from the fifteen countries that were then part of the EU. Initially, one book was chosen to represent each country, including four from the component parts of the United Kingdom. The book chosen from Scotland was Mairi Hedderwick's *Katie Morag and the New Pier*.[5] It was deemed extremely important to include Scottish visual narratives in a European collection of picturebooks to try to help all European children, including those in the rest of the UK, to realise not only that Scotland is an important part of Great Britain but also that it has its own culture, literature and languages. The same applied for Wales and, when using the Collection in Welsh schools, teachers said that one of the main reasons they wanted to use it was to help their children to see that Wales is an important part of both the UK and Europe, and that their language was not the only one that was different from English.

The EPBC was shortly followed by several other EU funded projects. The first of these (2001–04) was ESET, an online European teacher-training course in several languages which uses the EPBC picturebooks to promote cultural understanding. Alongside this, BARFIE, an intercultural picturebook collection, was developed, as well as a Catalan picturebook collection based in Barcelona. Between 2004 and 2007, the EDMR project was created which focused on European children's literature websites containing picturebook collections.[6] The following year, a second European picturebook collection was created in Cyprus, promoting the structured pedagogical use of picturebooks and focusing on second language teaching and learning. After this, picturebook collections began to assume a more global perspective with the creation of the New Zealand PictureBook Collection and the Pacific PictureBook Collection. The use of Māori loanwords in both the collections invites children to explore not only the Māori language but also several community languages,[7] rather like many of Itchy Coo's publications. As the world scene is ever changing and there is more and more movement between cultures, IBBY Italia launched another picturebook collection: *Silent Books, from the World to Lampedusa and Back*, in 2012 using wordless picturebooks with visual narratives that could be understood and enjoyed by children regardless of language.

Much of the work undertaken in all these projects has at its heart the same philosophy as those working with Scottish picturebooks, namely to 'suggest ways in which future generations of children might be helped to acknowledge their own identities, and understand what it means to be European' as well as world citizens).[8]

The Place of Scottish Picturebooks

Representations of Scotland, its languages, literatures and cultures are naturally part of the European scene now and their images in picturebooks are an extremely important catalyst not only for young Scottish children in the quest for their own identities but also an opportunity for children and young people in the rest of the world to learn more about the Scottish way of life. Scottish picturebooks, therefore, play a crucial role in this learning process. Maureen Farrell suggests that 'A Scottish picturebook is one that deals centrally with issues of life and experience in Scotland, is set in Scotland, or exhibits recognisably Scottish attitudes towards Scotland or the world at large'.[9] She also believes that they should engage 'the reader in the identification of and reflection on the wide range of cultural communities and individual experiences which constitute a distinctive national culture'. For Farrell, Scottish picturebooks fall into three main categories: (a) those produced by Scottish writers and illustrators that are inherently Scottish, such as picturebooks by Mairi Hedderwick and Aileen Paterson; (b) those written and illustrated by picturebook creators who are 'non-Scots living and working in Scotland or commenting on Scottish life and culture from outside', such as the Australian team of Tania McCartney and Tina Snerling who have travelled widely and present their view of Scotland in *A Scottish Year*;[10] finally (c) Scottish writers and illustrators whose material 'is not overtly Scottish in nature but if told in their own true and unique Scots voice then it should be considered a Scottish text' – picturebook creators such as Debbie Gliori, Ross Collins and Lynn Mercer would fall into this category.

Farrell's broad definition of what constitutes a distinctly Scottish picturebook in a multicultural/international society is very helpful in trying to establish the role of the genre in constructing a national identity through its literature, particularly that which focuses on the Scottish view of life, customs and languages.

Language Awareness

Building an awareness of the many languages spoken in Scotland today builds a confidence in young people and helps them to be proud of the languages they speak, as well as developing their understanding of other languages. Scottish picturebooks can, therefore, play a crucial role in reinforcing Scotland's languages for its young citizens. Karen Coates highlights the fact that the English-speaking world needs to promote the translation and marketing of books that transcend national and cultural boundaries.[11] Scotland is now beginning to address this, and it is publishers like Floris and Itchy Coo who are leading the way, together with a number of education projects such as *Itchy Coo Education* which is designed for the benefit of all schools throughout Scotland. Additionally, individual authors and translators, like Shetland's Christine De Luca (Edinburgh's Makar – poet laureate – 2014–17) are making waves not only with their own creative picturebooks but also in the translation of other Scottish writers who currently write in English. De Luca has suggested that her 2008 Shetlandic version of Roald Dahl's *George's Marvellous Medicine*[12] (*Dodie's Phenomenal Pheesic*)[13] 'may have helped broaden the approach from just Lallans Scots, which is as foreign to Shetland children as English', to include the other Scots dialects, too.'[14] She signed contracts for a Shetlandic version of two of Julia Donaldson's books, project-managed by Itchy Coo. Donaldson's *The Gruffalo*[15] had already been translated into four variants of Scots, including Shetlandic, and many of her other books either make visual references to Scottish culture or are dedicated to Scottish primary schools.

Transmitting Scotland's Cultural Heritage through Picturebooks

A nation's culture has traditionally been seen as a reflection of the values, tensions, myths, and psychology that identify a national character,[16] and children's literature plays an important role in helping to create a national identity, distinguishing it from others. Scottish picturebooks are instrumental in doing this as they are social, cultural and historical documents. In January 2006, in fact, Scotland's new cultural policy gave Scottish literature a prominent place by acknowledging the importance of education as a catalyst towards accessing Scotland's literary heritage. The time, therefore, was ripe for a corpus of Scottish children's literature to be highlighted that could be used in schools by teachers and read by children in order to explore and interrogate their own cultural history and identity. Farrell suggests this corpus of work should be 'recognisable as Scottish Children's Literature [and exist] separately from [but be] complementary to English Children's literature'.[17] She intimates that picturebooks 'far from comprising a mere afterthought in Scotland's creative psyche, play a fundamental role in the shaping of that collectively imagined space known as Scotland'.[18]

Anne Dolan likens culture to an iceberg.[19] The visible part, she suggests, symbolises elements of culture that can clearly be seen, such as food or clothes; whilst those elements that are less obvious, such as why someone eats or dresses the way they do, are represented by the much larger underwater portion. It is these observable and non-observable parts of culture that need to be understood as part of one's identity, and culturally relevant picturebooks can 'help children to identify with their own culture, as well as exposing them to others'.[20] Farrell considers that 'multicultural literature in its most authentic form is an area of literature that focuses on the reality of various cultures', and she suggests that certain Scottish picturebooks can help readers to 'recognize themes, topics, values, social conventions, and language – those elements that characterize a culturally specific body of literature'.[21] Her argument is supported by many of the academics cited in this chapter. Evelyn Arizpe looks at the responses of readers from different countries and backgrounds, and highlights the potential of picturebooks for exploring places and cultures.[22] Bettina Kummerling-Meibauer discusses the fact that many picturebooks 'demand cultural knowledge, as well as the ability to decipher multiple layers of visual information [in order to understand] the close relation between verbal text and illustration':[23] she believes that readers must acquire cultural knowledge in order to comprehend the complexity of intertextual and intra-textual codes in contemporary picturebooks. Maria Nikolajeva and Liz Taylor are more precise when they probe into 'the function of objects in picturebooks, their cultural connotations and their significance for the narrative' and hence a reader's interpretation of the visual story as it interacts with the written narrative.[24]

Children's Engagement with Picturebooks

The drama of turning the page in a picturebook and the ways in which young readers engage with enmeshed and entwined texts (through reading both words and pictures) is, as in other multimodal literacies, instrumental in developing the knowledge and skills that lead children towards spoken, printed, visual and digital texts. By listening to and using spoken language when they play, young children learn that printed language carries meanings. When they enjoy stories and rhymes, become familiar with literacies that are valued by their own communities and learn about symbols and numeric sign systems, they can also learn to navigate around images, symbols, sounds, languages and layouts they encounter on digital screens. Through all the visual narratives that are presented to them, children can be encouraged to develop 'critical literacy' in terms of thinking about the most effective ways to communicate, which modes of media to use, and how best to learn more about their own and other cultures.

Sandra Beckett argues that complex visual narratives in picturebooks 'with their many cultural allusions fascinate readers of all ages'.[25] Sandie Mourao takes this further by suggesting that our own cultural frame will 'influence what we see' and socially constructed ideas will contribute to children's 'interpretation' of the images they see in a picturebook.[26] This is why, if Scottish culture is to become more widely appreciated, it is important to discuss Scottish books with young readers from both Scotland and further afield. It is also why children's existing shared awareness of common cultural archetypes can play a vital role in interpreting texts from many cultures. As Kerenza Ghosh unpicks the complexities of classroom discussions, she stresses the importance of children 'working as a team'; thus reinforcing the need for individuals to makes sense of visual narratives.[27] These interpretations, of course, may vary from group to group and culture to culture but what remains constant, if carefully selected picturebooks are chosen, is the fact that young children are able to appreciate the ways in which the visual and verbal texts are 'manipulated to convey meaning'.[28]

The interaction between picture and text in *A Scottish Year* allows young children to experience the sights and sounds of Scotland. Five Scots children take their readers on a journey through a year of celebrations and traditions which exemplify everyday Scottish life. The story integrates modern-day culture and lifestyle with past traditions and heritage; visually depicting the diverse faces of Scotland from the heather-strewn Highlands to its historical cities, isolated outer islands, and fascinating rural towns. This visual narrative exemplifies how cultural allusions can lead to fruitful classroom discussions and can open up new worlds for young readers, both above and below the surface of the iceberg. Presented with this situation, children are able to relate much of what they see to their own experiences whilst, at the same time, being aware of cultural similarities and differences. Much of Janet Evans's work demonstrates this when she discusses an Australian book with a group of nine-year-olds in the UK.[29] Her research shows clearly that children are able not only to use their own socially constructed ideas, developed from personal experiences, but also share their joint knowledge of common cultural archetypes. This helps them to empathise with characters and disclose their 'developing critical viewpoints'[30] of how another culture's experiences might align with their own.

Publishers' Cultural Involvement with Scottish Picturebooks in Schools

Language clearly plays an important part in all these discussions and children need to be able to read and understand visual texts in order to benefit from this sort of cultural exchange. It must be realised, however, that picturebooks are items of manufacture and commercial products, and publishers play an extremely important role in providing quality materials. What is exciting for children in Scotland is the way in which the production of Scottish picturebooks is progressing and incorporating many different aspects of Scottish culture, including its linguistic diversity. *Itchy Coo*'s publishing company appears to be leading in terms of revitalising the Scottish language, particularly in schools. They have published numerous picturebooks in Scots, which entwine images with words to enhance understanding. With these visually supported Scots narratives, the editors have worked closely with teachers and provided many support activities to be used alongside their books. These range from picturebooks for 'wee folk', to Scottish rhymes and tales and 'bandes dessinées' or comic-strip visual narratives.

Linguistic Input

Back in contemporary Scotland, there is never a dull moment in *Blethertoun Braes*,[31] a town that is full of exaggeratedly Scottish characters who take their readers through a day in their lives. Provost Pawkie, Mrs Nae Offence, the Reverend 'Soapy' Sheen, Colonel Swithering-Gitt and all their pals and neebors make *Blethertoun Braes* an amusing reflection on Scottish culture as well as an enjoyable romp for older readers. Comic-strip narratives are another amusing way for older readers to find out about the Scottish culture. In *Asterix and the Pechts*,[32] however, not only can they visually enjoy the fun-loving Asterix's epic voyage to a land rich in traditions, but they can also be auditorily immersed in the Scots language through Matthew Fitt's engaging translation. As Asterix and his friend Obelix journey on, they begin to discover a people whose cultural differences can cause them to have troubles of their own, often resulting in memorable gags and wordplay. In this translation, Asterix and Obelix visit *Pechtland*, the ancient kingdom of northern and eastern

Scotland. Instead of producing a text in a single or standard Scots, Fitt chooses to write in a number of forms reflecting the regional dialects of Scotland. For instance, Asterix and Obelix speak Glaswegian, the Picts speak Doric or Northeast Scots, and the Romans speak Dundonian Scots.

The idea of comic-strip translations in Scots is one that is not new. Alasdair Allan, former Minister for Learning, Science and Scotland's Languages in the Scottish Government, produced a version in Scots of *Asterix an the Muckle Fecht* during the 1990s. While that was unfortunately never published, now that comic-strips are being made available in the Scots language, alongside many other picturebook texts, it is fitting that Itchy-Coo should provide *The Compact Coo*.[33] This CD contains extracts from a large number of their books for older readers and encourages them to listen to the verbal alongside the visual, thus facilitating the recognition of Scots words on the page – often one of the biggest barriers to the creative use of Scots in the classroom.

Environmental Visual Narratives

The literary publisher *Floris* realises that picturebooks are, first and foremost, an experience for the child, and tends to focus on excellent visual narratives that tell a good story, interwoven with texts in English which incorporate selected Scottish loanwords. This applies to many of their *Wee Kelpies* and *Picture Kelpies*, as well as their *Traditional Scottish Tales* and *Kelpies* for older readers, many of which can be partially accessed on the Floris website. A large majority of these stories have their roots in Scottish culture and help children to either identify with their own cultural heritage or explore a fascinatingly new world. This is made possible because the majority of Floris's picturebook creators are Scottish, and so are ideally placed to draw on their cultural inheritance to imbue their written and verbal texts with Scottish life, whether it be contemporary tales or those that are more of a folkloric nature.

A large number of their books, particularly those in the *Picture Kelpie* series, focus on Scotland's bird and animal life; introducing young readers to a myriad of delightful characters who inhabit the Scottish islands. In *Harris the Hero*,[34] for example, we are introduced to a young 'puffling' puffin called Harris who, joined by his brother Lewis (also named after a Scottish island) and numerous other animal friends, helps a lost baby seal. The blues and greens of the detailed island scene, together with the clusters of puffins clearly at home in their marine setting, contrasts with the dilemma of the young seal who cannot find his way home. The simultaneous display of each set of facing pages makes this picturebook an excellent visual introduction to the Scottish islands of Harris and Lewis, as well as Scottish wildlife. *Skye the Puffling*[35] also introduces young readers to Scotland's island habitat, this time the Isle of May, North Berwick and the Bass Rock in the Firth of Forth, where the emerging puffin chick is surrounded by Scotland's seascapes, drawn using gentle watercolour.

The Grouse and the Mouse[36] and *Can't Dance Cameron*[37] offer opportunities to encounter other Scottish birds. Although these two tales are somewhat different, they both give further insights into the Scottish culture and stress the importance of being who you are. The first, starring Bagpipe, an endangered black grouse who is a bit of a show-off, and Squeaker, a wood mouse – quietly confident but not pushy. It is an amusing tale which, as well as introducing young children to two Loch Lomond and Trossachs residents, is also about valuing difference and being yourself. The second introduces Cameron, a capercaillie, one of the largest members of the grouse family. His story is set in the Scottish Cairngorms and includes a host of Scottish animals. In complete contrast, *Hairy Hettie, the Highland Cow*[38] presents a rather hairy highland cow and explains to readers that, as it is usually cold in Scotland, Hettie needs a thick coat to keep her warm. Hettie's numerous adventures not only show a humorous side of the Scottish Highlands that may be unfamiliar to many children, but also reinforces both the climate and the diversity of terrain that can be found in Scotland.

How to Make a Heron Happy[39] gives readers a rather different visual insight into the Scottish environment, as it is set in a drab, neglected, Scottish inner-city park. Hamish, used to interpreting his friends' moods by their facial expressions and body gestures, thinks that the heron in his park does not look very happy because he has long, frowning eyebrows and his shoulders are hunched. He thinks this is probably due to the bird's miserable environment, and so decides to try to cheer it up by getting his friends to clean up his park. The transformation from the neglected inner-city park to one that is vibrant and full of life not only sheds light on a Scottish inner-city but also, through its contrasting use of colours and hues as the story progresses, has an environmental implication. Details such as these, particularly in picturebook illustrations, play a vital part in transmitting aspects of Scottish cultural life.

The revered Scottish picturebook creator Aileen Paterson, who also tends to focus more on urban aspects of Scottish culture, draws strongly on her childhood experience, paying homage to her Kirkcaldy granny's

Scots tongue, to focus on minute details which can give young readers insights into the Scottish way of life. In *Maisie comes to Morningside*,[40] for example, Maisie Mackenzie, a kilt-wearing kitten and heroine of Paterson's series, lives in Morningside, a suburb of Edinburgh. Many of her adventures take place in different parts of Edinburgh or Glasgow, where the minutiae of Scottish life are reflected in Paterson's finely tuned socially observed illustrations.

Musical Adventures

Ayrshire's Elizabeth McKay's Granny stories depict many other aspects of Scottish culture. In *Wee Granny and the Ceilidh*,[41] as well as helping her readers with pronunciation of Ceilidh – Kay-lee – McKay includes a plethora of circumstantial details that are truly Scottish and introduces important musical elements of Scots life. *Bagpipes, Beasties and Bogles*,[42] as the title implies, not only familiarises young readers with perhaps the most well-known Scottish instrument – the bagpipes – but confronts them with Charlie McCandlewick, a night sweep who not only sweeps chimneys but also takes care of the bogle creatures of the night who 'blackened our bread and puggled our porridge' (p. 4), the Nippers and Nabbers who hide under children's bed, the Croakies who flap about in cupboards and the Whigmaleeries who wail at windows. These rather eccentric creatures apparently come from a story of 'Scotland long ago' (p. 2).

Traditional Tales

Also deeply rooted in Scotland's mythology are its many traditional tales, a large number of which are associated with creatures that inhabit its sizeable body of waters. Every one of Scotland's myriad of waters appears to have its cold, dark depths and every loch in Scotland seems to have its kelpie, in any number of different guises. In *The Secret of the Kelpie*,[43] young Flora discovers a stunning white horse emerging from a loch. Initially, she is fascinated by the animal's beauty but later, when she discovers that it is a kelpie – a shape-shifting water horse from Scottish folklore known to steal children – she has to decide if she should reveal this secret in order to save her family. *The Selkie Girl*,[44] however, focuses on a very different type of shape-shifter: a selkie, a seal who can become human. As young Fergus walks along the beach, he finds a beautiful fur blanket hidden in the rocks but does not realise that this belongs to a selkie girl who has lost her seal skin and cannot get back to her sea-home without it. These two tales are among a number of Picture Kelpies that bring classic Scottish folk and fairy tales to life. *The Tale of Tam Linn*[45] and *The Dragon Stoorworm*[46] are two very different stories. The first invites young readers to share a mythical tale of magic and evil overpowered, and can be viewed on YouTube, whilst the second explains the origins of Scotland's many islands. Theresa Breslin's *Illustrated Treasury of Scottish Mythical Creatures*,[47] on the other hand, delves into the mysteries of Scottish folklore and brings together tales of enigmatic selkies, bad-tempered giants, devious fairies, and even Loch Ness's most famous resident. As an art form, picturebooks hinge on the interdependence of pictures and words; in Breslin's book the creatures intertwine themselves with the text to add an outer worldly beauty which brings to life Scottish folklore, making it accessible to all. Like many of the Floris books, it is possible to 'read' these visually impressive tales in the 'See Inside' section of the Floris website.

Mairi Hedderwick, whose Katie Morag stories have already been mentioned, also illustrates for several other Scottish writers in a much more light-hearted way. One of these is Moira Miller who, before she died, wrote numerous stories for children which live on in her absence. The *Adventures of Hamish and Mirren*[48] is one of these. Hamish and his canny wife live in a picturesque farmhouse beside a Scottish loch in an area of Scotland that one would think was quiet and peaceful. Unfortunately, the loch is inhabited by a talking sea urchin, singing sand, hungry fairies, a sad bogle and a grumpy witch, all of whom add a cultural flavour to these short stories. Miller's humorous text interacts with Hedderwick's usual flair for creating visual delights of her homeland and offers introductory insights for younger children into folkloric Scotland.

A Historical Perspective

Birlinn publishers cater for a much wider audience and tend to focus more on historical and mythical texts for junior readers, many of which are available to download in their iBookstore. *1314 And All That*[49] is an irreverent take on Scotland's history, and the interaction between perceptive drawings and lively text bring this period of Scottish history amusingly alive for young readers. It is complemented by *1745 And All That*[50] which highlights key areas of Highland history from the earliest times to the present day and offers unique facets of Highland life, such as clanship, sheep, shinty and whisky. Allan Burnett's *Scottish Tales of Adventure*[51] takes on a more serious note and brings to life the stubborn determination of Elsie Inglis and the Scottish Women's Hospitals during the First World War, reinforcing the role that women played during this period. Conversely, Joan Lennon's folkloric tale *Silver Skin*[52] set in Skara Brae, Orkney at the end of the Stone Age, transmits an island mythology about selkies that is timeless.

For centuries, classic Scottish folk tales have been passed down from storyteller to storyteller and have transported young listeners and readers to magical realms where mermaids and men, selkies and sailors, ogres and princesses are miraculously transformed. Scottish poet William Montgomerie and his wife Norah first published these captivating stories from all parts of Scotland in 1956. Their collection *The Folk Tales of Scotland*[53] became a classic of the storytelling tradition and has been published by Birlinn with Norah Montgomerie's own original drawings.

Developments

The Scottish Book Trust has also been instrumental in promoting Scotland's culture through visual narratives and most of the books mentioned in this chapter are highlighted on their website. As well as focusing on picturebooks, the Trust has also begun to bring graphic novels to the forefront of older readers' attention. One of their publications is a graphic novel biography of the pioneering environmentalist, John Muir – a Scottish-born inventor, naturalist, artist, mountaineer, geologist, glaciologist and writer who spent his life exploring wild places and was the founding father of national parks in the United States. After the novel's publication in 2014, copies of *John Muir, Earth – Planet, Universe*[54] were distributed to schools across Scotland. These books, accompanied by online teaching support notes, are likely to help ensure that John Muir's legacy of protecting the environment is upheld in Scotland and perhaps more globally. Graphic novels can of course include fiction, non-fiction, and anthologised work as well as distinguished comic-strip narratives such as *Asterix and the Pechts*, already discussed. *John Muir, Earth – Planet, Universe*, however, presents older readers with an opportunity to find out about a more serious yet true side of Scottish culture; a PDF of this can be downloaded via the Scottish Book Trust website.

Cultural Progress

All cultures develop and change over time, but they must also retain a certain amount of continuity for the process to be effective. In modernising the picturebook world, the internet has greatly influenced what is currently available: new digital interactive picturebooks are just one example of multi-media progress. They are rapidly becoming part of the twenty-first century's landmarks in the world of children's literature: young readers are now able to choose between 'analogue' and digital modes of reading. The Scottish Book Trust appears to be forging ahead with ideas of how these interactive narratives can be accessed. Their website embraces the two reading modes and makes a number of suggestions for accessing both 'virtual' reality materials (where a simulated world takes the place of the real one) and 'augmented' reality (which adds to the reader's experience of the real world). Either could use sounds, graphics, video or any other media which makes the visual and auditory reading experience enriching and enjoyable.

Conclusion

A culture, such as that of Scotland, authenticates and replicates itself in the stories written for children, and picturebooks, in all forms, are quite naturally paramount in this process. Those from Scotland are no exception, as the small selection discussed here indicates. These primarily visual narratives, that interweave picture and text, allow young readers to become immersed in Scotland's languages, literature and culture whilst absorbing important beliefs and values that are universal. For this reason, carefully selected Scottish picturebooks can become not only mirrors to help young Scottish readers see reflections of their own culture, but also windows through which children from around the world can experience certain aspects of Scottish life. The picturebook world has changed considerably since Hill's 1996 article, but his perceptive thoughts on the material children should read have not. What is needed, he suggests, are 'books in which the story is to a great extent determined by the kind of people the characters are – books in which the readers can recognise the characters and situations'.[55] Current trends and the interplay of picturebooks with other multimodal art forms, such as *bandes dessinées*, graphic novels and digital texts, are facilitating this, but the potential for Scottish picturebooks in the future could be limitless, thus allowing all readers even greater opportunity to learn more about Scotland's cultural heritage as the twenty-first century progresses.

Acknowledgements

With grateful thanks to Tracy Cooper and her team at the Scottish Book Trust; Katy Lockwood-Holmes at Floris Books; Matthew Fitt at Itchy Coo; Christine De Luca, William Goldsmith and Margaret Donaldson for their support when writing this chapter.

CHAPTER ELEVEN

Ambition and Identity: Scottish Children's Literary Prizewinners

Morna Fleming

There is an impressive number of awards for children's literature. Some, like The Guardian Children's Fiction Prize, the Costa Children's Book Award (formerly the Whitbread, 1971–2005) and the National Book Awards (or Nibbies) choose from books submitted by publishers and voted for by adult readers or writers. The Federation of Children's Book Groups' Children's Book Award is voted for solely by children from start to finish. Others, such as the Blue Peter Book of the Year, the Nestlé Children's Book Prize and the Smarties Book Prize are hybrids, with readers voting for the books submitted by publishers. Scottish writers have not had a high degree of success in these competitions although there are some notable exceptions. These include the all-conquering J. K. Rowling with some earlier Harry Potter novels, Anne Fine – both for her young readers' stories *Bill's New Frock* and *Ivan the Terrible* (Nestlé/Smarties 1989 and 2007 respectively) and Young Adult novels *Goggle-Eyes* (Guardian 1990), *Flour Babies* and *The Tulip Touch* (Whitbread 1993 and 1996 respectively) – and the adopted Scot Julia Donaldson of the Gruffalo stories. Relatively recently, however, Scots writers have seen a breakthrough: the Coatbridge-born Brian Conaghan won the Costa in 2016 with *The Bombs That Brought Us Together*, Renfrew's Ross Mackenzie took the Blue Peter with *The Nowhere Emporium* in the same year, while Dundee-based Pamela Butchart won the Blue Peter with *The Spy Who Loved School Dinners* in 2015.

The oldest and most venerated of the awards are the CILIP (Chartered Institute of Library and Information Professionals) Carnegie and Kate Greenaway Medals for children's novels and illustrations respectively. Described on the award website as the one[s] authors and illustrators 'want to win', they are seen as the gold standard in children's literature. The Carnegie Medal was instituted in 1936 by the Library Association to mark the centenary of the birth of Andrew Carnegie, philanthropist and benefactor of libraries, to be awarded 'for the best book for children published in the British Empire in 1936'. The first award was to *Pigeon Post* by Arthur Ransome, which was followed in 1937 by Eve Garnett's *The Family from One End Street*, and in 1938 by Noel Streatfield's *The Circus is Coming*. Recognition that non-fiction could be worthy of 'best' status came in 1939 with the award to Eleanor Doorly for *Radium Woman*, an account of Marie Curie. However, by 1941, the Library Association recognised that assigning 'best' was a hostage to fortune, and the criterion was changed to 'the outstanding book for children', while the publishing arena shrank from the British Empire to 'England'. Although this was probably not designed to exclude writers and publishers from Scotland, Wales and Northern Ireland, particularly given Carnegie's Scottish ancestry, that was the apparent effect, such that when the Welsh-born, Scottish nationalist parliamentary candidate and Orcadian resident Eric Linklater was the proposed awardee in 1944, the terms were changed again:

> The Library Association Carnegie Medal will be awarded for an outstanding book for children by a British subject domiciled in the United Kingdom (Great Britain and Northern Ireland) published in Great Britain during the year in which it is considered worthy of the award.

The detailed criteria for judgement specified

> a book for children between 9 and 12, with universal appeal, appealing to both sexes, in the best English, its story following the line of the possible if not the probable, its characters alive, its situations credible, its tone in keeping with generally accepted standards of good behaviour and right thinking.[1]

It is notable that there was no award in 1943 or 1945, with no book in those years considered worthy of consideration.

The four novels to be discussed in this chapter are all products of their time, but, with the possible exception of the first, are in no way time-bound or dated. They are Eric Linklater's *The Wind on the Moon*, which won in 1944, Mollie Hunter's *The Stronghold*, winner in 1974, Anne Fine's *Goggle-Eyes*, the 1989 medallist (and winner of the Guardian Children's Fiction Prize the following year – the only novel to achieve the double) and Theresa Breslin's *Whispers in the Graveyard*, medal-winner in 1994. They all deal with issues that were and are current and in the public interest, and all have all the criteria for a successful, engaging story. All are in their own way family stories, all involving some kind of disruption to the nuclear family through the removal of a parent through service overseas, death or divorce. In nineteenth-century family stories, where the father has been removed (such as Mr March's military service in Louisa M. Alcott's *Little Women* (1868) and Father's unjust imprisonment in E. Nesbit's *The Railway Children* (1906)), '[m]others in particular have a constricting effect on the plot and on the children's activities; their love is so embarrassingly obvious that it can't be overlooked. It stands in the way of that independence that children like to imagine'.[2] In contrast, the mothers in these four novels are either useless, or absent, or actually encouraging of self-development and independence.

Two of the novels involve elements of fantasy, 'that extensive, amorphous and ambiguous genre [...] incorporat[ing] the serious and the comic, the scary and the whimsical, the moral and the anarchic',[3] but the fantasy overlaps the main narrative thread rather than being the central feature. M. O. Grenby has characterised 'Ptolemaic' fantasy as that where the world of the novel revolves around the actions of the protagonists, which is the case for Linklater's female protagonists, while in a 'Copernican' fantasy the protagonists move, disorientated, travelling through a fixed universe, like Breslin's Solomon.[4] In the former, child characters become powerful and important figures, although in their own worlds they have been weak, as is seen supremely in C. S. Lewis's *Narnia* tales, while Solomon finds himself falling into a universe of evil which he cannot understand but has to fight and conquer if he is to save himself and those he cares for.

Mollie Hunter's historical fiction, discussed in detail in an earlier chapter, gives children a sense of the past which has contributed to their present, and tends towards the adventure genre, but overlaps frequently with the family story, fantasy, fairy and folk tale. In the adventure story, a powerless and dependent individual can be developed into the centre of important events, as Coll becomes the saviour of his tribe through his design of the Stronghold of the title – the first broch in Scotland – and the reader comes to appreciate the tension between the marginal and (to outsiders) insignificant Sol in Breslin's novel, who becomes central and crucial to the fantasy world.

Linklater's, Hunter's and Breslin's novels are variously characteristic of the adventure story in the form of a quest, often beginning with a domestic crisis of some kind which means the protagonists have to leave the safety of home. They have a minor (or a series of minor) adventure(s) where they prove their worth, then the quest opens, generally structured as a series of smaller crises which culminate in the completion of the mission: finding the treasure, solving the crime, freeing the hostage, and so on. The protagonists are born with, or come into possession of, a special asset – a special skill, clever (or magical) pet, or a weapon. Generally, the protagonists are not alone, often accompanied by a faithful adult who acts as a surrogate parent, as is the case of Linklater's Mr Corvo, Hunter's Niall (although he is the same age as Coll), and Breslin's Ms Talmur.[5]

None of the novels presents a conventional account of 'home' as in the middle-class group seated round the table, in a room with a dresser and pictures on the walls, eating a meal which has been cooked by the mother (figure). Whereas in the nineteenth and early twentieth centuries the family was seen as nurturing and protecting the child, more recent children's novels, from the mid-twentieth century, see threats to the child's well-being coming even from within the family. The protagonists may come from families where the parents are apparently indifferent to the fate of their offspring, which is seen to extreme effect in Breslin's novel, but to a lesser extent in Fine's.[6] Linklater's family is essentially binary, with the children in a schoolroom setting ruled (quite ineffectively) by the governess, while Hunter's is, with essential differences owing to its pre-Christian era setting, not at all alien to the modern reader. Both Fine and Breslin depict family homes which are chaotic in different ways where the children, although undoubtedly loved, are frequently required to be self-reliant.

In terms of the protagonists themselves, they are a breed apart from the conventional. The heroes of adventure stories in the nineteenth and most of the twentieth century tended to be male, like Jack Harkaway, the hero of Bracebridge Hemyng's paper *Boys of England* (1871), with spectacular skills and abilities to counteract whatever plot device could be thrown at him. The corresponding *Girls' Own Paper* (from 1880) celebrated family and home, domesticity, conformity to authority, any naughtiness simply a phase the girls must outgrow.[7] In this way, Linklater's Dinah and Dorinda are conventional female protagonists, as they are still in the naughty phase, although apparently constrained to that by elements outwith their control:

> 'There is wind on the moon,' [their father] said. 'I don't like the look of it at all. Where there is wind on the moon you must be very careful how

you behave. Because if it is an ill wind, and you behave badly, it will blow straight into your heart, and then you will behave badly for a long time to come.' (p. 7)

Gender dissonance within a rigidly gendered society is appreciated by readers, as exemplified in the female character George, in the *Famous Five* books by Enid Blyton, who hates being a girl and tries her best to match Julian and Dick in their exploits. Nowadays, it is more usual for gender dissonance to be exemplified through boys who are not heroic adventurers, like Hunter's crippled Coll, or Breslin's dyslexic Sol, who are forced by circumstances into confronting a danger that only they can defeat.

Unlike Hunter's and Fine's heroes, Linklater's and Breslin's are small children, of primary school age, who have been forced by circumstances to take on adult roles. Linklater's girls undertake a journey in a furniture van east across Europe to rescue their father, in a rather kinder parody of the cattle-truck journeys that many were making at the time, and, incidentally, reminding present-day readers of the desperate flights of migrants westward from war zones. Breslin's Sol has to look after himself as his workless father is frequently drunk, useless in a paternal role, and there is rarely enough money for proper food in the house. At school he is bullied mercilessly by his teacher, Warrior Watkins, and frequently bunks off to his hideaway in the local graveyard, where he confronts the horror from the past which is unleashed by the unthinking events of the present. Hunter's Coll who is now eighteen, and of age to be part of the ruling council of the tribe of the Boar, was crippled in a Roman raid when he was a small child, the Roman tearing him from his mother's grasp and dashing him against the rocks of the shore. As a member of a warrior tribe, and having been adopted by the chief, Nectan, he is very aware of his physical shortcomings. Although not taunted or bullied because of them (at least, not by those who know him) he feels the only way he can play a full role in the tribe is through exercising his brainpower, to construct a means of protecting the tribe against the raiders. Fine's Kitty is perhaps superficially the strongest character of the four, but this is a mask, as she has come through a desperately unhappy situation: her divorced mother has taken up with a new man that Kitty cannot stand and who appears to be everything that her father, her mother's previous partner, was not. Fine gives Kitty a storytelling facility which she uses to comfort and empathise with a classmate who is going through the same situation. All four of these protagonists become involved in a quest, with varying degrees of willingness and ability, and with very different outcomes, although all four are ultimately successful, for themselves and for those they care for.

Linklater's *The Wind on the Moon* challenges the Carnegie Medal criteria of the time in a number of aspects, not least the credibility of the plot and the standard of behaviour of the protagonists. Dinah and Dorinda – tutored at home by the ridiculously over-informative Miss Serendip (who presumably serendipitously has at her fingertips facts about every aspect of daily life encountered) – are the daughters of a particularly unsympathetic father (apparently based on Linklater himself, according to his daughters)[8] and a largely ineffective and absent mother. Briefly, the plot is that Major Palfrey, the girls' father, very shortly into his year-long mission overseas, is captured and imprisoned by Count Hulagu Bloot, the Tyrant of Bombardy, and the girls decide that they will rescue him. In a series of improbable events, the girls change themselves into kangaroos using a potion from the local witch, which enables them to talk to animals. They are thus able to free the Golden Puma and Silver Falcon from the local private zoo so that they can accompany them on their journey on their way to gaining their own freedom. The girls do, of course, rescue their father, who is, however, spectacularly ungrateful to them.

Although there is no overt reference to the war which was raging world-wide at the time of writing, it is clear that Major Palfrey is engaged in some kind of major conflict; Count Hulagu Bloot bears more than a passing resemblance to Adolf Hitler. Names in the novel are the stuff of fairy tale and fantasy, as most of the inhabitants of Midmeddlecum appear to have gravitated by what has been called nominative determinism to appropriate professions: the butcher is Mr Leathercow, the grocer Mr Fullalove, the baker Mr Crumb, the Vicar is Mr Steeple, the Judge Mr Justice Rumple. (Could John Mortimer possibly have read this and remembered the name for his character Rumpole? The fact that Rumpole attended Linklater's, a fictional minor public school – it is called 'Mulstead' in the first story – perhaps suggests that he did.)

While the episodic nature of much of the novel exemplifies a mixture of fantasy, Dr Dolittle-like talking to the animals, a detective story and a thoroughgoing adventure story, it is always narrated absolutely seriously, with no suggestion of the adult writer condescending to the child readers. Linklater may have been an unsatisfactory father, but he was an expert story-teller, and frequently produces incidents which are outrageously comic. The cumulative effect of the multifarious stories leading up to the main plot narrative creates an atmosphere resembling an adult's telling a series of night-time tale to his children. These tales are populated by characters apparently adapted from Linklater's own reading, such as the giraffe who had previously been Detective Parker, taken from Dorothy L. Sayers's Peter Wimsey mysteries, and the *Times*-reading Bendigo the bear, who appears to be modelled on a bare-knuckle boxer of the nineteenth century, William Bendigo Thompson, who turned evangelist Methodist preacher after his retirement.

Hunter's narrative is essentially linear, opening with the confrontation between Nectan, Chief of the tribe of the Boar, and Domnall, the Chief Druid, but early on interrupted by the first of what will be periodic replays in italicised script of Coll's memory of the Roman raid when he was crippled, the readers being given rather more and slightly different information each time. These repetitions highlight the brutality of the raiders, and the very real danger to the people of the next incursion. Only Coll holds the possibility of a middle way between Nectan's desire to flee from the Romans to save the tribe, and Domnall's demand that they stand and fight. As is conventional in this type of narrative, there is a series of more minor confrontations and conflicts before the main conflict which will give Coll his opportunity to prove himself.

Fine has used the framing narrative of Kitty's giving her account of her experience to Helen while the two girls are closeted (literally) in the lost property cupboard. The reader (and the listening Helen) is presented with the whole account of Goggle-Eyes's wooing of Kitty's mother and Kitty's final change of attitude in the course of a single school morning, with periodic interruptions by classmates wondering when they will ever emerge. Such is Fine's storytelling ability, transmitted through Kitty, that the reader willingly suspends disbelief.

Breslin has also chosen a linear narrative, but punctuates it with fragments of song lyrics, and fairy tales which Sol recalls in difficult situations. The novel opens on the conflict between Sol and his bullying teacher, a situation which will be repeated several times until he is removed from the classroom altogether. Events from the past threaten to intrude into the narrative, but are incorporated into it, such that the time-frame does not change: the past events are read about and discussed in the present, and the evil from the past resurrects itself totally in the present.

Each protagonist has a worthy adversary, or indeed a number of adversaries, who must be defeated in order for the mission to succeed and the story to be told. Linklater's Dinah and Dorinda find their nemesis in their father's captor, Count Hulagu Bloot. The Count is described as somewhat of a pantomime villain character, but this is highly misleading:

> Count Hulagu Bloot hated all the countries of the earth except his own, and his own he despised [...] for two reasons. When he was young, his fellow-countrymen had never been able to see how clever he was; and after he became the Tyrant of Bombardy – by various cruel, dastardly, ingenious, and horrible means – they never saw how easy it would be to get rid of him, but allowed him to rule them as he liked. And what he liked more than anything else was to make people suffer. (p. 199)

After all the fairy tale, fantasy, slapstick and pantomime of the rest of the novel, this final section really brings us to the heart of what is effectively Linklater's satire on Hitler's Germany. The name 'Hulagu' may relate to the grandson of Genghis Khan, Hulagu Khan, a Mongol ruler who conquered much of Western Asia, the surname Bloot reducing him to a comic figure (although it could be from the Dutch *bloot*, which means naked or, figuratively, uncomplicated, as Bloot is an uncomplicated tyrant). As Hitler's recent biographer, Volker Ullrich,[9] has stated, Hitler was enthroned by a sinister plot of stupid elite politicians just at the moment when the Nazis were at last losing strength. It did not have to happen. Ullrich constantly reminds his readers that Hitler did not reach the chancellorship by his own efforts but was put there by supercilious idiots who assumed they could manage this vulgarian.

The Count's Castle of Gliedermannheim is a fairy-tale castle, looking 'something like a crown on a king's head: a little crown perched on the summit of a huge, knobbly, sallow-coloured bald head [...] enormously strong and rather ugly' (p. 240) and in situation somewhat resembling the Kehlsteinhaus or Eagle's Nest built for Hitler in 1938. Count Hulagu Bloot's private suite, next to the magnificent banqueting hall, has walls

> hung with disgusting pictures of people being tortured [...] In one corner were dumb-bells, a skipping-rope, and a Sandow developer for the muscles; and in another corner a book-case with a book in it called *How to Make Friends and Influence People*. (p. 241)

Body-building, persuasive writing and ranting speeches as advocated by Dale Carnegie in *How to Make Friends and Influence People* were characteristic of Hitler's early development into the tyrant.

In a Hansel-and-Gretel-like twist in the plot, Dorinda finds that she has been leaving a trail of peppermint creams, to which the Count is addicted, as it was said Hitler was, right to their father's dungeon, leading the Count directly to them, and the whole family to be endungeoned. While the witch in the Grimm fairy tale wanted to fatten her prisoner, the Count enjoys starving his prisoners, and regularly feeling their thinning arms and more prominent ribs. The reminder of the work camps of Nazi Germany is inescapable. In the end, it is the indefatigable tunnelling of two ancient sappers from the First World War which enables the liberation of the group, their improbable tunnels criss-crossing Europe as did the resistance railroads.

It was not war, but another outbreak of nationalism, that would see the next Scottish winner of the Carnegie Medal, Mollie Hunter, chiming with the national mood in 1974. In this year of two elections the Scottish National Party achieved a breakthrough with seven seats in February, and eleven in October, prompting Idi Amin of Uganda to proclaim his support of Scottish independence. This was also the year of the television version of John McGrath's 1973 ground-breaking *The Cheviot, the Stag and the Black Black Oil*. *The Stronghold*, with its narrative of the Scottish nation emerging from what is now acknowledged to be anything but 'the dark ages', must have struck a chord. It is a challenging read, with multiple plot strands and interlocking narratives.

This is not just a quest narrative, where the reader knows that the broch is going to be built, and simply must find out how the process is resolved through Coll's trials. Coll's description of the building of the broch – with a solid base of stone built around an inner circular courtyard, upon which successive hollow galleries are constructed, again of stone, the builders standing on the rising construction to build the galleries around themselves (there is a helpful schematic of the inside of the broch presented as part of the preamble to the novel) – seems to the modern reader obvious. Bran, Coll's brother who has been adopted by the Druids, expresses that thought for the reader:

> And yet, it was such a simple [concept ...] Why had no one ever thought of that before? Why had no one else in these treeless islands realised that the structure of a stone building could provide its own scaffolding? [...] Because that was the way with all great ideas [...] They seemed simple only because they rested on principles that could be demonstrated to be true. But it took a really great mind in the first place to recognize the mere existence of such principles! (pp. 47–48)

It was this thought, that '*one single brilliant mind*' had originated the design that proliferated all over the north of Scotland and the islands that gave Hunter, as she explains in the Foreword, the source of her novel.

Coll has several adversaries to address, principally Domnall, the Chief Druid, who is opposed to anything other than standing and fighting the Romans, but increasingly Taran, who has returned to the tribe having apparently escaped from his slave-master in Gaul and has designs on taking over the leadership of the tribe. The battle is won, exactly as planned and predicted by Coll as he built the Stronghold and convinced Nectan of the best way to defend it. But Domnall's confidence when cursing the retreating Romans is his downfall, as he is struck in the neck by a Roman javelin, and falls, apparently dead on the instant. This is Taran's chance to prove himself, with a shout of '"*Ave! Ave! Amicus Romae sum! Amicus Romae sum!*"' (p. 187). Again, this challenges the modern reader. There will be few who have been taught Latin nowadays, although at the time of writing it would have been a given, at least for certain streams in Scottish schools. Those who have been so taught recognise Taran's perfidy immediately, as he is shouting, 'Hail! Hail! I am a friend of Rome!' Inevitably, Domnall has not been killed, and Clodha, Taran's nemesis, having heard the translation of his treasonous words from the old man, snatches the javelin and plunges it into Taran's heart.

A very different kind of problem is presented by Anne Fine in *Goggle-Eyes*. Set at the height of the Faslane anti-nuclear protest, and the peace camp set up at the main gate over a long period, the Trident missiles based there are opposed by the Scottish National Party, the Scottish Socialist Party and the Scottish Green Party. As is depicted in the novel, there are occasional breaches of the perimeter fence, some considerably more serious than the rather perfunctory ones depicted. The issue confronting the protagonist, Kitty, however, is considerably closer to home. Her mother is a divorcée, and a new man has just come into her life. Ostensibly a school story, themes of friendship and loyalty, strength and solidarity among the sisterhood come to the fore. The framing narrative of the two girls in the cupboard, periodically interrupted by people wondering when they are ever coming out, neatly divides Kitty's narrative into the developing parts of the relationship.

Fine's writing is leavened throughout with humour and irreverence towards authority. Kitty Killin is unexceptional, except for her gift with language, and she tells a good story, which is why her teacher, Mrs Lupey, sends her after her classmate Helen, who is, like Kitty, faced with a mother planning to re-marry, and to a man that she cannot stand. In Kitty's case, this is Gerald Faulkner, the Goggle-Eyes of the title, who has turned her mother into 'some radiant, energetic fashion plate who doesn't even *hear* when you tell her it's the last episode of her favourite series' (p. 16) and who has even abandoned the Thursday evening meetings, about which she was previously 'fanatical'. The depiction of the difficult teenage daughter is achieved to perfection. The moodiness, the determination not to be 'nice' while not being objectionably rude, the sense of impatience with the younger sister who appears to take these new situations very much in her stride, and the longing to have time on her own with her mother even if it is only on the drive to a meeting, ring sensitively true. The political involvement, too, is typical of the mid-teens, when 'causes' loom large, in this case, the campaign for nuclear disarmament. Predictably, Gerald Faulkner sees nuclear weapons as the best defence against a future war, as he can remember the aftermath of the Second World War and its horrors caused by conventional weapons. But it is the way he looks at her mother, 'goggling at her' as she checks her dress in the mirror, and the fact that he seems to be so comfortable in their house that infuriates Kitty so much.

The visit to the nuclear submarine base is a fine set piece. The statistics on the power of weaponry currently deployed in the world are staggering and make sense of this, admittedly rather perfunctory, protest. Otherwise, the description of the event is somewhat ludicrous, as the protesters tell the police they are coming, and make ritual cuts in the fence wire before being arrested and retreating. The sentiment behind it, however, is genuine.

> 'Why do we bother to do *anything*?' [Kitty's mother] asked. 'Why do we reclaim hills and hand over petitions? Why do we march and hold silent candlelight vigils? Why do we write to politicians and wear our badges and send letters to the newspapers? [...] There are millions who think the way we do. *Millions*. People of all sorts. And this way the police and the courts and the newspapers get to see that we're not all the sorts of loonies and layabouts that can be safety ignored. They get to see growing numbers of sensible citizens who object to these places. And from our statements in court, they get to hear *why*.' (p. 78)

Gerald, a small businessman obsessed with Stock Exchange reports and Building Society handbooks, has observations to make about the protesters which even Kitty realises make sense. Reinforcing what was said earlier about the anti-nuclear people not being 'loonies and layabouts', he points out that if they dressed professionally rather than warmly and comfortably for the protests they would probably get a better reception, and if they were to protest outside government offices or in shopping centres, then more people would see them and their banners, rather than the 'most politically informed sheep in the world' at the bases themselves. They should be organising a letter-writing campaign instead of singing protest songs in the bus. Kitty is definitely coming to see Gerald in a different light, and genuinely wants to know when she asks him whether, with all his reading of Stock Exchange reports and Building Society handbooks, his way of thinking about things is a little bit boring? 'I meant thin, miserable, unimaginative, blind, stupid! But being polite I said "boring"', (p. 114) and Gerald responded that yes, he probably was boring, and had been boring all his life, but was also reliable, and predictable, and perhaps that was what had attracted their mother to him.

Theresa Breslin wrote *Whispers in the Graveyard* in response to a rise in requests of her as a librarian for books about dyslexia. Her dyslexic protagonist, Solomon, lives in a chaotic household with his father who is frequently workless, and who, when he does have a bit of money, is too ready to spend it on alcohol. This had become too much for his mother, who had eventually left, giving Sol the choice of where to live. As he did not at that time understand how difficult his father was going to be to live with, he chose to stay with him. His father refuses to believe that Sol has a problem which is preventing his reading, largely because he suffers in the same way himself, but gets by through using his memory, leaving 'messages' with neighbours, and using tricks to conceal his inability. Sol has picked up some of these himself but is very aware that he cannot cope with letters, numbers and words in the way that the youngest children in the school can, despite dedicated help from the infant teacher, Ms Talmur. The antagonists Sol must confront in his young life are multifarious and variously threatening. His father becomes violent when drunk, or when Sol has hidden the bottles, and cannot protect Sol from what life is throwing at him. He is at the mercy of his class teacher, who simply dismisses him as thick and unteachable, and takes every opportunity to bully him mentally and physically. However, the most threatening force is that awakened in the graveyard, the ancient evil which was buried there in the eighteenth century, and which has been brought back to life by the plan to divert the river back to its original course, ironically the cause of the centuries-old curse.

Sol as a character is very reminiscent of Susan Cooper's Barney Drew in *Over Sea, Under Stone* (1965) who, seeking the Grail which will help him to keep the Dark at bay, hears voices in his head:

> Who are you to intrude here, the voice seemed to whisper; one small boy, prying into something that is so much bigger than he can understand, that has remained undisturbed for so many years? Go away, go back where you are safe, leave such ancient things alone [...][10]

Sol is confronted by the disturbance of 'his' corner of the graveyard, which has produced 'a great disquiet' (p. 13). The adults concentrate on the possibility of a cholera pit in the graveyard which will require special treatment, but Sol is aware that there is more in the disturbed earth than cholera or even smallpox. The rowan tree which has been uprooted, but which has refused to come free of the soil – and which has already inflicted an injury on Sol's arm, which we later find is the route into his mind for the hidden memory in the earth – is symbolic of the protection against evil which is being removed. He gradually becomes more and more aware of the voice of the witch in his head, drawing him to her. Not only does Sol have to save himself; he has to save Amy, Professor Miller's daughter, whom the witch is also attacking:

> the woman who was burned as a witch [...] lived where the kirkyard is now. No wonder there is a bad atmosphere there. They burned her within sight of the mill itself. They had diverted the river when they built the mill and it took away her water supply. She is supposed to have put a curse on the miller and all of his family. (pp. 126–27)

The final denouement in this novel sees Sol's father as the saviour, using his brute strength to break the witch's spell and save not only Sol, but Amy and Ms Talmur. He has accepted his reading issues, has agreed to attend what are presumably Alcoholics Anonymous meetings, and Sol has decided to visit his mother.

The preoccupation with language in Breslin's novel is in fact another common feature of the other three. Kitty Killin's storytelling skills are the vehicle Fine uses to pursue an authentically rendered portrait of an unconventional family life, with all that entails in terms of the naturalistic idioms which clearly differentiate the characters. Hunter's differentiation of the language of the Men of the Boar and the Druids, and ultimately Taran's treacherous use of Latin creates a vividly believable setting which conveys the sense of a distant time and an alien set of beliefs. Linklater's use of rhymes, fairy-tale idioms, and, of course, the very fact of the girls' being able to talk to the animals in their own languages endows the novel with a continually changing narrative effect.

All four novels have an 'all's well that ends well' conclusion, although each is very different. The Palfrey girls are already bored with their life back in Midmeddlecum, but are left a message by the local witch which (with echoes of Miss Serendip's tireless educating) effectively tells them that they have all the resources for their own adventures if they simply use their own wits and intelligence. Coll, having shown that the Stronghold can be built and can work successfully against the raiders

> saw his dream of the Stronghold enlarged to a vision of coastline after coastline dominated by towering, impregnable defences; defences strong enough to stand for generation upon generation, until Rome was finally defeated and there was no further need of his Strongholds [...] But even then they would still stand for a wonder and a sign of those who had lived long ago. The dream would last. Those who came after would be aware it had once been [...] (p. 203)

At the end of *Goggle-Eyes*, which has covered a school morning, Mrs Lupey breaks the spell, but she understands the power of the storyteller: 'Living your life is a long and doggy business, says Mrs Lupey. And stories and books help. Some help you with the living itself. Some help you just take a break. The best do both at the same time' (p. 139).

Breslin's close is rather more ambivalent. Solomon has, with the guidance of Ms Talmur, accepted his dyslexia, and with her promotion to another school, will have to find his own way of dealing with it. She leaves him with a visual formula for writing his own name – the S of the river, the sun and moon for the three 'o's, the new three arched bridge for the 'm' and 'n' (p. 165). His father has agreed to attend Alcoholics Anonymous, but we leave Solomon waiting for his father at the meeting place, tracing out his name on the steamed-up window using the visual imagery of river, sun, moon and bridge.

Writing for children and young adults is sometimes more challenging than writing for adults, especially when there are so many distractions available to young readers. Three of these novels are to be found in many English department book stores, their appeal and quality attested by the Carnegie award, but also by the expertise of the storytelling which captures and holds the imagination. Whether it is likely that Eric Linklater's achievement will be recognised by the purchase of class sets of *The Wind on the Moon* is rather doubtful, but it has proved itself worthy of a place in the school library at least.

CHAPTER TWELVE

Scottish Poetry in the Scottish Secondary Classroom: Seeing Beyond the Set Texts

Jennifer Farrar

How children experience Scottish poetry during their school years in Scotland is, to a large extent, dependent on their teacher's knowledge, taste and inclination. Their experience is also – it seems inevitably – subject to the vagaries of changes in education policy and organisational structure. As an example, during the preparation of this chapter it was announced that the Scottish Qualifications Authority (SQA) would be closed down and an alternative body would take on its role. Inevitably, this chapter is written in a context when the SQA still operated and is presented as an overview of the current curriculum in order to illustrate the general principles that would prevail under any curricular guidance set up in future.

While educators are encouraged to introduce learners of all ages to the 'richness and breadth of Scotland's literary heritage',[1] just how that should be done is primarily left to the discretion of schools and individual class teachers. This can mean that for some pupils, Scottish poetry infuses diverse aspects of their learning, while for others, it is reserved only for special occasions such as Burns Night or standalone projects about Scotland's culture and history. While it is possible that some young people will encounter and enjoy Scottish poetry in their out-of-school lives, it is nevertheless the case that children's knowledge of this literature is heavily influenced by what they read or listen to within their classroom walls. For this reason, education can be seen to occupy a custodian-like role in relation to Scottish poetry by continuing to ensure that learners do gain access to the texts that are considered to be so fundamental to Scotland's cultural, national identity. Yet this custodial role is also curatorial, given the unavoidable need to prioritise certain texts, voices and themes above others. The 'tradition' of Scottish poetry that emerges in and through schooling is therefore always selective in its nature and should be recognised as such, parallelling a view set out eloquently by Raymond Williams.[2]

For pupils entering the senior phase of their secondary education (age 15–18), Scottish poetry now plays a more prominent and formalised role as a result of the Scottish Government's decision to introduce a mandatory question on Scottish literature into the externally assessed National 5 and Higher English examinations. Since 2014, candidates have been required to study a text – or, in the case of poetry, a selection of Scottish texts – from a set list of pre-agreed titles and authors issued by the SQA. (See Appendix A for the most recent table of set Scottish poetry.) Following a consultation process with teachers and other stakeholders – the views of teachers and other stakeholders were consulted when the SQA generated the original 2014 set text list, the list being subsequently refreshed for the start of the 2018 academic session – work by the following poets was identified as 'highly suitable' for study by senior pupils through a series of questionnaires and focus groups: Carol Ann Duffy, Norman MacCaig, Edwin Morgan, Liz Lochhead, Sorley MacLean, Jackie Kay, Don Paterson and Robert Burns. Yet the emergence of these names as key representatives of Scottish poetry was met with some regret by teacher respondents to the consultation process, who were reported to have expressed disappointment at the predictability and outdated nature of the final selection.[3]

Behind this prescriptive shift is the hope that learners can be supported towards deeper understandings of their own cultural and social identities through the study of texts that have been deliberately judged and categorised as 'Scottish'. Yet, as the use of inverted commas is intended to suggest, the question of what makes these texts Scottish is problematic. Does 'Scottishness' relate to the identity or nationality of the author? The subject matter or themes presented? The place of publication or presentation? With Williams's idea of a selective tradition, already referred to, in mind, similar sorts of questions can be asked about the aspects of Scottish life and culture that are foregrounded by the selected texts and the limits this inevitably imposes on the perspective we offer to children. Whose voices and experiences are privileged? What spaces, places and topics are picked out as most relevant for young people today? What other ideas and themes could be explored?

Beginning from such questions, this chapter sets out to consider what aspects of Scottish culture and society are presented and promoted by the SQA's current selection of Scottish poetry. Yet it also aims to look 'beyond the list', by offering an equally subjective selection of poets whose voices resonate, complement and complicate those already found on the 'official' list, where those poems likely to be examined may constitute a teacher's focus. Given the large number of individual poems selected by the SQA, it has not been possible to deal with each one in a chapter of this length. Instead, some of the poems have been grouped together, using categories that reflect general themes and key approaches found across the selection. While not exhaustive, they are intended to offer a general flavour of what 'Scottishness' looks like, both in the poetry found 'on the list' and also 'off the list', from within the growing field of Scottish poets who write about aspects of Scotland's language, identity and culture. Again, the 'off-list' suggestions are presented as merely that: suggestions that are in no way definitive and it is recognised that many other poets and texts could be included. The first section on the 'use of Scots' is followed by an exploration of how 'urban places and spaces' are represented in Scottish poetry, which is, in turn, followed by a consideration of how 'Scotland's geology, landscape and nature' is depicted. In the final section, poems and poets dealing explicitly with issues and themes connected to 'Scotland's past and future' are presented.

On the List – Use of Scots

As one of the most instantly recognisable markers, the use of Scots helps to anchor several poems in the SQA selection to an obvious Scottish-sounding voice or accent. Many poets can be seen to achieve this effect through the scattering of occasional Scots words here and there in ways that do not prevent readers without any knowledge of Scots language and culture from accessing the poems' meaning. For some poets, Scots plays a far more dominant role in the proceedings. In Edwin Morgan's 'Good Friday', the language and speech patterns used by the drunk man on the bus dominate the text and help to provide its location, while creating a vivid, authentic-sounding record of a chance encounter that can be read with deeper significance:

> You're an educatit man, you can tell me –
> Aye, well. There you are. It's been seen
> time and again, the working man
> has nae education, he jist canny – jist
> hasny got it – know what I mean
> he's jist bliddy ignorant ...

Morgan's decision to let the Scots' voice take centre stage in this poem makes it possible to interrogate attitudes towards the use of Scots as well as stereotypical assumptions linked to class. It is also possible to explore the conversational cadences that Morgan achieves by reporting speech in this way and to consider the impact they may have on the reader.

It is interesting that Jackie Kay's 'Bed', a poem written entirely in Scots, was removed from the 2014 set text list in the 2018 refresh. In this dramatic monologue, the persona explains how age and increased infirmity have led to an acute sense of marginalisation from her daughter and daily life, as well as a heightened metaphysical awareness of the 'skeleton underneath ma night goon'. Like Morgan, Kay uses Scots as a vehicle to deliver a voice that will sound recognisable to many readers:

> She is that guid to me so she is
> an Am a burden tae her, I know Am ur.
> Stuck here in this big blastit bed
> year in, year out, ony saint wuid complain.

'Bed' has been replaced with Kay's 'Old Tongue', a poem in which Standard Scottish English is used to carry the main meaning, with Scots occupying a powerfully evocative but much more illustrative role. In 'Old Tongue', Kay presents a voice that has lost its sense of 'Scottishness' as a result of a move south to England. She lists some of the words that she feels have 'fallen off' her tongue through lack of use, such as 'eedyit, dreich, wabbit, crabbit', and considers, with intense sadness, the identity loss that can also accompany such geographical and linguistic shifts. Unlike 'Bed', in which Scots is used to convey themes of age, time and society, in 'Old Tongue', Scots and its use (or lack thereof) becomes the theme, raising questions about the significance of accent and language to the construction of an individual's identity. A similar idea of identity loss is explored by Carol Ann Duffy in 'Originally', although not explicitly about Scotland or the Scots language. In 'The Way My Mother Speaks', Duffy does reflect, with some poignancy, upon several phrases commonly used by her mother – 'what like is it' and 'the day and ever' – that seem to remind her of her long-lost childhood in Scotland and cause her to experience painful pangs of love and longing for the past.

The use of Scots as a theme features less prominently in the set of poems selected as representative of Robert Burns, which explore ideas that can be considered universal but are delivered in a language the poet described proudly as his own native tongue. The questions about religion and hypocrisy raised in 'Address to the Deil' and 'Holy Willie's Prayer' still resonate today, while the issues of legitimacy and environmental concern found in 'A Poet's Welcome to his Love-Begotten Daughter' and 'To a Mouse' respectively can be easily translated into a modern context for secondary-aged readers.

Off the List – Use of Scots

As a modern-day response to Burns's 'Address of Beelzebub', James Roberston's 'Beelzebub Resurfaces' shows how the original poem's concerns with corruption and abuses of power can be translated into a contemporary context that sees Beelzebub delighting in the misery human beings have inflicted on one another through their predilection for terrorism, war and environmental destruction. With a careful use of humour to balance out the bleak and angry reality that Robertson depicts ('For man had made his paradise / A stinkin, scabbit cowp'), this poem also illustrates the powerful insights that can come from considering alternative viewpoints, no matter how distasteful:

> And aw ye haly terrorists
> Be bauld and fou o faith
> And whaur ye ding doun tyranny
> Raise misery and daith.

Writing in the same collection,[4] Matthew Fitt's 'Kate o Shanter's Tale' presents a voice unheard in Burns's original 'Tam o' Shanter', by offering a much-beleaguered wife's response to her drunk husband's late return home. We have to imagine whether Tam is present (or indeed conscious) for Kate's weary and frustrated monologue: perhaps she is preparing her line of argument for when he does surface, or perhaps she is addressing the now-sleeping lump who

> cam in here
> four in the bliddy moarnan
> an ye wur buckled.

Given that Fitt labels this poem as an extract, perhaps we are to see it as merely one example from a marriage that is frequently tested by alcohol abuse, an idea that effectively increases sympathy for Kate's position in a way not found in Burns's original. Kate's sense of anger builds as she considers how her husband would probably have excused his selfish actions to himself: 'well dinnae gie's it, shanter / juist dinnae gie's it'.

Yet the poem's ending reads ambiguously, with Kate's final use of the conversational Scots phrase 'sae ye ur' sounding almost affectionate in its reprimand, suggesting she is once again willing to forgive him his 'bletherin, blusterin, drunken' behaviour.

Just as Jackie Kay illustrated in 'Bed', Roberston and Fitt's poems show how Scots can be used to give voice to perspectives that speak to a whole range of contemporary concerns, without explicitly addressing the linguistic power dynamics that are also at play. Taking on the idea of Scots as an expression of identity, as found in Kay's 'Old Tongue', spoken word poet Katie Ailes explores how Scots words and phrases have made their way into her American-English vocabulary, including the peculiarly Scottish preposition 'outwith'. In 'Outwith', Ailes describes with pleasure how some of her mid-Atlantic vowel sounds have lengthened in response to Scotland's linguistic climate:

> Glasgow rolled itself under my tongue,
> a grey marble lolling my mouth open with Os:
> Glasgow, Kelvingrove, going to Tesco.

Other, sharper-sounding vocal changes are conveyed by Ailes's wonderful use of 'thistling': 'then thistling my speech with sleekit lisps, / wee packets of crisps ...'. As Ailes observes in the closing lines, those on the outside of Scotland's language and culture can start to feel at home when words such 'aye' and 'outwith' begin to occur naturally within their speech, a comfortable realisation that leads her to conclude succinctly and with some certainty: 'I may be from out / But I am now with.'

On the List – Urban Places and Spaces

Grouped together under this next heading are the poems in which depictions of urban Scotland come across either explicitly, through direct reference to place names or locations, or implicitly, through the evocation of settings that identify strongly with well-known aspects of Scottish society and culture.

Edwin Morgan's 'Trio', a poem that is situated squarely on one of Glasgow's busiest shopping streets at Christmas time, offers a Scottish-tinged rumination on the importance of human love and joy that reaches out beyond its Buchanan Street location, while seeming to foreshadow the idea of Glasgow as a place that 'smiles better' which would emerge the next decade in a 1980s municipal advertising campaign. This positive view of humanity is accompanied by a pair of Morgan poems that explore some of the less 'smiley' parts of Glasgow's reputation, such as the shattering presentation of violent crime found in 'Glasgow 5 March 1971', and the grim portrayal of poverty and tenement life in 'Glasgow Sonnet i', in which:

> The kettle whimpers on a crazy hob.
> Roses of mould grow from ceiling to wall.
> The man lies late since he has lost his job,
> smokes on one elbow, letting his coughs fall
> thinly into an air too poor to rob.

While it is dispiriting that Morgan's portraits of the hopelessness caused by social inequalities are still relevant today, they can offer effective 'ways in' to these often challenging topics. It is hard not to respond to the cruel inhumanity found in the closing lines of 'Glasgow 5 March 1971', in which 'two drivers keep their eyes on the road' and ignore the glass-shredded, blood-splattered victims of the violent assault who lie on the pavement just feet away from their closed car doors.

In 'The Bargain', by Liz Lochhead, Glasgow's famous Barras Market provides the backdrop – both metaphorical and literal – to a poem about relationships, while also conveying Lochhead's obvious affection for the city. In addition to key colloquial phrases ('Somebody absolutely steamboats he says'), Lochhead peppers this poem with references to aspects of place that will resonate with those who know the city well, such as 'the Tron end of London Road and / Gallowgate' and 'Paddy's Market'.

Several of Don Paterson's poems similarly evoke an urban sense of place through the use of geographical and cultural references, but without using Scots or Glaswegian to the same extent as Lochhead, Morgan and Kay. In '11:00: Baldovan', Paterson explores themes of growing up and change through the eyes of two small boys who take a bus journey, unsupervised by parents, from one part of Dundee (Baldovan) to another (Hilltown) in search of 'comics / sweeties and magic tricks', crucial Saturday morning pocket-money purchases for many children in the Western world. In 'Nil Nil', Paterson weaves in references to Scottish football (including the very Scottish-sounding McGrandle) and contrasts the slow demise of a local football club with the sudden death of a fighter pilot on his return to the Leuchars air base in Fife. While Paterson frames his musings on life and death within a specifically Scottish context, they are universal enough to transcend the geographical and cultural limits to be transposed or applied elsewhere.

Off the List – Urban Places and Spaces

As a contrast (or companion) to Morgan's Glasgow-based poems, Valerie Gillies's 'To Edinburgh' offers a love poem to Scotland's capital city, a place she describes variously as 'a spatchcock town', a 'guttit haddie' and finally, as a geological miracle of heavens, hills, 'spires and tenements' that both shapes and inspires those who live within its walls.

A more politically challenging view of Scotland's urban landscape can be found in Jim Monaghan's 'United Colours of Cumnock', in which the poet and political activist ruminates on the social changes that have transformed his East Ayrshire home-town. Lying only a few miles away from Mossgiel, where Robert Burns once farmed, Cumnock is depicted as a town that has now lost its colour, or sense of political and cultural identity, due to social changes that are outwith the inhabitants' control. Once a verdant, 'tree in every scene town' with a proudly unionised community, prepared to stand up for one another – 'That's red that came from meeting rooms, / from folk that worked the pumps and looms' – Cumnock is now depicted as a grey place weakened by poverty and made ill by its loss of vibrancy and political spirit:

> But now my town's a grey town,
> a fifty mils a day town,
> a watch life slip away town,
> a tunnel wae nae light.

Beginning from a similar position of poverty and despair to Monaghan ('Skint, baw ragged, poackets ful eh ma / fingers, cannae afford tae burn toast'), William Letford's 'This Is It' finds a moment of joy in the midst of a depressingly familiar urban scene. Letford's persona finds himself 'outside Greggs eating a macaroni pie' when a busker starts to play a guitar and sing, and while Letford does not have a pound to spare, he is inspired by the sound of the young busker's musical ambitions:

> I'd like tae tell um that this is it, this is
> where the hammer hits the stane and sparks
> ur made.

Witnessing such 'sparks' – or moments of creativity – in the midst of the mundane causes Letford to feel suddenly alive and we too are encouraged to be inspired by the young man's gift and obvious dedication to his music: 'Eez young an the dreams thit wur boarn in eez bedroom wake me up.' As Letford notes in the final lines, while the busker's audience might consist of only one – the poet – and while his stage is a town centre precinct, the main thing is that the busker is pursuing his dreams: 'bit singin, wee man, yur singin'.

On the List – Geology, Landscape and Nature

Moving outwards from the city and townscapes discussed above, another set of poems describe Scotland's wilder landscapes. Dominant in this category are the poems of Sorley MacLean, a writer who has been described by Emma Dymock and Scott Lyall as both Gaelic and European in his outlook and as someone who was heavily influenced by the northern landscape that surrounded him.[5] It is striking that his poetry is usually taught in schools not in his original Gaelic, but in his translation of the texts into English. In 'Tràighean' ('Shores'), MacLean names a succession of Scottish beaches as the backdrop for a love poem, conjuring up powerful comparisons about the size and scale of the ocean in relation to his own feelings and passions. In 'Ceann Loch Aoineart' ('Kinloch Ainort'), MacLean uses an extended military metaphor to evoke the strength and power of a set of rugged mountain peaks:

> Eachraidh bheanntan, marcachd mhullaichean,
> deann-ruith shruthanach càthair,
> sleamhnachd leacannan, seangachd chreachainnean,
> srannraich leacanach àrd-bheann.

A cavalry of mountains, horse-riding summits, / a streaming headlong haste of foam, / a slipperiness of smooth flat rocks, small-bellied bare summits, / flat-rock snoring of high mountains.

By labelling his poems with specific geographical references, either in the title or within the text, MacLean anchors his poems to particular parts of the Scottish landscape. The same cannot necessarily be said of Norman MacCaig's 'Basking Shark', amongst the most 'natural' of his poems picked out for study by the SQA. In 'Basking Shark', the poet is out rowing in an unnamed sea when he 'stub[s] an oar on a rock where none should be', prompting him to contemplate the evolutionary process:

> Swish up the dirt and, when it settles, a spring
> Is all the clearer. I saw me, in one fling,
> Emerging from the slime of everything.

While MacCaig's use of a gently lilting rhythm and rhyme in these lines evokes a Scottish-sounding voice, it could be argued that the 'tin-tacked' sea he describes could be located anywhere a basking shark might roam. Indeed, MacCaig's use of natural imagery in 'Sounds of the Day' achieves the same local and universal effects through its use of softly Scottish-sounding word choice ('snuffling puff') that could be understood (and interpreted differently) anywhere else in the English-speaking world.

Off the List – Geology, Landscape and Nature

Using an approach that resonates with MacLean's use of the list in 'Tràighean' ('Shores'), Valerie Gillies's 'Stream Rhythm' describes the pattern of streams that feed the River Tweed as it journeys though the south of Scotland. Weaving together placenames and stream-names with personified detail and fragments taken from myth and legend, Gillies's repeated use of rhyming couplets contributes to a cumulative sense of the streams' energy and shared history as they tumble and rush along together:

> Manor's stony settlements rise,
> Posso the pleasance, earthly paradise,
> Hundleshope and Waddenhope,
> a man's name in hollow court.

In the final stanza, Gillies considers the feeling of 'stability' or longevity that can come from the centuries-old human habit of naming (or possibly renaming) aspects of the surrounding wilderness, such as the streams and pockets of woodland she catalogues in this poem.

Pursuing this idea from almost the opposite direction, Ken Cockburn's 'Shandwick Stone' depicts nature as resisting the human tendency to label and define in order to keep its mysteries intact. The swirling patterns and symbols that can be found on the Shandwick Stone – a Class II Pictish stone located in Easter Ross – seem designed to confuse the 'stone hunters' who eagerly seek out their centuries-old secrets. A description of the Pictish beast as an impossible 'bird-fish-mammal' that 'harbours a smile' helps to confirm the personified Stone's pleasure when its visitors feel confused by the weathered stone imagery they find. The idea of nature conspiring against humans occurs again in the closing stanza, when the rain clouds gather in order to send the unwelcome guests home once again, while the grey sea remains 'unyielding', keeping all secrets close.

Moving even further north, Christine De Luca's 'Soondscape' uses the onomatopoeia-rich Shetlandic dialect to evoke a sense of the easy relationship between nature and the island's power-generating windmills. The constant thrum of the wind turbines – described as sounding like 'kert-wheelin alleluias' – exists in harmony with the incessant noise of the seabirds on their granite posts, a sound De Luca records memorably as 'an oorie whirr, a vimmerin / o' whaaps an peewits' ('an eerie whirr, tremulous sounds / of curlews and lapwings'). Taken together with the sounds of the wind as it rattles through bits of broken farm machinery, the overall effect is a 'hushie hubbelskyu' or 'an uproarious lullaby', a phrase that appears to be contradiction in terms, but one that also suggests the life-affirming effects of experiencing such a wonderful landscape of sounds: 'da haert lifts'.

On the List – Scotland's Past and Scotland's Future

Of all the categories of 'Scottishness' presented here, this final heading is one of the busiest, dealing as it does with tradition and history, family, politics and culture across the centuries, generations and language barriers.

Aspects of Scotland's history and politics are visible in Sorley MacLean's 'Hallaig' and 'Sgreapadal', although the latter was dropped from the set text list in the 2018 refresh. Both poems deal with the impact of the Highland Clearances and offer insights into Gaelic traditions and culture. In 'Sgreapadal', MacLean also considers the current threat posed by the development of nuclear weapons, something he describes with some certainty as '[…] an lèirsgrios obann / a thuiteas às an iarmailt' ('[…] the sudden holocaust / that will fall from the sky'). As with so many of the poems selected by SQA that date from earlier decades, it is possible to see how easily they could be connected to contemporary issues and debates still facing Scotland.

In contrast to MacLean's insider perspective, MacCaig's 'Aunt Julia' presents an outsider's view of Gaelic culture through the poet's overwhelming sense of regret at not being able to connect with his aunt across the language barrier until it is too late. Part of the appeal of 'Aunt Julia' comes from its blend of Scottish traditions and landscapes within cherished childhood memories. The aunt that MacCaig remembers has a peat-stained foot, could make expert use of a spinning wheel and was a 'keeper of threepennybits in a teapot', a most evocative image. As a result of the communication frustrations the speaker faced as a child and then later an adult, MacCaig's message seems to be to prize the culture and traditions from Scotland's island life and to prevent them becoming nothing more than 'so many questions unanswered', like his own to Aunt Julia.

Turning finally to Liz Lochhead, whose three poems 'View of Scotland/Love Poem', 'Some Old Photographs' and 'For My Grandmother Knitting' all offer poignant and nostalgic snapshots of Scottish culture and traditions, past and present. Like 'Aunt Julia', and, to some extent, the persona in Kay's 'Bed', Lochhead uses 'For My Grandmother Knitting' as a space to consider not only the cruelty of the ageing process but also the traditions and skills that can be left behind or rejected as older generations fade and recede. The grandmother we meet here was once a nimble-fingered fisher girl whose hands 'made do and mended / scraped and slaved and slapped sometimes' as a wife and mother but has now become someone whose restless fingers produce more knitted products than her family can use or desire. In 'View of Scotland/Love Poem', Lochhead recalls some of the family traditions and social practices that have made Hogmanay a special time for so many generations of Scots. Her mother is depicted as busy 'jiffywaxing the vinolay' at the start of the poem, before preparing a spread of tinned salmon, a 'slab of black bun', shortbread and steak pies for the Hogmanay first-footers and family guests who may or may not arrive. By documenting these traditions in poetic form, Lochhead extends their lifespan while also inviting wider discussions about how other families and cultures mark such occasions, both inside and outside of Scotland. In a similar way, 'Some Old Photographs' transports the reader back to a glamorous-looking Glasgow of the past and causes us to reflect on what has been gained and lost by the passage of time, while reminding us of the stories that can be tucked away inside dusty old photo albums.

Off the List – Scotland's Past and Scotland's Future

Looking beyond the list, it is not hard to extend this final theme outwards from the SQA's sometimes overtly nostalgic focus on history and tradition in order to encompasses some of the contemporary socio-political issues that are arguably of relevance and significance to current and future generations of young people at school in Scotland.

Scotland's changing political landscape has presented poets with opportunities to engage with aspects of national identity both explicitly and implicitly. In 'A Manifesto for MSPs', one of a series of sonnets about Scotland's Parliament, James Robertson provides a list of the ideal (and not so ideal) behaviours for the politicians who have been charged with leading the country forward into a new era. In the octet, Roberston urges MSPs to lead by example by resisting the temptation to be 'glaikit', 'sleekit' or 'ower smert' in their political dealings. In the sestet, he sets out his template for a more compassionate and principled politics, one that includes a commitment to truth, freedom and loyalty: 'heeze up the banner o humanity, / seek oot the truth and tae the truth be leal'.

In 'Scotland the More', Catherine Wilson also issues a rallying cry for change, but this time addresses it to the nation as a whole. An award-winning slam poet, Wilson's text comprises a long list of Scotland's many positive qualities and success stories that include the natural, the cultural and the idiosyncratic: 'We have strong opinions over who should win best sheep'. As a relatively new Scottish voice, Wilson makes a playfully frustrated reference to the dominance of certain national stereotypes ('we are more / than *just* Burns poetry') but her concern also seems to be with limiting the damage that the underdog complex might continue to do to Scotland's collective national consciousness, hence her repeated, emphatic use of 'more'.

Many of Kathleen Jamie's poems fit into this category, although the label of 'Scottish poet' is one she has resisted. In 'The Republic of Fife', Jamie toys with the freedoms that could emerge from a confident republic of citizens who grow and gain strength from supporting one another. In 'Mr and Mrs Scotland Are Dead', Jamie explores another aspect of Scottish identity through the discovery of some outdated personal artefacts found discarded at a local dump that once belonged to a couple called Mr and Mrs Scotland.

> [...] his shaving brush, her button tin.
> Do we save this toolbox, these old-fashioned views
> addressed after all, to Mr and Mrs Scotland?

While considering what to do with the once-valued objects next, Jamie's thoughts turn to the inevitable 'turning out' that happens with the old to make way for the new. This includes the disposal of 'old-fashioned views' as mentioned above, a phrase that at first glance seems to refer to the outdatedness of the Scotlands' opinions, but literally refers to a small pile of picture postcards received from a variety of Scottish seaside towns. Yet the metaphorical point about outdated views remains and, like Robertson (and to some extent Wilson), Jamie's concerns seem to be with *what else?* and *what's next?* for Scotland, a point I return to in the conclusion.

Other voices focus on more problematic aspects of Scotland's national identity. Looking backwards in order to suggest new ways of moving forwards, Kate Tough's 'People Made Glasgow' offers harsh and uncompromising truths about the city's difficult connection to the slave trade:

> Brutalised Africans made Glasgow
> amazing disgrace, how sweet
> the civic amnesia ...
> mansions without plaques
> unrevised street names
> no memorial

In the footnotes that accompany the poem, Tough describes her sense of horror at Glasgow's failure to adequately redress its past wrongs, especially when contrasted with civic marketing campaigns (such as 2013's 'People Make Glasgow') that persistently portray the city as a champion of equality and the common people. Looking around her, Tough observes the unhappiness and cruelty of city life that exists for so many:

> why else would we drink to incoherence
> jump on the heads of passing men
> punch our women
> tell our children in a checkout queue,
> 'Ah hate bank holidays cuz it means
> Ah huftae look at youse fir three days no two.'

Consequently, Tough wonders if the contemporary problems for which Glasgow is now infamous, such as the domestic violence mentioned above, poor health and lower-life expectancy, are somehow rooted in, or are a consequence of, the city's problematic past:

> The whip's crack
> comes a little after
> the whip's stroke.

Difficult home truths of a different sort are explored in 'Hopscotch', a spoken word poem by Nadine Aisha Jassat, in which the poet describes the everyday racism and sustained sexualised verbal abuse she has endured as both a girl and as a woman of mixed heritage growing up in Scotland, highlighting the kind of abusive racist language she has suffered:

> 'Is your Dad in the Taliban?'
>   'You should go back home now,'
>   'go back home,'
>   'go back to –'
> Where?
>   'Your mum.'
>   'Your mum's a paki lover.'
> I am 14.
>   'Slut.'
> She was 43.

Like Kate Tough, Jassat's account is unstintingly honest in its exposure of the racism, sexism and ignorance that can be found on Scotland's streets. Such attacks have occurred so frequently over the years that she uses her memories of them 'like a guidebook / to my own hometown', an image that increases our horrified understanding of Jassat's feeling of isolation within the country of her birth.

> 'But your hair,
>   but your eyes,
>   but your skin,
>   but you don't look Scottish,
>   and where,
>   where,
>   where are your family from,
>   originally.'

Jassat provides no solutions in this poem. Instead, in the final line, she offers up her words to the reader ('I'm leaving them here') as evidence or as a shocking reminder that is intended to inspire us into thought or action. Both Jassat and Tough help to problematise aspects of Scotland's national identity by giving voice to less listened-to narratives and by showing how and why these experiences matter to a twenty-first-century Scotland.

What these poems also emphasise is the scope or possibility that can come from understanding this notion of 'Scottishness', or what it means to be Scottish, so that it is less about Scottish identity *per se* and more about the contemporary issues that Scottish writers identify with. Such an approach can be seen in Catherine Wilson's 'Facts', a poem in which she recounts the experience of losing her sister in the 1996 Dunblane Massacre when a gunman walked into a Scottish primary school and murdered seventeen people before killing himself – a horrendous local event with national and international repercussions. It can also be seen in 'The Gap', a poem written in response to Jackie Kay's 'Gap Year', in which Jenny Lindsay grapples with the issues that living with Alzheimer's Disease can bring to a family. In 'I'm Sorry', MiKo Berry, another award-winning Scottish slam poet, explores issues relating to mental health and self-harm. All of these issues and poems can be labelled Scottish in their provenance, yet like so many of the poems on the SQA list, their relevance and reach extends far beyond Scotland's national boundaries.

Conclusion

What all of the poems discussed here have in common is that they have something tangibly Scottish about their content, whether it is a theme, a setting, issue or use of Scots. To re-use Robert Louis Stevenson's well-known phrase, perhaps what unites them all is that they have 'a strong Scots accent of the mind', something that can manifest itself in different ways and to differing extents according to the poet and, in the context of education, according to the teacher-mediated interpretation and the understandings that students bring with them to the text.

By exploring poems from the SQA list in relation to other Scottish texts that either echo or extend the ideas they contain, this chapter's purposes have been two-fold: first, to make visible the limits, constraints and definitions that are imposed by any selection process, especially one with a label that appears to apply the notion of a singular culture to an expanding multicultural society; and second, to consider how pupils' experiences of Scottish poetry could fruitfully be enriched and broadened through an exploration of other poets who write 'off-list' about similar ideas and themes. As the summaries that follow each subheading illustrate, there is much to commend and enjoy from within the SQA selection, yet, as evidenced above, the tendency towards nostalgia and towards a sense of 'Scottishness' that simply may not be accessible or tangible to Scotland's increasingly diverse younger population has its disadvantages as well as advantages. Respondents to the original SQA consultation were not convinced that the poets 'on the list' were reflective of 'modern Scottish poetry',[6] meaning that teachers in agreement with this are tasked with finding and providing children with access to alternative, contemporary voices.

As this chapter has tried to show, playing around with the notion of identity so that it can also encompass some of the issues that young Scots currently identity with and have experience of may make it possible to keep poetry relevant and vibrant in our classrooms and beyond. From such a perspective, Scottish poetry for young people becomes a body of writing that looks outwards as well as inwards, can scrutinise current issues through a distinctly Scottish contextual lens and, by doing so, can connect the local with the global. The samples drawn from Scotland's flourishing spoken word and slam poetry movements provide ample evidence of just how vital, varied and engaging these voices can be, even if they do depart from traditional poetic conventions and assumptions of what a poem ought to do or say. In addition, these texts can offer teachers important opportunities to engage directly with both contemporary and historical issues related to racism, prejudice and poverty in ways that may help to deflect and combat their pernicious influence over future generations of Scots.

It is clear that, after considering the selections in this way, there is no simple answer to the question what makes a text Scottish, just as it also seems evident that there are both advantages and disadvantages associated with learners experiencing Scottish poetry via a mandatory, prescriptive list. For some pupils, engaging with Scottish texts for the high-stakes purpose of an exam might be one of their only experiences of Scottish literature, or certainly one that stands out in their memories, for reasons that are hopefully good but possibly bad. Preparing students for an exam on set poets is no easy task and it is all too easy for teachers to inadvertently commit, in Kelly Gallagher's terminology, 'readicide'[7] by murdering a poem through over-analysis or a heightened attention to examination rubric at the expense of pleasure. This task is made even harder if the poems being studied do not resonate culturally or socially with all of the learners in a class. By drawing from the far wider pool of poets and poems that extends far beyond the list, perhaps teachers will be able to energise and enthuse learners into exploring – and perhaps even writing – Scottish poetry for themselves.

It is hoped that the structure of this chapter has helped to draw attention to the 'canonising effect' of the set text list, a feature of any curriculum that could open up exciting critical possibilities if interrogated and explored in classrooms rather than simply ignored or accepted as normative and unproblematic. By asking questions about what Scottishness looks like in poetry and considering what else is possible and how it could be represented, it might be possible to use poetry about Scotland's culture and cultural identity as a springboard, or as a 'way in' to the sorts of intercultural and multifaceted discussions about citizenship, social justice and identity that should be taking place in classrooms across the country.

List of Scottish poems set for National 5 and Higher English for 2018 onwards (at time of going to press)

Robert Burns
'Holy Willie's Prayer'; 'Tam o' Shanter'; 'To a Mouse'; 'A Poet's Welcome to his Love-Begotten Daughter'; 'To a Louse'; 'A Red, Red Rose'.

Carol Ann Duffy
'War Photographer'; 'Valentine'; 'Originally'; 'Mrs Midas'; 'In Mrs Tilscher's Class'; 'The Way My Mother Speaks'.

Jackie Kay
'My Grandmother's Houses'; 'Lucozade'; 'Gap Year'; 'Keeping Orchids'; 'Old Tongue'; 'Whilst Leila Sleeps'.

Liz Lochead
'The Bargain'; 'My Rival's House'; 'View of Scotland/ Love Poem'; 'Last Supper'; 'Revelation'; 'Box Room'.

Norman MacCaig
'Assisi'; 'Visiting Hour'; 'Aunt Julia'; 'Basking Shark'; 'Hotel Room, 12th Floor'; 'Brooklyn Cop'.

Sorley MacLean (in self-translation)
'Hallaig'; 'Shores'; 'An Autumn Day'; 'I give you Immortality'; 'Kinloch Ainort'; 'Girl of the red-gold hair'.

Edwin Morgan
'In the Snack-Bar'; 'Trio'; 'Good Friday'; 'Winter'; 'Glasgow 5 March 1971'; 'Glasgow Sonnet i'.

Don Paterson
'Waking With Russell'; '11:00 Baldovan'; 'The Ferryman's Arms'; 'Nil Nil'; 'Rain'; 'The Circle'.

CHAPTER THIRTEEN

Scottish Children's Literature: Where Are We Now?

Maureen A. Farrell

A volume such as this one – an International Companion – never sets out to do the work of an encyclopaedia. It sets out instead to provide chapters covering key topics on the subject in question, in this case Scottish children's literature, to showcase and spotlight areas of growth and interest or to re-visit previously acknowledged areas of strength with a contemporary perspective. Its coverage does not purport to be comprehensive but its purpose should encourage surprise, interest, delight and curiosity on the part of the reader and scholar. It should facilitate new study and research and encourage the celebration of the amazing body of work that is Scottish children's literature as currently understood. The intended effect would be to acknowledge the place of Scottish children's literature in the world canon and to present a fertile area for reading for pleasure and for further scholarly research. It is hoped that previous chapters have accomplished some of this as we draw to a conclusion. So, at this point consideration should be given to a short review of some of the recent advances in the field and some of the areas for development that still need to be addressed.

Scottish authors have always been published, very often by publishing companies that are located outside Scotland and at times this has brought particular challenges, especially when the author has sought either to write completely in Scots or to include Scots language within the work. The added challenge of course is that one of Scotland's other languages, Gaelic, is still badly under-represented in Scottish children's literature. The Scottish Languages Bill referred to in the Introduction should go some way towards strengthening parity of esteem for both Scots and Gaelic. However, the decisions writers make in terms of language use may still be thwarted by priorities at the editorial and publishing levels, held perhaps with the best of intentions. Publishers are, of course, looking for the greatest commercial potential and may see the publication of Scots and Gaelic material as being only intended for a niche market. Nevertheless, it is vital that linguistic independence and diversity are supported and encouraged in terms of the languages of Scotland. The growth of publishing companies located in Scotland, and with a commitment to Scottish children's and young adult literature, has been touched on earlier in this volume in the Origins of Scottish Children's Literature chapter; Itchy Coo, Black and White publishing and the Canongate Kelpies imprint have been considered there.

However, it would be important to mention also that Itchy Coo has become an established imprint in Scottish publishing and has sold almost a quarter of a million books. It also has an important and well-established education programme working with schools, libraries and teacher education establishments promoting Scots within education. In the same broad space, Floris is the largest children's book publisher in Scotland and is particularly known for its Kelpies range of Scottish children's books. Kelpies publish books for children in the early years up to material for young adults and include both fiction and non-fiction. They publish a catalogue twice a year and have significantly increased the number of books in recent years. They also revived the Canongate Classics imprint in an effort to get neglected Scottish literature back into print. Kathleen Fidler's *The Desperate Journey* and *The Boy with the Bronze Axe*, both originally published in 1964, were reprinted in 2012 and George Mackay Brown's 1980 *Fankle the Cat* (republished 2012) remains in print. But the hugely rich back catalogue of the work of people like Mollie Hunter, Allan Campbell MacLean and Frances Mary Hendry is still largely neglected.

Sadly, our backlists of classic Scottish children's literature texts more generally are still not managed, studied or promoted as they should be. The publisher Birlinn has an imprint, BC Books, which focuses on writing and illustration for young readers and Black and White publishing has an imprint, Ink Road, which focuses on young adult fiction. What is interesting about these companies, some well established, some emerging in the 1990s and after, is their recognition of the need for secure publication of Scottish children's material. Some of this may come from the growing recognition of the place of children's literature more generally and some may be a result of the resumption of the Scottish parliament and the growing attention at political and educational levels of the importance of the Scots language and of indigenous publishing more generally in an era of increasingly corporatised and financialised literary production. This is shown by Ilda Erkoçi's discussion of 'Narrative Cities' and Publishing Scotland's film *Forever Lands – The Growth of Children's Writing and Publishing in Scotland*, both appearing in 2023.[1]

Of equal importance but significantly lower profile is the case of Gaelic children's literature. Despite being recognised officially as one of Scotland's languages in 2005 and a manifest and acclaimed commitment from the Scottish Government to raise the stakes for Gaelic, the editors of this book struggled to identify writers to address Gaelic children's literature and were only successful at the eleventh hour, thankfully at the highest level of commitment and insight. Mairi Kidd's chapter provides a more detailed consideration of Gaelic books, their history and challenges – in particular the challenge of Gaelic translation. Unlike Itchy Coo's success with Scots translations of hugely popular children's writers like Roald Dahl, David Walliams, A. A. Milne and Julia Donaldson, the fact that it takes approximately thirty per cent more words to translate English to Gaelic presents significant problems, to say nothing of the difficulty of trying to manage rhymes, as in the case of translating *The Gruffalo*. Of particular importance in this area is the lack of translated or original material for children beyond the age of twelve, especially if they are learning Gaelic as a second language. Scotland already boasts an important publishing house, Barrington Stoke, who for twenty-five years have been publishing age-appropriate books for dyslexic and reluctant readers. They publish 'unpatronizing content matched to the age of the reader not their reading level',[2] ensuring the material is properly edited to ensure comprehension and accessibility. Surely it must be possible to support a similar initiative in Gaelic books for young adult Gaelic learners. It seems this is a goal for which we should be striving.

As well as these long-established languages of Scotland, we should not forget incoming home languages such as Polish, Urdu, Arabic, Farsi, Mandarin, Makaton, to name only a few of the 170 languages spoken in Scotland.[3] For example, Polish-born illustrator Kasia Matyjaszek has taken her beautiful work out to Polish-speaking families via Glasgow's book festival Aye Write and other platforms. She is definitely someone to watch out for – see her work in *I Am A Very Clever Cat* (Templar, 2016) and *The Fourth Bonniest Baby in Dundee* (Floris, 2016). We need to see many more languages represented within this provision.

Since this book was commissioned, Scotland, like many other countries, has undergone swift and far-reaching changes. Some of the changes and developments have a longer history than others. Echoing children's literature in the UK generally, Scotland has not had a particularly edifying history in terms of inclusion of Black and ethnic minority representation in children's and young adult literature. The Centre for Literacy in Primary Education (CLPE) has for the last six years provided an annual report

CLPE Reflecting Realities – a survey of Ethnic Representation within UK Children's Literature. The annual CLPE survey was launched in 2017 with the key focus of determining the extent and quality of ethnic minority characters featured within Picturebooks, Fiction and Non-Fiction for ages 3–11 published in the UK. This year's (2023) report shows a sustained upward trend in the volume of inclusive and representative literature published for children in the UK. Of particular note is the fact that thirty per cent of the children's titles published in 2022 featured ethnically minoritised characters, up from four per cent in the first report in 2017.[4] This statistic should be celebrated, but the situation in Scotland needs to be disarticulated from the UK so that accurate national information can be reported. The Literature Alliance of Scotland's *Breaking New Ground* (2019) publication[5] found only one writer of colour working in children's and young adult's literature in Scotland at the time – and she was a university student originally from London. Since then, the British Asian writer Maisie Chan has re-located to Scotland and credits that move with the occasion of completing her first full-length children's book. Her debut novel *Danny Chung Does Not Do Maths* (2022) won the Jhalak Prize and the Branford Boase Award that same year. She was the Dr Gavin Wallace Fellow in Moat Brae in 2020–21, their first writer in residence. From 2023 to 2024, she undertook an author residency with Howden St Andrew's Primary in Livingston. Chan also runs the Bubble Tea Writers Network to support and encourage writers of East and Southeast Asian descent in the UK. Despite this notable and high-profile success story, we need a concerted effort to encourage and develop more Scottish BAME authors.

Study of the traditions of children's literature in Scotland and of the 'classic' works closely identified with them has also in recent times entailed a fresh appraisal of the presence and the negotiation of gender politics within these texts: applying full critical attention to the narrative roles of significant girl and women characters, their often unexpected or overlooked agency as sources of moral and existential interest, and their frequently conflicted or painful communication of the experience of female marginalisation and subordination. In the last fifty years, feminist readings of Scottish literature have had a transformative effect upon literary critical and popular understanding of an enormously wide range of texts, and the growing application of such ways of reading to Scottish children's literature has had, as Carole Jones has argued, a comparably important influence on the interpretation and popular appreciation of texts long held as central to the national literary heritage.[6]

Changing perceptions of gender and sexuality – and the cultural and political arguments surrounding it – are of course not merely reflected in Scottish children's literature. They are, rather, reproduced, critiqued and circulated through it and through its reception in the acts of private and shared reading. This is especially relevant to a literature so closely bound up with the tasks of mass education and the acquisition of literacy. Scottish children's literature of the modern and contemporary periods, which is of course now so indebted to women writers, has, as Jones suggests, been deeply interwoven with the social and cultural reframing of gender expectations and relations, gender politics and – latterly – the radical and systematic interrogation of seemingly bedrock gender essentialism and heteronormativity. This has freed contemporary Scottish children's literature in its current diversity to be active in the navigation of these questions in ways which challenge, subvert and reimagine gender identity and exchange in both present and future contexts. Nor is this liberation of perspective and approach confined to the (nonetheless still urgent) issue of female equality. Important works of Scottish children's literature have returned in recent times with both pathos and humour to the celebrated and deep-rooted imagery of Scottish masculinity, in both adult and juvenile settings – examining how this masculinity is acquired and fashioned; its costs and limitations; its relationship to sexism, homophobia and aggression; and even how it might be somehow redeemed or remade as the socio-economic structures which generated and sustained it over many generations appear at last irretrievably to fade.

Scottish children's literature needs to incorporate, highlight and invest in other protected characteristics. Scottish children's books showcasing disability and neurodiversity should be much more visible than they are currently. In relation to this area, the work of e.g. Pamela Buchart and Elle McNicoll is to be welcomed for their significant contributions in these areas both in terms of their own different abilities and in their writing of books where neurodivergent characters take centre stage – such as McNicoll's award-winning 2020 novel *A Kind of Spark*. She is an advocate for better representation of neurodiversity and disability in publishing and the media and founded The Adrien Prize to recognise children's fiction that explores the disability experience. McNicoll is an outspoken champion of better representations of neurodiversity in publishing as well as in its products. LGBTQ+ topics also need a higher profile and this aspect is being taken very seriously by organisations such as LGBT Youth Scotland who, in 2016, commissioned Rachel Plummer to write a book of poems retelling traditional Scottish stories from an LGBT+ perspective. The book *Wain* was published in 2019. It is a collection of LGBT-themed poetry for teens based on retellings of Scottish myths. The collection contains stories about kelpies, selkies, the Loch Ness monster, alongside lesser-known mythical people and creatures such as wulvers, Ghillie Dhu and the Cat Sith. The poems in the collection are fun and surprising and are a magical mix of myth and contemporary LGBT themes. *Wain* is beautifully illustrated and suitable for readers of all ages.

Scottish literature, including children's literature, frequently presents the Scots as having a multifaceted reputation for hospitality, dry wit, strength of feeling, industry, socialist convictions and a keen desire for social equality and justice as well as having a well-developed social conscience showing awareness of current sustainability and climate change issues. Other long-established themes in children's literature include the continuing spectres of poverty and disadvantage, but these are lent added sharpness by their current and continuing damaging impact on the lives of large numbers of Scotland's children, despite considerable national energy devoted to their remedy. One contemporary author whose work covers many of these themes for varied age ranges is Victoria Williamson. Her writing makes an interesting case study of the varied ways in which these topics can be tackled and how she makes the subjects interesting, relevant and engaging for young readers. Her most recent books deal with issues of disability, climate change, homelessness, terminal illness and a worrying dystopian future.

Williamson's *War of the Wind* (2022) is a powerful eco-adventure driven by four teenagers who have additional support needs. Deaf because of a boating accident, Max is horrified by the bullying he begins to experience as a result of his disability. While all of this is happening, he and his friends also have to contend with the unexpected consequences of a new wind farm on the island, one which was supposed to improve internet access but instead results in beaches strewn with dead bats and platoons of soldiers occupying the power station. When Max and his friends find out that the lethargy and violent outbursts occurring in the community are the result of sinister experiments, it falls to them to fight back. Targeted at a younger age group her *Norah's Ark* (2023) is a story told by two very different people. Norah and her father are living in a B&B having lost their home. Delays in benefit payments mean they are often hungry and Norah is bullied at school where she also struggles with reading. Her love of animals provides some consolation. Caring for some orphaned baby birds brings her into contact with Adam who also loves animals but whose background is very different. His family are wealthy but he too is frustrated as he recovers from leukaemia and the restrictions his parents place upon him. In direct accessible prose this story holds the reader's attention while at the same time opening their eyes to the ways the deeply disadvantaged in modern society have to live.

Williamson's most recent book is her first foray into young adult (YA) fiction. This dystopian novel explores sustainability and the self-serving greed of global corporations through a story of family, friendship survival and hope. *Feast of Ashes* (2023) is set one hundred years in the future. The earth's eco-systems have been obliterated and Adina has been raised in the safe haven of Eden Five, the huge greenhouse of a colossal corporation. In a truly shocking opening, Adina admits to having killed 14,756 people as a result of a terrible error which wrecks Eden Five. She and her fellow survivors are forced out into the wastelands beyond the dome of the greenhouse. In the course of their pursuit of Sanctuary they find they are not alone as they had expected and the corporation is not as they thought either. This is the first novel kicking off a new series guaranteed to capture the interests of young adult readers. While Williamson may be charged with trying to include every manner of protected characteristic and all the 'hot' themes and topics of the day in her work, she manages to do this while crafting genuinely exciting stories and portraying the authentic struggles of the central characters.

Other contemporary Scottish authors are tackling these important topics and themes in our society but, as with all areas of diversity in Scottish children's literature, we cannot rest on our laurels; more needs to be done and Scottish writers are responding well to these new possibilities and emancipated forms of experience in providing interesting, relevant and engaging material for readers in Scotland and beyond.

Alongside the celebration of Scottish Children's Literature in these chapters, another recent initiative needs to be identified and lauded. In 2019 Moat Brae, the National Centre for Children's Literature and Storytelling, was opened in Dumfries. J. M. Barrie lived in Dumfries from 1873 to 1878. During his time there he often visited Moat Brae house and he said that the gardens were 'enchanted lands' to him and inspired the world of Peter Pan. In 2009 a dedicated group of people committed themselves to finding a way to keep J. M. Barrie, Moat Brae, and Barrie's childhood hometown of Dumfries at the forefront of children's literature. Ten years of fundraising and dedication resulted in the re-opening of Moat Brae as a literary destination for all ages in 2019. Two of its key aims are of particular importance in the context of this book. These are:

1. To establish itself as the National Centre for Children's Literature and storytelling with a remit of nurturing the love of reading and storytelling across the country.
2. To set best practices in the Scottish Children's Literature sector and support its development across all genres and in Scotland's three national languages (Scots, Gaelic and English).

Unfortunately, faced with a combination of factors, including the Covid-19 pandemic and difficulties in obtaining sponsorship and funding, Moat Brae was forced to close its doors in August 2024. In just five years, however, it performed a huge amount of work highlighting the importance of reading for children; other such initiatives will be vital to ensure that Scottish children's literature continues to thrive even in testing economic times.

As has been stated above, a volume such as this is not intended to be exhaustive but rather to act as both a showcase and a catalyst for Scottish children's literature. Its intention is to recognise the longevity and richness of a long-established body of literature in Scotland intended for children and young adults; to foreground the potential of Scottish children's and young adult literature for future enjoyment and reward; to acknowledge its potential critical, civic and educational impact, and simply to rejoice in the wonderful body of work that is currently available. Our aspiration is that readers will use the chapters here to renew old acquaintances and encounter unfamiliar and enlivening authors and materials. We further hope they will then find themselves inspired to read more widely and engage more fully with the wealth of provocative, self-confident and exciting Scottish children's literature celebrated by what we trust will be seen as a genuinely pioneering collection.

Endnotes

Introduction

1. Sarah M. Dunnigan, 'Children's Literature', in Gerard Carruthers (ed.), *A Companion to Scottish Literature* (Hoboken NJ: Wiley Blackwell, 2024), pp. 271–85.
2. Ibid., p. 272.
3. Peter Hunt, 'Poetics and practicality: Children's literature and theory in Britain', *The Lion and the Unicorn*, 19.1 (1995), p. 41.
4. F. J. Harvey Darton, *Children's Books in England: Five Centuries of Social Life*, 3rd ed., revised by Brian Alderson (London: Oak Knoll Press, 1999 [1932]).
5. Gerry Hassan and Russell Gunson, *Scotland, the UK and Brexit: a Guide to the Future* (Edinburgh: Luath Press, 2017).
6. Marie-Odile Pittin-Hedon, Camille Manfredi and Scott Hames (eds), *Scottish Writing after Devolution: Edges of the New* (Edinburgh: Edinburgh University Press, 2022).
7. Wilson McLeod and Jeremy Smith, 'Resistance to Monolinguality: The Languages of Scotland since 1918', in Ian Brown (ed.), *The Edinburgh History of Scottish Literature* (Edinburgh, Edinburgh University Press, 2007), vol. 3, pp. 21–30.
8. Robert McColl Millar, *A History of the Scots Language* (Oxford: Oxford University Press, 2023).
9. Charles Jones, *The Edinburgh History of the Scots Language* (Edinburgh: Edinburgh University Press, 1997).
10. Derrick McClure, *Scots and its Literature* (Amsterdam: John Benjamins, 1996), ch. 1, passim.
11. Ronald Macaulay, *Extremely Common Eloquence: Constructing Scottish Identity through Narrative* (Amsterdam: Rodopi, 2005), p. 24.
12. Scottish Education Department, *Primary Education: A Report of the Advisory Council on Education in Scotland* (Edinburgh: His Majesty's Stationery Office, 1946), p. 76.

13. Ibid., p. 77.
14. Bronagh Ní Chonaill, 'Fosterage: Child-Rearing in Medieval Ireland', *History Ireland*, 5.1 (Spring 1997), pp. 28–31; Gilbert Markus (ed.), *Cáin Adomnáin: a seventh-century law for the protection of non-combatants* (Kilmartin: Kilmartin House Trust, 2008).
15. Thomas Christopher Smout, *A Century of the Scottish People 1830–1950* (London: Fontana, 1990).
16. Nicholas Orme, *Medieval Children* (New Haven: Yale University Press, 2001); Nicholas Orme, *Medieval Schools* (New Haven: Yale University Press, 2006); Nicholas Orme, *Tudor Children* (New Haven: Yale University Press, 2023); Elizabeth Ewan and Janay Nugent (eds), *Finding the Family in Medieval and Early Modern Scotland* (London: Routledge, 2008); Janay Nugent and Elizabeth Ewan (eds), *Children and Youth in Pre-Modern Scotland* (Martlesham: Boydell, 2015).
17. Thomas M. Devine, *The Scottish Nation: A Modern History* (Harmondsworth: Penguin, 2012).
18. Robert Anderson, Mark Freeman and Lindsay Paterson, *The Edinburgh History of Education in Scotland* (Edinburgh: Edinburgh University Press, 2015).
19. Donald Witherington, 'Scotland, a half-educated nation in 1834? Reliable critique or persuasive polemic', in Walter M. Humes and Hamish M. Paterson (eds), *Scottish Culture and Scottish Education 1800–1980* (Edinburgh John Donald Publishing, 1982).
20. C. J. Wright, 'Academics and their aims: English and Scottish Approaches to University Education in the 19th Century', in *History of Education*, 8.2 (1979), pp. 91–97.
21. Robert A. Davis and Frank O'Hagan, *Robert Owen* (London: Bloomsbury, 2014).
22. Michael Shapira, *The War Inside* (Cambridge: Cambridge University Press, 2013).
23. Kasey McCall-Smith, 'Entrenching Children's Participation through UNCRC Incorporation in Scotland', *The International Journal of Human Rights*, 27.8 (2023), pp. 1181–204.
24. Maureen A. Farrell, *Culture and Identity in Scottish Children's Fiction* (PhD Thesis, University of Glasgow, 2009).
25. Douglas Gifford, 'Breaking Boundaries: From Modern to Contemporary in Scottish Fiction', in Brown (ed.), *The Edinburgh History of Scottish Literature* (Edinburgh: Edinburgh University Press, 2007), vol. 3, p. 251.

1. The Origins of Scottish Children's Literature

1. Sheila Ray, 'The World of Children's Literature: An Introduction', in Peter Hunt (ed.), *The International Companion Encyclopedia of Children's Literature.* (London: Routledge, 2004 [1996]), pp. 849–58.
2. Maria Nikolajeva, *Children's Literature Comes of Age: Towards a New Aesthetic* (London: Routledge, 1996).
3. Sandra L. Beckett, *Reflections of Change: Children's Literature since 1945* (Westport, CT: Greenwood Press, 1997).
4. F. J. Harvey Darton, *Children's Books in England: Five Centuries of Social Life* (London: Oak Knoll Press, 1998 [1932]).
5. Julia Briggs, 'Transitions 1890–1914', in Peter Hunt (ed.), *Children's Literature: An Illustrated History* (Oxford: Oxford University Press, 1995).
6. Stuart Hannabuss, in Hunt (ed.), *The International Companion Encyclopedia of Children's Literature* (2004), pp. 688–91.
7. Jane Potter and Helen Williams, 'Children's Books', in David Finkelstein and Alistair McCleary (eds), *The Edinburgh History of the Book in Scotland* (Edinburgh: Edinburgh University Press, 2007), vol. 4, pp. 352–67.
8. Joseph McAleer, 'Magazines and Comics', in Finkelstein and McCleary (eds), vol. 4, pp. 368–84.
9. Hunt (ed.), *The International Companion Encyclopedia of Children's Literature* (2004).
10. Jack Zipes (ed.), The Oxford Encyclopedia of Children's Literature (Oxford: Oxford University Press, 2006).
11. Matthew Grenby, 'Bibliography: the resources of children's literature', in Peter Hunt (ed.), *Understanding Children's Literature* (London: Routledge, 2005), pp. 140–58.
12. Heather Scutter, 'Children's Literature, outside, over there, and down under', *Ariel: A Review of English Literature*, 28 (1997), pp. 21–36.
13. Walter Scott, *Tales of a Grandfather* (Edinburgh: Cadell, 1828–31).
14. Catherine Sinclair, *Holiday House* (Edinburgh: William Whyte and Co., 1839).
15. Colin Milton, '"Half a trade and half an art": Adult and Juvenile Fiction in the Victorian Period', in Susan Manning (ed.), *The Edinburgh History of Scottish Literature: Volume 2, Enlightenment, Britain and Empire* (Edinburgh: Edinburgh University Press, 2007).
16. John Newbery, *A Little Pretty Pocket Book* (London: John Newbery, 1744).

17 John Wilson Croker, *Stories Selected from the History of England* (London: John Murray, 1822).
18 Walter Scott, *The Letters of Sir Walter Scott*, ed. Herbert J. C. Grierson et al. (London: Constable, 1932–37).
19 Sinclair, *Holiday House*, p. xiv.
20 Walter Scott, *The Journal of Sir Walter Scott*, ed. William E. Kinloch Anderson (Oxford: The Clarendon Press, 1972), pp. 411–12.
21 George MacDonald, *At the Back of the North Wind* (London: Everyman Publishers, 1871).
22 See Milton.
23 Helen Williams, *Printing in Scotland 1508–2008* (Edinburgh: Scottish Printing Archival Trust, 2009).
24 Norah and William Montgomerie, *The Hogarth Book of Scottish Nursery Rhymes* (London: Hogarth Press, 1964).
25 Anne Forsyth (ed.), *Scots Poems for Children* (Edinburgh: Mercat Press, 2001).
26 Alan Macdonald and Ian Brison (eds), *Ram, Tam, Toosh: An Anthology of Scottish Verse for Children* (Edinburgh: Oliver & Boyd, 1982).
27 Julia Donaldson, *The Gruffalo* (London: Macmillan Children's Books, 1999).
28 Claire McFall, *Ferryman* (Dorking, Surrey: Templar Publishing, 2013).
29 Elle McNicoll, *A Kind of Spark* (London: Knights Of, 2020).
30 Julia Bertagna, *Exodus* (London: Picador, 2002), p. 195.
31 Carla Sassi, *Why Scottish Literature Matters* (Edinburgh: The Saltire Society, 2005), pp. 114–15.
32 Victoria Kiechel, 'Extraction and the Built Environment: Violence and Other Social Consequences of the Built Environment', in Judith Shapiro and John-Andrew McNeish (eds), *Our Extractive Age: Expressions of Violence and Resistance* (London: Routledge, 2021), pp. 114–32; Stanislav Roudavski, 'Interspecies Design', in John Parham (ed.), *The Cambridge Companion to Literature and the Anthropocene* (Cambridge: Cambridge University Press, 2021), pp. 147–62.
33 Teresa Breslin, 'The Power of Place', *Ibbylink*, 20 (2007), p. 2.
34 Maria Nikolajeva, *Children's Literature Comes of Age: Towards a New Aesthetic* (London: Routledge, 1996), p. 7.

2. 'Through the Midnight Sea': Some Dimensions of Scottish Children's Poetry

1 Julie Johnstone, *The Thing That Mattered Most: Scottish Poems for Children* (Edinburgh: Black and White Publishing, 2006), p. 38.

2   Kirstie Blair, 'The Scottish Nursery Muse: Scottish Poetry and the Children's Verse Tradition in the Victorian Period', in Sarah Dunnigan and Shu-Fang Lai (eds), *The Land of Storybooks: Scottish Children's Literature in the Long Nineteenth Century* (Glasgow: Scottish Literature International, 2019), pp. 84–106.

3   Friedrich A. Kittler (trans. Michael Metteer and Chris Cullens), *Discourse Networks 1800/1900* (Stanford CA: Stanford University Press, 1990); Marina Warner, *No Go The Bogeyman: Scaring, Lulling and Making Mock* (London: Chatto & Windus, 1998).

4   Hugh MacDiarmid, 'Introduction', William Soutar, *Collected Poems*, ed. Hugh MacDiarmid (London: Andrew Dakers, 1948), pp. 16–17.

5   David Robertson (ed.), *Songs for the Nursery* (Glasgow: David Robertson, 1844); Peter Opie and Iona Archibald Opie, *The Oxford Dictionary of Nursery Rhymes* (Oxford: Clarendon Press, 1997), pp. 424–25.

6   Kirstie Blair, *Working Verse in Victorian Scotland: Poetry, Press, Community* (Oxford: Oxford University Press, 2019), pp. 63–100.

7   David Buchan, *Scottish Tradition: A Collection of Scottish Folk Literature* (London: Routledge, 1984).

8   Robert A. Davis, 'Mother at the Source: Romanticism and Infant Education', in Martin Domines Veliki and Cian Duffy (eds), *Romanticism and the Cultures of Infancy* (Cham: Palgrave Macmillan, 2020), pp. 91–113.

9   Fredrik Albritton Jonsson, *Enlightenment's Frontier: The Scottish Highlands and the Origins of Environmentalism* (New Haven, CT: Yale University Press, 2013), pp. 11–43.

10 Gill Plain (ed.), *Scotland and the First World War: Myth, Memory, and the Legacy of Bannockburn* (Lanham, MD: Rowman and Littlefield, 2016).

11 Joanne Lewis, 'How Far From Babylon? The Voices of Stevenson's Garden', in Charlotte F. Otten and Gary D. Schmidt (eds), *The Voice of the Narrator in Children's Literature: Insights from Writers and Critics* (NY: Greenwood, 1989), pp. 239–51; Michael Rosen, 'R. L. Stevenson and Children's Play: The Contexts of *A Child's Garden of Verses*', *Children's Literature in Education*, 26.1 (1995), pp. 53–72; Morag Styles, *From the Garden to the Street: An Introduction to 300 Years of Poetry for Children* (London: Cassell, 1998), pp. 170–186.

12 Julia Reid, 'Robert Louis Stevenson and the "Romance of Anthropology"', *Journal of Victorian Culture*, 10.1 (2005), pp. 46–71.

13 David Kennedy, *The Well of Being: Childhood, Subjectivity and Education* (New York: SUNY Press, 2006); Robert A. Davis, 'Brilliance

of a Fire: Innocence, Experience and the Theory of Childhood', *Journal of Philosophy of Education*, 45.2 (2011), pp. 379–97.
14 Lewis, 'How Far From Babylon? The Voices of Stevenson's Garden', in Otten and Schmidt (eds), *The Voice of the Narrator in Children's Literature* (1989), pp. 239–51.
15 Javier Moscoso, *Arc of Feeling: The History of the Swing* (London: Reaktion, 2023).
16 Ann C. Colley, '"Writing Towards Home": The Landscape of *A Child's Garden of Verses*', *Victorian Poetry*, 35.3 (Fall 1997), pp. 303–18.
17 Jean Webb, 'Conceptualizing Childhood: Robert Louis Stevenson's *A Child's Garden of Verses*', *Cambridge Journal of Education*, 32.3 (2002), pp. 359–65; Adam Kozaczka, 'Symbolism and Empire: Stevenson, Scott, and Toy Soldiers', in Sarah Dunnigan and Shu-Fang Lai (eds), *The Land of Storybooks: Scottish Children's Literature in the Long Nineteenth Century* (Glasgow: Scottish Literature International, 2019), pp. 174–92.
18 Elizabeth Waterston, 'Going for Eternity: *A Child's Garden of Verses*', *Canadian Children's Literature*, 25.4 (Winter 1999), pp. 5–10.
19 Shaun Holland, '"The Land of Play" – Robert Louis Stevenson's *A Child's Garden of Verses*', in Morag Styles, Louise Joy and David Whitley (eds), *Poetry and Childhood* (Stoke-on-Trent: Trentham Books, 2010), pp. 63–71.
20 Amanda Norman, *Transitional Objects in Early Childhood: The Value of Transitional Objects in Early Years* (Abingdon: Routledge, 2024).
21 Michel Foucault and Jay Miskowiec, 'Of Other Spaces', *Diacritics*, 16 (1986), pp. 22–27.
22 Malika Pedley, '*Mother Tongue Other Tongue* poetry competition: insights for language education', *Scottish Languages Review*, 36 (2021), pp. 9–20.
23 W. (William) R. Aitken (ed.), *Poems of William Soutar: A New Selection* (Edinburgh: Scottish Academic Press, 1988), pp. 63–121.
24 John Jamieson, *An Etymological Dictionary of the Scottish Language* (Edinburgh, 1808), p. 268.
25 Chloé Germaine, *The Dark Matter of Children's 'Fantastika' Literature: Speculative Entanglements* (London: Bloomsbury, 2023).
26 Jackie Kay, *Red, Cherry Red* (London: Bloomsbury, 2007), pp. 36–37.
27 Bette Boyd (ed.), *Anither Hantle o Verse: Poems in Scots for Children* (Edinburgh: NMS Enterprises Publishing, 2008), pp. 49–50.
28 Ibid., pp. 77–78.
29 Ibid., p. 35.

30. Johnstone, *The Thing That Mattered Most*, p. 95.
31. Ibid., pp. 34–35.
32. Jane Dowson, *Carol Anne Duffy: Poet for our Times* (London: Palgrave Macmillan, 2016), p. 198.
33. Carol Ann Duffy, *New and Collected Poems for Children* (London: Faber & Faber, 2009), p. 79.
34. David Whitley, 'Childhood and Modernity: Dark Themes in Carol Ann Duffy's Poetry for Children', *Children's Literature in Education*, 38, (2007), pp. 103–13.
35. Eva Müller-Zettlemann, 'Skeleton, Moon, Poet: Carol Ann Duffy's Poetry for Children', in Angelica Michelis and Antony Rowland (eds), *'Choosing Tough Words': The Poetry of Carol Ann Duffy* (Manchester: Manchester University Press, 2003), pp. 186–202.

3. Children's Scottish Historical Fiction

1. György Lukacs, *The Historical Novel* (London: Merlin Press, 1955, trans. 1962).
2. Jerome De Groot, *The Historical Novel* (London: Routledge, 2010), p. 18.
3. Review from 'Christian Recorder', December 1821, in Grace Kennedy, *Anna Ross: a story for children* (Edinburgh: William Oliphant, 1826, 3rd edition [1824]), p. 172.
4. J. M., 'Some account of the authoress', in Grace Kennedy, *Dunallan, or Know What You Judge* (London: Ward, Lock and Tyler, n.d. [1870?], orig. pub. Edinburgh: W. Oliphant, 1825), p. v.
5. Walter Scott, *Tales of a Grandfather*, p. vii.
6. www.literacytrust.org.uk/about/faqs/710_how_can_i_assess_the_readability_of_my_document_or_write_more_clearly [accessed 20 March 2024].
7. R. (Robert) M. Ballantyne, *The Lighthouse: being the story of a great fight between man and the sea* (Edinburgh: Chambers, 1865), p. 207.
8. Kate Flint, *The Woman Reader* (Oxford: Oxford University Press, 1993).
9. The key source for this information is the main catalogue of the National Library of Scotland and it is not clear whether Kennedy published all her novels in her lifetime or whether some manuscripts were published posthumously. Her works went through multiple editions until the end of the nineteenth century. Interestingly, the pioneering Victorian naturalist, Philip Gosse (1810–1888) remembers reading *Anna Ross* and works by Mary Martha Sherwood in his Dorset

childhood: see Douglas Lloyd Wertheimer, 'Philip Henry Gosse: Science and Revelation in the Crucible' (unpublished PhD thesis, University of Toronto, 1977) p. 33.
10. De Groot, p. 16.
11. Kennedy, *Anna Ross* (Edinburgh 1826), p. 143.
12. Deirdre H. McMahon, '"Quick, Ethel, your rifle!": portable Britishness and flexible gender roles in G. A. Henty's books for boys', *Studies in the Novel*, 42.1–2 (2010), p. 154 and ff.
13. Jan de Maeyer et al. (eds), *Religion, Children's Literature and Modernity in Western Europe 1750–2000* (Leuven: University of Leuven Press, 2005).
14. Peter Hunt, 'The Loss of the Father and the Loss of God in English-Language Children's Literature 1800–2000', in Maeyer et al., p. 295.

4. A 'Spell of Stories': Scottish Children's Fantasy

1. Ross MacKenzie, *The Otherwhere Emporium* (Edinburgh: Floris Books, 2021), p. 276. This is the third and final volume of the *Emporium* trilogy; his other YA series include *Evernight* (2020) and *Feast of the Evernight* (2021); *Shadowsmith* (2016).
2. Naomi Mitchison, *The Big House* (London: Faber and Faber, 1950), p. 123; it was reprinted, with an introduction by Moira Burgess, by Kennedy & Boyd in 2010.
3. An extensive critical literature has grown up around Rowling's series; for this reason, the present chapter does not discuss the work in detail in favour of enabling other contemporary Scottish fantasy writers to be explored, though its influence and importance is obviously profound. See, for example, Fiona McCulloch's excellent chapter on Rowling in *Contemporary British Children's Fiction and Cosmopolitanism* (Children's Literature and Culture) (London: Routledge, 2016).
4. The genre-crossing boundaries of fantasy are frequently discussed cf. Lucie Armitt, *Fantasy Fiction: An Introduction* (New York: Continuum, 2005), p. 1, and Ceri Sullivan and Barbara White (eds), *Writing and Fantasy* (London: Longman, 1999). Mitchison's *The Big House*, for instance, blends fairy tale with a miracle narrative that seems deliberately to allude to medieval Celtic saints' lives.
5. Armitt, p. 3.
6. Mackenzie, *Otherworld*, p. 88. The Potter series is an obvious example whilst a crossover audience can be found in other popular fantasy fiction series of the last two decades e.g. Philip Pullman's *His Dark Materials*. See Margaret Zeegers, Charlotte Pass, Ellen Jampole, 'A

Clash of Chronotopes: Adult Reading of Children's and Young Adult Literature', *International Journal of the Book*, 7.4 (2010), pp. 89–97.

7   See Roderick McGillis, 'Investigating the Reading Subject: Response Criticism', in Roderick McGillis (ed.), *The Nimble Reader: Literary Theory and Children's Literature* (New York: Twayne, 1996), pp. 177–200; Evelyn Arizpe (ed.), *Children as Readers in Children's Literature: The power of texts and the importance of reading* (London: Routledge, 2015); Poonam Arya and Karen M. Feathers, 'Reconsidering Children's Readings: Insights into the Reading Process', *Reading Psychology*, 33.4 (2012), pp. 301–22.

8   Tolkien's classic essay is 'On Fairy Stories', in *Tree and Leaf* (London: HarperCollins, 2001), pp. 1–81; cf. Verlyn Flieger and Douglas A. Anderson's edition, *Tolkien on Fairy-Stories* (London: HarperCollins, 2014).

9   cf. Farah Mendlesohn, *Rhetorics of Fantasy* (Wesleyan University Press, 2008); see also Tzvetan Todorov's classic study for classifications of the category of 'the marvellous', *The Fantastic: A Structural Approach to a Literary Genre*, trans. Richard Howard (Ithaca: Cornell University Press, 1975). There is an extensive critical literature on fantasy writing but Lucie Armitt in *Theorising the Fantastic* (London: Arnold, 1996) offers an insightful conceptual overview. See also Christine Brooke-Rose, *A Rhetoric of the Unreal: Studies in Narrative and Structure, Especially of the Fantastic* (Cambridge: Cambridge University Press, 1981); Rosemary Jackson, *Fantasy: The Literature of Subversion* (London: Methuen, 1981); Kathryn Hume, *Fantasy and Mimesis: Responses to Reality in Western Literature* (New York: Methuen, 1984); Edward James and Farah Mendlesohn (eds), *The Cambridge Companion to Fantasy Literature* (Cambridge: Cambridge University Press, 2012); Brian Attebery, *Stories about Stories: Fantasy and the Remaking of Myth* (Oxford: Oxford University Press, 2014). Ursula K. Le Guin's own writing about fantasy is also illuminating: cf. *The Language of the Night: Essays on fantasy and science fiction*, ed. and intro. Susan Wood (New York: Putnam, 1979).

10 Julie Bertagna, *Exodus* (London: Picador, 2002), p. 26. All subsequent references are to this edition.

11 The 'vial' is from the *Emporium*; the box from Mitchison's *The Big House*.

12 The only sustained discussion to date has been by Maureen Farrell in 'The lost boys and girls of Scottish children's fiction', in *The Edinburgh History of Scottish Literature*, ed. Ian Brown, Thomas

Clancy, Susan Manning, and Murray Pittock, 3 vols (Edinburgh: Edinburgh University Press, 2007), vol 3, pp. 198–206; 'Culture and Identity in Scottish Children's Fiction', unpublished PhD thesis, University of Glasgow, 2009, which has an entire separate chapter devoted to the study of Scottish children's fantasy (pp. 120–63). In her chapters on Rowling and Bertagna in Contemporary British Children's Fiction, Fiona McCulloch also discusses Scottish fantasy writing in the context of writing for children and young adults.

13 For helpful overviews of a vast field, see Maria Nikolajeva, 'The development of children's fantasy', in Edward James and Farah Mendlesohn (eds), *The Cambridge Companion to Fantasy Literature* (Cambridge: Cambridge University Press, 2012), pp. 50–61, and Catherine Butler, 'Modern children's fantasy', in James and Mendlesohn, pp. 224–35.

14 In *An Anthology of Scottish Fantasy Literature* (Edinburgh: Polygon, 1996), Manlove suggests that 'doubles and dream structure', the profound influence of Calvinism, social non-conformism, 'a levelling down' (p. 14), the prevalence for a fantastical underworld (rather than 'over', p. 15), and 'a continual sense of undertow, of a greater gravitational force that will absorb the self' (p. 15), might be considered defining qualities of Scottish fantasy; Margaret Elphinstone, 'Scottish Fantasy Today', *Ecloga Online Journal*, 1 (2001), pp. 1–13 [accessed 20 March 2024]; for related work on Scottish fantasy in the context of Gothic, see, for example, Monica Germanà, *Scottish Women's Gothic and Fantastic Writing: Fiction since 1978* (Edinburgh: Edinburgh University Press, 2010), and Kirsty MacDonald, 'Against Realism: Contemporary Scottish Literature and the Supernatural', in Bertold Schoene (ed.), *The Edinburgh Companion to Contemporary Scottish Literature* (Edinburgh: Edinburgh University Press, 2007), pp. 328–35.

15 The work of Susan Cooper (*The Boggart* [1993]) or Susan Price (*The Sterkarm Handshake* [1998]) are good examples of this imaginative and historical transposition.

16 cf. Margaret Bennett, 'The Roots of Living Tradition', in Sarah Dunnigan and Suzanne Gilbert (eds), *The Edinburgh Companion to Scottish Traditional Literatures* (Edinburgh: Edinburgh University Press, 2013), pp. 7–13 (p. 7); Donald Smith, *Storytelling Scotland: A Nation in Narrative* (Edinburgh: Polygon, 2001).

17 See further, Sarah Dunnigan, 'The Early Modern Period', in Dunnigan and Gilbert (eds), *Scottish Traditional Literatures*, pp. 63–73 (pp. 63, 66).

18 The tales of *Beauty and the Beast* and *Sleeping Beauty* seemed especially popular, often in single printings or collections, frequently listed in the records of Glasgow, Edinburgh, and Paisley chapbook publishers; cf. Kirsteen Connor, 'Youth's poison?: The creation and evolution of children's chapbooks in Scotland, 1800–1870', unpublished MPhil(R) thesis, University of Glasgow (2010).
19 Edward J. Cowan and Mike Paterson, *Folk in Print: Scotland's Chapbook Heritage 1750–1850* (Edinburgh: John Donald, 2007), p. 22.
20 See Valentina Bold, 'Entertaining and Instructing Histories: Children's Chapbook Literature in the Nineteenth Century', in Sarah Dunnigan and Shu-Fang Lai (eds), *The Land of Story Books: Scottish Children's Literature in the Nineteenth Century* (Glasgow: Scottish Literature International, 2019), pp. 42–61.
21 Harvey, p. 23; Cowan and Paterson, pp. 22–24.
22 *Letters on the Elementary Principles of Education*, vol. 1, 6th edn (London: Baldwin, Cradock and Joy, 1818), p. 292. The work was first published in 1801 as Letters on Education and subsequently republished in expanded editions; see Pam Perkins, 'Hamilton, Elizabeth (1756?–1816)', in David Cannadine (ed.), *Oxford Dictionary of National Biography*, online ed. (Oxford: Oxford University Press, 2004), www.oxforddnb.com/view/article/12062 [accessed 20 March 2024]. On the controversy in general see, for example, Nicholas Tucker, *Suitable for Children? Controversies in Children's Literature* (London: Chatto & Windus for Sussex University Press, 1976); Torben Weinrich, *Children's Literature – Art or Pedagogy?* (Copenhagen: Rothskilde University Press, 2000); Andrea Immel and Michael Witmore (eds), *Childhood and Children's Books in Early Modern Europe, 1550–1800* (New York and London: Routledge, 2006); Dennis M. Welch, 'Blake and Rousseau on Children's Reading, Pleasure, and Imagination', *Lion and the Unicorn*, 35.3 (2011), pp. 199–226.
23 Charlotte Mitchell, 'Sinclair, Catherine (1800–1864)', in David Cannadine (ed.), *Oxford Dictionary of National Biography*, online ed., (Oxford: Oxford University Press, 2004), www.oxforddnb.com/view/article/25612 [accessed 20 March 2024]. See further Farrell, *Culture and Identity*, pp. 54–58; Robin A. Hoffmann, 'Holiday House, Childhood, and the End(s) of Time', in *Children's Literature: Annual of The Modern Language Association Division on Children's Literature and The Children's Literature Association*, 41 (2013), pp. 115–39; Alexandra Rae Valint, 'Mischief, Gender, and Empire: Raising Imperial Bachelors and Spinsters in Catherine Sinclair's Holiday House',

Children's Literature Association Quarterly, 36.1 (2011), pp. 64–88; David Rudd, 'The Froebellious Child in Catherine Sinclair's Holiday House', *The Lion and the Unicorn*, 28.1 (2004), pp. 53–69; Jackie C. Horne, 'Punishment as Performance in Catherine Sinclair's Holiday House', *Children's Literature Association Quarterly*, 26.1 (2001), pp. 22–32.

24 Catherine Sinclair, *Holiday House. A Book for the Young*, intro. Barbara Willard (London: Hamish Hamilton, 1972), pp. 124, 128.
25 'The Fantastic Imagination', in George MacDonald, *The Complete Fairy Tales*, ed. Ulrich C. Knoepflmacher (London: Penguin, 1999), p. 7. Unless otherwise stated, all subsequent MacDonald references are to this edition.
26 *Scottish Folk and Fairy Tales* (1892; Bath: Lomond Books, 2005), p. 18. This is a version of 'The Kind and Unkind Girls' (ATU 480).
27 Mary MacGregor, *Stories from the Ballads told to the Children*, with pictures by Katharine Cameron (London: T. C. and E. C. Jack, 1908), p. viii.
28 Ibid., p. 15.
29 Ibid., p. 4.
30 Elizabeth W. Grierson, *The Scottish Fairy Book*, with illustrations by Morris Meredith Williams (New York: Frederick A. Stokes Company, 1910), 'Preface', n.p.
31 Jacqueline Rose, *The Case of Peter Pan, or, The Impossibility of Children's Fiction* (London: Macmillan, 1984); cf. David Rudd and Anthony Pavlik (eds), 'The (Im)possibility of Children's Fiction: Rose Twenty-Five Years On', *Children's Literature Association Quarterly*, 35.3 (2010).
32 *Peter and Wendy*, in J. M. Barrie, *Peter Pan: Peter and Wendy and Peter Pan in Kensington Gardens*, ed. with Introduction and Notes by Jack Zipes (London: Penguin, 2004), p. 12.
33 Jacob's *The Golden Heart* is republished by Kennedy and Boyd (2011).
34 See further Maureen Farrell, 'Culture and Identity', pp. 142–46; Moira Burgess, *Mitchison's Ghosts: Supernatural elements in the Scottish fiction of Naomi Mitchison* (Humming Earth, 2008) and 'Naomi Mitchison and the Supernatural', *The Bottle Imp*, 19, www.thebottleimp.org.uk/2016/06/naomi-mitchison-and-the-supernatural/ [accessed 20 March 2024].
35 Naomi Mitchison, *The Fourth Pig*, with a new introduction by Marina Warner (Princeton: Princeton University Press, 2014), p. 16.
36 Andrew Lang, *The Gold of Fairnilee and other stories*, intro. Gillian Avery (London: Victor Gollancz Ltd, 1967), p. 47.

37 Martin Stewart, *Riverkeep* (London: Penguin, 2016). All subsequent references are to this edition.
38 All subsequent references to Bertagna's trilogy are to the following editions: *Exodus* (London: Young Picador, 2002); *Zenith* (London: Young Picador, 2007); *Aurora* (London: Macmillan Children's, 2011).
39 'The Gold of Fairnilee', p. 51: 'The Fairy Queen, that had seemed so happy and beautiful in her bright dress, was a weary, pale woman in black, with a melancholy face and melancholy eyes. She looked as if she had been there for thousands of years, always longing for the sunlight and the earth, and the wind and rain' (p. 51).
40 Ross McKenzie, *The Nowhere Emporium* (Edinburgh: Floris Books, 2015), p. 42; p. 64. All subsequent references are to this edition.
41 This is the first of the 'Edinburgh Nights' series; see 'T. L. Huchu talks witch-hunting aunties and the Zimbabwean magic in Scotland that inspired his fantasy novel', www.panmacmillan.com/blogs/young-adult/library-of-the-dead-inspiration-t-l-huchu [accessed 3 August 2023].
42 Jackie Kay, *Strawgirl* (London: Macmillan Children's Books, 2003), pp. 62, 103.
43 George MacDonald, *At the Back of the North Wind*, ed. Roderick McGillis and John Pennington, with a preface by Stephen Prickett (Broadview Press, 2011), pp. 122–24. All subsequent references are to this edition.
44 *The Princess and the Goblin* (London: Puffin, 1996), p. 177.
45 *Aurora*, p. 143. Interestingly, the 'Midnight Storyteller' also includes *Beowulf*, *Brave New World*, *The Time Machine*, *Gormenghast*, *Wuthering Heights*, *The Tempest*, *Frankenstein*, *Gulliver's Travels*, *The Grapes of Wrath*, and *War and Peace* amongst his narrations (cf. p. 249).
46 Huchu, p. 88.
47 Quoted in Seth Lerer, *Children's Literature: A Reader's History, from Aesop to Harry Potter* (Chicago: University of Chicago Press, 2008), 'From Islands to Empire', p. 151.
48 Mollie Hunter, *The Kelpie's Pearls* (Edinburgh: Merchiston Publishing, 2011). All subsequent references are to this edition.
49 Debi Gliori, *Night Shift* (London: Hot Key Books, 2017), n.p. It was shortlisted for the Kate Greenaway Medal and received a nomination for IBBY's selection of Outstanding Books for Young People with Disabilities.
50 McCulloch, *British Children's Fiction*; see also Farrell, 'Lost Boys and Girls', p. 203. See further in general Carrie Hintz and Elaine Ostry

(eds), *Utopian and Dystopian Writing for Children and Young Adults* (London: Routledge, 2003).

51 On ecocritical and environmentalist concerns as portrayed in children's and young adult literature more generally, see Greta Gaard, 'Children's Environmental Literature: From Ecocriticism to Ecopedagogy', *Neohelicon: Acta Comparationis Litterarum Universarum*, 36.2 (2009), pp. 321–34; Sidney I. Dobrin and Kenneth B. Kidd (eds), *Wild Things: Children's Culture and Ecocriticism* (Detroit: Wayne State University Press, 2004); Geraldine Massey and Clare Bradford, 'Children as Ecocitizens: Ecocriticism and Environmental Texts', in Kerry Mallan and Clare Bradford (eds), *Contemporary Children's Literature and Film: Engaging with Theory* (New York: Palgrave Macmillan, 2011), pp. 109–26.

52 Farrell, *Culture and Identity*, p. 163.

53 See Lizanne Henderson and Edward J. Cowan, *Scottish Fairy Belief: A History* (East Linton: Tuckwell Press, 2001).

54 For extensive discussion, see further Farrell, *Culture and Identity*, pp. 138–63.

55 See also Janis Dawson, 'Expanding a Traditional Ballad: Tam Lin in the Picture Book Fantasies of Jane Yolen and Susan Cooper', *Children's Folklore Review*, 25.1–2 (2002–03), pp. 23–38; Ginger Mullen, 'Transformations of "Tam Lin": An Analysis of Folktale Picture Books', *Looking Glass: New Perspectives on Children's Literature*, 8.3 (2004); Evelyn M. Perry, 'The Ever-Vigilant Hero: Revaluing the Tale of Tam Lin', *Children's Folklore Review*, 19.2 (1997), pp. 31–49; Martha P. Hixon, 'Tam Lin, Fair Janet, and the Sexual Revolution: Traditional Ballads, Fairy Tales, and Twentieth Century Children's Literature', *Marvels & Tales: Journal of Fairy-Tale Studies*, 18.1 (2004), pp. 67–92; Kallie George, 'An Earthly Knight and Fire and Hemlock: Two "Tam Lin" Retellings', *Looking Glass: New Perspectives on Children's Literature*, 11.1 (2007).

56 Duncan and Linda Williamson, *A Thorn in the King's Foot: Stories of the Scottish Travelling People* (London: Penguin, 1987); Duncan Williamson, *The Coming of the Unicorn: Scottish Folk Tales for Children* (Edinburgh: Floris Books, 2012) and *The Flight of the Golden Bird: Scottish Folk Tales for Children* (Edinburgh: Floris Books, 2013).

57 Matthew Fitt and James Robertson, *A Wee Book o Fairy Tales in Scots*, illus. Deborah Campbell (Edinburgh: Itchy Coo, 2003); Donald Smith, *Wee Folk Tales in Scots*, illus. Annalisa Salis (Edinburgh: Luath Press Ltd, 2018).

58 George Mackay Brown, *The Two Fiddlers: Tales from Orkney* (London: Chatto and Windus, 1974).
59 Ibid.

5. Gaelic Plays for Children 1900–1950

1 My thanks to Sheila Kidd, Geraldine Parsons, Peadar Ó Muircheartaigh and Eleanor Thomson for their valuable comments.
2 Jason Marc Harris, *Folklore and the Fantastic in Nineteenth-Century British Fiction* (Aldershot: Ashgate, 2008).
3 Michael Shaw, *The Fin-de-Siècle Scottish Revival: Romance, Decadence and Celtic Identity* (Edinburgh: Edinburgh University Press, 2020).
4 Charles W. J. Withers, *Gaelic in Scotland: 1698–1981: The Geographical History of a Language* (Edinburgh: John Donald, 2021), p. 162; Jonathan Dembling, 'Gaelic in Canada: New Evidence from an Old Census', in Wilson McLeod et al. (eds), *Cànan & Cultar/Language & Culture: Rannsachadh na Gàidhlig 3* (Edinburgh: Dunedin Academic Press, 2006), pp. 57–71.
5 Fiona O'Hanlon and Lindsay Paterson, 'Gaelic Education since 1872', in Robert Anderson, Mark Freeman and Lindsay Paterson (eds), *The Edinburgh History of Education in Scotland* (Edinburgh: Edinburgh University Press, 2015), pp. 304–25.
6 Charles W. J. Withers, *Gaelic Scotland: The Transformation of a Culture Region* (Abingdon: Routledge, 2016), pp. 145–66.
7 Ealasaid Chaimbeul, *Air Mo Chuairt* (Steòrnabhagh: Acair, 1982), p. 4. All translations from Gaelic into English in this chapter are by Sìm Innes unless otherwise stated.
8 Chaimbeul, *Air Mo Chuairt*, p. 11.
9 Aonghas Caimbeul, *Suathadh ri Iomadh Rubha*, ed. by Iain Moireach (Glaschu: Gairm, 1973), pp. 21–22. Partial translation in Meg Bateman, 'The Autobiography in Scottish Gaelic', in Ian Brown et al. (eds), *The Edinburgh History of Scottish Literature, Vol. 3: Modern Transformations – New Identities (from 1918)* (Edinburgh: Edinburgh University Press, 2007), pp. 225–30 (p. 228).
10 For a discussion of the time period involved and for further reading see Michael McAteer, 'Celtic and Irish Revival' (2019), available via www.oxfordbibliographies.com. For Scotland in particular see Derick S. Thomson, 'Gaelic renaissance c. 1900–1930', *Transactions of the Gaelic Society of Inverness*, 60 (1997–98), pp. 285–301.
11 William Gillies, 'Alexander Carmichael and the Folklore of the MacMhuirich Poets', in Domhnall Uilleam Stiùbhart (ed.), *The Life*

    and Legacy of Alexander Carmichael (Port of Ness: The Islands Book Trust, 2018), pp. 96–114 (p. 112).
12 Fiona Macleod, *The House of Usna* (Portland, Maine: Thomas B. Mosher, 1903); Fiona Macleod, *The Immortal Hour* (Portland, Maine: Thomas B. Mosher, 1907).
13 Bessie J. B. MacArthur, *The Clan of Lochlan and Silis: Two Celtic Plays* (Edinburgh: W. M. Urquhart and Son, 1928).
14 Sìm Innes, 'Translated drama in Gaelic in Scotland to c. 1950', *International Journal of Scottish Theatre and Screen*, 9 (2016), pp. 61–88.
15 Pauline Turner Strong, *American Indians and the American Imaginary: Cultural Representation Across the Centuries* (Abingdon: Routledge, 2016), p. 2.
16 Sìm Innes and Kate Louise Mathis, 'Gaelic Tradition and the Celtic Revival in Children's Literature in Scottish Gaelic and English', in Sarah Dunnigan and Shu-Fang Lai (eds), *The Land of Story-Books: Scottish Children's Literature in the Long Nineteenth Century* (Glasgow: Scottish Literature International, 2019), pp. 107–57.
17 Alexander M'Laurin, *The First Book for Children in the Gaelic Language* (Edinburgh: Printed for the Society for the Support of Gaelic Schools, by A. Balfour, 1811).
18 Iain Mac Phàidein, *Companach na Cloinne: Leabhran Sgoil anns am bheil Sgeòil Thaitneach, fo làimh Chaluim Mhic Phàrlain* (Stirling: Aonghas Mac Aoidh, 1912).
19 Ian MacDonald, 'Publishing for Children in Gaelic', in Jeffrey Garrett (ed.), *Children's Books of the Celtic World* (Munich: Erasmus Grasser Verlag, 1988), pp. 4–11 (p. 4).
20 Wilson McLeod, *Gaelic in Scotland: Policies, Movements, Ideologies* (Edinburgh: Edinburgh University Press, 2020).
21 Allan MacDonald, 'An Sithean Ruadh', *The Celtic Review*, 3.9 (1906), pp. 77–83.
22 Roger Hutchinson, *Father Allan: the life and legacy of a Hebridean priest* (Edinburgh: Birlinn, 2010).
23 Tiber Falzett, '"Cuir Dhachaigh E" ("Send It Home"): The Gifts of the Little People, the Bob of Fettercairn and the aesthetics of a tale and a tune', in C. Ó Baoill and N. McGuire (eds), *Rannsachadh na Gàidhlig 6* (Aberdeen: An Clò Gàidhealach, 2013), pp. 93–120.
24 MacDonald, 'An Sithean Ruadh', pp. 77–78.
25 Ibid., p. 81.
26 Ibid., p. 82.

27 Sìm Innes, 'Dùsgadh na Féinne (1908): Katherine Whyte Grant's Scottish Gaelic kinderspiel', in Sharon J. Arbuthnot et al. (eds), *The Gaelic Finn Tradition II* (Dublin: Four Courts Press, 2022), pp. 197–210.
28 Ibid., p. 200.
29 Joseph Falaky Nagy, 'Fiannaíocht', in John T. Koch et al. (eds), *Celtic Culture: A Historical Encylopedia* (Santa Barbara: ABC-CLIO, 2006), pp. 744–46.
30 John Sobieski and Charles Edward Stuart, *Lays of the Deer Forest with Sketches of Olden and Modern Deer-Hunting; Traits of Natural History in the Forest: Traditions of the Clans; Miscellaneous Notes*, 2 vols (Edinburgh and London: William Blackwood and Sons, 1848), vol. 2, pp. 525–27.
31 Susan Ross, 'Identity in Gaelic Drama 1900–1949', *International Journal of Scottish Theatre and Screen*, 9 (2016), online at www.ijosts.glasgow.ac.uk/volume-9/
32 Katherine Whyte Grant, *Dùsgadh na Féinne* (Paisley: J. & R. Parlane, 1908) p. 14.
33 Malcolm MacFarlane, 'Am Mosgladh Mòr', *The Celtic Monthly*, 22.7 (July 1914), pp. 136–39; 22.8 (August 1914), pp. 156–58; 22.9 (September 1914), pp. 171–74. [Malcom MacFarlane], 'Am Mosgladh Mòr', *The Celtic Monthly*, 23.3 (March 1915), pp. 54–57; 23.4 (April 1915), pp. 74–77; 23.5 (May 1915), pp. 82–86. This introduction is on p. 130 of the first instalment.
34 Calum MacPhàrlain, *Am Mosgladh Mòr* (Glascho: An Comunn Gaidhealach, 1925).
35 Innes and Mathis, 'Gaelic Tradition and the Celtic Revival', p. 118.
36 L. Macbean, 'The Mission of the Celt', *Transactions of the Gaelic Society of Inverness*, 21 (1896–97), pp. 56–69 (p. 69). See Innes and Mathis, 'Gaelic Tradition and the Celtic Revival'.
37 *Am Mosgladh Mòr*, p. 56.
38 Ibid., pp. 83–84.
39 Roderick MacLeod, 'Malcolm Macfarlane (1853–1931) of Dalavich and Elderslie: Writer, Editor, Composer, Correspondent and Controversialist', *Transactions of the Gaelic Society of Inverness*, 64 (2006), pp. 299–315.
40 McLeod, *Gaelic in Scotland*, p. 59.
41 On Sinclair see Aonghas MacLeòid, 'Forgetting Donald Sinclair 1885–1932: The Passage between Celtic Revival and Scottish Renaissance', *Scottish Language*, 37 (2018), pp. 55–72.

42 Donald Archie MacDonald, 'Migratory Legends of the Supernatural in Scotland: A General Survey', *Béaloideas*, 62/63 (1994–95), pp. 29–78 (p. 46).

43 See for instance, 'Fear aig an robh leannan sìth uaireigin agus mar a dh'fheuch i ri cur às dha bhean', on *Tobar an Dualchais*, Tape ID SA1965.006, recorded March 1965: www.tobarandualchais.co.uk/track/62850?l=gd; Tale 72, 'A Man with a Fairy Lover', in Alan Bruford and Donald A. MacDonald (eds), *Scottish Traditional Tales* (Edinburgh: Polygon, 1994), pp. 247–48.

44 Alexander Carmichael, *Carmina Gadelica* (Edinburgh: T. and A. Constable, 1900), pp. 248–49.

45 Ronald Black, 'I thought he made it all up: Context and Controversy', in D. U. Stiùbhart (ed.), *The Life and Legacy of Alexander Carmichael* (Port of Ness: The Island Book Trust, 2008), pp. 57–81.

46 Michelle Macleod, 'Three Centuries of Gaelic Language Manipulation on Stage', *Scottish Studies*, 33 (2014), pp. 9–25 (p. 15).

47 Sheila Kidd, 'The Forgotten First: John MacCormick's *Dùn-Àluinn*', *Scottish Gaelic Studies*, 22 (2006), pp. 197–219; Sìm Innes, 'Shakespeare's Scottish play in Scottish Gaelic', *Scottish Language*, 33 (2014), pp. 26–50.

48 Dòmhnall Budge (ed.), *Sàr-Òrain le Catrìona Dhùghlas: Na h-Òrain is an Ceòl gu h-uile Catrìona Dhùghlas* (Dùn Bheagan, n.p. 1971), pp. 4–5.

49 Dòmhnall Buidse, 'Bàird an Eilean Sgiathanach Clann-an-Aba, Throdairnis', *Transactions of the Gaelic Society of Inverness*, 48 (1976), pp. 584–601 and projects.handsupfortrad.scot/hall-of-fame/jonathan-macdonald-mbe/

50 'Skye Provincial Mod', *An Gaidheal*, 28 (1933), p. 190; 'Mod Prize List', *An Gaidheal*, 43 (1947), pp. 25–28 (p. 25).

51 Thomas McKean, 'Celtic Music and the Growth of the Féis Movement in the Scottish Highlands', *Western Folklore*, 57 (1998), pp. 245–59 (n. 6, pp. 256–57).

52 D. Budge (ed.), *Pein-Ora* (Dùn Bheagan: Budge, 1972), p. 15.

53 Tape ID SA1954.069, recorded July 1954 www.tobarandualchais.co.uk/track/68075?l=en

54 Anna NicIain, 'Sgeulachd a' Ghamhna Dhuinn', *Béaloideas*, 6 (1930), pp. 293–97. For an English translation see 'The Tale of the Brown Calf', in Alan Bruford and Donald A. MacDonald (eds), *Scottish Traditional Tales* (Edinburgh: Polygon, 1994), pp. 64–69. See also 'A' Chaora Bhiorach Ghlas' ('The Sharp Grey Sheep'), in John Francis

Campbell (ed.), *Popular Tales of the West Highlands*, new edition, 4 vols (1890–93), vol. II, pp. 300–06.
55 Ross, 'Identity in Gaelic Drama 1900–1949', pp. 39–60.

6. Stevenson's Junior Fiction

1 David Daiches, *Robert Louis Stevenson* (Norfolk, Connecticut: New Directions, 1947), pp. 28–29.
2 R. H. Hutton, Unsigned Review, *Spectator*, 11 August 1888, lxi, pp. 1099–100, reprinted in Paul Maixner (ed.), *Robert Louis Stevenson: The Critical Heritage* (London, Boston and Henley: Routledge & Kegan Paul, 1981), pp. 318–20 (p. 319).
3 Robert Louis Stevenson, 'A Gossip on Romance', reprinted in Jeremy Treglown (ed.), *The Lantern-Bearers and other essays: Robert Louis Stevenson* (New York: Farrar Straus Giroux, 1988), pp. 172–82 (p. 172).
4 Ibid., p. 175.
5 George MacDonald, 'The Fantastic Imagination', in *A Dish of Orts: Chiefly Papers on the Imagination and on Shakespeare* (London: George Newnes, 1905), pp. 313–22 (p. 317).
6 John Rowe Townsend, *Written for Children: An Outline of English Children's Literature* (London: Garnet Miller, 1965), pp. 43–54.
7 Oliver S. Buckton, '"Faithful to his Map": Profit and Desire in Robert Louis Stevenson's *Treasure Island*', *Journal of Stevenson Studies*, 1 (2004), pp. 138–49.
8 Treglown, pp. 194–95.
9 Ibid., p. 279.
10 Robert Louis Stevenson, *Treasure Island*, ed. Peter Hunt (Oxford: Oxford University Press, 2011), p. 117. Further quotations are from this edition.
11 Robert Louis Stevenson, *The Black Arrow*, ed. John Sutherland (London: Penguin Books, 2007), pp. viii-ix. Further quotations are from this edition.
12 Robert Louis Stevenson, *Kidnapped*, ed. Ian Duncan (Oxford: Oxford University Press, 2014), p. 156. Further quotations are from this edition.
13 Daiches, p. 55.
14 Edward J. Cowan, '"Intent upon my own race and place I wrote": Robert Louis Stevenson and Scottish History', in Edward J. Cowan and Douglas Gifford (eds), *The Polar Twins* (Edinburgh: John Donald Publishers, 1999), pp. 187–214.
15 Ibid., pp. 201–02.
16 Treglown, p. 282.

17 Robert Crawford, *Scotland's Books: The Penguin History of Scottish Literature* (London: Penguin Books, 2007), p. 497.
18 Treglown, pp. 283–84.
19 Sutherland, p. xxvii.
20 Ibid., p. xlvi.
21 *The Letters of Robert Louis Stevenson*, 8 volumes, ed. Bradford A. Booth and Ernest Mehew (New Haven, Connecticut and London: Yale University Press, 1994–95). Further quotations are from this edition.
22 Robert Louis Stevenson, *Kidnapped* and *Catriona*, ed. Emma Letley (Oxford and New York: Oxford University Press, 1986), p. 425.

7. Mollie Hunter's Teen Fiction: Transitioning through Enchanted Humanness to Adulthood

1 Peter Hollindale, 'World enough and time: The Work of Mollie Hunter', *Children's Literature in Education*, 8.3 (1977), pp. 109–19, p. 109.
2 Valerie Bierman, Obituary, *The Scotsman*, 7 August 2012.
3 Hollindale, 'World enough and time: The Work of Mollie Hunter', pp. 117–18, strongly lauds Hunter's *The Haunted Mountain*, and *A Sound of Chariots*.
4 Betty Greenway, *A Stranger Shore: A Critical Introduction to the Work of Mollie Hunter* (Lanham, Maryland: Scarecrow Press, 1998).
5 A notable exception being Maureen Anne Farrell, 'Culture and Identity in Scottish Children's Fiction' (unpublished PhD thesis, University of Glasgow, 2009).
6 Mollie Hunter, *Talent is Not Enough* (New York: Harper & Row, [1976]).
7 Hollindale, 'World enough and time: The Work of Mollie Hunter', discusses several ways in which Hunter's work is not constricted by its Scottishness, including the socialism in *A Sound of Chariots*, and several other considerations, such as their grounding values of, especially, love. He also briefly mentions their 'humanness' (pp. 111–12, 115, 117).
8 Mollie Hunter, *A Sound of Chariots* (London: Collins, 1983 [1973]).
9 Mollie Hunter, *The Third Eye* (Glasgow: Richard Drew, 1988 [1979]).
10 Mollie Hunter, *The Stronghold* (London: Hamish Hamilton [1974]).
11 Mollie Hunter, *A Stranger Came Ashore* (London: Hamish Hamilton, 1975).
12 Mollie Hunter, *I'll Go My Own Way* (London: Fontana Lions, 1987 [1985]). On such highly sensitive subjects, including rape, compare *TINE*, pp. 20–22.

13 Mollie Hunter, *The Thirteenth Member* (Edinburgh: Canongate, 1986 [1971]).
14 Mollie Hunter, *A Pistol in Greenyards* (London: Hamish Hamilton [1965]).
15 Philip Pullman, *Northern Lights* (London: Scholastic, 1995).
16 See Mollie Hunter's comments on why she chose to write about ordinary people (*TINE*, p. 14). Roni Natov, 'The Truth of Ordinary Lives: Autobiographical Fiction for Children', *Children's Literature in Education*, 17.2 (1986), pp. 112–25 (p. 117), draws attention to how Bridie, in Hunter's *A Sound of Chariots*, finds 'in her admiration and sympathy for the bravery and fineness of ordinary people a new feeling of community'.
17 See Mollie Hunter, 'A Need for Heroes', *Children's Literature Association Quarterly* (1979), Proceedings, pp. 52–66 (p. 56).
18 Mollie Hunter, *You Never Knew Her as I Did* (London: Hamish Hamilton, 1981).
19 Mollie Hunter, *Escape from Loch Leven* (Hamish Hamilton, 1981).
20 Plato, *The Republic*, 2nd edn (London: Penguin, 2003), pp. 240–44 (514a–17a).
21 Mollie Hunter, *The Ghosts of Glencoe* (London: Hamish Hamilton, 1976 [1966]), pp. 159–60.
22 Hannah Arendt, *Eichmann in Jerusalem: A Report on the Banality of Evil*, rev. edn (Harmondsworth: Penguin, 1964).
23 Mollie Hunter, *The Enchanted Whistle* (London: Magnet, 1985; first pub. 1968 under the title *The Ferlie*).
24 M. Sarah Smedman, 'Springs of Hope: Recovery of Primordial Time in "Mythic"', *Children's Literature*, 16 (1988), pp. 91–107 (pp. 99–102), discusses hope in relation to what is probably Hunter's most emotionally harrowing and yet life-affirming/hopeful novel, her semi-autobiographical *A Sound of Chariots*.
25 Mollie Hunter, *The Kelpie's Pearls* (London: Hamish Hamilton, 1983 [1964]).

8. Adolescent Citizenship in Cathy MacPhail's *Mosi's War* and Claire McFall's *Bombmaker*

1 See Fiona McCulloch, *Contemporary British Children's Fiction and Cosmopolitanism* (New York and London: Routledge 2017); '"Daughter of an Outcast Queen": Defying State Expectations in Jenni Fagan's *The Panopticon*', *Scottish Literary Review*, 7.1 (Spring/Summer 2015), pp. 113–31; '"The Future of the Planet": Scottish Cosmopolitanism/

Cosmofeminism and Environmentalism in Theresa Breslin's *Saskia's Journey*', *Studies in Scottish Literature*, 40 (2014), pp. 183–204; 'Dismembering "Patriotism": Cosmopolitan Haunting in Theresa Breslin's *Remembrance*', *The Lion and the Unicorn*, 38.3 (Sep. 2014), pp. 342–59; '"Many Different Voices and Accents" – Cosmopolitan Time-Travel in Catherine Forde's *Think Me Back*', *International Review of Scottish Studies*, 39 (2014), pp. 55–80; '"A New Home in the World": Scottish Devolution, Nomadic Writing, and Supranational Citizenship in Julie Bertagna's *Exodus* and *Zenith*', *Ariel*, 38.4 (2007), pp. 69–96.

2   Maria Jose Botelho and Masha Kabakow Rudman, *Critical Multicultural Analysis of Children's Literature* (Abingdon and New York: Routledge, 2009), p. 1.

3   Michael Gardiner, 'Literature, Theory, Politics: Devolution as Iteration', in Berthold Schoene (ed.), *The Edinburgh Companion to Contemporary Scottish Literature* (Edinburgh: Edinburgh University Press, 2007), p. 48.

4   Michael Gardiner, *Modern Scottish Culture* (Edinburgh: Edinburgh University Press, 2005), p. 1.

5   Michael O'Neill, *Devolution and British Politics* (Harlow: Pearson Longman, 2004), p. 366.

6   Ibid., p. 327.

7   Fiona McCulloch, 'Julie Bertagna Interview' (unpublished typescript, 4 October 2006), n.p.

8   Claire McFall, *Bombmaker* (Dorking: Templar, 2014), p. 24. All references to this text will be cited by pagination throughout.

9   Judith Torney-Purta and Jo-Ann Amadeo, 'Participatory Niches for Emergent Citizenship in Early Adolescence: An International Perspective', *The Annals of the American Academy of Political and Social Science*, 633, The Child as Citizen (January 2011), pp. 180–200 (p. 197).

10 Cathy MacPhail, *Mosi's War* (London and New York: Bloomsbury, 2013), p. 59. All references to this text will be cited by pagination throughout.

11 John Stephens, *Language and Ideology in Children's Fiction* (London and New York: Longman, 1992), p. 246.

12 Ibid., p. 68.

13 Glenda Norquay, '"Transitory Thresholds": Geographic Imaginings of Adolescence in Women's Fiction from North-east Scotland', *Scottish Literary Review*, 3.2 (2011), pp. 81–99 (p. 84).

14 Angela McRobbie, 'Young Women and Consumer Culture', *Cultural Studies*, 22.5, pp. 531–50 (p. 533).

15 Alison MacKenzie, Penny Enslin and Nicki Hedge, 'Education for global citizenship in Scotland: Reciprocal partnership or politics of benevolence?', *International Journal of Educational Research*, 77 (2016), pp. 128–35 (p. 128).
16 Peter Hopkins, 'Young people and the Scottish Independence Referendum', *Political Geography*, 46 (2015), pp. 91–92.
17 Ibid., p. 92.
18 Ebbi Ferguson, 'EU referendum: The fact 16 and 17-year-olds couldn't vote on the most important decision of their lives is a disgrace', *Independent*, 27 June 2016: www.independent.co.uk/student/istudents/eu-referendum-result-brexit-student-votes-at-16-remain-leave-europe-a7101736.html [accessed 20 March 2024].
19 Ibid, n.p.
20 John W. Robertson, Neil Blain and Paula Cowan, 'Who Decides? What Matters? Scottish Adolescents' Perceptions of the Importance and Influence of Media Personalities, Parents and Peers', *Citizenship, Social and Economics Education: An International Journal*, 6.1 (2005), pp. 73–87 (p. 82).
21 McCulloch (2007), 2016.
22 Ursula Le Guin and Susan Wood, *The Language of the Night: Essays on Fantasy and Science Fiction* (London: Putnam, 1979), p. 31.
23 Maria Nikolajeva, *Reading for Learning: Cognitive Approaches to Children's Literature* (Amsterdam and Philadelphia: John Benjamins., 2014), p. 79
24 Bogdan Draganski, Christian Gaser, Gerd Kempermann, H. Georg Kuhn, Jürgen Winkler, Christian Büchel, and Ame May, 'Temporal and Spatial Dynamics of Brain Structure Changes during Extensive Learning', *The Journal of Neuroscience*, 26.23 (June 2006), pp. 6314–17 (p. 6317).
25 Gardiner (2007), p. 48.
26 Rosi Braidotti, *Transpositions* (Cambridge and Malden: Polity Press, 2008 [2006]), p. 17.
27 Ulrich Beck, *World Risk Society* (Cambridge: Polity, 1999).
28 Audre Lorde (1985) cited in Susan Stanford Friedman, *Mappings: Feminism and the Cultural Geographies of Encounter* (Princeton and Chichester: Princeton University Press, 1998), p. 3.
29 Benedict Anderson, *Imagined Communities: Reflections on the Origin and Spread of Nationalism* (London: Verso, 1983).
30 Aileen Christianson and Alison Lumsden. *Contemporary Scottish Women Writers* (Edinburgh: Edinburgh University Press 2000), p. 2.

31　Judith Butler, *Frames of War: When is Life Grievable?* (London and New York: Verso 2010 [2009]), p. 38.
32　Lorna Sage, *Women in the House of Fiction: Post-War Women Novelists* (Basingstoke and New York: Palgrave Macmillan, 1992), p. ix.
33　Roberta Seelinger Trites, *Disturbing the Universe: Power and Repression in Adolescent Literature* (Iowa City: University of Iowa Press, 2000), pp. 18–19.
34　Benjamin Lefebvre, 'Agency, Belonging, Citizenship: The ABCs of Nation-Building in Contemporary Canadian Texts for Adolescents', *Canadian Literature: A Quarterly of Criticism and Review*, 198 (Autumn 2008), pp. 91–101 (p. 99).

9. From Fairy Cauldrons to *An Gruffalo*: The Development and Challenges of Scottish Gaelic Children's Literature

1　Iain Mac Phàidein, *Companach na Cloinne: Leabhran Sgoil anns am bheil Sgeòil Thaitneach, fo làimh Chaluim Mhic Phàrlain* (Stirling: Aonghas Mac Aoidh, 1912).
2　J. G. MacKay, *Sgeulachd a' Choire: The Tale of the Cauldron* (Dundee: Malcolm C. MacLeod, 1927).
3　Fiona O'Hanlon and Lindsay Paterson, 'Gaelic Education since 1872', in Robert Anderson, Mark Freeman and Lindsay Paterson (eds), *The Edinburgh History of Education in Scotland* (Edinburgh: Edinburgh University Press, 2015), pp. 304–25.
4　Ruaraidh MacThòmais, 'Am Bòdach Ròcais' (The Scarecrow), in *An Rathad Cian* (The Far Road), self-translated, (Glasgow: Gairm, 1970), p. 18.
5　Joanne L. Lynn, 'Runes to ward off sorrow: rhetoric of the English nursery rhyme', in Rhonda Brock-Servais, Catherine Butler, Victoria de Rijke (eds), *Children's Literature in Education 16* (London: Ward Lock Educational, 1985), pp. 3–14.
6　Douglas Beck, illus. Mairi Kidd, *Biorachan Beag Agus Biorachan Mòr – Big Tappietoorie an Wee Tappietoorie: Sgeulachd an Gàidhlig is Albais – a Story in Gaelic and Scots*, trans. J. Derrick McClure (Portree: Fèisean nan Gàidheal, 2004).
7　Alasdair MacNeacail (ed.), *Oideas na Cloinne* ('Children's Learning') (Glasgow: A. Sinclair, 1947).
8　Scottish Council for Research in Education (ed.), *Aithris is Oideas* ('Telling and Learning') (London: University of London Press, 1964).
9　Tormod Caimbeul (ed.), *Air do Bhonnagan, a Ghaoil* ('On Your Bare Feet, Sweetheart') (Stornoway: Acair, 2005).

10 Lisa Storey, *Bha Siod ann Reimhid* ('Once Upon a Time') (Inverness: Club Leabhar, 1975).
11 Murchadh MacLeòid, *Am Bloigh Beag le Beannachd* ('The Little Portion with a Blessing'), (PRG-Cànan, 1997).
12 Mairi Kidd, illus. Nicola O'Byrne, *Mar a Chuala Mise E* ('As I Heard It') (Stornoway: Stòrlann, 2011).
13 Seònaid Walker, illus. Heather Insh, *Am Peata Bàn* ('The White Pet Sheep') (Inverness: Clàr, 1997).
14 Catrìona Mhoireach, illus. Heather Insh, *Lasair Dhearg* ('Red Flame') (Inverness: Clàr, 1997).
15 Ruairidh MacIlleathain, illus. Heather Insh, *Conachar agus an Torc* ('Conachar and the Boar') (Inverness: Clàr, 1997).
16 Malachy Doyle, illus. Jane Ray, *An Gille Bragail* ('The Bold Boy'), uncredited translator (Stornoway: Acair, 2001).
17 Cailean Spencer and Cruinneachadh an Luchd-teagaisg Ghàidhlig 1968, Inbhir Nis, *Fear nam Fiaclan* ('The Dentist') etc. (Glasgow: Gairm, 1971).
18 Iain Mac a' Ghobhainn, *Iain am Measg nan Reultan* ('John Among the Stars') (Glasgow: Gairm, 1970).
19 Maoilios Caimbeul, illus. Nick Hesketh, *Clann a' Phroifeasair* ('The Professor's Children') (Glasgow: Gairm, 1988).
20 e.g. Iain Mac a' Ghobhainn, *Little Red Riding Hood agus an Dorus Iaruinn* ('Little Red Riding Hood and the Iron Door') (Glasgow: Gairm, 1977).
21 Eilidh Watt, *Latha a' Choin Duibh* ('The Black Dog's Day'), (Inverness: Club Leabhar, 1972).
22 Fionnlagh MacLeòid, illus. Michael Healey and Criosabel NicLeòid, *Tothan* ('Tothan') (Inverness: Club Leabhar, 1975).
23 Judith Kerr, *Mog an Cat Dìochuimhneach* ('Mog the Forgetful Cat'), uncredited translator (Inverness: Club Leabhar, 1973).
24 John Murray and Catherine Morrison, *Bilingual Primary Education in the Western Isles Scotland* (Stornoway: Acair, 1984), p. 28.
25 Fionnlagh MacLeòid, illus. Jewel B. Smith, *Tugainn Cuairt* ('Let's Go for a Walk') (Inverness: An Comunn Gàidhealach, 1976).
26 Tormod Caimbeul, illus. Donald Smith, *Uilleam Bàn agus an Iolaire* ('Fair-haired William and the Eagle') (Inverness: An Comunn Gàidhealach and The Highlands and Islands Development Board, 1977).
27 Ellen Blance and Ann Cook, illus. Quentin Blake, *Spàgan agus am Bike Ùr* ('Monster and the New Bike') etc., Gaelic adaptations by John Murray, Catherine Morrison, Annie MacDonald and Finlay MacLeod

(London: Longman in Association with the Bilingual Project for the Western Isles Council, 1978).
28 Lisa Storey, illus. Roy Pederson, *Coinneach* ('Kenneth'); Fionnlagh MacLeòid, *O Tractar!* ('Oh Tractor!'); Fionnlagh MacLeòid, *Am Fear a Thàinig a Chunntadh nan Taighean* ('The Man Who Came to Count the Houses'); all (Stornoway: Acair, 1979).
29 Carinne MacKenzie, *Às a' Bhìobull: Gideon* (From the Bible: Gideon), etc., ill. Mackay Design Associates, trans. Christina MacKenzie (Stornoway: Acair, 1980).
30 Bilingual Project, illus. Katherine Barr, Jewel Smith et al., *Bàtaichean* ('Boats') etc. (Stornoway: Acair, 1982–83).
31 Fionnlagh MacLeòid, illus. Aonghas MacDhòmhnaill, *Mac an t-Strònaich* ('Stronach') (Stornoway: Acair, 1994).
32 Anna NicDhòmhnaill, illus. Aonghas MacDhòmhnaill, *Stamh* ('Tangle') (Stornoway: Acair, 1991).
33 John Murray and Catherine Morrison, *Bilingual Primary Education in the Western Isles Scotland* (Stornoway: Acair, 1984), p. 76.
34 Eric Hill, *Nollaig Spot* ('Spot's Christmas') etc., trans. Iain Moireach (Stornoway: Acair, 1983).
35 Carol Watson, *An Taigh* ('The House') etc., trans. Iain MacDhòmhnaill (Stornoway: Acair, 1986).
36 e.g. Angharad Tomos, *Rala Rwdins* ('Rala Rudins') (Talybont, Ceredigion: Y Lolfa, 1983).
37 e.g. Angharad Tomos, *Na Rinn I Orra* ('What She Did to Them'), trans. Fionnlagh MacLeòid (Stornoway: Acair, 1986).
38 e.g. Penelope Lively, illus. Valerie Littlewood, *Na Dràgoin Chrosda* ('Dragon Trouble') (Stornoway: Acair, 1989).
39 e.g. Anne Lorne Gillies, *Am Muncaidh Frangach* ('The French Monkey') (Stornoway: Acair, 1990).
40 Julia Donaldson, illus. Axel Scheffler, *An Gruffalo* ('The Gruffalo'), trans. Tormod Caimbeul (Stornoway: Acair, 2018), spread 1.
41 Joseph Coelho, illus. Fiona Lumbers, *Lùna agus Latha na Leabharlainn* ('Luna Loves Library Day'), trans. Mòrag Anna NicNèill (Stornoway: Acair, 2019).
42 Ross Collins, *Tha Mathan air mo Chathair* ('There's a Bear in my Chair'), trans. Morag Stewart (Stornoway: Acair, 2016).
43 Morag Hood, *Is Mise Ialtag* ('I am Bat'), uncredited translator (Stornoway: Acair, 2018) .
44 Julia Donaldson, illus. Axel Scheffler, *The Gruffalo* (London: MacMillan, 1999), spread 1.

45 Donaldson and Scheffler, *An Gruffalo*, trans. Tormod Caimbeul.
46 Katrina Charman, illus. Nick Sharratt, *Tha Mucan-Mara air Bus* ('The Whales on the Bus'), uncredited translator (Stornoway: Acair, 2023).
47 David Melling, *Cudail Chan Fhaigh Mi* ('Hugless Douglas'), trans. Norma NicLeòid (Stornoway: Acair, 2012).
48 Marie C. NicAmhlaigh, illus. Robin Bans, *Teàrlag agus na Spàinean* ('Charlotte and the Spoons') etc. (Stornoway: Acair, 1998).
49 Catrìona NicIlleDhuibh, *An Tractar agus an Liobht* ('The Tractor and the Lift') (Stornoway: Acair, 2010).
50 e.g. Ceitidh Hutton, *Rona is a Caraidean* ('Rona and Friends') (Inverness: Leabhraichean Beaga, 2011).
51 e.g. Lisa Storey, *Angaidh agus Am Baidhsagail aig Donna Banana* ('Angus and Donna Banana's Bike') (Inveness [?]: Clò Phabaigh, 2022).
52 e.g. Gracie Summers, illus. Veronica Petrie, *Seo Agaibh Morse* ('Here We Have Morse') (Stornoway: Acair, 2016).
53 Chris Bradford, illus. Sonia Leong, *Ninja: A' Chiad Dùbhlan* ('Ninja: The First Mission') etc., trans. Dòmhnall Uilleam Stiùbhart (Edinburgh: Cuilean Craicte, 2015).
54 Michael Morpurgo, illus. Catherine Rayner, *Ceit agus an Caiptean* ('Clare and the Captain'), trans. Màiri Kidd (Edinburgh: Cuilean Craicte, 2015).
55 *Oor Wullie Gaelic Annual*, trans. Dòmhnall Uilleam Stiùbhart and Màiri Kidd (Edinburgh: Cuilean Craicte, 2016).
56 Ishi NicIlleathain, *Am Bann* ('The Band') (Stornoway: Acair, 2014).
57 Elaine NicFhearghais, *A' Chlach-Ghealaich* ('The Moon Rock'), (Stornoway: Acair, 2014).
58 Catrìona Leagsaidh Chaimbeul, *An t-Ionnsachadh Bòidheach: Am Fuachd Ghorm* ('Learning Young: The Blue Cold'), etc. (Stornoway: Acair, 2014).
59 Ó Laighléis, Ré, *Punk agus Sgeulachdan Eile* ('Punk and Other Stories') (Inverness: Leabhraichean Beaga, 2006).

10. Scottish Children's Picturebooks within a European and Global Context

1 Barbara Bader, *American Picturebooks from Noah's Ark to the Beast Within* (New York: Macmillan, 1976), p. 1.
2 Alan Hill, 'Talking about Reading in Scotland', in Penni Cotton, *European Children's Literature I* (Kingston: Kingston University Press, 1996), pp. 145–51.
3 Ibid., p. 145.

4   Penni Cotton, 'The European Picture Book Collection: A Multicultural Catalyst for the 21st Century', *Interjuli* (January 2016), pp. 54–71 (p. 58).
5   Mairi Hedderwick, *Katie Morag and the New Pier* (London: Bodley Head, 1993); Penni Cotton, *Picture Books sans Frontières* (London: Trentham Press, 2000), pp. 78–79.
6   Lilia Ratcheva, *EDM Reporter: Surfing the Net: A European Survey into Children's Use of the Internet* (Vienna: International Institute for Children's Literature and Reading Research, 2008), p. 5.
7   Penni Cotton and Nicola Daly, 'Visualising Cultures: The "European Picture Book Collection" Moves "Down Under"', *Children's Literature in Education*, 46.1 (2015), pp. 88–106 (p. 91).
8   Penni Cotton, 'The Europeanness of Picture Books', in Margaret Meek (ed.), *Children's Literature and National Identity* (Stoke on Trent: Trentham, 2001), p. 111.
9   Maureen A. Farrell, '"Jings! Crivens! Help Ma Boab!" – It's a Scottish Picturebook', *New Review of Children's Literature and Librarianship*, 17.2 (2011), pp. 176–88 (p. 179).
10 Tania McCartney, illus. Tina Snerling, *A Scottish Year: Twelve Months* (Wollombi: Exisle Publishing, 2015).
11 Karen Coates. 'Picturebooks: Beyond the Borders of Art, Narrative and Culture ed. by Evelyn Arizpe, Maureen Farrell, and Julie McAdam (review)', *Children's Literature*, 42 (2014), pp. 305–15 (p. 308).
12 Roald Dahl, illus. Quentin Blake, *George's Marvellous Medicine* (London: Jonathan Cape, 1981).
13 Roald Dahl, illus. Quentin Blake, trans. Christine De Luca, *Dodie's Phenomenal Pheesic* (Edinburgh: Itchy Coo Publications, 2008).
14 Personal email, May 2016.
15 Margaret Donaldson, illus. Axel Scheffler, *The Gruffalo*.
16 Joyce Bainbridge and Brenda Wolodko, 'Canadian Picture Books: Shaping and Reflecting National Identity', *Bookbird*, 40.2 (2002), pp. 21–27 (p. 21).
17 Maureen A. Farrell, *Culture and Identity in Scottish Children's Fiction* (unpublished PhD thesis, University of Glasgow, 2009), p. 1.
18 Ibid., p. 187.
19 Anne M. Dolan, *You, Me and Diversity: Picturebooks for teaching development and intercultural Education* (London: Trentham, 2014), p. 25.
20 Susan A. Colby and Anna F. Lyon, 'Heightening awareness about the importance of using multicultural literature', *Multicultural Education*, 11.3 (2004), pp. 24–28 (p. 24).

21 Farrell, '"Jings! Crivens! Help Ma Boab!"', p. 185.
22 Evelyn Arizpe, Maureen A. Farrell and Julie McAdam (eds), *Picture books: Beyond the Borders of Art, Narrative and Culture* (Abingdon: Routledge, 2013), p. 15.
23 Bettina Kummerling-Meibauer (ed.), *Picturebooks: Representation and Narration* (London: Routledge, 2014), p. 10.
24 Maria Nikolajeva and Liz Taylor, 'Must We to Bed Indeed? Beds as Cultural Signifiers in Picturebooks for Children', *New Review of Children's Literature and Librarianship*, 17.2 (November 2011), pp. 144–63 (p. 144).
25 Sandra L. Beckett, *Crossover Picturebooks: A Genre for All Ages* (New York: Routledge, 2012), p. 85.
26 Sandie Mourao, 'What's real and what's not', in Janet Evans (ed.), *Challenging and Controversial Picturebooks* (London: Routledge, 2015), p. 183.
27 Kerenza Ghosh, 'Who's Afraid of the Big Bad Wolf?', in Evans, *Challenging and Controversial Picturebooks*, p. 211.
28 Ibid.
29 Janet Evans, p. 249.
30 Ibid., p. 258.
31 Matthew Fitt and James Robertson (eds), illus. Bob Dewar, *Blethertoun Braes* (Edinburgh: Itchy Coo Publications, 2004).
32 Didier Conrad and Jean-Yves Ferri, trans. Matthew Fitt, *Asterix and the Pechts* (Edinburgh: Itchy Coo Publishing, 2013).
33 Matthew Fitt and James Robertson (eds), *The Compact Coo* (Edinburgh: Itchy Coo Publishing, 2003).
34 Lynne Rickards, illus. Gabby Grant, *Harris the Hero* (Edinburgh: Floris Books, 2013).
35 Lynne Rickards, illus. Jon Mitchell, *Skye the Puffling* (Edinburgh: Floris Books, 2016).
36 Emily Dodd, illus. Kirsteen Harris-Jones, *The Grouse and the Mouse* (Edinburgh: Floris Books, 2015).
37 Emily Dodd, illus. Katie Pamment, *Can't Dance Cameron* (Edinburgh: Floris Books 2015).
38 Polly Lawson, illus. Jo Allan, *Hairy Hettie, the Highland Cow* (Edinburgh: Floris Books, 2012).
39 Lari Don, illus. Nicola O'Byrne, *How to Make a Heron Happy* (Edinburgh: Floris Books, 2011).
40 Aileen Paterson, *Maisie comes to Morningside* (Selkirk: Three Hills Books, 1989).

41 Elizabeth McKay, illus. Maria Bogade, *Wee Granny and the Ceilidh* (Edinburgh: Floris Books, 2015).
42 Tim Archbold, *Bagpipes, Beasties and Bogles* (Edinburgh: Floris Books: 2012).
43 Lari Don, illus. Philip Longson, *The Secret of the Kelpie* (Edinburgh: Floris Books, 2016).
44 Janis Mackay, illus. Ruchi Mhasane, *The Selkie Girl* (Edinburgh: Floris Books, 2014).
45 Lari Don, illus. Philip Longson, *The Tale of Tam Linn* (Edinburgh: Floris Books, 2014).
46 Theresa Breslin, illus. Matthew Land, *The Dragon Stoorworm* (Edinburgh: Floris Books, 2014).
47 Theresa Breslin, illus. Kate Leiper, *Illustrated Treasury of Scottish Mythical Creatures* (Edinburgh: Floris Books, 2015).
48 Moira Miller, illus. Mairi Hedderwick, *Adventures of Hamish and Mirren* (Edinburgh: Floris Books, 2015).
49 Scoular Anderson, *1314 And All That* (Edinburgh: Birlinn, 2000).
50 Scoular Anderson, *1745 And All That* (Edinburgh: Birlinn, 2001).
51 Allan Burnett, *Scottish Tales of Adventure* (Edinburgh: Birlinn, 2014).
52 Joan Lennon, *Silver Skin* (Edinburgh: Birlinn, 2015).
53 Norah and William Montgomerie, *The Folk Tales of Scotland* (Edinburgh: Birlinn, 2008).
54 Julie Bertagna, illus. William Goldsmith, *John Muir, Earth – Planet, Universe* (Edinburgh: The Scottish Book Trust, 2014).
55 Hill, 'Talking about Reading in Scotland', in *Cotton* (1996), p. 151.

11. Ambition and Identity: Scottish Children's Literary Prizewinners

1 Owen Dudley Edwards, *British Children's Fiction in the Second World War* (Edinburgh: University Press, 2007), pp. 250–52.
2 Gillian Avery, *Childhood's Pattern: A Study of the Heroes and Heroines of Children's Fiction 1770–1950* (London: Hodder & Stoughton, 1975), p. 224.
3 Matthew O. Grenby, *Children's Literature* (Edinburgh: University Press, 2008), p. 144.
4 Ibid., pp. 159–60.
5 Joan Aitken, 'Interpreting the Past: Reflection of an historical novelist', in Sheila A. Egoff, Gordon Stubbs and Ralph Ashley (eds), *Only Connect: Readings in Children's Literature* (Toronto: Oxford University Press, 1996), pp. 62–73.

6   Kimberley Reynolds, 'Changing Families in Children's Fiction', in Sebastian Chapleau (ed.), *New Voices in Children's Literature Criticism* (Lichfield: Pied Piper, 2004), pp. 193–208.
7   Judy Simons, 'Gender Roles in Children's Fiction', in Matthew O. Grenby and Andrea Immel (eds), *The Cambridge Companion to Children's Literature* (Cambridge: Cambridge University Press, 2009), pp. 143–58.
8   Owen Dudley Edwards, p. 214.
9   Volker Ullrich, *Hitler: Ascent, 1889–1939*, trans. Jefferson S. Chase (London: Bodley Head, 2016).
10 Susan Cooper, *Over Sea, Under Stone* (London: Puffin, 1968 [1965]), p. 194.

12. Scottish Poetry in the Scottish Secondary Classroom: Seeing Beyond the Set Texts

1   Education Scotland, *Curriculum for Excellence: Literacy and English: Principles and Practice*: www.education.gov.scot/media/uwpg245f/literacy-english-pp.pdf (p. 1).
2   Raymond Williams, 'The Analysis of Culture', in John Storey (ed.), *Cultural Theory and Popular Culture: A Reader* [2nd ed.] (Georgia: The University of Georgia Press, 1998), p. 55.
3   Ashbrook, *Final Report: Engagement for Scottish Texts in English Courses* (Glasgow: Ashbrook Research and Consultancy, 2012): www.sqa.org.uk/files_ccc/AshbrookReportEnglish.pdf (p. 61).
4   Douglas Gifford, *Addressing the Bard: Twelve Contemporary Poets respond to Robert Burns* (Edinburgh: Scottish Poetry Library, 2009). This poem was also published earlier in Matthew Fitt, *Kate o Shanter's Tale and Other Poems* (Edinburgh: Luath Press, 2003).
5   Emma Dymock and Scott Lyall, 'The Poetry of Modernity', in Carla Sassi (ed.), *The International Companion to Scottish Poetry* (Glasgow: Scottish Literature International, 2015), pp. 74–82.
6   Ashbrook, p. 38.
7   Kelly Gallagher, *Readicide: How Schools Are Killing Reading and What You Can Do About It* (London: Routledge, 2009).

13. Scottish Children's Literature: Where Are We Now?

1   Ilda Erkoçi, 'Narrative Cities – Literary Edinburgh: A Model to Follow', *Academicus International Scientific Journal*, 14.27 (2023), pp. 42–56; Publishing Scotland, *Forever Lands – The Growth of Children's Writing*

and *Publishing in Scotland*, film (2023): www.youtube.com/watch?v=b5YCzVlQyzc

2 Barrington Stoke Publishing: www.barringtonstoke.co.uk/dyslexic-reluctant-readers/

3 Scotland.org: www.scotland.org/about-scotland/culture/language

4 Centre for Literacy in Primary Education (2023), *Reflecting Realities – Survey of Ethnic Representation within UK Children's Literature*: www.clpe.org.uk/research/clpe-reflecting-realities-survey-ethnic-representation-within-uk-childrens-literature-1

5 Literature Alliance Scotland (2019), *Breaking New Ground: celebrating children's authors and illustrators of colour*: www.literaturealliancescotland.co.uk/breaking-new-ground/

6 Carole Jones, 'Gender and Sexuality', in Gerard Carruthers (ed.), *A Companion to Scottish Literature* (Hoboken, NJ: Wiley Blackwell, 2024), pp. 299–311.

Further Reading

Robert Anderson, Mark Freeman and Lindsay Paterson, *The Edinburgh History of Education in Scotland* (Edinburgh: Edinburgh University Press, 2015).

Evelyn Arizpe, Maureen A. Farrell and Julie McAdam (eds), *Picture books: Beyond the Borders of Art, Narrative and Culture* (Abingdon: Routledge, 2013).

Evelyn Arizpe (ed.), *Children as Readers in Children's Literature: The Power of Texts and the Importance of Reading* (London: Routledge, 2015).

Ashbrook, *Final Report: Engagement for Scottish Texts in English Courses* (Glasgow: Ashbrook Research and Consultancy, 2012).

Gillian Avery, *Childhood's Pattern: A Study of the Heroes and Heroines of Children's Fiction 1770–1950* (London: Hodder & Stoughton, 1975).

Sandra L. Beckett, *Reflections of Change: Children's Literature since 1945* (Westport, CT: Greenwood Press, 1997).

Kirstie Blair, *Working Verse in Victorian Scotland: Poetry, Press, Community* (Oxford: Oxford University Press, 2019).

Maria Jose Botelho and Masha Kabakow Rudman, *Critical Multicultural Analysis of Children's Literature* (Abingdon and New York: Routledge, 2009).

Rhonda Brock-Servais, Butler and Victoria de Rijke (eds), *Children's Literature in Education 16* (London: Ward Lock Educational, 1985).

Gerard Carruthers (ed.), *A Companion to Scottish Literature* (Hoboken, NJ: Wiley Blackwell, 2024).

Centre for Literacy in Primary Education, *Reflecting Realities – Survey of Ethnic Representation within UK Children's Literature* clpe.org.uk/research/clpe-reflecting-realities-survey-ethnic-representation-within-uk-childrens-literature-1 (2023).

Sebastian Chapleau (ed.), *New Voices in Children's Literature Criticism* (Lichfield: Pied Piper, 2004).

Kirsteen Connor, *Youth's poison?: The creation and evolution of children's chapbooks in Scotland, 1800–1870*, unpublished MPhil(R) thesis, University of Glasgow (2010).

Penni Cotton, *European Children's Literature I* (Kingston: Kingston University Press, 1996).

Edward J. Cowan and Douglas Gifford (eds), *The Polar Twins* (Edinburgh: John Donald, 1999).

Edward J. Cowan and Mike Paterson, *Folk in Print: Scotland's Chapbook Heritage 1750–1850* (Edinburgh: John Donald, 2007).

Robert Crawford, *Scotland's Books: The Penguin History of Scottish Literature* (London: Penguin Books, 2007).

F. J. Harvey Darton, *Children's Books in England: Five Centuries of Social Life*, 3rd ed., revised by Brian Alderson (London: Oak Knoll Press, 1998 [1932]).

Jerome De Groot, *The Historical Novel* (London: Routledge, 2010).

Sidney I. Dobrin and Kenneth B. Kidd (eds), *Wild Things: Children's Culture and Ecocriticism* (Detroit: Wayne State University Press, 2004).

Sarah Dunnigan and Shu-Fang Lai (eds), *The Land of Story-Books: Scottish Children's Literature in the Long Nineteenth Century* (Glasgow: Scottish Literature International, 2019).

Owen Dudley Edwards, *British Children's Fiction in the Second World War* (Edinburgh: Edinburgh University Press, 2007).

Elizabeth Ewan and Janay Nugent (eds), *Finding the Family in Medieval and Early Modern Scotland* (London: Routledge, 2008).

Maureen A. Farrell, *Culture and Identity in Scottish Children's Fiction*, PhD Thesis, University of Glasgow (2009).

Penny Fielding (ed.), *The Edinburgh Companion to Robert Louis Stevenson* (Edinburgh: Edinburgh University Press, 2010).

David Finkelstein and Alistair McCleary (eds), *The Edinburgh History of the Book in Scotland* (Edinburgh: Edinburgh University Press, 2007).

Kate Flint, *The Woman Reader* (Oxford: Oxford University Press, 1993).

Michael Gardiner, *Modern Scottish Culture* (Edinburgh: Edinburgh University Press, 2005).

Chloé Germaine, *The Dark Matter of Children's 'Fantastika' Literature: Speculative Entanglements* (London: Bloomsbury, 2023).

Betty Greenway, *A Stranger Shore: A Critical Introduction to the Work of Mollie Hunter* (Lanham, Maryland: Scarecrow Press, 1998).

Matthew O. Grenby, *Children's Literature* (Edinburgh: Edinburgh University Press, 2008).
Matthew O. Grenby and Andrea Immel (eds), *The Cambridge Companion to Children's Literature* (Cambridge: Cambridge University Press, 2009).
Carrie Hintz and Elaine Ostry (eds), *Utopian and Dystopian Writing for Children and Young Adults* (London: Routledge, 2003).
Peter Hunt (ed.), *The International Companion Encyclopedia of Children's Literature* (London: Routledge, 2004 [1996]).
Andrea Immel and Michael Witmore (eds), *Childhood and Children's Books in Early Modern Europe, 1550–1800* (London: Routledge, 2006).
Edward James and Farah Mendlesohn (eds), *The Cambridge Companion to Fantasy Literature* (Cambridge: Cambridge University Press, 2012).
Charles Jones, *The Edinburgh History of the Scots Language* (Edinburgh: Edinburgh University Press, 1997).
David Kennedy, *The Well of Being: Childhood, Subjectivity and Education* (New York: SUNY Press, 2006).
Bettina Kummerling-Meibauer (ed.), *Picturebooks: Representation and Narration* (London: Routledge, 2014).
Seth Lerer, *Children's Literature: A Reader's History, from Aesop to Harry Potter* (Chicago: University of Chicago Press, 2008).
Literature Alliance Scotland, *Breaking New Ground: celebrating children's authors and illustrators of colour*: www.literaturealliancescotland.co.uk/breaking-new-ground/ (2019).
Jan de Maeyer et al. (eds), *Religion, Children's Literature and Modernity in Western Europe 1750–2000* (Leuven: University of Leuven Press, 2005).
Kerry Mallan and Clare Bradford (eds), *Contemporary Children's Literature and Film: Engaging with Theory* (New York: Palgrave Macmillan, 2011).
Robert McColl Millar, *A History of the Scots Language* (Oxford: Oxford University Press, 2023).
Fiona McCulloch, *Contemporary British Children's Fiction and Cosmopolitanism* (London: Routledge 2017).
Roderick McGillis (ed.), *The Nimble Reader: Literary Theory and Children's Literature* (New York: Twayne, 1996).
Margaret Meek (ed.), *Children's Literature and National Identity* (Stoke on Trent: Trentham Books, 2001).
John Murray and Catherine Morrison, *Bilingual Primary Education in the Western Isles Scotland* (Stornoway: Acair, 1984).
Maria Nikolajeva, *Children's Literature Comes of Age: T1owards a New Aesthetic* (London: Routledge, 1996).

Maria Nikolajeva, *Reading for Learning: Cognitive Approaches to Children's Literature* (Amsterdam and Philadelphia: John Benjamins, 2014).

Janay Nugent and Elizabeth Ewan (eds), *Children and Youth in Pre-Modern Scotland* (Martlesham: Boydell, 2015).

Peter Opie and Iona Archibald Opie, *The Oxford Dictionary of Nursery Rhymes* (Oxford: Clarendon Press, 1997).

Nicholas Orme, *Medieval Children* (New Haven: Yale University Press, 2001).

Nicholas Orme, *Medieval Schools* (New Haven: Yale University Press, 2006).

Nicholas Orme, *Tudor Children* (New Haven: Yale University Press, 2023).

Charlotte F. Otten and Gary D. Schmidt (eds), *The Voice of the Narrator in Children's Literature: Insights from Writers and Critics* (New York: Greenwood, 1989).

Marie-Odile Pittin-Hedon, Camille Manfredi and Scott Hames (eds), *Scottish Writing after Devolution: Edges of the New* (Edinburgh: Edinburgh University Press, 2022).

Lilia Ratcheva, *EDM Reporter: Surfing the Net: A European Survey into Children's Use of the Internet* (Vienna: International Institute for Children's Literature and Reading Research, 2008).

Jacqueline Rose, *The Case of Peter Pan, or, The Impossibility of Children's Fiction* (London: Macmillan, 1984).

Carla Sassi, *Why Scottish Literature Matters* (Edinburgh: The Saltire Society, 2005).

Carla Sassi (ed.), *The International Companion to Scottish Poetry* (Glasgow: Scottish Literature International, 2015), pp. 74–82.

John Stephens, *Language and Ideology in Children's Fiction* (London and New York: Longman, 1992).

Morag Styles, *From the Garden to the Street: An Introduction to 300 years of Poetry for Children* (London: Cassell, 1998).

Morag Styles, Louise Joy and David Whitley (eds), *Poetry and Childhood* (Stoke-on-Trent: Trentham Books, 2010).

John Rowe Townsend, *Written for Children: An Outline of English Children's Literature* (London: Garnet Miller, 1965).

Nicholas Tucker, *Suitable for Children? Controversies in Children's Literature* (London: Chatto & Windus for Sussex University Press, 1976).

Marina Warner, *No Go The Bogeyman: Scaring, Lulling and Making Mock* (London: Chatto & Windus, 1998).

Torben Weinrich, *Children's Literature – Art or Pedagogy?* (Copenhagen: Roskilde University Press, 2000).

Martin Domines Veliki and Cian Duffy (eds), *Romanticism and the Cultures of Infancy* (London: Palgrave Macmillan, 2020).

Jack Zipes (ed.), *The Oxford Encyclopedia of Children's Literature* (Oxford: Oxford University Press, 2006).

Notes on Contributors

Penni Cotton is Senior Research Fellow at the National Centre for Research in Children's Literature, responsible for European research projects. Author of numerous articles and organiser of many conferences, her first book, *Picture Books sans Frontières* (2000), explains the rationale behind her work, focusing on the importance of visual narratives world-wide in helping create imaginative minds and cross-cultural boundaries.

Robert A. Davis is Professor of Religious and Cultural Education in the University of Glasgow. He has taught, written and broadcast widely on literature, religion and the cultural history of childhood. His recent work includes studies of the British lullaby traditions and explorations of the educational experiments of Robert Owen.

Beth Dickson, formerly Deputy Head of the University of Glasgow School of Education, has twin research interests in Scottish Literature, including Catherine Carswell, and teacher education, writing with Moyra Boland 'Co-existing sites of teacher education: a university and school partnership in Glasgow' (2023). She is currently a member of the Board of Teacher Education at the Education Workforce Council, Wales.

Sarah Dunnigan, Senior Lecturer in English Literature at Edinburgh University, writes about traditional ballads, fairy tales, early-modern Scottish literature, especially women's writing, and history of Scottish children's literature. Co-founding, with Valentina Bold, SELCIE (Scotland's Early Literature for Children Initiative), a collaboration between Edinburgh University and Edinburgh's Museum of Childhood, she co-edited, with Shu-Fang Lai, *The Land of StoryBooks. Scottish Children's Literature in the Long Nineteenth Century* (2019).

Jennifer Farrar is Senior Lecturer in children's literature and English in the University of Glasgow's School of Education. Originally a secondary English teacher, she now works with undergraduate and postgraduate students. Her research interests include student teachers' identities as reading teachers, critical literacies and picturebooks.

Maureen A. Farrell is a Senior Lecturer in the University of Glasgow School of Education. A teacher educator, she teaches on the Masters programmes in Children's Literature and Literacies. Her specialist area is Scottish Children's Literature and the representation of cultural identity in fiction and picturebooks.

Morna Fleming is an independent scholar, having spent her working life in secondary schools in Fife and Edinburgh. She first developed an interest in Scottish literature through Glasgow University's distance-taught MPhil, continuing to a PhD, completed in 1997. Contributing widely to scholarly volumes, she has addressed a variety of local, national and international conferences.

Sìm Innes, Senior Lecturer in Celtic and Gaelic at the University of Glasgow, works on Scottish Gaelic literature with a particular interest in transmission, borrowing and translation of culture and ideas. He has published on a wide range of periods and topics: from late-medieval Gaelic religious poetry to twentieth-century Gaelic drama.

Ralph Jessop was Senior Lecturer in Literature and Philosophy at Glasgow University's Dumfries Campus from 1999 to 2023. His publications include *Carlyle and Scottish Thought* (1997), 'Peter Pan's Make-Believe' (*Gateway to the Modern*, 2014) and 'Learned Ignorance' (*Journal of Philosophy of Education*, 2021).

Mairi Kidd, a children's publisher, literature development specialist, published writer for children and adults, and translator of children's fiction into Gaelic, is Director of the Saltire Society, having headed Moat Brae, Scotland's National Centre for Children's Books, and been CEO of Seven Stories, Creative Scotland's Head of Literature, Managing Director of Barrington Stoke and CEO of Stòrlann.

Fiona McCulloch, an independent scholar, was Lynn Wood Neag Distinguished Visiting Professor of British Literature (University of

Connecticut, 2015). Her books include *The Fictional Role of Childhood in Victorian and Early Twentieth-Century Children's Literature* (2004), *Cosmopolitanism in Contemporary British Fiction* (2012), and *Contemporary British Children's Fiction and Cosmopolitanism* (2017), and articles and chapters include '"Connected to time": Ali Smith's Anachronistic Scottish Cosmopolitanism' (2022).

David Robb, a Research Fellow in English at the University of Dundee, has published on Hogg, Sydney Goodsir Smith, Robin Jenkins and George MacDonald. His book on Robert Louis Stevenson was published in 2016. He is again writing on MacDonald and preparing further work on the plays of Alexander Scott.

Index

Acair (publishing house), 170, 171, 172–73, 175
Adrien Prize, 24, 228
adventure stories, 193–97
Aesop fables, 17
Ailein, Maighstir (Allen MacDonald), *An Sìthean Ruadh*, 103–05
Ailes, Kate, 'Outwith', 211
Allan, Alasdair, 184
Amadeo, Jo-Ann, 151, 158
Andersen, Hans Christian, 25, 84, 90
Anderson, Benedict, *Imagined Communities*, 161–62
Annand, James King (J. K.), 45–46
    A Wale o Rhymes, 50–54
Arbuthnott, Gill, 96
Arendt, Hannah, 139
Aries, Philippe, 6
Armitt, Lucie, 78
Armstrong, Anne, 'Cat Food Rap', 55
Asterix and Obelix (fictional characters), 24, 183–84, 188
asylum seekers, Western media's representations of, 162

Atalanta (periodical for girls), 127
authority, deference to, 139–40
Aye Write, 174, 226

ballads
    collections of, 83–84
    as material for chapbooks, 95
Ballantyne, James, 22
Ballantyne, R. M.
    The Coral Island, 115
    The Lighthouse, 65–66, 68, 72–73
Bans, Robin, 173
Barbour, John, 23
Barrie, J. M., 15, 230
    Peter Pan, 20
Barrington Stoke (publishing house), 174, 226
Beck, Ulrich, 161
Beckett, Sandra, 13, 182
'becoming', 149–50, 161
'bedroom' poems, 38
Bell, J. J., 22
Berry, MiKo, 'I'm Sorry', 221
Bertagna, Julie
    Exodus trilogy, 28, 86, 88, 93–94, 95, 150, 159
    Soundtrack, 26–27

Bible stories, 17, 170
Bilingual Education Project, 169–72
Birlinn (publishing house)
   1314 And All That, 187
   1745 And All That, 187–88
   BC Books, 225
Black, Catrìona, 173
Black and ethnic minorities, 226–27
   See also *specific names of authors*
Black and White Publishing, 24–25
Blackhall, Sheena, 'Skyscraper Family', 54–55
Blackwell publishers, 24
Blain, Neil, 159
Blair, Kirstie, 31–32
Blake, William, 34
Blance, Ellen, *Spàgan* (*Monster* series), 170
Blue Peter Book of the Year, 191
Blyton, Enid, *Famous Five* books, 195
Bookbug bags, 173
Boppert, Helene, *Wain*, 95
Botelho, Maria José, 149
Boyd, Zachary, 81
Boys of England, 197
Bradford, Chris, 'Ninja' series, 174
Braidotti, Rosi, 161
Breslin, Theresa, 29–30, 95
   Caged, 9
   Divided City, 150
   Illustrated Treasury of Scottish Mythical Creatures, 187
   Remembrance, 152
   Saskia's Journey, 27
   Whispers in the Graveyard, 193–94, 195, 197, 202–04
Brexit referendum, 2, 154, 158–59

Briggs, Julia, 14
Brison, Ian, 22
British children's literature, 15
Broons, The, 23
Bruce, Dorita Fairlie, *The King's Curate*, 65, 68, 73–74
Buchan, John, 117
Buchart, Pamela, 228
Buckton, Oliver S., 117–18
Burnett, Allan, *Scottish Tales of Adventure*, 188
Burns, Robert, 4, 34, 213
   'Address of Beelzebub', 210
   'Address to the Deil', 209
   'Holy Willie's Prayer', 209
   'To a Mouse', 210
   'A Poet's Welcome to his Love-Begotten Daughter', 210
   'Tam o' Shanter', 210
Butchart, Pamela, 24
   The Spy Who Loved School Dinners, 191
Butler, Judith, 162

Caimbeul, Aonghas (Angus Campbell), 100–01
Caimbeul, Maoilios (Myles Campbell), 168
Cameron, Katharine, 83–84
Campbell, Elizabeth. See Chaimbeul, Ealasaid
Campbell, J. F., 84
Campbell, Marion, 22
   'Lord Ullin's Daughter', 32
   The Wide Blue Road, 74
Campbell, Myles. see Caimbeul, Maoilios
Canongate Classics imprint, 225
Canongate Kelpies imprint, 24

Carmichael, Alexander, *Carmina Gadelica*, 109
Carnegie, Andrew, 17–18, 191–92
Carnegie Medal, 21, 85, 130, 191–92, 196
Carroll, Lewis, 19
Caveney, Philip
  One for Sorrow, 70–71, 75–76
  Seventeen Coffins, 70
caves, as symbols, 138, 140
Celtic Revival, 83, 99, 101–02, 109
Celts/Celtic rights, in McFall's *Bombmaker*, 151, 154, 163
Centre for Literacy in Primary Education (CLPE), *Reflecting Realities* (report), 226–27
Chaimbeul, Ealasaid (Elizabeth Campbell), 100
Chambers, Robert, *Popular Rhymes of Scotland*, 83
Chan, Maisie, *Danny Chung Does Not Do Maths*, 227
chapbooks, 81, 95
'child-centredness', 8
childhood
  figurative site of in nursery verse, 33–34
  the psychology and anthropology of, 35
  in Scotland, historic narrative of, 6–7
children's literature
  definition, 14
  'golden age', 19
  see also Scottish children's literature
Christianson, Aileen, 162
CILIP (Chartered Institute of Library and Information Professionals), 191

'Cinderella' type, 83, 112–13, 167
citizenship, Scottish adolescent, 151, 153
  and YA fiction, 159, 164
Club Leabhar, 169
Coates, Karen, 179–80
Cockburn, Ken, 'Shandwick Stone', 215–16
cognitive criticism, 159
Collins, Ross, 179
Colvin, Sidney, 123, 128
Comhairle nan Eilean Siar (Western Isles Council), 169
Comhairle nan Leabhraichean (Gaelic Books Council), 102–03, 169, 175
comics and comic strips, 23, 183–84
Comunn Gàidhealach, An (The Highland Association), 108, 111, 169
Conaghan, Brian, *The Bombs That Brought Us Together*, 191
contingency, 132–33
Cook, Ann, *Spàgan* (Monster series), 170
corporal punishment, 47
cortical remapping, 160–61
cosmopolitanism, 161
Costa Children's Book Award, 191
Cowan, Edward, 121, 159
cradle-song poetry, 34
Crawford, Robert, 122
Creative Scotland, 174
Crichton Smith, Iain. *see* Mac a' Ghobhainn, Iain
'critical literacy', 182–83
Crocker, John Wilson, *Stories Selected from the History of England for Children*, 18

Cuilean Craicte ('Mad Puppy'), 174–75
cultural archetypes, children's awareness of, 182–83
cultural heritage, and picturebooks, 180–81

Dahl, Roald, 24, 180
Dandy, The, 23
Darton, Harvey, *Children's Books in England*, 14
De Luca, Christine
  Dodie's Phenomenal Pheesic, 180
  'Soondscape', 216
Defoe, Daniel, *Robinson Crusoe*, 115, 116
Deleuze, G., 150, 161
devolution, Scottish, 149, 150, 153
Dhùghlas, Catrìona (Katherine Douglas)
  Greusaiche nam Bròigan, 111–13, 114
  plays, vignettes and songs, 111–13
digital technologies, 76
disability, representation of, 228, 229
Doherty, Berlie, 9
Dolan, Anne, 181
Don, Lari, 95
  selkie stories, 96
  The Tale of Tam Linn, 96
Donaldson, Julia, 23
  The Gruffalo, translations, 25, 172–73, 180, 226
  prizewinning books, 191
Doorly, Eleanor, 192
Douglas, George, 'Nursery Stories', 83

Douglas, Katherine. *see* Dhùghlas, Catrìona
Doyle, Arthur Conan, 117
Doyle, Malachy, *An Gille Bragail*, 168
Draganski, Bogdan, 160
Duffy, Carol Anne, 22
  children's poetry, 57–61
  'Originally', 209
  'The Way My Mother Speaks', 209
Dumfries. *see* Moat Brae
dyslexia, 174, 226

eco-novels, 28
  see also Bertagna, Julie, *Exodus* trilogy
Edinburgh
  International Book Festival, 174
  Scottish National Portrait Gallery, 130
education
  and the 1872 Education (Scotland) Act, 17, 99–100, 166
  1946 government report on languages, 4–5
  development of universal education, 13
  and Knox, 7–8, 17
  secondary education, poetry, 206–23
  spread of literacy in Britain, 20–21
  see also Bilingual Education Project
English (language)
  and the 1872 Education (Scotland) Act, 17, 99–100
  Scottish Standard, 4, 16
  Standard, 16

Enlightenment, 8, 35
Enslin, Penny, 158
environmental narratives, 184–86
    see also Bertagna, Julie,
        Exodus trilogy
Erkoçi, Ilda, 225
ethnic minorities. see Black and
    ethnic minorities; specific
    names of authors
European Union (EU)
    and Brexit, 154, 158–59
    picturebook collection,
        177–78
Evans, Janet, 182

fairy and folk tales
    anthologies, 80–81
    and the Celtic Revival, 83
    chapbooks, 81
    edited by Lang, 19
    intertextuality in fantasy
        stories, 87
    translations, 25
'Fairyland', heterotopia of, 42
fantasy, 26, 78–98
    alternative and redemptive
        worlds, 92–95
    brief history, 80–89
    child protagonists, 89–92
    'Copernican', 193
    folkloric heritage, 95–97
    'Ptolemaic', 193
Farrell, Maureen, 95, 179, 180, 181
Federation of Children's Book
    Groups' Children's Book
    Award, 191
female readership. see gender
    issues/themes
feminist perspectives, historical
    fiction, 67–68

Ferguson, Ebbi, 158
Ferguson, Elaine. see
    NicFhearghais, Elaine
Fidler, Kathleen
    The Boy with the Bronze Axe,
        225
    The Desperate Journey, 225
Fine, Anne
    Goggle-Eyes, 191, 194, 195–96,
        197, 200–02, 204
    prizewinning books for
        younger readers and
        young adults, 191
Finlay, Alec, 23
Fionn mac Cumhaill (fictional
    character), 105, 110
Fitt, Matthew, 22
    Asterix and the Pechts,
        translation, 183–84, 188
    'Captain Puggle', 57
    'Kate o Shanter's Tale', 210–11
    Wee Book o Fairy Tales, 96
Fleming, Morna, 22–23
Flint, Kate, 66
Floris (publishing house), 180,
    184, 225
    Kelpies (for older readers), 184
    Picture Kelpies series, 184–85,
        186–87
    Traditional Scottish Tales, 184
    Wee Kelpies, 184
folk collecting movement, 83
Ford, Robert, 33
    Ballads of Bairnhood, 31–32
Forde, Catherine (Cathy)
    Tug O' War, 28
    young adult literature, 24
Forsyth, Anne, Poems for
    Children, 22
Foucault, Michel, 42

Fraser, Bashabi, 'My mum's sari', 56
Frazer, James, 33

Gaelic, 16, 226
    and the 1872 Education (Scotland) Act, 166
    in children's fantasy stories, 93
    early readers, 102
    and education, 99–101
    Language (Scotland) Act, 2005, 25
    legal status of, 4
    revival movement, 101
    see also plays, Scottish Gaelic children's
Gaelic Books Council. *see* Comhairle nan Leabhraichean
Gaelic folklore ecotypes, 113
Gairm (periodical), 168
Gairm (publishing house), 168–69
Gallagher, Kelly, 222
Gardiner, Michael, 149, 150, 160–61
Garnett, Eve, *The Family from One End Street*, 192
gender issues/themes, 65–71, 227–28
    female sexuality and identity, 153
    and girls' political agency, 158
    in prizewinning fiction, 194–95
    and Stevenson's audience for *Kidnapped* and *Catriona*, 128–29
Gillies, Anne Lorne. *see* Latharna NicIllIosa, Anna
Gillies, Valerie
    'To Edinburgh', 213
    'Stream Rhythm', 215
Gillies, William, 101
Girls' Own Paper, 197
Glasgow
    book festival, 226
    civic marketing campaigns, 219
Gliori, Debi, 23, 179
    Night Shift, 92
    Scottish Gothic novels, 27–28
Good Words for the Young (magazine), 19
Gothic tradition, 27–28, 152
Grahame, Kenneth
    other children's fantasy stories, 84
    The Wind in the Willows, 20, 84
graphic novels, 25, 188
Greenway, Betty, 130
Grenby, M. O., 193
Grenby, Matthew, 15
Grierson, Elizabeth, 84
Guardian Children's Fiction Prize, 191

Haggard, H. Rider, *King Solomon's Mines*, 117
Haldane, J. B. S., 22
Hamilton, Elizabeth
    The Cottagers of Glenburnie, 81
    Letters on Elementary Principles of Education, 81
Hannabuss, Stuart, 14
Hedderwick, Mairi, 23, 179
    Adventures of Hamish and Mirren, 187
    Katie Morag and the New Pier, 178
Hedge, Nicki, 158
Hemyng, Bracebridge, *Boys of England*, 197

Henderson, Barbara, 9
    Wilderness Wars, 28–29
Henderson, James, 125
Hendry, Mary, *Chains*, 29
Henley, W. E., 118
Henryson, Robert, *Morall Fabillis*, 17
Henty, G. A., *In Freedom's Cause*, 65, 67–68, 72
Highland Association, The. see Comunn Gàidhealach, An
Highland Clearances, 105–06, 216
Hill, Alan, 176–77
Hill, Eric, 171
historical fiction, 62–77
    'adult' writing for children, 116, 117
    gender issues in, 65–71
    ideology, 71–76
    production, 63–65
Hollingdale, Peter, 130
Hope, Anthony, 117
Hopkins, Peter, 158
Huchu, T. L., *The Library of the Dead*, 80, 86, 89
Hunt, Peter, 75
Hunter, Mollie, 22, 85, 193
    The Enchanted Whistle, 140–42
    The Ghosts of Glencoe, 138–40
    I'll Go My Own Way, 133, 134–35, 142–43
    The Kelpie's Pearls, 89, 97–98, 133, 143–44
    A Pistol in Greenyards, 133
    A Sound of Chariots, 133, 137
    A Stranger Came Ashore, 133, 143, 144
    The Stronghold, 130, 132–33, 135, 192, 193–94, 195, 197, 199–200, 204
    Talent is Not Enough (published lectures), 130, 133–34, 136
    The Third Eye, 133, 134–35, 138, 144–47
    The Thirteenth Member, 133, 146
    works, overview, 130
    You Never Knew Her as I Did (Escape from Loch Leven), 133, 137
Hutton, R. H., 116

illustrated children's books, and aesthetic movements, 84
imperial themes, children's poetry, 39–42
independence referendum, Scottish (2014), 149, 155, 158, 165
Ink Road imprint, 225
Innes, Sìm, 25–26
intellectual development. see cortical remapping
intertextuality, 26, 87, 110
Irish children's literature, 15, 175
Itchy Coo imprint, 24–25, 225, 226
    The Compact Coo, 184
    picturebooks in Scots, 183

Jacob, Violet, 84
Jacobs, Joseph, 83
Jamie, Kathleen
    'Mr and Mrs Scotland Are Dead', 218–19
    'The Republic of Fife', 218
Jassat, Nadine Aisha, 'Hopscotch', 219
Jauncey, James, 26
    The Witness, 28

Kabakow Rudman, Masha, 149
Kate Greenaway Medal, 191
Kay, Jackie, 22
   'Bed', 209
   'Gap Year', 221
   'Hauf A Dozen', 54
   'Old Tongue', 209, 211
   Strawgirl, 27, 86–87, 91–92, 95
Kelpies, 24
kelpies, 167, 229
Kennedy, Grace, *Anna Ross*, 63–64, 65, 68
Kerr, Judith, 169
Kidd, Mairi, 25–26
King, Jessie M., 84
Kirk, Robert, *The Secret Commonwealth*, 44
Knox, John, 17
Kummerling-Meibauer, Bettina, 181

Laird, Elizabeth
   The Secrets of the Fearless, 29
   Welcome to Nowhere, 9
landlordism, critique of, 105–06
Lang, Andrew, 83
   The Blue Fairy Book, 19
   The Blue Poetry Book, 31–32
   'The Gold of Fairnliee', 85, 96
   Prince Prigio, 19
language(s)
   in the development of Scottish children's literature, 15–16
   diversity, and publishers, 224–25
   Scotland's Languages Bill (2024), 3–4
   in Scottish picturebooks, 179–80
   see also English (language); Gaelic; Scots (language)
Latharna NicIllIosa, Anna (Anne Lorne Gillies), 171

Le Guin, Ursula, 159
Leabhraichean Beaga (publishing house), 169, 173, 175
Leavis, F. R., 4
Lefebvre, Benjamin, 164
Lennon, Joan, 96
   Silver Skin, 188
Letford, William, 'This Is It', 213–14
Lewis, C. S., *Narnia* tales, 193
Lexy Chaimbeul, Catrìona (Catriona Lexy Campbell), 175
LGBTQ+ topics, 65, 228–29
libraries, public, 17–18
Library Association, 191–92
Lightwood, Donald, *The Baillie's Daughter*, 69–70, 74
Lindsay, Jenny, 'The Gap', 221
Lingard, Joan, 22
Linklater, Eric
   The Pirates in the Deep Blue Sea, 85
   The Wind on the Moon, 21–22, 85, 192, 193, 194–97, 198–99, 204
literacy. *see* education
literary criticism, 19
   and Stevenson's *Garden of Verses*, 34–44
literary magazines, 13
Literature Alliance Scotland, *Breaking New Ground*, 227
Lochhead, Liz
   'The Bargain', 212
   'For My Grandmother Knitting', 217
   'Some Old Photographs', 217
   'View of Scotland/Love Poem', 217
Lorde, Audre, 161

INDEX 283

Lorne Gillies, Anne. *see* Latharna NicIllIosa, Anna
Low, R. D., 23
lullabies, 167
Lumsden, Alison, 162

Mac a' Ghobhainn, Iain (Iain Crichton Smith), 169
   at *Gairm*, 168
MacArthur, Bessie J. B., *The Clan of Lochlan*, 101
MacAulay, Marie C. *see* NicAmhlaigh, Mairi C.
Macbean, Lachlan, 106–07
MacCaig, Norman
   'Aunt Julia', 216–17
   'Basking Shark', 214–15
   'Sounds of the Day', 215
MacCormaig, Iain (John MacCormick)
   An Ceòl-Sìthe, 109–11
   Dùn-Aluinn, 110
MacDhòmhnaill, Aonghas (Angus MacDonald), *Mac an t-Srònaich*, 170
MacDonald, Allen. *see* Ailein, Maighstir
MacDonald, George, 20
   At the Back of the North Wind, 19, 89–90
   children's fantasy stories, 82, 85, 86, 87–88, 89–91, 94–95, 95–96
   'The Fantastic Imagination', 82, 117
   Good Words for the Young (magazine), 19
MacDonald, Ian, 102–03
MacFarlane, Malcolm. *see* MacPhàrlain, Calum

Macgregor, Mary, ballad anthology, 83–84
MacKay, J. G., *Sgeulachd a' Choire* ('The Tale of the Cauldron'), 166–67
Mackay, Janis, 96
   The Accidental Time Traveller, 64, 65, 70, 75, 76
Mackay Brown, George, 85, 87
   'The Everlasting Battle', 93
   Fankle the Cat, 225
   The Two Fiddlers, 96–97
MacKenzie, Alison, 158
MacKenzie, Ross
   The Colour of Hope, 80
   Emporium trilogy, 78–79, 86, 88–89, 91
Mackenzie, Ross, *The Nowhere Emporium*, 191
MacLean, Ishi. *see* NicIlleathain, Ishi
MacLean, Sorley
   'Ceann Loch Aoineart' ('Kinloch Ainort'), 214
   'Hallaig', 216
   'Sgreapadal', 216
   'Tràighean ('Shores'), 214
MacLeod, Fiona (William Sharp), 101
MacLeòid, Fionnlagh (Findlay Macleod)
   Mac an t-Srònaich, 170
   Tothan, 169
Mac-na-Ceàrdaich, Dòmhnall (Donald Sinclair), *Ruaireachan*, 108–09
MacPhail, Catherine, 26
   Mosi's War, 150–51, 152, 157–58, 162–63

MacPhàrlain, Calum (Malcolm
  MacFarlane)
  Am Mosgladh Mòr, 106–08
  Companach na Cloinne, 102,
    166
MacThòmais, Ruaraidh (Derick
  Thomson), 'Am Bodach
  Ròcais', 166–67
magic realism, 27
Manlove, Colin, 79
Marryat, Frederick, *Masterman
  Ready*, 115
masculinity, 161, 228
  see also gender issues/themes
materialist ideologies, 76
Matyjaszek, Kasia
  *The Fourth Bonniest Baby in
    Dundee*, 226
  I Am A Very Clever Cat, 226
McAleer, Joseph, 14
McCall Smith, Alexander,
  Precious and the Puggies,
  24–25
McCartney, Tania, *A Scottish
  Year*, 179
McClure, Derrick, 4
McFall, Claire
  Bombmaker, 151, 152–57, 163–64
  Ferryman, 24
McGregor, Iona, *An Edinburgh
  Reel*, 68–69
McKay, Elizabeth
  Bagpipes, Beasties and Bogles,
    186
  Granny stories, 186
McMahon, Deirdre H., 67
McNicoll, Elle, *A Kind of Spark*,
  24, 228
'Meade, L. T.' (Elizabeth
  Thomasina Meade Smith), 127

Melling, David, *Cudail Chan
  Fhaigh Mi*, 173
Mendlesohn, Farah, 79
Mercer, Lynn, 179
Milgram, Stanley, 138
Miller, Moira, *Adventures of
  Hamish and Mirren*, 187
Miller, William, 22
  'Wee Willie Winkie', 33
Milne, A. A., 24
Mitchison, Naomi, 21
  The Big House, 78, 84, 92, 93
  The Fourth Pig, 84
  'Kate Crackernuts' (play
    adaptation), 85
Moat Brae, 227, 230–31
modernity
  disenchanted, 143
  and Mollie Hunter's teen
    fiction, 131, 132, 134
Mòds, 111
Moireach, Iain (John Murray), 169
Monaghan, Jim, 'United Colours
  of Cumnock', 213
Montgomerie, Norah and
  William
  Folk Tales of Scotland, 188
  *Hogarth Book of Nursery
    Rhymes*, 22
Morgan, Edwin
  'Glasgow 5 March 1971', 212
  'Glasgow Sonnet i', 212
  'Good Friday', 208
  'Trio', 211
Morgan, Nicola, 9–10
  Fleshmarket, 29
  The Highwayman's Curse, 29
Morpurgo, Michael, 174
Moscoso, Javier, 37
Mourao, Sandie, 182

Muir, John, 188
Murray, John. *see* Moireach, Iain

National Book Awards, 191
National Centre for Children's Literature and Storytelling, Moat Brae. *see* Moat Brae
National Gaelic Education Resource Agency, 172
nationhood, and identity, Scottish
 alternative constructions, 161–62
 in poetry, 218, 219–20
Native Americans, 102
Nestlé Children's Book Prize, 191
neurodivergency, 228
Newbery, John, *A Little Pretty Pocket Book*, 18, 166
NicAmhlaigh, Mairi C. (Marie C. MacAulay), 173
NicDhòmhnaill, Anna, 170
NicFhearghais, Elaine (Elaine Ferguson), 175
NicIlleathain, Ishi (Ishi MacLean), 175
NicIlleBhàin Ghrannd, Catrìona (Katherine Whyte Grant), *Dùsgadh na Féinne*, 105
NicIlleDhuibh, Catrìona, 173
night-time poems, in Stevenson's *Garden of Verses*, 43–44
Nikolajeva, Maria, 12, 30, 159, 181
Niven, Liz, 'Feart', 55–56
Norquay, Glenda, 153, 164
Northern Lights, the, 144
Nosy Crow (publishers), 24
nursery verse, 33–34, 44–45, 167
 see also poetry, children's; *individual writers*
Nye, Alex, *Darker Ends*, 75, 76

Old English, 4
Oor Wullie, 23, 174
oral tradition (Scottish), 17, 80, 166–67
Orme, Nicholas, 6

pastoral genre, and nursery verse, 33–34
Paterson, Aileen, *Maisie comes to Morningside*, 185–86
Paterson, Don
 '11:00: Baldovan', 212
 'Nil Nil', 212–13
Peter Pan (fictional character), 84, 87
Phillips, Alfred R., 124
 Don Zalva the Brave, 124–25
picturebooks, 23, 176–90
 European collection, 177–78
 fantasy, 92
 Gaelic, 170, 172–73
 see also specific names of authors/illustrators
Plato, *Republic*, 138, 140–43
plays, Scottish Gaelic children's, 99–114
Plummer, Rachel, *Wain*, 95, 229
poetry, children's, 22–23
 anthologies, 22–23, 31–33
 see also individual writers
Potter, Jane, 14
Presbyterianism, 21, 71, 73
Pròiseact Foghlam Dà-Chànanach/Bilingual Education Project, 169–72
Protestantism
 and educational reform, 7
 in Scott's historical fiction, 71–72, 75
Prue, Sally, *Cold Prue*, 9

psychology of childhood. *see* childhood
publishing houses, Scottish, 21
Publishing Scotland, 225

queer representation, 95, 165, 228–29
quests, 193–94, 196, 199

Ram Tam Toosh (ASLS anthology), 22
Ransome, Arthur, *Pigeon Post*, 192
Ray, Jane, *An Gille Bragail*, 168
Ray, Sheila, 12
reading scheme/easy readers, Gaelic, 171, 172
Reid, Julia, 35
religious themes
    Gaelic folklore, 109
    historical fiction, 65, 66–67, 71–76
Robertson, James, 24–25, 159
    'Beelzebub Resurfaces', 210–11
    'A Manifesto for MSPs', 218
    Wee Book o Fairy Tales, 96
Rodger, Alexander, 22
romance genre, historical fiction, 62
Romanticism, 8, 37, 90
Rowling, J. K., *Harry Potter* books, 9, 191

Sassi, Carla, 28
Saxby, Jessie, 84
science fiction genre, Gaelic, 168
Scotland's Languages Bill (2024), 3–4
Scots (language), 16, 19
    attitudes to, 4–5
    ballad anthology, 84

children's poetry, 45–56
    Itchy Coo imprint, translations, 24–25
    official attitudes to, 25
    picturebooks, 183–84
    Scottish poetry, 208–11
Scott, Sir Walter
    intended audience, 65
    Ivanhoe, 116
    'tale' of the Massacre of Glencoe, 71–72, 75
    Tales of a Grandfather, 17, 18, 63, 64, 68
    the Waverley Novels, 124
    on writing for children, 18–19
    'Young Lochinvar', 32
Scottish Book Trust, 188
    John Muir, Earth – Planet, Universe, 188
    website, 189
Scottish children's literature
    and language issues, 15–16
    origins and development of, 14–15, 17–23
    in twenty-first century, 23–30
    see also specific names of authors
Scottish devolution. *see* devolution, Scottish
Scottish Education Department, 1946 report on languages, 4–5
Scottish Gothic. *see* Gothic tradition
Scottish independence referendum. *see* independence referendum, Scottish (2014)
Scottish National Players, 102
Scottish Poetry Library, 22
Scottish Qualifications Authority (SQA), 206, 207, 217, 221–22

Scottish Standard English (SSE). see English (language), Scottish Standard
Scutter, Heather, 15
seal-wife tales, 168
secondary education, Scottish poetry, 206–23
selkie stories, 96–97, 187, 229
Shakespeare, William, 125
Sharp, Willliam. see MacLeod, Fiona
Sherwood, Mary Martha, 66
Shetlantic dialect
  in picturebooks, 180
  in poetry, 216
Sinclair, Catherine, *Holiday House*, 17, 18–19, 81–82
Sinclair, Donald. see Mac-na-Ceàrdaich, Dòmhnall
slam poets, 218, 221, 222
Smarties Book Prize, 191
Smith, Donald, *Wee Folk Tales in Scots*, 96
Smith, Lorna, 22–23
Snerling, Tina, *A Scottish Year*, 179
Snicket, Lemony, 25
'Snow White' type, 167
Soutar, William, 22
  Bairnrhymes, 46–50, 53–54
Southall, Ivan, 171
spoken word poets, 211
  see also slam poets
Stephens, John, 151–52, 160
Stevenson, R. L., 49, 89, 221
  The Black Arrow, 115, 117, 119–21, 123–25, 126, 128
  Catriona (*David Balfour*), 115, 116, 119, 120, 123, 127–28
  A Child's Garden of Verses, 22, 34–44

essays on the developing child, 35
  'A Gossip on Romance', 116–17
  'A Humble Remonstrance', 118
  intended audience, 65
  junior fiction, 115–29
  Kidnapped, 115, 116, 117, 119, 123, 126–29
  'My First Book', 122–23
  New Arabian Nights, 124
  Prince Otto, 127
  Treasure Island, 19, 115, 117–19, 121–23
Stewart, Martin, *Riverkeep*, 85–86, 88, 91
Stòrlann Nàiseanta na Gàidhlig/National Gaelic Education Resource Agency, 172
Streatfield, Noel, *The Circus is Coming*, 192
suffrage, 158–59
Sunday Post, comic strips, 23
Sutcliff, Rosemary, 171

Tam Lin (fictional character), 96, 187
Taylor, Liz, 181
Thompson, D. C., 23
Thomson, Derick. see MacThòmais, Ruaraidh
Tolkien, J. R. R., 79
Tom Thumb, his life and death (chapbook), 81
Torney-Purta, Judith, 151, 158
Tough, Kate, 'People Made Glasgow', 219
traditional tales, Scottish, 186–88
Trites, Roberta Seelinger, 164
TV and radio, Gaelic-language adaptations, 171

uncanny, the, 43, 48, 49
United Nations, Rights of the Child, 8
urban realism, 26–27

Wales, Welsh
    and the EPBC picturebook collection, 178
    Gaelic translations, 171
Walliams, David, 25
war poetry, Scottish, 34
Warner, Marina, 84
Watkins, Dudley D., 23
Watson, Carole, 171
Watt, Eilidh, *Latha a' Choin Duibh*, 169
Wells, H. G., 117
Welsh children's literature, 15
Whistle Binkie, 22
'whistle binkies', 32, 45
Whyte Grant, Katherine, *Dùsgadh na Féinne*, 105
Williams, Helen, 14
Williams, Raymond, 206

Williamson, Victoria
    Feast of Ashes, 230
    Norah's Ark, 229–30
    War of the Wind, 229
Wilson, Catherine
    'Facts', 221
    'Scotland the More', 218
women
    women's writing as alternative perspective, 162
    see also gender issues/themes
Wynne Jones, Dianne, *Fire and Hemlock*, 96
Wyss, Johan David, 115

young adult (YA) literature, 79, 149–50
    concern with agency and empowerment, 164–65
    definition, 14
    see also specific names of authors
Young Folks paper (periodical), 117, 124–25

www.ingramcontent.com/pod-product-compliance
Lightning Source LLC
Chambersburg PA
CBHW052103230426
43671CB00011B/1913